# DOUGLAS HAIG

# DOUGLAS HAIG

The Preparatory Prologue

*1861–1914*

Diaries and Letters

Edited by

## Douglas Scott

Pen & Sword
**MILITARY**

First published in Great Britain in 2006 by
Pen & Sword Military
an imprint of
Pen & Sword Books Ltd
47 Church Street
Barnsley
South Yorkshire
S70 2AS

ISBN 1 84415 404 1
978 184415 404 3

A CIP catalogue record for this book is
available from the British Library

Typeset in Sabon and Bernhard Modern by
Phoenix Typesetting, Auldgirth, Dumfriesshire

Printed and bound in England by
Biddles Ltd, King's Lynn


Pen & Sword Books Ltd incorporates the Imprints of Pen & Sword
Aviation, Pen & Sword Maritime, Pen & Sword Military, Wharncliffe
Local History, Pen & Sword Select, Pen & Sword Military Classics and
Leo Cooper.

For a complete list of Pen & Sword titles please contact
PEN & SWORD BOOKS LIMITED
47 Church Street, Barnsley, South Yorkshire, S70 2AS, England
E-mail: enquiries@pen-and-sword.co.uk
Website: www.pen-and-sword.co.uk

This book is dedicated to the memory
of my grandmother Doris Haig

# Contents

# Preface

by

Major The Earl Haig OBE

I am happy to introduce my nephew Douglas Montagu-Douglas-Scott, who has put together extracts from my father's early letters and diaries. These include interesting descriptions of life in the Sudan during the River War and of friends and colleagues with whom he served in the Boer War, also later in India. They go back to his early days as an undergraduate at Oxford.

Douglas's book completes my mother's work, which she intended to publish in the 1930s. For reasons of space he has had to omit many passages, but in his selection he has included extracts which reveal my father's evolving personality on the way to maturity. They demonstrate his warm personality, his devotion to family and friends and his love of the army. They mention his criticisms, which are generally apt and to the point.

Most of the letters are addressed to his sister Henrietta who, to a great extent, replaced their beloved mother Rachel Veitch, after her death. I remember Henrietta, who was supportive of her brother and later of our generation as well.

When my father married my mother Dorothy Vivian in 1905 he realised his wife came from a different background, in fact diplomacy. However they were each servants of the Crown – one an army officer, the other a Maid of Honour first to Queen Victoria and then to Queen Alexandra. And they were both horse-lovers and golfers; it was a golf course which gave him the opportunity to propose! So my mother took on the responsibilities and cares as the wife of a seriously involved army officer.

After my father died in 1928 I can testify to my mother's devotion to his memory and to her continuing work for disabled ex-servicemen and their dependents. In 1934 she decided to embark on her selection of my father's diaries up to 1914. It is that work which provided the original manuscript, which was the basis for much of this book. How I remember the night time sounds of her typewriter which began rather jerkily about 4 a.m.! The walls of our flat in Learmonth Terrace, Edinburgh, were not thick enough to protect me from the irritating noise! Typing the diaries, particularly the 1914–1918 ones, was one of the achievements of her life. She typed her manuscript of the wartime diaries from the originals when they reached her by King's Messenger and then again twice over.

On the fly leaf of my mother's copy of my father's dispatches, my father wrote:

> To my wife Doris in grateful recollection of all she was to me during the Great War. Although she regularly received instalments of my daily diary and knew more than those at home what was taking place at the Front, yet no one has ever been able to say 'Lady Haig told me that'.

I know my parents would have been deeply grateful to their grandson for adding the final touches to their accounts of events, which are of such importance to present day readers.

Haig of Bemersyde
April 2006

# Acknowledgements

The inspiration for this book came from my uncle, the present Earl Haig, who knew very well the tremendous amount of work done by his mother in preparing her late husband's diaries and letters for publication. He drew my attention to the 'Advance Proof Copy', which she had received, but which never went to the final stage of actual publication. This document has been invaluable in putting together my book. He has also been very helpful in telling me his recollections of his father and other members of the Haig family, notably his aunt Henrietta. In addition I could not have done without his help in understanding the history of the Haigs. Andrea De Pree, married to my kinsman Peter De Pree, gave me a most scholarly family tree, which also helped.

I spent many constructive hours in the National Library of Scotland, in Edinburgh, the home of the Haig papers. I was tremendously helped by Colm McLaughlin, the main custodian and expert on the papers. He drew my attention to many things I would otherwise have missed and conjured up some of my grandfather's fascinating photographs of India at the end of the nineteenth and beginning of the twentieth centuries. Some of these have been used here as illustrations. The staff in the National Library were always pleasant and helpful.

I am grateful also to Simon Moody of the National Army Museum, who showed me the album of the Sudan Campaign, from which came the photographs of the Emir Mahmoud and the paddle steamer carrying the 21 Lancers south towards Omdurman. I am also grateful to Denise Brace of the Museum of Edinburgh, which houses the main collection of Haig photographs. She endured with equanimity my exclamations of surprise as one interesting photograph after another was produced from the Museum's well-kept archive. A number have been used as illustrations.

John Hussey, a walking encyclopaedia on warfare in general and Douglas Haig in particular, has been immensely helpful. Whenever I was puzzled by something I rang John and he always knew the answer.

Gary Sheffield and John Bourne, the editors of the recent re-issue of the 1914–1918 Diaries, have also been most helpful. Chris Pugsley checked the facts about Sandhurst in the 1880s for me. Ken Gillings and Willie Mahon helped me with the facts about some of the participants in the South African War. Walter Reid, whose life of Douglas Haig is due for publication in 2006, and I exchanged ideas and information on a number of occasions.

My wife, Monica, has been a tower of strength, in helping me with research both in the National Library and on the Internet and in putting up with me disappearing into my studio for hours on end. Finally I would like to thank Susan Econicoff, my editor at Pen & Sword, for her patience and calm as we struggled to reduce the manuscript to the size acceptable to Pen & Sword.

I am most grateful to all the above.

D.M-D-S.

# Glossary

## Military

| | |
|---|---|
| AAG | Assistant Adjutant General |
| ADC | Aide-de-Camp |
| AG | Adjutant General |
| AIF | Australian Imperial Forces |
| ASC | Army Service Corps |
| Batt | Battery |
| Bde | Brigade |
| BGS/BGGS | Brigadier General General Staff |
| BGRA | Brigadier General Royal Artillery |
| Bn. | Battalion |
| CGS | Chief of the General Staff |
| CIGS | Chief of the Imperial General Staff |
| C.-in-C. | Commander in Chief |
| CO | Commanding Officer |
| CoS | Chief of Staff |
| CRA | Commander Royal Artillery |
| CRE | Commander Royal Engineers |
| DAAG | Deputy Assistant Adjutant General |
| DAQMG | Deputy Assistant Quartermaster General |
| DGs | Dragoon Guards |
| DMI | Director of Military Intelligence |
| DMO | Director of Military Operations |
| DMS | Director of Medical Services |
| DMT | Director of Military Training |
| DSD | Director of Staff Duties |
| FM | Field Marshal |
| FSR | Field Service Regulations |

| | |
|---|---|
| GHQ | General Headquarters |
| GOC | General Officer Commanding |
| GOC.-in-C. | General Officer Commanding-in-Chief |
| GSO | General Staff Officer, Grades 1,2 and 3 |
| HLI | Highland Light Infantry |
| i/c | in command as in 2i/c |
| IG | Inspector General |
| IGC | Inspector General of Cavalry |
| ILH | Imperial Light Horse |
| KOSB | King's Own Scottish Borders |
| KRRC | King's Royal Rifle Corps |
| MGGS | Major General General Staff |
| MGRA | Major General Royal Artillery |
| MS | Military Secretary |
| NCO | Non-Commissioned Officer |
| OC | Officer Commanding |
| QMG | Quartermaster General |
| RA | Royal Artillery |
| RE | Royal Engineers |
| RFA | Royal Field Artillery |
| RHA | Royal Horse Artillery |
| RHG | Royal Horse Guards (The Blues) |
| Sqn. | Squadron |

## Orders and Decorations

| | |
|---|---|
| KG | Knight of the Garter |
| KT | Knight of the Thistle |
| KP | Knight of St. Patrick |
| GCB | Knight Grand Cross of the Order of the Bath |
| KCB | Knight of the Order of the Bath |
| CB | Companion of the Order of the Bath |
| OM | Member of the Order of Merit |
| GCSI | Knight Grand Commander of the Star of India |
| KCSI | Knight Commander of the Star of India |
| CSI | Companion of the Star of India |
| GCMG | Knight Grand Cross of St. Michael and St. George |
| KCMG | Knight Commander of St. Michael and St. George |
| CMG | Companion of St. Michael and St. George |
| GCIE | Knight Grand Commander of the Indian Empire |
| KCIE | Knight Commander of the Indian Empire |
| CIE | Companion of the Indian Empire |

| | |
|---|---|
| GCVO | Knight Grand Cross of the Royal Victorian Order |
| KCVO | Knight Commander of the Victorian Order |
| CVO | Commander of the Victorian Order |
| MVO | Member of the Victorian Order |
| VC | Victoria Cross |
| DSO | Companion of the Distinguished Service Order |
| ISO | Companion of the Imperial Service Order |

# Introduction

In his biography of Douglas Haig, published in 1935 by Faber and Faber, Duff Cooper wrote:

> . . . the life of Lord Haig . . . is an epic drama of four years and one hundred days. There is also a preparatory prologue of fifty-three years and an epilogue of ten.

This book covers the fifty-three years of the preparatory prologue with selections from Douglas Haig's diaries and his letters to a number of people.

Until his marriage Haig wrote almost daily to his sister Henrietta, who was ten years older than him and one of the formative influences in his life. When his mother died in 1879, when Haig was eighteen, Henrietta took over some of her role and was his main confidante. There are only a few letters to Henrietta after Douglas Haig married Dorothy Vivian (Doris). Other recipients of Douglas Haig's letters included Field Marshal Sir Evelyn Wood, Oliver Haig (his nephew), Lord Haldane, Secretary of State for War when Haig was at the War Office, General Sir Gerald Ellison (Haldane's Principal Private Secretary), Sir Lonsdale Hale, with whom he collaborated in writing 'Cavalry Studies' in 1907, and Lord Jessel, an influential Member of Parliament, when the future armament of Cavalry Regiments was being considered. (He had served in the 17 Lancers as a junior officer).

Very few of the diary entries over this long period, or of the letters reproduced here have been published before. Doris Haig collected letters after her husband's death and had intended to publish them together with his diaries in about 1935, but she was prevented from doing so because it was thought such a book would conflict with Duff Cooper's official biography. When she published her own book, *The*

*Man I Knew* in 1936 it included no extracts from the diaries and none of Haig's letters.

She had worked with great diligence and conscientiousness for several years to type the diaries and letters and this book would have been much more difficult to compile had her typescript not been available. She had no help in carrying out this work and every word was typed by her – it is said she even typed everything twice! But given the enormous amount of material and the fact that her husband's writing is not always easy to read, just to have done it once was heroic and a labour of love. To have done it twice is beyond belief. She must have been bitterly disappointed that her work did not end with publication. In consequence this book of Douglas Haig's diaries and letters before the First World War is dedicated to her memory.

Haig's life before the 'epic drama' can quite easily be split into a number of phases, all of which were important to his subsequent career, all of which contained lessons, which he learnt and from which he benefited later. Each phase is represented by a chapter in this book.

All the phases of his career were important militarily, but some were more important than others. For example the Sudan campaign gave him his first experience of hostile fire and in South Africa he had great responsibilities beyond what nowadays would be called his job specification, partly because of the inadequacies of his superiors, but mainly because he found that responsibility came easily to him. St John Brodrick's letter of 30 June 1905, written during his time as Secretary of State for War, to Doris Haig makes this point very well in relation to Haig's performance in South Africa. He wrote;

> . . . I used to hear from returning officers one chorus of panegyric of the ideal staff officer, who from the first made the reputation of his chiefs, and I always knew whose name would follow the preamble . . .

Haig's career had been slow before Sudan – he went there as a rather elderly captain – but that campaign and the South African War made his name, not just as a staff officer, but also as a leader of troops in battle. From then on promotion came exceptionally fast. Arguably the most important phase of the Prologue, however, was his time as right hand man to Haldane, Secretary of State for War. He worked with Haldane from 1906-08 in the reorganization of the British Army, the formation of the Territorial Army, the establishment of the role of Chief of the Imperial General Staff and the preparation of Field Service Regulations, published in 1909. The result of these achieve-

2

ments were that the 'Great Little Army' of 1914 went to war in a state of efficiency which was unrecognizable, when compared with the army that fought in South Africa. Had the reorganization not been carried through, the First World War might well have been over rather quickly and the result might well have been different. At best there might have been an ignominious withdrawal through a Channel port, as happened to a far less well organized, trained and equipped Expeditionary Force in the Second World War. And, dare one say it of an Army which included Generals Alanbrooke, Alexander and Montgomery, less well led.

There is a sea change in the diaries around the time of Haig's return from India in order to join Haldane at the War Office. The earlier diaries and the letters to Henrietta are full of accounts where he was involved, either as a spectator or a participant, in incidents which he found amusing, and his dry, Scottish sense of humour comes through on many occasions. Examples are his comments about his friends at Oxford, the great tiger shoot in India, the chaotic polo game in New South Wales, the laughable behaviour of the Germans on the Nile steamer, his description of Kitchener's 'Roman triumph' at Berber, the departure of French and staff by the last train out of Ladysmith, and the description of the Kadir Cup to quote merely a few incidents. The diary entries are frequently lighthearted and full of life and the letters to Henrietta particularly so. They show an interest in the people he meets, particularly if there is a Scottish connection. He was obviously surprised to find that the father of a Dutch Reformed Church Minister had been a prominent citizen in Inverness and was called Fraser. He probably also discovered – although this is not mentioned – that the Reverend Fraser's son – was a Boer Commando leader!

After his arrival at the War Office the diary becomes much more a record of his day-to-day engagements and there are no further letters to Henrietta, for obvious reasons. The range of people, whom he met at this phase of his life is remarkable, including the main Government and Opposition leaders, most of the British Royal family, the Empress Eugenie and Grand Duchess Vladimir, Sidney and Beatrice Webb and Sir James Gildea, founder of SSAFA. It is interesting that both Douglas and Doris Haig were at this stage thinking about the well-being of troops and their families, particularly the welfare of widows and families of soldiers who had been casualties. These thoughts led ultimately to the Earl Haig Fund and British Legion.

An insight into Douglas Haig's mind and his attitude to other people can be gathered from his favourite verse. It was:

3

Question not, but live and labour
Till the goal is won;
Helping every feeble neighbour,
Seeking help from none;
Life is mostly froth and bubble,
Two things stand like stone;
Kindness in another's trouble,
Courage in your own.

This is part of a poem by Adam Lindsay Gordon (1833–70) entitled *Ye Wearie Wayfarer*. The choice is not too surprising for the Founder of the Earl Haig Fund and the British Legion. Perhaps more surprising is that he knew the poem. Adam Lindsay Gordon was a remittance man in South Australia. For numerous misdemeanours in Aberdeenshire his family gave him a one-way ticket to Australia. He became a Trooper in the South Australian Mounted Police and lived in the south-east of the state near Mount Gambier. Is it possible that Haig heard the poem when he was in South Australia in 1889?

There are a number of clear themes running through the diaries and letters. Of these perhaps the most obvious is Haig's determination to achieve the highest possible level of professionalism in his own preparation for the future, but also that the troops under him should be as professional as possible. In his time as a junior officer with the 7 Hussars he is surprised that some of his fellow subalterns do not know how to handle a piece of equipment which he considered simple and part of every young officer's basic military knowledge. For himself, he recognized the need to go to the Staff College, not something an officer in the 7 Hussars was expected to do. When he told his Commanding Officer that that was his intention, the latter is reputed to have replied that no 7 Hussar officer had ever been to the Staff College and that he should think carefully about the consequences before deciding to do so! One of the consequences was that he would never serve in the 7th again – one of the reasons why he commanded the 17 Lancers.

Haig also made sure that he had some militarily worthwhile extra regimental appointments (not ADC jobs!). This brought his ability to the notice of senior officers, who helped to promote his career. The most obvious example of this was Field Marshal Sir Evelyn Wood, who was impressed by Haig's wish to improve his knowledge of the cavalry of the two main Continental armies, the French and the German. It was Wood who selected him for the Egyptian Army in 1898. Apart from Sir Evelyn, Field Marshal French and Generals

Greaves, Bengough, Luck and Fraser all did what they could to help Haig to achieve his potential. Haig's partnership with French was extremely productive for both men as long as it was confined to the leadership of cavalry. French eventually was a victim of the Peter Principle, in which the talented executive is promoted to the level above the one at which he is able to perform effectively.

During his life Douglas Haig had a close relationship, in each case of a different nature, with three exceptional women. The first was Rachel Veitch his mother, who saw his potential and encouraged and generally advised him until her death in 1879. A number of her letters have survived. Rachel was very religious and did her best to instil in her youngest son a sense of reverence for Christianity and the Church. She was determined that he would go to Oxford or Cambridge as a prelude to deciding what he would do to earn his living. One letter to her from Douglas, which has survived, was written at Clifton in 1879, although it is only dated Monday. He tells her in it that John Percival, the Headmaster, would like him to stay on until the end of the year, rather than leave in the summer and that he should not go to a crammer before taking the entrance exam into Oxford. Rather, Percival said it would be better that he himself coach Douglas. Following the death of Rachel Haig in March 1879, it was thought better that Douglas should go up to Brasenose in October 1880 after spending some time with his brother Hugo in California and also attending Rhodes the crammer, working up the subjects in which he was less strong.

After Rachel's death, Henrietta Haig, the second exceptional woman in Douglas Haig's life, became a great influence on his career, helping him in many ways, and in Sudan and South Africa supplying him with many luxuries, which greatly improved his comfort. (He shared the food and drink with his brother officers.) Henrietta married William G. Jameson, the Irish whiskey distiller, in 1876; they had no children. Through yachting he was a friend of the Prince of Wales (King Edward VII) and it was through the Jamesons that Haig became friendly with the Royal Family. For Douglas, Henrietta gave him some of the love and care that he had had from his mother. For Henrietta, Douglas gave her some of the devotion that a son gives to his mother. It was an exceptional and loving relationship. Haig asked her advice on many aspects of his life and he trusted her to look after his business and financial interests when he was abroad. Douglas Haig's son remembers Aunt Henrietta as exceptionally kind, gentle, intelligent and sweet.

In 1905 Douglas Haig married Dorothy Vivian (Doris), the third exceptional woman in his life. They had a very happy marriage and four children. She devoted her life to him and after his death to his memory and to preserving his reputation. Her work on his papers undermined her health and she died before she was sixty years old. All historians, who have studied Haig's private papers, owe her a tremendous debt of gratitude.

Their 'courtship' is recorded below and it was certainly unusual to say the least. Doris had been told by her brother George, an officer in the 17 Lancers, that Haig was a 'woman hater' and he seems to have made every effort not to introduce her to his Commanding Officer. His reason for keeping a low profile may have been that he was in trouble with the regiment because he was in the process of ending his marriage by divorce. This was unheard of for an officer in a good regiment such as the 17 Lancers and many officers in this position felt obliged to resign their commission. George did not resign, but he was anxious to keep a safe distance from his colonel. Doris and Douglas did not meet until they were both staying at Windsor Castle for Ascot Races.

But was Douglas Haig a 'woman hater'? The evidence of his diary does not suggest any such thing. There is one comment, not made with any seriousness, that women always seemed to be at the bottom of any trouble (on the Nile steamer). What man hasn't made such a remark more or less in jest? Later, when he was in India as Chief of Staff, and a married man, he comments that he had formed a committee without any women on it to avoid any quarrelling – again not too serious an indictment for the charge of women hating. Certainly there is no evidence of passionate affairs although his children believed that he had a remarkably close relationship with Lady Warwick; the beautiful Daisy. He would have met her frequently through hunting with the Warwickshire hounds. Many an affair has been started out hunting, but again there is no evidence.

His brother officers in the 7 Hussars did not think of him as a 'woman hater'. His friend J.G. Beresford wrote him a note, which is undated but was tucked into the diary for 1888 and probably dates from around the time the two of them went shooting ibex and other game in Kashmir. The note says:

> . . . Sly rascal, I knew you could not keep off the females and I am glad you got the other two . . .

This seems to suggest a score line of Haig 2, Beresford 1! Curiously, there are several entries in this particular diary, which have been carefully cut out. Did they perhaps record meetings with young ladies and were the excisions made by Doris?

He was also a popular dinner guest of the officers' wives at Secunderabad. Mrs Amy Cochran, wife of Colonel Cochran, commanding the Hampshire Regiment at Secunderabad wrote the following to Doris in 1929;

> I would so like you to tell your son that his dear father was the most delightful young officer that I ever came across, so modest and selfless. I remember saying to him several times; 'Oh! Mr Haig, you rode so splendidly this afternoon' and his replying, 'Wasn't it another fellow?'
>
> My husband and I lived with the General in the next lines to the 7th Hussars and I had to arrange all his (the General's) dinner parties. I nearly always used to say; 'Mayn't I ask Mr Haig?' I was always so delighted when he came.

Surely Mrs Cochran wouldn't have had such a 'crush' on a woman hater. Another thread going through the diaries and letters is Haig's health. He was badly asthmatic as a boy, but grew out of this debilitating disease before he went to Oxford. But the disease caused him to be careful of his health, to eat and drink in moderation and to take exercise. His health worries were compounded by attacks of typhoid and malaria during his first tour in India. The malaria came back from time to time throughout the remainder of his life, usually at a thoroughly inconvenient moment, and the diaries record sudden 'agues' and very high temperatures. He consulted several medical specialists and regularly took the waters in Germany, Switzerland and even Wales.

There can be no doubt that India affected the health of the majority of the British, who served there. Typhoid (enteric fever) and malaria were India's gifts to Haig. He took great care to ensure that they did not totally undermine his health. He kept some verses, written possibly by Oliver Haig, about the upshot of long service in India. The following is the final verse.

> Thus wags the long, long day
> From year to year away,
> Until we've earned our pay,
> One paltry pound a day:
> Then home to die in England,
> A worthy recompense

For loss of health and sense.
So end's my story
Of India's glory.

These verses doubtless provided Haig with the awful example of what might have happened had he not been concerned with his own well-being, through sensible living and plenty of exercise.

As to exercise; he started playing polo at Oxford in 1883 and became sufficiently proficient to be selected to play for England against the United States. He also played in the 7 Hussars side which was arguably the most successful regimental team in the Army at that time. He was evidently good at training polo teams as is shown by the success of the 17 Lancers team under his leadership. He continued to play polo, although not competitively until he returned to England to command at Aldershot in 1912. By then he had become a golfer, playing in India, Scotland and England regularly; he became an efficient player, very rarely leaving the fairway. He also played tennis; the diary records him being hit in the eye by a tennis ball in India, which was both painful and embarrassing. He hunted regularly with the Warwickshire every winter he was in England and rode before breakfast most days. It was his and Doris's choice to live near Farnborough and commute to London, when he was with Haldane at the War Office, so that he could ride each morning. He shot as well, but not a great deal; again this activity is referred to in the diary, when he stayed with his nephew Oliver Haig at his home, Ramornie in Fife.

This book does not attempt to prove or disprove anything concerned with Douglas Haig's life. It sets down a selection of Haig's diaries and his letters, the most numerous being to his sister, for what they are worth. It has been a privilege to read them; it has also been most enjoyable. It is to be hoped that they give the same pleasure to others.

# Chapter 1

# Childhood, School, Oxford, Sandhurst.

### 1861 – 1885

In the mid-twelfth century King David I of Scotland invited a powerful Norman knight, Hugo de Morville[1] to take up land in the Scottish Borders. Together King David and de Morville founded Dryburgh Abbey. Amongst de Morville's retinue was a young knight from the same part of Normandy, now known as the Cap de la Hague.

His Latin name was Petrus de Haga (or in French, Pierre de la Hague). He was granted land at Bemersyde, some three miles from Dryburgh, where he built a defensive tower in which he lived. His descendants are still there more than 800 years later. By the fourteenth century the de Hagas had become Haigs, with the ninth laird of Bemersyde being known as Sir Andrew Haig. They had also become so well established at Bemersyde that the thirteenth century poet and seer, Thomas the Rhymer, proclaimed that:

> Tyde what may, whate'er betyde
> Haig will be Haig of Bemersyde.

When Bemersyde came into the ownership of Douglas Haig in 1923, following its purchase from a cousin, he became the twenty-ninth laird. This is certainly a remarkable example of continuity, but one has to say that the mortality rate of the earlier lairds through battle against the English was fairly high and rather accelerated the numbers.

The sixth laird was at Bannockburn and killed at Halidon Hill in 1333. The eighth laird was killed at Otterburn in 1388, the tenth at Piperdean in 1436. The thirteenth laird was killed at Flodden in 1513. At least three fought and survived, the fifth at Stirling Bridge and the eleventh at Sark. The fourteenth commanded some of the light horse from the Borders at Ancrum Moor and captured one of the English commanders, Sir Ralph Eure (or Evers). Badly wounded, Eure was taken back to Bemersyde, where sadly he died – his ransom would have been well worth having. At least one de Haga went to the Crusades, which is why the Saltire appears on the Haig coat of arms. Possibly the ancient Spanish chestnut tree in front of the house at Bemersyde was brought back by a Crusader; it may be over 700 years old, planted well before the date at which this species was officially brought to Scotland.

The Haigs were never large landowners on the scale of the Scotts of Buccleuch, the Kerrs, the Douglases or the Homes. They never became grandees or enobled. They were, however, more than 'bonnet' lairds, in the sense that they had, for centuries, had more land than could be encompassed by a sweep of the bonnet. There are several examples of gifts of land and woodland to Dryburgh Abbey or Old Melrose, with not much in return – a stone of wax a year from Old Melrose seems to have been the only physical benefit, but one hopes that generations of Haigs felt a spiritual benefit.

This, then, is the family into which Douglas Haig was born in Charlotte Square, Edinburgh, on 19 June 1861. He was descended from the sevcenteenth laird, James Haig, through his eldest surviving son Robert. James Haig virtually ruined the estate through poor management and general extravagance. He passed the estate to his brother William, fled to Holland and died shortly afterwards in 1619. William, King's Solicitor of Scotland, made an extremely shrewd settlement, cutting out Robert and passing the estate to his nephew, David, the seventh son of James Haig, who had a rich Dutch/German wife. Their son, Anthony, with money from his Dutch/German inheritance, made many improvements to Bemersyde. The house still benefits from them.

Meantime poor Robert, who should have succeeded to the estate, became a tenant farmer in Stirlingshire and then farmed his own land in Clackmannanshire. He had, however, previously visited his relations in Holland and had learnt modern methods of distilling. As a result, he started to make and sell excellent whisky for local consumption. (He got into trouble with the local kirk for making it on the Sabbath day.) Four generations later, John Haig of Gartlands, Clackmannanshire, married Margaret Stein, daughter of Scotland's leading whisky distiller. John died at the age of fifty-three and the widow, desperate to make ends meet, apprenticed her five sons to learn to become distillers in her father's two distilleries at Kilbagie and Kennetpans. One of these sons, William, was Douglas Haig's grand-father. William and his son John created a highly successful whisky business in Fife, which became one of the world's leading brands until it was taken over in the late twentieth century by the Guinness organ-ization and disappeared from the British market.

Because of the whisky business Douglas was born into an extremely well off family. Far from being an obscure cadet branch of the Bemersyde Haigs they were in fact descended from the eldest surviving son of the seventeeth laird and should, under the normal laws of inheritance, have continued to own the estate. For entirely sensible reasons their ancestor, Robert Haig, had been dispossessed, but in the end Robert's descendants have triumphed. When Bemersyde went to Field Marshal Earl Haig, it was in effect going back to the part of the Haig family, to which it rightly belonged.

Douglas's mother, Rachel Veitch, also came from a long established Borders family. She was the 'heraldic' heir of Eliock, near Perth and Dawyck, near Peebles, (which explains why the subsidiary title to the Haig Earldom is Viscount Dawick), and a descendant of 'the De'il o' Dawyck' one of King Gustavus Adolphus's commanders in the Thirty Years War. His sword, still remarkably sharp, can be seen at Bemersyde. Douglas was the eleventh child to be born to John and Rachel Haig, of which eight survived into adulthood.[2] William, the eldest, was twenty years older than Douglas, Henrietta his closest friend, confidante and mentor was ten years older. John Haig, his father, died in 1878 followed, a year later, by his much loved mother. After her death, Henrietta became almost a substitute mother and certainly was the greatest influence on his life until he married in 1905. He was always on good terms with his brothers and sisters; their names appear regularly in his diaries, as do the names of various other relatives.

As a small child Douglas Haig suffered badly from asthma. It must have affected much of his young life, making him quick tempered and impatient; it was probably the cause of his apparent slowness in learning. It is not easy to concentrate when every breath is difficult. The photograph of Douglas, aged perhaps three, still in a dress, with long blonde curls, shows him looking furious and carrying a pistol. In the next photograph, taken two years later, he is wearing his kilt and looks a good deal happier. In the meantime his brothers and sisters had cut off his long curls and this together with the kilt gives him a much more masculine appearance. The only person, who was

11

unhappy, needless to say, was his mother, who carefully kept the curls. (They are now in the Huntly House Museum in Edinburgh.) A relative, visiting the family when Douglas was seven or eight, wrote:

> The boy was sitting up in bed with a shawl round his shoulders fighting for breath and smoking datura tatula cigarettes, which seemed to do him good. He continued to suffer from asthma for many years, but undoubtedly cured himself by his determination always to avoid anything that might bring on a fresh attack.

Putting on one side one's amazement that cigarettes could have been prescribed for asthma, it seems from the evidence of his school career that he managed to bring this debilitating disease under control by the time he was seventeen. He appears by then to have become a more than competent rugby footballer and you cannot play rugby or any other kind of football with asthma.

The Haig family lived at Cameron House in Fife, which was convenient for the Haig Distillery at Markinch. This meant that when Douglas went to his first school, a day school in Edinburgh, he and his older brother John boarded with a Miss Hepburn in Castle Terrace. Apart from a governess at some stage in his earlier childhood, this, in 1869, when he was eight, was his first experience of education. He moved from there to Orwell House, near Rugby, a typical boarding school preparing boys for their public school. Orwell House specialized in preparing boys for Rugby School. What with his asthma and the delayed start in his education, it was decided that Douglas would not succeed in passing the entrance examination into Rugby and, even if he did, would find the work too hard. In particular his knowledge of Greek was not up to standard. Rugby at the time had a high reputation academically; as the Eton song has it:

> Rugby may be more clever,
> Harrow may make more row . . .

There was no suggestion of sending Douglas to Eton or Harrow and so he went to Clifton College in Bristol in 1875, aged fourteen – again rather late for entry into a public school. His older brother John (Bee) was already there. Clifton was a relatively new school, having been founded in 1862; it was modelled on Rugby and its headmaster, John Percival, had taught at Rugby. Percival, aged only twenty-eight when he was appointed, was an inspirational headmaster and the school was an excellent choice for Douglas. His academic ability was allowed

12

to develop at his own pace, rather than being pushed too hard. By the time he was seventeen he was starting to learn well and in his last year came top in Latin, a subject in which he had been exceptionally slow initially. He did not develop into an outstanding schoolboy – how many outstanding schoolboys did we know who were burnt out at twenty? But he was clearly more than adequate at both academic work and games, particularly rugby football. Contemporaries at Clifton[3] told Lady Haig, when she was writing her book, *The Man I Knew* in 1935–6, the following:

> I remember Douglas Haig proposing a motion in the School House Debating Society – 'That the Army has done the country more service than the Navy'.
>
> . . . My recollections of him are of a very determined young-ster, whose clean appearance was merely the anticipation of the day when he became the smartest of smart cavalry officers. He was a fine character of a gentleman then as he was to the end of his days.
>
> My recollection of him has always been of a boy particularly genial and sociable. His brain was alert and active. He was very popular in the Schoolhouse. I can see him now playing half-back (School XV) as active as a cat and as brave as a lion. To me he was a lovable boy, full of guts and by no means lacking in fun. We were often side by side in the scrum and a dour fighter he was.
>
> Quite contrary to the general opinion, it was at Clifton that he first began to think of his future career.

The recollection that he proposed a motion extolling the Army at the expense of the Navy is in itself not proof that he was thinking of going into the Army as his profession. This, after all, was simply a house debating society, not really to be taken seriously. The other comment that Douglas was already thinking of a military career is interesting, but probably represents a generally vague idea, rather than a firm intention and plan. After all, if he really was intent on the Army at that stage he would have prepared for and taken the Army exam there and then. Instead, he went off after school to California with his brother, Hugo, before going to a crammer to help him to pass into Oxford, which he did successfully.

It has been suggested that Oxford was an academically easier option than Sandhurst and that Douglas would find entry into the Army as a university entrant, a scheme only recently introduced, much easier than taking the Army exam immediately after leaving school. In fact Sandhurst [4] had no entrance exam before 1877 and it seems unlikely that, within two years, the standard should have become superior to Oxford entry. It seems much more likely that Douglas wanted a gap between school and the next stage – nowadays known as 'the gap year'. Also his mother, the most important influence in his life, had recently died and this too may have caused him to delay entering into the next phase of his life. He no doubt wanted to go to university, as did many young men with his background and wealth, without necessarily taking academia too seriously. He had been advised to go to university by his eldest brother, Willie, and very strongly by his mother.[5] It seems unlikely that he was thinking seriously of the Army until later, otherwise he would certainly have taken the Army exam at the earliest possible moment, so as to be as high up the Army List as possible. As it happened he decided not to stay on at Oxford another term in order to achieve the residence requirement for his degree – he had missed a term through illness, but had passed all the necessary examinations evidently with some ease – because he realized that time was marching on and if he delayed any longer he might be too old to be eligible for entry. It is hard to accept that he thought seriously about the Army until well into his time at Oxford. In fact the correspondence between Douglas Haig, his brother Willie and his mother makes it quite clear that the whole family was keen for him to go to Oxford as a prelude to entering into a 'profession or trade' as soon as possible after completing his degree. There was no suggestion that that profession should be the Army.

Haig went to Brasenose College in October 1880 and obviously enjoyed his time there. He worked hard, but hunted, played polo and was a member of the leading clubs for undergraduates, including the Bullingdon and Vincent's. Polo, at which he became exceptionally good in later years, indeed representing England in the United States, being part of the highly successful 7 Hussars team and leading the 17 Lancers to win the Army championship, had only recently come to England and had not been played at Oxford. Having become a founder member of the University Polo Club he tried to persuade the authorities that they should be allowed to play in the parks by referring to the ancient history of the game, claiming that it had been brought to Europe by Marco Polo. The authorities were not falling for this very dubious provenance and refused permission. They did, however, play in Port Meadow and the club was a success. One can conclude from the following description of the first Inter-Varsity match against Cambridge that the standard was not high. Haig had

14

started to keep a diary whilst at Oxford, with this entry being dated Saturday, 17 June 1882, two days before his twenty-first birthday, but written from memory as the diary actually starts in 1883.

> I played at Hurlingham at polo for Oxford University v. Cambridge. Our team consisted of 1. Harry Portman, Captain. 2. Jack Cator. 3. Gosling. 4. Charrington – and self. (Polo was five-a-side at that time.) Portman's two ponies inferior. Cator had only one. Gosling two, but he himself as well as ponies was moderate player – Charrington had two excellent ponies, but being himself such a duffer he might as well have been off the ground! I had one very good pony and another moderately good one. I got the only goal on our side, but we ought to have had several had our fellows backed me up. The Cam. Team only got one also, so the match was a draw.

Presumably the match was only four chukkas, but one feels sorry for Cator's wretched pony. What Haig confided to his diary makes it clear that he considered his contribution to the Oxford side in the game was easily the most valuable. We can perhaps put this boastfulness down to youthful exuberance. He was not, by nature, a boastful man. A return match was played, at which Cambridge won. Haig said his ponies were tired, having been played by someone else mid-week.

Haig's contemporary at Brasenose, Lord Askwith,[6] wrote a long article for the *Oxford Magazine* in February 1928, shortly after Douglas Haig had died It covers, both fully and amusingly, life at Oxford in 1880–83. The following are extracts:

> On the first evening of that October day, he from Clifton and I from Marlborough, lads of the same age, sat side by side in the Old Hall, facing the large picture of Principal Frodsham Hudson; and afterwards in my room, as his wine had not arrived, sipped a bottle of claret together. We laughed over our interviews held that morning with Dr. Cradock, who had been Principal at that date for twenty-seven years. To me he had finally ended by saying, 'Drink plenty of port, sir. You want port in this damp climate.' To him he had remarked, 'Ride, sir, ride. I like to see the gentlemen of Brasenose in top boots.' Such jerked out and unexpected pieces of advice to lads fresh from school endeared Principal Craddock to generations of B.N.C. men from their day of entry. Haig said that being too old to try to enter in the usual way, he had determined to try to enter the

15

Army through the university, an opportunity but lately, I think, introduced.

Little during the evening could that youth have foretold that he would be Commander-in-Chief of the greatest Army the Empire had ever produced, in the greatest war known to history. On December 16th 1927, after he had presided over a dinner given to the Principal, Mr. Sampson, and the Fellows of B.N.C., I had with him a long talk; he made plans for future visits to Oxford, spoke of old days, said he remembered every word of our forty-seven-year-old talk as if it had been yesterday, and before the end of January he passed away.

Haig's lodgings in Brasenose apparently were almost squalid. Lord Askwith's recollections continue:

. . . and here Haig lived for two terms, not liking these meagre quarters (in a building put up temporarily in the Peninsular War). In athletics he started on the river, but his frame and weight were too slight, and he could not bear the monotony of tubbings or the upbraidings of coaches, and soon left it for the hunting field. I can see him now, then, as ever, scrupulously dressed, walking through the 'Quad', with tails showing beneath a short covert coat, as was then the fashion.

For the Schools he read French Literature and the Elements of Political Economy under (Sir) Richard Lodge, and in other subjects, such as Homer, dealt with Walter Pater. Mr Sampson, the present principal, tells me that Haig said Pater taught him how to write English. [ What Haig actually said in his speech of 16 December 1927 was that Walter Pater had had the 'unenviable' task of trying to teach him to write good English.]

His special tutor was Dr. Heberden, the late Principal of B.N.C. and a famous Vice-Chancellor, whom he held in real affection, and my own impression is that Dr. Heberden, by example, showed him the duty of thinking of others.

In social life Haig was elected to the (now defunct) Octagon Wine Club, but soon left it to become a member of the Junior Common Room or Phoenix Club; and later was also elected to the Bullingdon, that Club famed beyond the University for its success in the support of interest in the horse, as well as of sport and hospitality generally. No dinner and no club, however, deterred Haig if he was not prepared for a particular lecture or essay. As to wine and cards, he was more than abstemious. His

16

object was to pass his Schools, and to pass them quickly, and he cut or left a social gathering for his books with singular tenacity of purpose. The College records and the remembrance of those who were his teachers show he sailed through his Schools with ease and speed, passing Moderations, the old 'Rudiments Examination', and three Groups, Ancient History, French, and Political Economy.

By ill-luck he missed the Summer Term of 1881 through an attack of influenza or similar illness, and though he had passed all his Schools, did not qualify by residence for the B.A. Degree. Of this he was aware, and scrupulously inquired, when advanced in 1915 to an Hon. Fellowship of Brasenose, and in 1919 to be an Hon. D.C.L. of the University, whether he had passed sufficient schools to entitle him to these honours!

The entries in Haig's diary for 1883 are full of the joys of being up at Oxford with a circle of amusing friends, luncheon and dinner parties, elections to the most desirable clubs, polo and hunting. He preferred the dinners to the lunches, because he did not usually eat lunch. He was sociable, even gregarious at this stage of his life and obviously much liked by his friends. Interestingly, he also attended the John Ruskin School of Art regularly, where he drew, rather than painted.

These contemporaries make an interesting and not undistinguished list. They are all mentioned in the diaries for 1882 and 1883 although not necessarily in the extracts included in this selection.

The entry for 18 April 1883 says:

Breakfast with Noll at 8.30 as usual and read till 1o'c. During the morning Walker the vet came to see me and advised blistering the mare's knee – I agree to this. The boy whom I engaged as groom yesterday for 16/- a week began work today. The two ponies arrived at 9.40 from Dublin. They left at 12.30 yesterday. I went to see them after lunch: the bay pony I bought in February last does not seem to have been much groomed, she did not eat her feed well. T.Turbett also sent a small black pony; he ate his grub well. T.T. paid £26 for this latter and he says in his letter received this morning – 'I hope I shall be able to sell him at a profit to satisfy.'

Dinner at 7 o'clock with Noll. Macdonnell and Lord Henry Bentinck dined with us. After dinner we have great argument on the present evils of the Church, notably the narrow-minded views of clergymen and their hypocrisy. Mac. talked loudly but did not listen to our arguments, he was all in favour of the 'good work done by the Church'. Jumbo (Bentinck) listened but said little; Noll stammered out his views on 'Charity' which, he said 'was never preached to the people.' I must say I thought he had right on his side tho' he could not express his feelings. Something does seem to be wrong in younger sons entering the Church because there is a living in the family and not because they have an inclination to it. Noll left and went to his couch at 10 p.m. I finished the argument amicably and we parted about eleven.

At dinner we had discussed the meanness of some fathers to their sons up here in the hopes of making them acquire the knowledge of the value of money – such as the Duke of Westminster to Harry Grosvenor who is obliged to bet a little to get some money and Puppy Weymouth who is allowed £300 a year by the Marquess of Bath his father. To bed about 11.30. Today the City and Suburban was run. Roisterer won – betting 50 to 1. Most people here backed Shotover but lost of course as he was nowhere.

The concept that you need to bet in order to increase your income is traditional and of very long standing. No doubt it is still alive and well today. Henry Grosvenor clearly failed to back Roisterer. He probably calculated that if the worst came to the worst the Duke, his father, would pay the bookmaker. That presumably is what the bookmaker thought too. In today's money Puppy Weymouth's allowance of £300 a year is the equivalent of £24,000 but, of course, purchasing values are very different now from what they were at the end of the nineteenth century. Nevertheless one cannot help feeling that young Weymouth was a very lucky Puppy.

Douglas Haig came down from Oxford in the summer of 1883, when he was twenty-two years old. If he was not to exceed the upper age limit for entry into Sandhurst, he had to miss a term at Oxford and, as pointed out above, also miss the residential qualification for his degree. This explains why he did not have time to go back to Oxford for the term that would have enabled him to receive his degree. After a short holiday in France, no doubt also to brush up his French, he went to a crammer in Hampton Court to prepare himself for the Sandhurst examination. He entered the Royal Military College, Sandhurst, in February 1884, when he was twenty-two years and eight months old.

18

Sandhurst, near Camberley, in those days consisted of ten divisions of gentleman cadets, all destined for the Cavalry, Guards or Infantry. They were all in what is now known as Old College, a splendid, early nineteenth century classical building. The Royal Military Academy Woolwich prepared the future officers in the Royal Artillery and Royal Engineers.

The present Sandhurst trains all professional officers in the British Army and, in addition, provides places for officers in the armies of a number of other friendly nations. There are three colleges, Old, New and Victory. Each company is named after a battle in which the British Army distinguished itself. The Old College companies are named after battles fought in the eighteenth and nineteenth centuries. Victory College companies all commemorate Second World War battles. New College are all from the First World War. The newly joined cadet, Douglas Haig, was to play a leading part in three of the battles. They are Ypres, Somme and Marne. The odd one out is Gaza.

Haig, obviously, was several years older than the majority of his intake, who had come to Sandhurst straight from school, and did not make many close friends as he had done at Oxford. He had already acquired the habit of hard work, much influenced by his mother, whose letters usually included advice about his studies, as well as a wholesome biblical text. He did not neglect sport and continued to play polo and hunt. He was always conscious of the need for exercise and fitness, typical of a former asthmatic, whose disease might return if he was not careful.

His hard work resulted in him passing out first in the order of merit, as now a combination of the highest marks in the examinations and a grading based on his general performance. An anonymous instructor told Lady Haig that, when asked in 1885 who was the most promising cadet, he had replied:

A Scottish lad, Douglas Haig, is top in everything – books, drill, riding and sports; he is to go into the cavalry, and, before he is finished, he will be top of the Army.

We do not know who the instructor was. There has been a suggestion that he was a senior NCO. Many ex-subalterns will recall being told 'You're the best officer we've ever had, Sir' by an NCO, who had consumed one or two pints too many! But this was quite different. Haig actually was top in everything. In consequence he won the Anson Memorial Sword. This was awarded to the best of the intake of 129 gentleman cadets, inevitably an Under Officer and was the precursor of the Sword of Honour, also invariably won by an Under Officer.

The Sandhurst course was only for one year, rather than eighteen months or two years. Possibly the university entrants were excused a term. Whatever the case, Haig was commissioned into the 7 Hussars in early February 1885. There was no family connection with the regiment but it had been raised in Scotland in 1690. Probably Haig had noted that the 7th was amongst the best polo playing regiments and similarly the officer talent-spotting on behalf of the 7th would have noted that young Douglas Haig was the best of the polo playing talent in that intake at Sandhurst.

Notes.
1.  The de Morville family tree (to be found on the Internet) seems to indicate that Hugo was the father of the de Morville, who was one of the murderers of Thomas a Becket.
2.  A boy and two girls died in infancy, leaving the following eight survivors: William (Willie) Henry Haig (1841–1884) who married Emily Martha Newman (1850–1929) and had one son and three daughters. Mary Elizabeth Haig (1843–1918) married, firstly, Colonel G. De Pree (1832–1887) and had two sons, and, secondly, John Jameson (1835–1920). Hugh (Hugo) Veitch Haig (1845–1902) married Archie Ann Lindesay Fraser (1849–1898) and had two sons and two daughters. Janet Stein Haig (1848–1924) married Charles Edwin Haig (1849–1917) and had one son and one daughter. Henrietta Frances Haig (1851–1928) married William (Willie) George Jameson (1847–1939). John (Bee) Alicius Haig (1857–1933) married Jessie Marion Purbrook, Lady Waller. George (Geordie) Ogilvy Haig (1859–1905) married Charlotte Augusta Astor. Douglas, Earl Haig (1861–1928) married the Hon. Dorothy Vivian (1880–1939) and had one son and three daughters.
3.  The Clifton contemporaries were Douglas J. Byard and C.C. Hoyer Miller. Sir Francis Younghusband (of Tibet fame) also wrote his recollection of Haig at Clifton, but possibly because there was a two year difference in age he does not seem to have remembered anything of note, except that young Douglas was good looking and always well turned out!
4.  The information on Sandhurst comes from Lieutenant Colonel Dr Chris Pugsley, a lecturer in Military History at Sandhurst.
5.  As early as June 1875 Rachel Haig was writing to her son saying that she hoped he would get into Oxford. She wrote more strongly on 28 February 1879 thanking Douglas for his letter, enclosing one from Willie about Douglas's future, and saying that she hoped that Dr Percival would be informed as soon as possible that Douglas's intention was 'to go to Oxford or Cambridge early – for as Willie says by going early you

will be finished early & ready to begin your Profession or Trade at once when you pass'. The letter is in the NLS.

6. George Rankin Askwith (1861–1942) became a distinguished lawyer and Government representative in international negotiations. He was also involved in British trade disputes. He became KC in 1908 and was awarded the CB in 1909. He was knighted (KCB) in 1911 and became the 1st (and last) Baron Askwith in 1919.

# Chapter 2

# 7 Hussars to Nomination
# for the Staff College

## 1885 – 1894

Douglas Haig was commissioned into the 7 Hussars in February 1885 and joined the Regiment at Aldershot. After a year or so he managed to introduce some variety into the humdrum life of a Subaltern in peacetime. Polo had occupied much of his leisure hours and his diary for 1886 contains records of matches played as part of the 7 Hussars team. At the same time he continued to work hard at being a soldier, passing off the square – the fate of all newly joined officers – in double-quick time. By this time the Regiment was at Hounslow. The first entry is as follows:

> Made honorary members of Ranelagh and Hurlingham Clubs. Both about 1hr. and 10 minutes drive.(from Hounslow) We have Regimental games regularly 2 or 3 times a week. Before the Derby, we played at Ranelagh, and, leaving after breakfasting in the Club House, were in time for the first race. Also during Ascot week we played Tuesday morning at Hurlingham and got to Ascot from Clapham Junction in time for first race.
>
> Hurlingham opens on 1st May – our first match was on Monday 7th against 'Freebooters'.
>
> Sides. 7th Hussars: Capt. Hon. RT Lawley,[1] Capt. Hone, Mr D Haig, Mr G Carew.[2]
>
> Freebooters: Mr J Watson, Capt. J Spicer, Capt. L Jones, Capt. Sinclair
>
> 7th Hussars win 5 goals to 1

Saturday, June 5th

Champion Open Cup. Final tie between 7th Hussars and 'Freebooters.

Sides. 7th Hussars – as above

Freebooters. Watson, Spicer, Jones and Major B. Gough (9th Lancers).

After half-an-hour 1st goal; was score by 7th Hussars (Carew). The Regiment had on three occasions v. bad luck in not getting a goal – once Watson saved the ball on goal line and said ball did not cross. There was a discussion and we gave in. Though at commencement of match most onlookers expected 7th to win, the luck was such that in the last 10 minutes the Freebooters scored four goals and thus won by 4 to 1.

> Carew played No. 1
> Hone played No. 2
> Lawley played No.3
> Haig played Back

These were the places throughout this season.

The 7 Hussars played in Dublin in July and Haig was able to stay with his brother Bee (John) at Kingstown. He was no doubt disappointed that the Freebooters won the Dublin Open Cup for the 2nd time in succession. 'They therefore keep it, and give another with "satisfactory and sportsmanlike rules".' In August he made his second visit to the USA as part of a British team to play the Americans at polo. They played two matches and won them both easily, despite the Americans including Haig's BNC friend Tommy Hitchcock in their team.

In September 1886 the 7 Hussars moved to Shorncliffe. Douglas Haig wrote:

About the 20th Sept. the Regt. Marches by 3 routes to Shorncliffe. I leave a couple of days before and go, accompanied by Bobby Houston (my servant) and Napper the Irish terrier, to Swalbach, Germany, where Henrietta is drinking the waters. After a fortnight's stay there, we leave, driving to Lorch on the Rhine, where we were recommended to the Hotel zum Schwann. Here they could not take us in, so we went on by train to Koenigswinter. George (brother) came to see us from Aix (Aachen) where he was drinking the waters. There is a railway up the Drackenfels now. We did not stay long in this place, as

23

my leave was nearly up and the Hotel was not very comfortable. We left on a Sunday from the station on the left bank of the Rhine. The train happened to be late and did not stay long in the station; the two servants were in consequence left on the platform. This was the train which ran in connection with the mail from Cologne. On arriving in Cologne I got a commissionaire at the Hotel du Nord to meet them and give them their tickets.

Henrietta, George and I leave at 1 o'clock. We drop him (George) at Aachen, and Henrietta and I go to Brussels. We reach there about 7, the servants about 11.30 at night. We are off next day by the forenoon express, 11 o'clock, a new train and much faster. Owing to better boats, we did the distance from Calais pier to Dover in the hour exactly.

I leave the train at Shorncliffe Camp and Henrietta goes up to London. Shorncliffe Camp is on the hill above Folkestone about a couple of miles distant. The Officers' huts have been condemned years ago as unfit, yet they are still standing. My quarters consisted of two small rooms about 8 feet square each; the roof let in the water when it rained; there was no lock on the doors and the wind came whistling through the cracks. At Shorncliffe it is always blowing a gale and one is perished with cold. The men's huts are of concrete and are most comfortable.

It was at Shorncliffe that all our accoutrements were taken over by Indian Government. The officer who examined the swords and carbines said he had seldom examined the carbines of a regiment going to India which were in such good order.

At the beginning of November I get leave and go to Scotland to say good-bye . . .

Thursday 25th November was a bitterly cold morning, snow on the ground and a biting wind, when the 7th Hussars fell in on the gravel in front of the Mess hut; the men with their sun helmets on looked weird-like in the grey morning light.

Haig's account of the journey to India on HMTS *Euphrates* comes from his diary:

The passengers are as a whole an uninteresting lot. Several newly married couples, greatly taken up with each other. One Colonel, going out to command a Battn. of the Rifle Brigade, is dubbed by the ladies 'the sentry' from the care he takes of his young wife. 5 or 6 doctors on board, mostly married. One, styled 'the dirty

Dr.' a German looking creature, excites the jealousy of an infantry captain; both have just lately entered the matrimonial state, and both men's wives are in the same cabin. The Dr. has the pull over the other, he can visit his wife's cabin to administer physic. The other feels annoyed no doubt; there are words and recourse is had to the Captain of the ship! But women are at the bottom of all quarrels . . .

We get to Bombay on Wednesday 22nd December about 1 o'clock. The voyage has been a smooth and prosperous one. We arrived too late to land that day at which we were pleased. The ship had hardly come to rest before HRH The Duke of Connaught,[3] C in Chief of Bombay Presidency, comes on board to welcome his old regiment to India. I am first to get off from the ship as I am sent to order dinner at Watson's Hotel: we are to entertain the officers of HMTS *Euphrates* – we all enjoy our dinner, our first in India, though I thought Bombay ought to have better cooks! We brought our own champagne from the ship with us; the hotel could not supply us with anything good! Such are Bombay hotels!

The Regiment was headed for Secunderabad in Hyderabad and this involved a long train journey via Poona and Wadi.

**Thursday, 23 December 1887**

The Duke of Connaught comes to see us off. We go in two trains about 7 o'clock and 7.30. I am in the first train. At 5 am we are told we have got to Poona. The stationmaster wants us to get out. It is cold on the platform. The other train arrives, and the regt. is formed up outside the station, but we can't move off as no staff officer has yet come to show us the way. So much for Indian management! The men too were disgracefully crowded in the carriages. We reach the rest camp about 8; all the officers are put up in the club – a very well managed place, and most comfortable. In the afternoon about 5pm the Duke and General Solly Flood[4] inspect the regt. And in the evening all the officers dine with HRH . . . .

On Sunday afternoon we leave Poona, about 5 pm in two detachments as before. The staff officer again at fault, he did not know the number that should go into each compartment. There was such a crush that we (the regt.) had to pay for an extra carriage to be put on. Next day we spend at Wadi, the junction of the Nizam's State Railway with the Gt. Indian Peninsular Ry.

We are off again after dinner about 8 and reach Trimulgherry about 7 next morning.

There is no permanent station here, but there is a platform, and when troops arrive tents are pitched. We found the officers of the Hampshire Regt. and the Gunners had sent down coffee, beer, etc. for officers and men. It was about 9 before we got off, and then there is a walk of 2½ miles to barracks. The road was v. dusty and the sun hot, so the march seemed a long one.

The men's bungalows are fine large buildings; the great drawback is, that there are not enough of them, having been built for regiments of 6 Troops while we have come out on the strong strength, viz. 8 Troops. In consequence of the want of space, the men's recreation rooms have to be used by one Troop as sleeping quarters. The officers find the same difficulty, want of house room, and several of the last joined have to share one subaltern's quarters between them. Had the regt. contained many married officers in place of only one (viz. Col. Peel), it would have been quite impossible to fit into the place!. The horses are all picketed out on the Maidan on account of 'anthrax' – they seem half starved and are in a wretched condition . . .

## 2 March 1887

General Gib inspects the regt. on the 19th, 21st and 22nd Feby. And we (the polo team) leave on Wednesday morning (23rd Feb. by the Bombay mail . . . At Ahmedabad, reached at 9.15 next morning, we change on to the metre gauge, and continue on this line till Saturday night at 8 pm when Delhi is reached. Here we have an hour for dinner and travel by the NW Ry. to Umballa which we reach about 6 next morning, Sunday . . . At breakfast Tom Hone tells me his best pony has come in from exercise lame! We go and have an inspection; the pony has sprained tendon of near foreleg, and won't be fit to play for months. The outlook at present is not hopeful! Only 10 sound ponies to begin the Tournament with! The Native Tournament fortunately begins next day and a number of ponies will be for sale after it.

So we make enquiries about the ponies and players, and next day we watch the match carefully and spot the best ponies in the losing team. It was a good match between XIth and IXth Bengal Cav., the former win. By the end of the week we have bought 9 ponies from the competing teams.

On Tuesday morning 2nd March, I had a bad head, but thinking it would go off I went about doing everything as usual.

26

Next morning we played a trial game of polo and after break-fast I felt I had fever. However, I thought it would wear off if I kept out of the sun. On Friday morning we played our third trial match before breakfast; I felt I was getting worse but as we had not a 5th player I thought there was nothing for it but to hold on.

Next night we went to dine with General McFarlane; I was in the drawing-room before dinner and felt so seedy I had to come away and go to bed. Next day the Dr. said my temperature was 105.6.

Haig had typhoid, one of the scourges of the British Army in India and, as we will see later, also in South Africa. Having recovered from the illness and convalesced in Simla, he was given leave to go to Kashmir, where he went shooting. He returned to Secunderabad at the end of August. He had been out of action for nearly five months.

He was again in Kashmir in April and May 1888 with Beresford,[5] a brother officer, who was an amusing and enjoyable companion. There was an unusual amount of snow, which inhibited the opportunity for sport, in this case shooting ibex and bears, but nevertheless a good time was had by both young officers. The diary records that a 'sahib' and his shooting party were buried by the snow. The problem which then arose was where and indeed how to bury the sahib. This caused Beresford, in particular, some amusement.

Haig was appointed adjutant of the 7 Hussars in July 1888. This was an important recognition of his ability; officers with such short service are seldom appointed adjutant. The diary then becomes more concerned with military matters. There was much training and a number of mock battles through the winter and spring of 1889 until the weather became too hot for both horses and men. As adjutant he was involved in an unusual disciplinary matter, when it was discovered that the paymaster, a Major Creighton, had insufficient funds in the treasury to pay the troops. A Court of Inquiry was held to determine whether the paymaster had had his hand in the till or had merely been unbelievably stupid and inefficient. We know that Creighton was in Close Arrest and that he was to face a court martial. Frustratingly the result is not recorded in Haig's diary, possibly because he was away in Europe on leave from the end of April to the end of June 1889.

Douglas Haig was clearly an efficient young officer with a growing reputation. His troop sergeant, S. Griffiths, wrote to Lady Haig in 1929:

As I was doing duty in 'C' Troop, that was Lieut. Haig's Troop, I saw a lot of the Lieut. in my duties. He was always kind and considerate to his men . . . .He was well liked by all the men. After I had a breakdown in health I was in hospital with enteric fever off and on for 12 months . . . During the time Lieut. Haig was appointed Adjutant of the Regiment in succession to Captain Ridley – a great responsibility for an officer with so little service, but the Lieut. was equal to the work he had to do, which was done in first-class military style . . . He would come down to hospital and talk to the serious cases, ask if he could do anything for you, he would write to your friends in England if you was not well enough . . . He was most kind to me.

The year ended with a tiger shoot, vividly recorded in the diary.

**Monday,30 December, 1889**
Went in morning to tank near camp. There is a kill beyond Gurrapoorum. After getting beaters etc. we start about 12o'clock – Beresford goes up first; Liebert second; self third; Crawley fourth. David (butler) comes up tree with me. Shortly after the beat commences, a bear comes near Crawley's tree. He fires at him. Then I hear some rustling in the bushes and Liebert fires; there is no roar. He says he has hit a tiger. After the beat is over Pechell comes to my tree and I get down. Crawley is already on the ground. We follow the wounded tiger. Pechell first, self second, then Jogira and Crawley with old David and my second rifle. Every coolie is up a tree on the top-most twig! Jungle is very thick so it is somewhat jumpy work; we go over some big stones, amongst thick jungle, and we come across the tiger – somewhat hard to see tho' I put on my spectacles and fire. The animal roars and rises up: this is a signal for all the gaspipe guns to be let off; in fact there is greater danger from the rear than in front. The tiger goes on about 40 or 50 yards and falls over. Again a discharge and he moves no more. The others then come up to see the animal. It must be noted that old David is a very brave man; he warned us not to run back should the tiger roar! However, the moment the shot was fired he rushed back upon those behind, carrying off my second rifle with him and spreading dismay into the ranks behind.

When all was over there was a great tamasha. A litter was made of boughs on which the tiger was carried by 16 coolies. In front of this came the band consisting of a couple of tomtoms and native minstrel singers, then at a suitable distance marched the great old man David mounted on my grey Arab pony, at present rather lean of flesh yet quite the charger as he has a flowing tail. On each side and in rear of the cortege came the populace of Caterpully and Gurrapoorum, Nagaunrum, and other neighbouring townships, making the jungle echo with their shouts. The arrival in camp is quite an event, all the boys, maty cook, etc., go out to see the bagh home amidst renewed yells.

During this time 'master' shivers in camp, waiting one hour for bath. Dinner comes about 7.45 and we drink Liebert's health in champagne.

In January 1890 he was again ill with fever, with a temperature of 104. He seems, however to have continued with his work as adjutant, without having time off in hospital or on sick leave. He attended the regimental sports three days later and the usual round of activities of regimental life. His diary complains about the chaplain's over-long sermon – 'Church in camp at 9 am. The Rev. Etty from Secunderabad kept us for an hour standing while he talked on. Such discomfort with a hot sun is not conducive to devotion.'

In 1890 he was once again able to take leave in Europe, returning to Britain in April by way of Monte Carlo, where he 'won about 25 Napoleons but lost them all again', and Paris, where he arrived on 30 April. The French capital was 'full of troops as a disturbance was expected. All the streets covered with sand to allow cavalry to charge if necessary. Only once required to charge, but patrols moved up and down at regular intervals.'

He went to his sister Mary's wedding in London, was in Scotland briefly, also Dublin and was at the Derby. By the end of June, after a whirlwind visit he was on the way back to India, reaching Secunderabad on 14 July.

Haig took no European leave in either 1891 or 1892, but travelled widely. In 1891 he and two brother officers went to Quetta and the North-West Frontier. This was followed by a visit to Ceylon, where once again he developed a high temperature, in this case 104.5, presumably the aftermath of typhoid or perhaps malaria, which he must have contracted during his first visit to India – he suffered bouts of malaria throughout his life. But, as in the previous year, he rose above it and carried on with his visit.

It seems that it was in Ceylon that he first played golf, rather surprisingly late in life for a Scotsman. He played with Lieutenant Colonel Dalgety, 7 Hussars, one of his travelling companions, having had 'a lesson in driving in the billiard room before starting. I found I got on v. well, much better than I expected.' It was in 1905 that he wooed his future wife, the Hon. Dorothy Vivian, on the golf course. So it was just as well that he had learnt how to play and, it seems, was a competent player. Eventually, he was elected Captain of the Royal and Ancient Golf Club at St Andrews and managed to drive efficiently off the first tee in his inaugural round under the gaze of the usual large crowd of members. Others, in the same situation, have not been so fortunate and an air shot or two is not unknown, particularly after lunch!

Haig arrived back in Secunderabad on 1 July, being met at the station by Beresford. As he said in his diary: '. . . to do this he missed his dinner. V. good of him. It is a v. wet night too!'

Haig stood out in comparison with the other young officers in the 7 Hussars. The Brigade Commander at Secunderabad, Brigadier General H.F. Bengough CB[6] evidently noted that he was somewhat different when compared with his contemporaries. He wrote in June 1891:

> I was most interested in your remarks on Cavalry Reconnaissance and in the little pamphlets that you sent me, all of which appear to me excellent. If all or most cavalry officers took as much interest in instructing their men, we should have our Cavalry, which General Luck says it now is, 'equal to any in Europe.' I should prefer to say best in the world.

He also caught the eye of General Luck[7] himself. Later in the year he was selected by the General to act as Brigade Major at the cavalry camp at Aligarh. In January the following year he was selected by his Commanding Officer to join General Sir George Greaves[8] as a staff officer at the Poona Camp and was attached to the headquarters of the Bombay Army.

In 1892 he took his leave in Australia rather than returning to Britain. He wrote on 2 May to Henrietta:

> The people here are extraordinarily hospitable; we only arrived (in Melbourne) last Tuesday and each day we have had invitations for lunch and dinner and theatre. The moment one is introduced to anyone, there is sure to be an invitation for some amusement or meal of sorts. The climate is fine and fresh here, and the eating and drinking is of the best! I mention this because you are always so afraid I don't take proper nourishment!

He and his brother officer, Beresford, had arrived in Adelaide on 22 April. They stayed at the Adelaide Club and visited Marble Hill,[9] the Governor's summer residence. Douglas Haig said of the visit:

At 3 pm (on Sunday 24th April) drive out to Marble Hill. A nice drive up hill after the first 3 miles. The house is about 12 miles from Adelaide and stands 2000 ft above sea. Well built but small for a Government House. Lord Kintore[10] met us as we arrived about 5. We took a little walk then had tea, and dinner at 7.30 pm. The Kintores were very kind and told us to be sure and let them know before we returned to Adelaide. We drove back about 10.30 pm. JG (Beresford) somewhat sleepy; night cold but the police horses took us along well.

The Governor had obviously been kind enough to provide Haig and Beresford with his carriage drawn along by a team of the Adelaide Police's splendid grey horses. They visited Larg's Bay Fort, '. . . Two 6" breech loading guns on disappearing carriages as well as 4 muzzle loaders . . .'. Then they went on to Melbourne, Ballarat, Sydney, the Blue Mountains and the New South Wales countryside around what is now Canberra.

All this was interspersed with visits to the theatre and opera. Haig was amused by the polo and even umpired and instructed on at least one occasion. It is interesting that he obviously got on well with the Australians. Maybe his enjoyable experience of Australia was a help to him years later when he had a large body of Australian troops under his command. They were marvellous troops, brave and full of initiative, but with a somewhat different concept of discipline compared with the average Pommy division!

When he returned to India in July he was posted to the Adjutant General's office in the Bombay Army. It was evidently clear that he was not going back to the 7 Hussars after this appointment finished. In fact it only lasted for a very few weeks.

### Diary Sunday, 14 August

Went to Church Parade and handed over Orderly Room to Graham afterwards. In the evening dine with Colonel Hunt and officers 7th Hussars – Colonel Hunt proposes my health. Amongst other things says, 'that whatever he undertakes he puts his whole heart and soul into it, and always, you may be sure, he makes things a success.' I find it hard to reply.

When he left for Poona by the 7.40 train on 15 August a party of seven brother officers, including the Commanding Officer, came to see him off. He wrote: 'I am v. sorry to say goodbye. Graham (the new Adjutant) puts a little note into the Tiffin baskets to bid farewell.'

Writing to Henrietta on 1 September 1892 from Poona he said:

I have found out all I want to know in the AG's office and as the examination for the Staff College is very hard, I think the sooner I come home the better and arrange what I am to do. I have therefore engaged a passage in the *Peninsula* which leaves Bombay on 9th Sept. and will therefore be home I hope a fortnight sooner than you expect! This ought I think to be my last letter to you from India for some time. I am going to wire to you that I am leaving before the 24th but is difficult to find a word to let you know that I have finished my business here and so am returning for that reason and not because I am unwell. I am really very fit and have little to do here except amuse myself but as I can do that better at home I think it best to start. The Chief is going on tour on the 5th, but won't hear of my leaving his house to stay in the Club; he bids me invite whoever I like to keep me company during his absence and just order his butler to provide dinner etc. for so many! V. hospitable of the old man, isn't it? I hope to go to Bombay on 7th as I have to get papers of all sorts in the way of pay and so on signed, and to receive others to give to pay people at home.

I should reach Brindisi about 23rd Sept. and will come home (as I have already told you) via Naples, Rome and Turin unless the weather is very hot, in which case I'll come straight, but Italy ought to be pleasant enough in the end of September. The cholera is also spreading I see, so maybe I'll have to make a detour for that. In any case you might drop me a line and tell me what you are doing because if you are paying visits I'll just take it easy on the continent till you are free. King & Co. have an agent at Brindisi so you might address there; if this reaches you too late for that perhaps you might find time for a line to Post Office, Naples. I'll call there and also at the one at Rome as I don't know the name of any hotel at present.

I got a letter from Bee saying he will look out for horses for me and offers me a share of Gerrardstown but suggests Stephen Kelly's as a good place for a residence! It was rather a shanty the last time I saw Stephen's house, good only for a cup of tea and toast, or whiskey: but perhaps the house has been 'remodelled', in any case I'll wait till I have seen you and discussed the Staff Coll. Exam. question with James (the crammer) before deciding where I'll go. Everyone goes to James or some coach for the Staff Coll. as he saves one so much trouble and knows whether one can pass or not. It seems quite odd leaving India so soon. My heavy baggage I am afraid will have to travel by itself a week or so later because I did not think I could have got away from this office so soon. I don't know what to do with it when I get to London because your house is already crammed to overflowing and there would be no room for books or clothes.

An extraordinary sign of the regard in which he was held in the 7 Hussars was that a party of brother officers and the Regimental Sergeant Major came to see him off at Bombay. It is not known whether or not they had other reasons for being in Bombay, but Mhow (near Indore), where, by then, the regiment was stationed, is many miles away and it is quite remarkable that they should have been given leave to undertake a journey of such length in order to see a relatively junior officer off to England.

**Haig's diary for 9 September 1892 says:**
Find Regimental Sergeant Major Humphries waiting at launch for me. We all go aboard *Peninsula* – quite melancholy parting. Humphries wrung my hand and said I was 'the best sort he had ever had to do with'. They go down the ladder into a small boat, the tide running very strong towards the lighthouse. I watched them with my glasses till they were quite a small speck, and were out near Coloba point. I feel quite sorry at leaving them all.

On arrival back from India, Douglas Haig moved into his sister's London flat at Albert Gate. At an early stage he consulted a doctor about his general health, to try to lay to rest Henrietta's fear that it might have been undermined by the recurring fever he had had in India.

On 30 October 1892 he wrote to Henrietta:

In order to set your mind at rest regarding my health, I went and saw a Dr. after leaving James (the crammer) tonight at 5 pm. one Hamilton Brown of a certain fame and certainly a most careful and painstaking physician. He looked at me all over! My tongue of course, chalked with a pencil the size of my liver, put things in his ears and listened to my lungs and heart and so forth. He said he would pass me as a 'thoroughly sound man' but a little below par. So I hope you will be satisfied now. All I want is plain food and a certain amount of exercise.

Haig went to Dusseldorf in March to improve his German. He seems to have taken Metcalfe, Henrietta and Willie Jameson's butler, with him. In one of his letters to Henrietta he said: 'Metcalfe does first rate. Brings me beef tea, by your orders at 11 am.'

On 17 March he wrote:

I was very sorry to leave you, but I fancy it is the best thing to do to come away by oneself in order to read up for this beastly exam . . . . Herr Carl Wagner is a man over 50, a kindly creature but can't speak a word of English. His Frau speaks English very well, and is a nice looking woman. She has taken a heap of trouble to make me comfortable . . . .I came in for the midday meal today; good soup (Scotch broth style) and roast mutton and a pudding. (a good leg which had not been boiled previously!) The old Frau says they don't live entirely in German style, having had so many acquaintances in England . . . It is no pleasure coming to these foreign parts, and you don't know how sorry I was to leave you last night . . .

Duesseldorf, 4 April 1893

I stayed with Boston's pal – 'Flossie' Oppenheim. The husband is a nice fellow, about 28, and has travelled in India and elsewhere. They insisted on my staying over Easter Monday and were really awfully hospitable. So were the parents who live in Coeln. On Sunday I dined with the Uncle and on Monday (last night) we had a big dinner at the father's about 50 couples at about 9 pm. This lasted till about 2 o'clock this morning. I was received by them all as if I was an old friend. Yesterday morning I drove out with Alfred (ie Flossie's husband) to see the Racing Stables about 6 miles from Coeln ; they have 22 horses in training. All the horses go to Berlin to-day for the racing season. The old people's houses in Coeln are most beautifully done up, and very large! I had no notion there were such fine places in the middle of dirty old Cologne . . . . You see I have taken Easter holidays like the rest of the world!

Duesseldorf, 27 April 1893

I am leaving this morning for Schwalbach . . . On thinking the matter over, regarding 'where I am to stay' I propose taking rooms for the fortnight before the exam. at some place near London, say Richmond, or Wimbledon or Windsor, so that I could come up to James's in the forenoon and go on the river or take a ride in the afternoon when I am free. I think this will be better than staying in London . . . . Just off to dine (5 pm) with the Lancer Regiment here. What an hour to eat, isn't it?

## Schwalbach, 6 May 1893

I am getting on nicely here thank you, and feeling all the better for the waters . . . I have not heard from Bee whether he sold my horses or not. He can do anything he likes with them, but wherever they are at, I must pay for their keep . . . If the bay pony is well enough I might have him over at Richmond . . . When do you propose to come here for your annual refresher? I might come here for a short time with you, and, when you go to your yacht, I might go on to Potsdam just to have a look at the cavalry regiments there for three or four weeks . . . .

The diary entries show that Haig had already established links with the German cavalry, as he did subsequently with the French later in the year. He obviously worked hard to improve his German before taking the Staff College examination. It is a pity that he didn't spend more time on mathematics. He took the examination in June 1893. Despite achieving 140 marks, more than the lowest successful candidate, he failed because he fell just below the 50 per cent pass mark in mathematics. It seems that there was a new examiner, who set a paper substantially different from previous papers and this caught out many candidates, including Haig, who had concentrated their revision efforts on previous papers and indeed had been advised to do so. As can be seen from the following account (draft) he wrote to support his possible entry by means of a nomination by the Commander-in-Chief, the Duke of Cambridge.[11]

1. At the exam. held in June '93 for entrance into the Staff College, I made a total of 2642 marks. The last successful candidate (Captain Taylor, Cheshire Regiment) only made 2503.

2. I am informed by Horse Guards letter of 8th inst., that I failed to qualify in the obligatory subject, mathematics, by 18 marks. Hence my name is not amongst the successful candidates.

3. The Secretary of State for War stated in the House of Commons that a new examiner had been detailed for the recent examination in mathematics and that the papers set were different to those set in previous years. Now, in every 'official' report on exam. for entrance to Staff College 'the attention of intending candidates is called to the papers previously set, and they are directed to take them as guides as to what is required of them'. This year candidates have been misled in the mathematics papers.

4. I am eligible for a 'nomination' by His Royal Highness the Commander-in-Chief, having been recommended by General Sir George Greaves on two occasions during the 2 years that the 7th Hussars were under his command, viz. in 1892 and again this year. Brigadier-General Bengough CB also recommended me for a nomination. He commanded at Secunderabad when the 7th Hussars were there.

As the result of the above recommendation I was informed by the Horse Guards in writing that my name would be submitted for approval by His Royal Highness whenever I had passed a 'qualifying' examination.

I request that the recent examination may be considered satisfactory enough to qualify me for a nomination.

5. Although I was allowed to compete at the recent exam. Sir R. Buller[12] informed me on 10th August that I was not fit for Staff work on account of a Medical Board having reported that I was colour blind. Notwithstanding this fact, I received an official communication from the Horse Guards in February last stating that the Medical Report was satisfactory and consequently I was allowed to compete at the last exam. Is it not rather late to fall back on the Medical Report now, because had I made 18 more marks in a paper which is acknowledged to be somewhat unfair, I would have entered the Staff College without further question?

6. I beg to submit that the Medical Board in examining me for colour blindness exceeded the orders contained in the Queen's Regulations regarding the Medical examination of candidates for the Staff College. The Board is not directed to test candidates for colour blindness and moreover only those candidates who appeared before a medical Board in London were so tested.

7. Professor Mohren (the great German oculist) has tested me for colour blindness and states that I am not colour blind.[13] The Medical Board in London asked me to match certain pale green and pink wools on a foggy day in January, and because I failed to do this to their satisfaction, I am pronounced unfit for the Staff employ altho' I have been in the Service nearly 10 years without ever the slightest doubt being cast upon my eyesight. My confidential reports will bear this out. I passed first out at Sandhurst in December 1884 and received a commission in the 7th (Queen's Own) Hussars on 7th February 1885.

This was clearly a considerable set-back to Haig's career. To have re-taken the exam a year later in order to get the required marks would not have been difficult. It seems, however, that the Adjutant General, Sir Redver Buller, put more importance on colour blindness and would not be prepared to allow Haig into the Staff College under any circumstances. Henrietta Jameson then wrote to Sir Evelyn Wood,[14] at that time Quartermaster General and General Keith Fraser,[15] the Inspector General of Cavalry, both of whom she knew. Fraser's response was that '. . . as a cavalry man I have no influence whatever. If your brother was a Rifleman, he could have a better chance. I am sorry.'

It is interesting to note that, even as early as the late nineteenth century, the myth of the 'black button mafia' was going strong. It was not until 1895 that a 'nomination' to the Staff College was secured for Haig for the course starting in January 1896. The nomination came from the Duke of Cambridge in his last year before retirement.

In the meantime he did not waste an opportunity to learn more about the way the cavalry in other armies operated and was able to attend the French army's cavalry manoeuvres in Touraine in September 1893. His visit was a considerable success and he got on well with the French officers, probably because unlike most British officers – indeed most British people – he spoke good French. He was impressed by the quality of the French troops and by their ability to perform intricate manoeuvres at speed, like 'a well disciplined polo team'. In his report, handed in to the British Military Attaché in Paris, he points out the need for such large-scale cavalry manoeuvres – two cavalry divisions were involved – to test in practice 'many regulations and instructions which seem excellent in theory'. His final paragraph says:

The French cavalry is composed of excellent material. Horses and men of all ranks stood the hard work well. The cavalry divisions reconnoitre, and are led to the attack, I venture to think, in accordance with common-sense principles. Still they might be a great deal better than they are. Napoleon has written that 'a cavalry force, to be of any use, must be composed of young generals and old captains'. Now the fault of the French Cavalry is that they have too many old officers in both ranks. In any case, whatever the short-comings of the French cavalry in the matter of precision and exactness in movement may be, I feel certain that their methods of reconnoitring and ideas on handling a cavalry division in the field deserve fully as much attention by thoughtful soldiers as do the actions of their neighbours across the Rhine.

Haig then returned to the 7 Hussars in Mhow (near Indore). This must have been a bitter pill to swallow, particularly as there was no vacancy for a squadron commander and he had to be content with the role of second in command of a squadron. In fact it must have been an embarrassing situation for the other officers in the 7th as well as for Haig. Being a pragmatist he got on with what needed to be done without sulking and to the best of his ability. Once again this earned him the respect of all ranks in his regiment. He was saved, from a long-drawn-out career and slow promotion through the regimental hierarchy with the possibility of commanding a regiment or at most a brigade, by being selected to become General Keith Fraser's ADC. The latter was still Inspector General of Cavalry and it gave Haig an excellent opportunity to learn something more generally about the British cavalry, although at thirty-three years old he was a bit long in the tooth to be an ADC. Fraser did already know how Haig had performed as adjutant and also when he was temporarily seconded to General Luck and to General Sir George Greaves at the Headquarters of the Bombay Army. Doubtless he had also read Haig's report on his attachment to the French Cavalry. Haig left India in April 1894. His Commanding Officer wrote to him as follows:

April 5 1894

My dear Douglas,

I cannot let you go away without saying how much I have appreciated what you have done for the Regiment. You came back to a position that a great many people would have disliked extremely, second fiddle in a Squadron. Instead of making a grievance of it all, I know what a lot of pains you have taken and how much the improvement in that Squadron has been owing to you and up to the last moment when you knew you were off you have taken just as much interest in the preliminary musketry in the Squadron as if you would be here to see the results. I cannot say how much you will be missed by all Officers, NCOs and men. Your example in the Regiment has been worth everything to the boys. You know I wish you every luck. You are, I think, bound to succeed because you mean to. I hate saying 'good-bye' as I am sadly afraid I shall never soldier with you again, but only hope I may.

Yours very sincerely,

Hamish Reid[16]

Haig's time in the 7 Hussars in India was also commented upon by RQMS Reginald Teale. He wrote to Haig in 1903 to congratulate him on his recent appointment as Inspector General of Cavalry in India.

Cav. Barracks
25/7/03

Sir,

Will you please pardon the liberty I am taking, but as I see that you are shortly going out to India (will you please accept my sincere congratulations on all your so well earned honours) I am taking the opportunity of saying how much Mrs. Teale and I would appreciate one of your photos, if it is not too much to ask for. You perhaps do not know, sir, how much I have to thank you for, but there was a time in India when I (a young fool) was being rapidly led away by bad companions, when suddenly the thought struck me 'what would Capt. Haig think of me if he saw me now' and I put down the glass and said 'I have done with drink'. That was 15 years ago, and I have touched none since. I am not a teetotaller, but I made up my mind and stuck to it. I have bitterly regretted those months I could not break from my so-called Friends. This will seem foolish to you, sir, no doubt, but I wanted to tell you how much I have to thank you for, and to tell you that it is through my deep respect for you that I have been enabled to raise myself to my present position. We have watched your splendid career throughout the last Soudan and African wars with so much interest and delight, for there is one little home in England where the name of Colonel Haig is loved and honoured above any other. I shall soon have completed my service and shall have to sever myself from the dear old

Regiment. How glad we were to see the 17th won the Polo Cup
– the big men can't beat the light ones.

Goodbye, Sir, and Good Luck,

Your most obedient servant

R. Teale

Haig went with the Inspector General on his visits to most of the cavalry regiments based in Britain. It gave him an insight into what was needed to improve their efficiency, so that they were ready for war. For comparison he had his experience of the French cavalry in 1893. As he wrote to Henrietta in July 1894 he clearly had a very full programme:

> . . . I cannot say exactly what I will be doing the week of the 28th, but as soon as I know Keith Fraser's movements, I will drop you a line. I am off to Frencham (near Aldershot) this afternoon to stay the night, as we have the 4th Hussars out for a reconnoitring day in that direction to-morrow. Tuesday we inspect the Greys in the morning and the 4th Hussars in the afternoon in the Field. On Wednesday we see the Greys reconnoitring in the forenoon, and then we come back to London. Thursday, Friday and Saturday we inspect the 1st and 2nd Life Guards here – so this week we are quite full up . . . reconnoitring means a scheme to be set which requires a little arrangement. Then, I have to look over the Reports and comment on what is done. This means time, so I am fairly busy.

In the meantime the War Office had decided that his colour blindness did not, after all, disqualify him from entering the Staff College. It is not known what caused Buller to have a change of heart; maybe he had finally come to realize that he was preventing an officer of considerable ability from reaching his full potential. Maybe Keith Fraser or Sir Evelyn Wood did actually manage to influence him and perhaps the report on the French cavalry manoeuvres had reached him. Whatever happened to ease Haig's path to the next step in his career, he was entered for the Staff College course starting January 1896. The remainder of 1894 was occupied with the British Autumn Manoeuvres on Salisbury Plain and the subsequent report writing. Haig also was able to pay another visit to the French. He watched a French reserve cavalry regiment mobilize at Limoges; his report to the War Office was considered to be worth printing.

1895 started with Haig working with Keith Fraser to complete the various tasks arising from the Autumn Manoeuvres. The entries in his diary for January and February include the following:

**Friday, 4 January 1895**
Write lengthy letter for General Fraser in reply to Director General of Military Education's remarks on method of Reconnoitring Instruction.

**Tuesday, 22 January**
After dinner went to see General Fraser at 43, Lowndes Square. Worked with him till nearly 1 am. Manoeuvre Report out. I sent copy to H. Jones of *Morning Post* and another to Chas. Williams at Constitutional Club; the latter of *Daily Chronicle*. Colonel Lonsdale Hale to get copy to-morrow.

**Monday, 11 February**
Heard from General Fraser that his successor had been appointed and that he was 'most grateful' to me for having come home to be his ADC.

**Wednesday, 13 February**
Received letter from General Fraser telling me of his disappointment at not getting an extension of Inspector Generalship of Cavalry . . . .

**Sunday, 17 February**
. . . Busy writing notes for French's lecture on Cavalry Manoeuvres.

Haig must also have been disappointed that Keith Fraser's appointment was not extended. It meant that he was effectively unemployed until the following January, when he was due to go to the Staff College. He spent the rest of the winter hunting with the Warwickshire Hunt from the house, Radway Grange,[17] which Willie and Henrietta Jameson used to take. Duff Cooper and John Terraine[18] both imply that Haig didn't really enjoy hunting and that he only did it because it was the right thing for a cavalry officer to do; also that he needed exercise for his health, which had been much undermined by his time in India. His diary, however, records details of the Warwickshire's runs with great enthusiasm. Duff Cooper says that:

If scent was bad and the prospects of sport seemed doubtful, he would often desert the field early in the day, and when his companions returned they would find that he had already settled down to the study of his military tomes.[19]

Surely this merely emphasizes his good judgement and usual sense of where the priorities lay.

For some time Haig had wanted to visit the German Cavalry to study them in comparison with the French and the British. 1895 provided that opportunity and he left London for Berlin on 24 April returning in June.

Notes:
1. Richard Lawley, son of 2nd Baron Wenlock, became a lieutenant colonel. He was a life-long friend of Haig – see his letter of 15 August 1902.
2. G.A.L. Carew D.S.O (1862–1937), retired as a major in 1902. For some reason he was known as 'Stodger'. 'Old Stodger' appears again in Chapter 6. After serving in Rhodesia, where he won his DSO, he was given command of a regiment of Australian Light Horse in South Africa, but chose that moment to accuse a senior officer in Rhodesia of graft. The general feeling was that he had been out too long in the midday sun and poor 'Old Stodger' was sent back to the 7th.
3. HRH Prince Arthur, Duke of Connaught was the son of Queen Victoria and Prince Albert. He was born in 1850, commissioned from Woolwich in 1866 into the RE, transferred into the RA and then into the Rifle Brigade. He evidently also served for a time with the 7 Hussars. He became a general in 1893 and a field marshal in 1902. He was Governor General of Canada from 1911–1916. He died in 1942.
4. General Sir Frederick Solly-Flood KCB, South Lancashire Regiment, was Colonel of the Regiment from 1905–1909.
5. Colonel The Hon. John Graham Beresford DSO was a close friend of Haig's both when they were in the 7 Hussars and afterwards. He was born in 1866 and became the 5th Baron Decies, an Irish title, in 1910. One of the Christian names given to his eldest son was Douglas. It seems possible that Haig was godfather. Beresford died in 1944.
6. Major General Sir Harcourt Mortimer Bengough KCB was born in 1837, appointed Major General in 1894 and retired in 1898. He died in 1922.
7. General Sir George Luck GCB was born in 1840, commissioned into the 15 Hussars in 1858, became a general in 1906 and retired in 1907. He was the first Inspector General of Cavalry in India in 1887–93. He succeeded Keith Fraser as IGC in GB and Ireland in 1895–98. He died in 1916.

8. General Sir George Richards Greaves GCB, CMG was born 1831, commissioned into the East Surrey Regiment in 1849, became a general in 1896 and retired the same year. He died in 1922.
9. Marble Hill, the summer residence of the Governor of South Australia was a solidly built stone house of the 1850s in the Adelaide Hills at Norton Summit. It had a wooden verandah on both floors, one of the reasons why it was destroyed in a bush fire in 1955.
10. The Earl of Kintore, 9th Earl, KT, GCMG was Governor of South Australia from 1889–1895. He was born in 1852 and died in 1930.
11. HRH Prince George Duke of Cambridge was the son of Prince Adolphus, Duke of Cambridge, and Princess Augusta of Hesse-Cassel. He was a grandson of King George III. Born in 1819 he joined the 12 Lancers in 1839 and subsequently the 17 Lancers and the Scots Fusilier Guards. He was appointed major general in 1845, general in 1854 and field marshal in 1862. He served in the Crimea in 1854, where he seems to have suffered from 'shellshock'. In 1887 he became Commander-in-Chief of the Army, from which he retired in 1895. He was much loved but universally considered to be a force of conservatism, making reforms extremely difficult to bring into effect. He died in 1904.
12. General Sir Redvers Buller VC, GCB. Born in 1838 he was commissioned into the 60 Rifles in 1858. He served in the Peking expedition of 1860, in Canada, Ashanti, the Kaffir War of 1878, the Zulu War of 1879, the first Boer War, the Egyptian Campaigns of 1882 and 1885. He became QMG then AG between 1887 and 1897. When the second Boer War started in 1899 he was GOC Aldershot and was given command of the Field Force for Natal. He was in effect superseded, when Roberts arrived in 1900. He retired in 1901 and died in 1908.
13. Haig probably was colour blind, despite the learned professor's opinion. Haig's niece, Ruth De Pree, left an unpublished memoir of her uncle, in which she records an occasion when he was wrong about the colour of her dress. The gene for colour blindness occurs to an above average extent in Haig's male descendants.
14. Field Marshal Sir Henry Evelyn Wood VC, GCB, GCMG originally joined the Navy and was a midshipman in the Crimea. He transferred in 1855 to the Army and was commissioned into the 13 Light Dragoons. He transferred from them into the 17 Lancers. He won his VC during the Indian Mutiny. During his highly distinguished career he was Sirdar of the Egyptian Army from 1883–1885, being succeeded by Kitchener. He had become Quartermaster General in 1893 and Adjutant General in 1897. He was a great admirer of Haig's abilities and helped to promote his career. He died in 1919.
15. Lieutenant General James Keith Fraser CMG was born 1832, and was in the Life Guards. He became Inspector General of Cavalry in 1891. He died at Cowes during Regatta week in 1895. His son Keith was in the 7 Hussars. Haig seems to have thought him somewhat hopeless and also

that his father treated him with some degree of meanness. In consequence there is reference in the diary to Haig bringing the young man back a coat from India. Keith (Jnr.) became the 5th Baronet of Ledeclune.

16. Lieutenant Colonel Hamish Reid appears as second in command of the 7 Hussars in the photograph taken at Secunderabad. Possibly the rather elderly and tired appearance of both Reid and Colonel Peel, his predecessor, may have been one of the factors, which caused Haig to move away from regimental soldiering.

17. Radway Grange is a substantial house at the foot of Edgehill in the heart of the Warwickshire Hunt's country. The diary for 4 March 1912 gives a fine description of driving a car up the hill from Radway to Banbury on a day when the road was icy!

18. *Douglas Haig – the educated soldier* by John Terraine, p21.

19. *Haig* by Duff Cooper, p40.

# Chapter 3

# German Visit and Staff College

## 1895 – 1897

**Friday, 26 April 1895**

Reached Bremerhaven about 11o'clock. Landed in tender as tide
v. low. B'haven about 1½ hours from Bremen. Reached Bremen
by train at 2 o'clock and left via Hamburg for Berlin at 4.07 . . .
Got to Hamburg 5.50 and changed stations. Left 6.20 – slowish
train – arrive Berlin 11.20. Go to Hotel Bristol on Unter-den-
Linden. Comfortable Hotel.

Thus started Haig's long visit to Germany. It was an important two
months in his career and gave him an insight into how the German
cavalry functioned and more generally into the workings of the High
Command. Sir Evelyn Wood was to say later that Haig knew more
about the German army than any other British officer.

He was received by the most senior German officers with quite exceptional kindness and courtesy. He was able to meet the Kaiser and was
invited to attend functions and military parades in a way that one finds
surprising bearing in mind that he was only a captain in a Hussar regiment, although an extremely personable one, who spoke some German.
To a great extent his reception must have been due to General Keith
Fraser, who as Inspector General of British Cavalry was well known
amongst the German High Command and also knew the Kaiser.

General Fraser had been Colonel of the 1st Life Guards and was a
friend of the Prince of Wales. He provided a number of important
letters of introduction. Possibly, also, knowledge of the reputation
Haig was starting to build up in the British army had found its way
to Germany. Whatever the cause, it was enough to put the nose of the
British Military Attaché, Colonel Swaine,[1] totally out of joint. The
following account of the visit comes from both letters to Henrietta,
and Haig's diary.

### Saturday, 27 April (diary)

. . . I went to the Embassy today but Colonel Swaine (Military Attaché) has gone to Darmstadt to receive the Queen. I found Rittmeister von Arnim, however, at home. I had a letter to him. He is in 1st Queen's Guard Dragoons. He seems a nice fellow; on Monday I am going out with his squadron. He is to mount me and supply an orderly to show me the way to the drill ground . . .

### Saturday, 4 May (to Henrietta)

. . . I am getting on very well here. All the German officers I have met do everything to make my stay agreeable and show me everything I want. The only officer who does not go out of his way to assist is Colonel Swaine, our own Military Attaché. He has been here nine years, is a friend of the Emperor's and can do pretty well anything he likes. He has been away at Darmstadt but returned three days ago. I did not want his help except once: that was yesterday. The Emperor inspected 4 Infantry battalions on the Templehofer Field where I go every morning. My regiment (the 1 Guards Dragoons) had been ordered to parade also to attack the Infantry or for some game of that sort. The officers said if I went with Swaine and the other Attaches I would see everything. I suggested this to Swaine. He said there would be nothing to see and that I would be better to be at the side of the field where the crowd is allowed to stand – in fact where you could see nothing. However I did not mind this, and got my horse from the regiment as usual. Luckily Von Loe, the Governor of Berlin, on whom I had called with a letter from old Keith met me on my way to the Templehofer Field, introduced himself and took me on to the ground. I rode about without molestation until the firing and tactical inspection began, when a mounted policeman of sorts rode up and said it was forbidden to be where I was. Old Von Loe saw the man coming and at once galloped up and rode beside me for the rest of the day. Asked senior officers what orders they had received, etc., simply for my information. I therefore saw everything and knew more about what was going on than if I had been with Swaine. Von Loe when he bade me good-bye said to be sure and let him know at any time if I wanted anything. He said on occasions like yesterday I should wear my uniform as then I could go anywhere without any trouble. Swaine says the authorities at home don't like it, so I am going to send and get leave from them. Again I have been asked by the officers in the 1st Guard Dragoons to go to the manoeuvres with them and live with them, etc. Swaine says, 'Oh, they may ask you, but this year the manoeuvres are on a very large scale and the Emperor would not allow you!' This is all rot. I fancy he

46

does not want me there, as he being an infantry man has never said much about cavalry matters in his reports home. However, I am independent of him: outwardly he pretends to be most friendly to me, offers to assist in anything I want, but when I ask a thing he throws obstacles in the way.

I am just off to see Field-Marshal Von Blumenthal.[2] He called on me at 7.10 am two days ago! I was in my bath. He must be 80 or more. He is to leave Berlin on Sunday and asked me to call on him to-day. He is also a friend of Keith's. I brought a letter to him from K. F. I also know Von der Planitz, the General of the Cavalry Division here . So you see I am quite at home now and get on, in spite of not having a house where I can swagger and entertain them! These are the essentials to success in a military profession according to H. V. (Hugo Haig), are they not?

## Diary for 4 May

Called on Field-Marshal Von Blumenthal, 11 Alsenstrasse, by his request. Spent nearly an hour with him. Now 85 years of age, and had influenza 3 times since 82 years old. He talks English well: his wife came from near Eyemouth. We discussed numerous topics – cavalry in England, in Germany, in India. He hoped I would not go back to India. When I said probably going to Staff College, he said, 'That is not hard work: it is very interesting: the training of recruits and horses is most fatiguing . . . .

## Diary for Tuesday, 14 May

. . . Dined with Von Bulow at 1st Guard Uhlans. Colonel v.d. Schulenburg most kind – was orderly to Prince Frederick Carl during '70 – carried flag of truce into Metz and saw Bazaine at Cissy not in Metz. Latter officer had nothing to do with the fortress he said, but Germans said 'We'll have "army and fortress".' Found only one sentry: the other fishing! – also cotton wool in gun, not cartridges. Von Hayseler now commands at Metz, under whom Schulenburg used to be. They visited Beaugency on leave etc. Met Von Pappenheim, Brigade Commander, and Von Bulow, Governor of Potsdam, at dinner.

Apropos of inspections. Even in Germany inspecting Generals are not always perfect. Some judge squadrons from a distance and are unable to estimate accurately the pace of the horses. What is wanted is a long even gallop and swinging but these are difficult to judge; the only way to estimate rate of pace is by riding with squadrons themselves. To-day it was deceptive how fast the Gardes du Corps were really going.

**To Henrietta he wrote on 19 May 1895:**

... I went to Potsdam on Friday by 7 am train and had a most pleasant morning. The Commander of a squadron of the Garde du Corps manoeuvred his squadron about for my benefit. The Colonel of the 1st Guard Uhlans also showed me his regiment and barracks etc. In the latter there is every article of equipment stored in the top storey for the Reserve regiment which would be formed as soon as war was declared. They gave a big lunch in my honour at the 1st Uhlans. Yesterday was inspection of squadrons of the Hussars of the Guard. The Colonel of the regiment, Von Mossner, gave me a horse. General von Winterfeldt, commanding the Guard Corps, was there; v.d.Planitz, commanding Guard Cavalry Division; both of these said they were delighted that I should attend all the inspections. At lunch these two bosses sat on each side of the Colonel and I was placed opposite. I stayed at Potsdam Friday night and made the acquaintance of all the Commanding Officers of Regiments – also of several of the Emperor's Aides-de-Camp, most of whom have been to England with him at one time or another and so are v. friendly to an English officer. Everyone asks me why I do not get presented to the Emperor. The real reason, of course, is that Swaine would not do it, though General Fraser says it is the custom to present all foreign officers to the Sovereign abroad. At present the Emperor is away but will be back soon. Old Keith has really taken a lot of trouble about my visit here and has written to the Ambassador about it. The latter has asked me to dine to-night, but I am going to Rathenow to be present at the inspection of squadrons there to-morrow. Thanks to Von Loe (the Governor of Berlin), I see all I want and do just what I please, but at the inspections I have to ride in a tall hat and frock coat, which is rather ridiculous, isn't it? If I had been presented to the Emperor he would have told me to wear my uniform . . . .

**Diary for Monday, 20 May**

Von Kayser (2nd. Lieut.) called for me at 7 am and Von Oppenheim sent me a horse – about 20 minutes' ride to drill ground. Ride round jumps which are wide enough for troops and well arranged. Also 3 jumps wide for squadron in the open. Squadron inspection commenced with 1 Troop sticking at post and dummy on ground at slow pace. 2 Troop going full speed and thrusting at head. 3 Troop advanced, charged and broke up sticking at dummies in ground. All recruits and young horses were seen. Men told to ride on right and left rein. Individual men made to charge past inspecting officer and shout 'Hurrah' and thrust with lance. The followed drill at trot and jumps, then gallop for ¼ hour. The CO rode with the Squadron leader, told him, to charge upon a certain point, then would say, 'You are now attacked from such a direction: rally and charge', etc. Tactical problems followed in each case. The usual flags – White Cav., Yellow Artillery, Red Infantry – were used. Subalterns lead squadrons, one flag per squadron.

1. Squadron advanced in flank offensive before regt. on right flank, marked enemy brought forward consisting of three flags and one whole squadron which then charged. Attack successful followed by pursuit and rally.
2. Squadron in second line advancing upon artillery when escort attacks suddenly in flank.
3. Squadron in extended formation against Infantry attacked unexpectedly.

Whole regiment then taken to a cliff where horses made to slide down on their hindquarters about 40 ft. high and very steep. One horse falls.

Lunched out there with all the celebrities. Had to drink out of horn presented by the Prince Fred. Charles – stag's antler with cups set in between the branches. Returned by 6 pm train. Graf Lehndorff dined with me at Bristol.

### Diary for Tuesday, 21 May

Inspection of Cuirassiers on Templehofer. The CO (v. Klinckowstroem) v. smart man . . . . Squadrons went well and galloped on the fast side as the Colonel desired it to, saying that the tendency is to decrease the pace gradually. Usual sort of inspection, but the Colonel very active and ready with sudden tactical situation:

1. Squadron advancing against flags when a superior force brought up on left flank from behind sand-hill. Troop detached from right of squadron and remainder move to the left. This v. well done as squadron going at full gallop.
2. Defile marked with lances. Squadron sent in sections at gallop thro' and ordered to form a flank and attack again and form to front and attack. Troops formed first, then squadrons . . . .

## Diary for Sunday, 26 May.

Dined with Sir Edward Malet[3] at Embassy in Wilhelm Str. Played whist till 12 o'c. Lady Ermyntrude and Sir E. very kind. Told Sir E. that his subordinates had put me in a fix by declaring that they knew nothing of me. He will send letter to Plessen.

## To Henrietta, 31 May.

Yesterday morning was the big Spring Review of the Berlin troops, and this morning of those in Potsdam before the Emperor. I went to Potsdam this morning, but not to the one here as I preferred to see the inspection of the Zieten Hussars in the Rathenow. I came back, however, for the 'Parade Tafel' at 6 pm yesterday in the Emperor's Schloss here. It was Von Plessen, the General in command of the Emperor's Military Household, who got me the invitation. I told you before of him: he is a nice fellow, and must have taken a lot of trouble about this business, as you see from the way I was treated.

I went in uniform of course, and on reaching the palace had a big staircase to go up and then through several galleries. In the latter there were Court officials with the names and places of the guests. I saw three or four of them but none knew about me, but passed me further along. Then a nice old boy came and asked me by name if he might show me my place at table. I found myself not amongst 'the foreign officers' but at the end of the table opposite the Emperor.

On my right was a Colonel Crosick, who commands the Fusilier Guards here, and a great friend of the Emperor. After we had been a certain time at dinner, the Emperor drank his health, then signalled to him that he wished to drink my health. So I stood up and emptied my glass to the Kaiser in the usual style – 'nae heeltaps'! He did the same. These were the only healths HM drank except of those quite close to him in the family, so to speak.

After dinner we went into the picture gallery and the Emperor came and asked me about my regiment, about Keith Fraser, and what I was anxious to do, and the length of leave which I had. Altogether he was most friendly.

On Wednesday night I dined with Princess Aribert of Anhalt ( daughter of Prince Christian)[4] Met her in London last year. She is really very friendly and nice. I had 3 invitations from her before I was able to go, and she always writes such civil notes . . . .

## To Henrietta, 9 June.

Last week I was busy looking at General v.d. Planitz inspecting the Cav. Regiments of the Guard Cav. Division – this week the Emperor starts his inspections. These will be over by Friday and then the regiments go in for reconnoitring and detached duties. I shall thus not have very much to interest me here after this week. On the other hand I have to be back in England for some Cavalry drills or manoeuvres which are to take place in August: they begin 12th August and last a month. I go as Brigade Major to Colonel French,[5] who commands a Brigade. You must not mention this till you see it in the papers as the AG has not approved of the details of the scheme, I believe. Well, taking the above points into consideration with reference to my going to Kissingen, where the cure lasts four weeks, and having regard to the fact that I cannot go direct from the waters to the manoeuvres, I have decided to go to Kissingen in about a fortnight's time, say 23rd., and get my cure done by 20th July.

**Also to Henrietta, asking her to buy some presents for him to give to his friends in Germany:**

You can spend £30 or more if you like, but I must have genuine articles that will last – for of course it would never do to say to me next time I come back 'what rubbishy things are made in England!' Get whatever you like; but you know they always wear uniform so pins and that sort of thing are no use, but of course they smoke considerably. Now as to the individuals: Arnim gives me a horse to ride here every day and through him I have got on so well; perhaps an English saddle – he is tall and thin, about WG's size I should think. Schmidt-Pauli has mounted me at Potsdam and entertained me there, so I would like something nice for him too. Thro him I have seen all the Potsdam inspections. Bulow gives me all information I want and is a capital fellow. He is a clever chap too; we ride together on the Templehofer Field – at the 'drills' in the morning. Blumenthal is the Chief Staff Officer of the Cavalry Division and has always kept me informed of every inspection and looked after me well. In fact, through him nothing has taken place since I came here which I have not seen. The others are just good fellows who have frequently fed me, and taken me to any show that has been going on . . . .

**To Henrietta, 12 June 1895.**

I heard this morning from Colonel French that Sir E. Wood is to conduct a 'Staff Tour' beginning on 21st June and lasting till 26th, and that Colonel French is to command the Cavalry on one side: the latter has kindly asked me to be his Staff Officer, hence my sudden decision to return . . . .

**To Henrietta, 21 June.**

I got here all right on Friday. On Saturday (y'day) we started at 8 am – French and I together. We rode from here (Hayward's Heath) towards the coast, over the Downs towards Shoreham, then to Brighton. We got there about 3 pm and lunched at 'The Old Ship' which seems a capital hotel and preferable to the Metropole (as ordered) and found all the Umpires and the officers of both sides (attackers and defenders). The Umpires are Buller, Sir E.Wood, and Hildyard (the Commandant of the Staff College).[6] Sir F. Grenfell was also there.

Once again Haig's health was causing concern to his family, particularly his sister Henrietta. He therefore returned to Germany to take an abbreviated version of the cure he had planned before returning unexpectedly to England for the manoeuvres. He went to Kissingen on 28 June.

**Diary for Sunday, 30 June**

Dr. Oscar Divuf Senr. Called on me at 12 noon. He said liver slightly enlarged on left lobe, spleen not much enlarged, heart a little weak. Course to be followed – Cure at 6 am and be at the spring by 7 am, drink one glass of Rakaczy, walk ¼ hour, then another glass and walk ½ hour. Breakfast of coffee and milk – no tea, no butter. Bath 11 o'c. – Soolen Bath of 26 R.(91F) Remain in it for 20 to 25 minutes. After bath, in fine weather walk ½ hour: in bad weather or in wind go to bed covered up for an hour. Dinner at 1. Supper at 7 – something small. Took first bath at 5 pm.

He probably found this regime less severe than the recommendation of an earlier doctor: 'He says I must live carefully – meat only once a day and ½ bottle of claret as a maximum allowance for a whole day!!! etc.'

Whilst at Kissingen he received a letter from Sir Evelyn Wood, who he met for the first time on the June Staff Tour, asking for his comments on certain aspects of training in the German army. Sir Evelyn's letter ended as follows:

It gave me great pleasure to meet you and have a talk, and the more so because I knew you pretty well on paper before. I think I may honestly say of you, what we cannot always say, that the expectation, though great, was even less than the pleasure you gave me by your conversation.

Douglas Haig's comment to his sister was: 'I told you that we got on very well together. Sir EW is a capital fellow to have upon one's side as he always gets his way!' To Sir Evelyn he wrote from Kissingen on 7 July:

I was greatly delighted to receive your kind letter and thank you very much for what you say about me. I shall always remember with more than pleasure the kindly way you spoke to me during the Staff Tour. I now enclose a few notes in answer to that question you asked me about the share taken by NCOs in polishing up the young soldier in Germany. I wish I could have given you more detailed information regarding the work done by NCOs in the Infantry. To tell you the truth, my time at Berlin was devoted entirely to Cavalry work, tho' what I have put down regarding the Infantry is what I know to be the fact. I hope however to find out in more detail the work of the Company before I return. I am drinking the waters here, as I have not got over the effects of fever which I used to get in India, but when this cure is finished I shall return to England via Berlin, where I know plenty of officers in the Infantry. There is an officer (Cavalry), Lieut. Von Bulow, of the General Staff (in Berlin) coming to England on leave for the month of August. He is anxious to see something of the manoeuvres in the New Forest, and the Cavalry Division which is to be formed at Aldershot. I take the liberty of asking whether you would get him permission to go to the New Forest. I am, I understand, to be a Brigade Major at the Aldershot drills so I can look after him and give him one of my horses to ride when he comes there. Please forgive the liberty I have taken in asking for Bulow, but I have received so much assistance and kindness from German officers of all ranks, that I feel sure you won't mind. It was from Bulow that I got two accounts of how Cavalry Staff Tours (Nebungreise) are carried out in Germany. I translated them and gave them to Colonel French with a request (if he thought fit) to ask you to look at them. The papers are not in the least confidential, but these Germans are so peculiar in some things, that I should not like it known how the papers came into my possession.

Again thanking you for your kindness to me and hoping the notes I now send may in some measure answer the question you asked me.

The notes were sent to Lady Haig in 1912 with a covering letter:

Sept 11th. 1912

My dear Lady Haig,

I got my exercise early today – hounds 5.39 – 9 miles distant so am tearing up letters. I doubt, you are so young, if you knew Douglas in 1895, but think you may like to see what I enclose herewith. It explains a part of the attraction that your man had for a keen soldier like

Yours sincerely

Evelyn Wood

In German Cavalry and Infantry how much do the Non-Commissioned Officers actually do in polishing up the young soldier, and where does the personal instruction of the Officer come in?

The Officer commanding a Squadron or Company is alone responsible for everything connected with that Squadron or Company. The goal to be reached is clearly indicated, namely 'Efficiency for War' but the methods by which that end is to be attended are left entirely to the discretion of Company & Squadron Commanders. This initiative of the Squadron & Company Leader is only limited by the necessity imposed on them, that their men within certain specified times attain certain degrees of efficiency.

The CO of a regiment (and a fortiori of a Brigade or Division) is not allowed to meddle with the instruction of Squadrons or to direct that the instruction of a Squadron shall be carried out in one way rather than another. The duty of these superior officers is to judge the results of the instruction given. They do this at the several inspections, and if need be, comment on any irregularity or omission which they have noticed in the body of troops inspected. Moreover, these senior officers have each a specified time in which they instruct the unit entrusted to them to command. Seeing then that each Squadron and Company Commander is at liberty to employ his officers and NCOs as he chooses in training the men, it is difficult to state precisely at what point the instruction of the NCO ceases, and that of the officer begins.

The general rule is that the first instruction both in the Infantry and Cavalry is given by the best NCOs available in each squadron, under the superintendence of an officer, and that upon the men reaching a certain state of proficiency in the several subjects, the officer then personally instructs. Recruits join in October and by the beginning of March (in Cavalry) they will be under the direct instruction of the officer charged with their training. To consider the question in detail, it is necessary to point out first of all, that the training of a squadron is divided into the following periods throughout the year, in which special attention is given to certain work, though practice in certain duties, such as Felddienst (detached duties), musketry practice, and gymnastics, goes on throughout the year without intermission.

| | |
|---|---|
| October to March | Winter Work |
| April to beginning of June | Squadron exercises concluding with Squadron Inspection by Regimental Commander. |
| 8 days in June | Regimental Drill followed by Regimental Inspection by Brigade General. |
| Thence to middle of August | Summer Work and leave season. |
| Thence to end of September | Manoeuvre period. |

For the purpose of winter instruction the Squadron is divided into, (1) Recruits; (2) Young horses; (3) Men in second and third year's service.

As a rule the senior 1st Lieutenant is given charge of the young horses, the next senior Officer trains the recruits and the next Officer the old soldiers. I would here point out that in the event of a Squadron (or Company) being short of Officers, the Non-Commissioned Officer next junior to the Wachtmeister (Squadron Sergeant Major), or to the Feldwebel in the Infantry (who holds nominally the same position as Wachtmeister, but has much less responsibility) does the ordinary work of a Lieutenant, but under no circumstances may such an individual superintend recruits: this duty must always be done by an officer.

The Squadron consists of 134 men and 133 horses, and each year some 28 to 34 recruits join between the 1st and 6th October. The Squadron Commander hands the recruits over to an Officer for training (usually the second Senior in the Squadron as stated above), and places at his disposal the best of the Non-Commissioned Officers in the Squadron.

The recruits are then divided into a suitable number of squads (usually three or four),which are drilled by Non-Commissioned-Officers. There is often a second Non-Commissioned-Officer with each squad whose business it is to take over awkward men who are slow at learning.

The chief duty of the Officer at first is to see that the recruits are not ill treated, and that the Squadron Commander's directions are carried out.

The recruits learn from the commencement.
1. Riding
2. Lance, sword and carbine drill on foot and then the use of lance and sword on wooden horses before executing the exercises mounted.
3. Gymnastics.
4. Musketry.
5. Theoretical instruction.

To begin with, the Non-Commissioned-Officers teach all these subjects while the officer simply directs in chief. After a few weeks the Officer himself gives the theoretical instruction and takes the recruits out for Felddienst (detached duties). Towards the end of the winter period (about March) all three or four squads are united for riding in the open and other work included in our 'Troop drill'.

I would point out that in some squadrons and regiments the Officer in charge of the recruits himself gives instruction in riding to each squad of recruits. This will take three to four hours daily. I give below the usual daily time-table of an officer when superintending the instruction of recruits. It is generally considered sufficient for the officer, if he has some experience in riding instruction, simply to superintend the Non-Commissioned-Officers who do the drilling; this takes one and a half hours daily as shown in the following table of work in winter.

| | |
|---|---|
| 7.30 am to 9. | Lance, sword and foot drill |
| 10 am to 11.30. | Riding School |
| 12 noon to 2 | The Officer had himself to ride with the other Officers. |
| 3 pm to 4.30. | Gymnastics and musketry instruction |
| 5 pm to 6. | Theoretical instruction. |

All four squads of recruits performed the same duty at the same times.

The recruits or lowest class of equitation is called 'The First Class': about fifty men usually ride in this class as all 'casuals' (such as cooks, clerks, orderlies, drivers, etc.), and bad riders join it.

Next there are the 'young horses'. These are divided into three squads as follows:

(1) Junge Remonten–       Horses of 5 years old.
(2) Alte Remonten  –      Horses of 6 years old.
(3) Vorjahrige Remonten  –       Horses of 7 years old.
(remounts of the preceding year)

Some thirteen to fourteen young horses join a squadron each year so there are about forty young horses in all. The senior 1st Lieutenant usually trains these.

Forty young horses – fifty ridden by recruits – Ninety horses accounted for. As there are one hundred and thirty-three horses in a Squadron, there are about forty-three available for men in their second and third year's service to ride. This class is called the 'Second Class' and consists of the following squads.

Abteilung A and B. The best horses with men serving their second year who are thought able to break horses the following year.

Abteilung C. Difficult horses with men serving a longer time than 2 years.

Abteilung D. All men serving their second year who do not ride in Abteilung A.

In April the whole Squadron goes out for the practice of the exercises contained in the Drill Book under 'Squadron Drill' – In the event of an insufficiency of Officers for four troop leaders, then a sergeant will lead the vacant troop.

After the inspection of Squadrons which takes place in the end of May, there are 8 days of Regimental drill followed by the inspection of the Regiment in drill.

Succeeding this period of instruction comes the summer period in which detached duties, swimming, pioneering work, field practices, shooting, with one day weekly for regimental drill in the open country or Squadron drill with lance and sword mounted combat. In all these exercises the officer instructs his men. This brings us to the middle of August when the manoeuvre period commences.

As regards the interior arrangements of the Squadron in barracks, the Squadron Commander holds his Squadron Sergeant Major responsible, who in turn holds the other Non-Commissioned-Officers responsible.

The Lieutenant thus has no responsibility in this respect. In barracks the Squadron is divided into divisions or squads (Beritt), each commanded by a Non-Commissioned-Officer; the number and strength of these varies greatly but usually depend upon the number and size of the rooms. These squads (Beritt) in barracks, have no connection with the squads (Abteilungen) for instruction.

The management of the horses and stable arrangements generally are managed by the Squadron Leader himself assisted by the Squadron Sergeant Major. The Lieutenants have nothing to do in this respect. It would seem as if so much is expected from the Lieutenants in the matter of instruction that no time is left for them to busy themselves with barrack duties. In the Cavalry this is entirely left by the Squadron Leader to his Non-Commissioned Officers.

On the other hand in the Infantry the internal arrangements (such as the cleanliness of the rooms, kits, etc.) are superintended by the Lieutenants who at least once or twice each day have some duty in this respect to perform.

There exist no written regulations upon the interior duties to be carried out by Squadrons, Companies or Regiments.

By 23 July Haig had permission for Von Bulow to attend the manoeuvres and wrote to him about the trip the trip to England in August.

**Diary for 14 August.**
Gave lunch to Bulow, Jensich and sundry other Germans at Cavalry Club. Left for Aldershot 3.45 pm. Went to Queen's Hotel. General Luck and Staff staying here. Brigadiers dined in evening. A little difficulty as to which Brigade I should go to. Brabazon was without a Brigade Major tomorrow and Combe, commanding cavalry Brigade here, said I was to join him,

Medium Brigade tomorrow. 'Then,' said Brabazon, 'he had better remain with me permanently.' Lord Dundonald, appointed to command Hussar Brigade, seemed angry. Wrote drill regulations at dictation of General Luck and Brigadiers present.

**Haig's notes for the day were:**
Drill of squadrons and regiments bad. COs too intent on looking at their commands in place of what is going on.

Direction seldom right; wished for Brigade Major to direct the base squadron as of old. The custom at Aldershot!

Pace uneven. It seems like trying to run before they can walk, doing Brigade movements before squadrons are trained!

Jumping by sections!! This should be done by squadrons at this time of year.

**Saturday, 31 August.**
Worked at Reconnaissance scheme for General Luck. Asked by him to make out the one of y'day to go in Drill Book. Rode with Marsham and Sudley to Hog's Back in afternoon to look at outpost line.

From the entry for 31 August it is clear that Haig was starting to become involved with the new Cavalry Drill Book, the first part of which had been written by Colonel John French. French had opted out of the project, gratefully one suspects, on being appointed AAG at the War Office. A press announcement about the new Cavalry Drill Book was made on 11 November 1895:

The New 'Cavalry Drill Book' will be issued in a few days. The present edition was only authorized in 1891, but it differed from its predecessors in but few respects. The new book has been thoroughly overhauled and revised. Indeed, these words are insufficient to express a tithe of what has been done; as a fact the whole has been re-written and boiled down into two small volumes. The first treats of equitation and foot drill, and is applicable to Artillery and other mounted services, and the second contains the drill of the Cavalry arm as apart from any other, and the details and instructions for manoeuvres, ceremonial, &c. It will be remembered that the Adjutant General entrusted the revision to Colonel JDP French, late 19th Hussars, in the early part of the year, but upon that officer subsequently being appointed an Assistant-Adjutant-General at Head-quarters, the work was but half finished, and Captain Douglas Haig, 7th Hussars, who was Aide-de-Camp to the late Lieut. General Keith Fraser, Inspector General of Cavalry, was nominated to complete the task. It is understood that Colonel French personally completed the first volume and that the second is entirely the work of Captain Haig.

It seems remarkable that so junior an officer as a captain should have been entrusted with such an important task as the revision of the Cavalry Drill Book. There must have dozens of more senior officers, including many who had been through the Staff College, who could, on paper, have had more experience and be better qualified for the work. Douglas Haig always 'punched above his weight' and this is yet another example.

He went to the Staff College in January 1896 and was there for the twenty-two months, a period of great value to his future career. The Commandant, Sir Henry Hildyard, turned out to be a competent Brigade Commander in South Africa (one of the few), outflanking the Boers at Laing's Nek and enabling Buller at last to be entitled to claim a victory. He reached the rank of full general and retired in 1911. Colonel G.F.R. Henderson,[7] the author of *Stonewall Jackson and The Science of War* was Chief Instructor and perhaps the leading military thinker of his generation in the British Army. He became Roberts's Director of Military Intelligence in South Africa and did a brilliant job, including making the plan for the surprise capture of Bloemfontein. His influence on Haig's thinking was considerable. It was also Henderson who said of Haig to some of Haig's fellow students; 'There is a fellow in your batch who one of these days will be Commander-in-Chief' The 'batch' included the future Field Marshal Allenby,[8] Lieutenant General Furse,[9] Brigadier General Edmonds,[10] Lieutenant General Macdonogh,[11] Major General Capper,[12] Lieutenant General Haking[13] and Brigadier General Blair;[14] surely a vintage intake. Field Marshal 'Wullie' Robertson[15] was in the following intake and Field Marshal Plumer[16] was an external examiner. With all this talent it was, nonetheless, Haig who stood out in the eyes of the Chief Instructor.

When, in 1911, Douglas Haig was appointed GOC Aldershot Command, Edmonds wrote to congratulate him and reminded him of Henderson's words. In a letter sent to Lady Haig after the Field

Marshal's death he, by then Sir James and the Official Historian of the First World War, said that his letter went on to remark:

> But, GOC is not the fulfilment of the prophecy; he said 'C-in-C'. So, on some future occasion I shall congratulate you again'. Further, in my letter, I begged him, as he had come to power, to try and get rid of the 'obese unholy old things who stifle and overlay us' and mentioned I still got on quite nicely without exercise. This explains his chaff about riding. I was at GHQ St Omer, where he arrived in December 1915, to take over as C-in-C, and congratulated him by word of mouth, adding, 'by the way, Henderson said you would be C-in-C. And he meant that you would be a successful one.'

Sir James gave Lady Haig her husband's response to his 1911 letter. It was written from Simla on 31 August 1911 and said:

My dear Edmonds,

I was delighted to get your letter by last mail. Thank you very much for your kind congratulations which I appreciate very much indeed.

I think dear old Henderson must have been talking through his hat when he said that he thought that I would ever be Commander-in-Chief of the British Army. I only wish to be of some use somewhere. I quite agree with you that there are a great many useless officers who 'smother and overlay us', as you put it, and who are just able to scrape along in peace time, but are quite unfit for the responsibilities which will come upon them in the event of war. I think that the first duty is to get good Battalion and Regimental Commanders, and also to see that they train their Companies and Squadrons on sound lines. I am very glad indeed that you are at last away from that War Office, and hope that you are taking lots of horse exercise and are galloping about the country with the best of them. I think we don't pay nearly enough attention to the physical fitness of the Staff Officers, especially at the War Office. What do you say?

We have had to cancel the Army Manoeuvres in November owing to failure to rain, so there will be a 'march past' at Delhi. This will please some of the 'old 'uns'. I shall look forward to hearing all your news and your views on how to beat the Germans when I get home in the winter.

It will be noted that already Haig knew who the enemy was to be! He also knew more than most about the enemy's army and High Command.

He and Edmonds (a Royal Engineer known to his friends as Archimedes) worked together during the final examination at the Staff College. Edmonds has left an amusing account of Haig's attitude to the work and the Directing Staff. He said that Haig never:

> made the slightest attempt to 'play up to' the instructors. If a scheme interested him he took tremendous pains with it; if he thought there was no profit in working it out, he sent in a perfunctory minimum. I remember a road reconnaissance sketch on which most of us had lavished extreme care, marking all the letter-boxes, pumps, gateways into fields and such-like. Haig handed in a sheet with a single brown chalk-line down the centre, the cross roads shown and the endorsement 'twenty miles long, good surface, wide enough for two columns with orderlies both ways'.

The Haig papers in the National Library of Scotland include a report he wrote in 1897 on how an invasion and re-conquest of Sudan could be accomplished. This is a very carefully thought out plan, written down in great detail with consideration given to the various options and conclusions almost exactly in line with Kitchener's campaign a year later. The 'Appreciation' had to be confined to '10 pages of foolscap' but a considerable number of appendices supply a wealth of detail to support the conclusions. Haig clearly found this exercise of interest and it no doubt proved of value to him when he joined the Anglo-Egyptian army a year later.

Notes.
1.  Sir Leopold Victor Swaine KCB, CMG was a highly successful Military Attaché in Berlin. He established a good relationship with the Kaiser and was used by the British Government as an unofficial point of contact with him. He described the young Kaiser as 'narrow minded' but 'a right good young fellow'. How wrong he was! Swaine was born in 1840 and commissioned into the Rifle Brigade in 1859. He retired as a Major General in 1902.
2.  Field Marshal Leonard, Graf von Blumenthal (1810–1900) was, with Moltke, one of the two leading German generals during the Bismarck period. He distinguished himself in the Schleswig War, the Austrian War of 1866 and the Franco-Prussian War of 1870. He is credited with developing the strategy of blitzkrieg. His British wife was called Delicia Vyner.
3.  The Rt. Hon. Sir Edward Malet Bt. GCMG, GCB was born in 1837. He married Lady Ermyntrude Russell, daughter of the 9th Duke of Bedford. They had no children. He was Ambassador in Berlin from 1884–95. He

was a member of the Court of Arbitration at The Hague from 1900–1906. He was also a Trustee of the Wallace Collection. He died in 1908.

4. Princess Aribert was Princess Marie Louise, granddaughter of Queen Victoria by Princess Helena's marriage to Prince Christian of Schleswig-Holstein. She was born in 1872 and died in 1956. She married Prince Aribert of Anhalt in 1891, but the marriage was annulled in 1900 because of non-consummation. Prince Aribert was a homosexual, who was discovered in bed with one of the male servants. When Princess Marie Louise returned to England, where she was brought up, King Edward is said to have remarked; 'Ah, poor Louise, she has returned as she went – a virgin'.

5. Field Marshal John French, Earl of Ypres KP, GCB, OM, GCVO, KCMG had been known to Haig since 1891; they collaborated on the Cavalry Drill Book in 1895. From that year their careers were extremely closely linked until 1915, when French was sacked and Haig took his place as Commander-in-Chief of the British forces in France. Although this obviously affected their relationship, it remained cordial and close enough for French to be one of the godfathers of Haig's son in 1918. Like Sir Evelyn Wood his career started in the Navy, before he transferred into the Army in 1874. His regiment was the 19 Hussars. He retired in 1921 after three years as Lord Lieutenant of Ireland. He died in 1925.

6. General Sir Henry John Thoroton Hildyard GCB was born in 1846 and commissioned into The Highland Light Infantry in 1867. As the Commandant of the Staff College in 1893–98, at the time when many of the future senior officers of the British Army in the First World War were there, his influence on British military thinking was considerable. He retired in 1911 and died in 1916.

7. Colonel George Francis Robert Henderson was an inspiring instructor when Haig was at the Staff College. He was a noted military writer, best known for his work on the American Civil War, *Stonewall Jackson and the American Civil War*. He was born in 1854 in Jersey, commissioned into the Royal Engineers in 1878. He served in the 1882 Egyptian campaign and subsequently in Gibraltar, Bermuda and Nova Scotia. He became an instructor at the Staff College in 1892 and was there until 1899. He then went to South Africa, where he was an effective Director of Military Intelligence. He died in 1903 in Aswan.

8. Field Marshal Edmund Henry Hynman Viscount Allenby GCB, GCMG, GCVO was born in 1861 and commissioned into the 6 Inniskilling Dragoons in 1881. He served in Bechuanaland and in the campaign of 1888 against the Zulus. He distinguished himself in the 2nd Boer War, serving with Haig in the Cavalry Division commanded by French. He ended the War as a colonel. He was promoted to major general in 1909 and was appointed Inspector General of Cavalry in 1910. Initially on the

63

Western Front in 1914–15 he became a corps commander in 1915. He was moved to the Middle East in 1917, conquering the Ottoman forces and capturing Jerusalem. His physical appearance and temper were such as to earn him the nickname 'The Bull'. He died in 1936.

9. Lieutenant General Sir William Thomas Furse KCB, DSO was born in 1865 and commissioned into the Royal Artillery in 1884. He served in the East Indies, South Africa and in Ireland before the First World War. He commanded 9th Division during the war before becoming Master General of the Ordnance in 1916. He died in 1953.

10. Brigadier General Sir James Edmonds CB, CMG. Born in 1861, he was commissioned into the Royal Engineers in 1881. He was an instructor at Woolwich from 1890–96. Thereafter his career was mainly as a staff officer, including being GSO1 of 4th Division in 1914. He suffered a nervous collapse and was replaced. He retired in 1914, and was promoted to brigadier general. He was the Official Historian of the First World War, a work of monumental scholarship. He died in 1956

11. Lieutenant General Sir George Mark Watson Macdonogh GBE, KCB, KGMG was born in 1865 and commissioned into the Royal Engineers in 1884. His pre-First World War career was entirely in the UK. He went to France in 1914 as DMI to French, the C.-in-C. He was transferred to the War Office as DMI to Robertson, the CIGS. He died in 1942.

12. Major General Thompson Capper KCMG, CB, DSO was born in 1863 and commissioned into the East Lancashire Regiment in 1882. He, together with Haig and Blair, was one of the officers recommended by Sir Evelyn Wood to Kitchener for employment in the Sudan campaign. He served in South Africa and India, where he became commandant of the Indian Staff College. After service in Ireland he was briefly Inspector of Infantry, before the start of the First World War, when he was given the command of the 7th Division. He was killed at Loos in 1915, one of the 100 or so General officers to be killed in the First World War.

13. Lieutenant General Sir Richard Cyril Byrne Haking GBE, KCB, KCMG, born in 1862 was commissioned into the Hampshire Regiment in 1881. He served in Ireland and South Africa. He commanded XI Corps during most of the First World War. After the war he had appointments in Russia and East Prussia. He retired in 1927 and died in 1945.

14. Brigadier General Arthur Blair DSO was born in 1869 and commissioned into the KOSB in 1890. He served in Egypt and South Africa, where he was severely wounded. In the First World War he became BGS of an Infantry Division. After the war he became the first General Secretary of the Earl Haig Fund, Scotland and The Officers Association, Scotland. He died in 1947.

15. Field Marshal Sir William Robert Robertson GCB, GCMG, KCVO, DSO, (1859–1933). He enlisted as a trooper in the 16 Lancers in 1877. He was commissioned into the 3 Dragoon Guards in 1888. Much of his early career was in Intelligence both in India and South Africa. He was

commandant of the Staff College from 1910 to 1913. He was QMG of the Expeditionary Force in France, then CGS, before returning to England as CIGS at the end of 1915. He was CIGS until February 1918, when he left the War Office as the result of Lloyd George's plot to remove him in order to give his favourite, Sir Henry Wilson, the job. After the war he commanded Rhine Army. He became a field marshal in 1920, the first and last man to have risen from the lowest to the highest rank in the British Army.

16. Field Marshal Herbert Charles Onslow, Viscount Plumer GCB, GCMG, GCVO, GBE was born in 1857 and commissioned into the York and Lancaster Regiment in 1876. He served in Jersey, South Africa, and the War Office as the first QMG on the Army Council established as the result of the Esher reforms in 1904. In the South African War he raised and commanded the Rhodesian Field Force, being promoted to major general at the end of hostilities in 1902. He commanded II Army during the First World War from 1915, with a break in November 1917 to March 1918 when he went to Italy to salvage the Allied campaign there after Italy's disastrous defeat at Caporetto. His great victory was the meticulously planned Battle of Messines in 1917. After the war he became Governor of Malta and High Commissioner in Palestine. He died in 1932.

# Chapter 4

# 'Bimbashi Haig Bey'

## The Sudan 1898

In 1881 the Mahdi,[1] a fundamentalist Sufi Muslim, and his followers, described as Dervishes, rose against Anglo-Egyptian rule in the Sudan. In 1883 his army virtually annihilated an Anglo-Egyptian army under the command of Hicks Pasha, an Indian Army officer. The Mahdi also enormously improved the firepower of his army by capturing thousands of Remington rifles and ammunition.

In 1885 the Governor General of the Sudan, Gordon,[2] was killed in Khartoum. The relieving army under Wolseley[3] arrived two days too late to save him and subsequently returned to Egypt. After the death of the Mahdi, he was succeeded by the Khalifa, who set about consolidating Dervish rule in the Sudan.

Meanwhile British officers were improving the efficiency of the Egyptian army. Kitchener[4] was appointed Sirdar or Commander-in-Chief in 1892. He started to improve the essential infrastructure, notably the existing railways and established a highly efficient telegraph system.

In 1897 Paliament voted him £240,000 to extend the railway across the desert from Wadi Halfa to Abu Hamed, a distance of 230 miles. (see map 1). This cut out a huge loop in the Nile and was probably the key decision in winning the Sudan campaign, because it meant he could use both river and rail for supplies. It cut out several cataracts, which were impassable when the river was low. The railway was built in ten months. Kitchener's engineers incidentally found the only two places on the route where there was water.

The distances involved in the campaign were huge, 1,500 miles or so from Alexandria to Khartoum, 1,350 from Cairo. Berber, some fifty miles south of Abu Hamed and the preferred jumping off point for the attack on Omdurman/Khartoum, is 570 miles from Aswan and ninety miles north of Khartoum.

66

By late 1897 Kitchener had increased the number of British officers in the Egyptian army and a British infantry brigade plus the 21 Lancers had arrived. Kitchener asked Sir Evelyn Wood to recommend three officers, who had recently completed the Staff College course, to come out to Egypt. Wood recommended Capper (East Lancs.), Blair (KOSB) and Haig (7 Hussars). Capper was killed at Loos as a major general, Blair, a personal friend of Douglas Haig, became BGS of a division in the First World War and, after the war, the first General Secretary of the Earl Haig Fund and the Officers' Association, Scotland.

In preparation for his secondment to the Egyptian army, Douglas Haig visited the Royal Ordnance Factory at Enfield on 19/20 January 1898 to learn the mechanism of the Maxim gun. The Maxim was an important weapon in both of the two main battles in the Sudan campaign, as will become clear later. Maxims were deployed in artillery batteries and were also mounted on to gunboats.

Before embarking for Egypt he had an important social engagement to fulfil; he had been invited to stay the weekend with the Prince and Princess of Wales at Sandringham. Unfortunately his usual efficiency and attention to detail deserted him and he went to Liverpool Street rather than St Pancras to catch the train. An embarrassing faux pas was avoided by the smooth-running flexibility of the Royal Household and staff!

### Diary for 22 January.

Go to Liverpool Street Station to catch 4.5 pm train for Wolverton, but train goes from St. Pancras. Start by 5.15 pm and get to Sandringham about quarter to nine. Dine in Equerry's room and join the party after dinner. Prince very kind and presents me to the Princess of Wales, Princess Victoria,[5] Duke and Duchess of York etc. The party included Sir E. Wood, Gen. Sir Richard Harrison,[6] Lt. Lord Claud Hamilton,[7] Mr Christopher Sykes, Boyd Carpenter (Bishop of Ripon).

### 23 January

Princess and some go to Church about 11.30. The Prince, Sykes and self go in at 12. Excellent sermon from the Bishop on Gordon. Text Hebrews 11th Chapter, 8th verse, 'And he (Abraham) went out and he knew not whither he went.' Before lunch see dogs, York Cottage. After lunch walk round with princess and see gardens, yearlings, mares in foal, etc. After dinner discuss Cavalry organization, Indian frontier, etc., with

HRH. Difficulty in finding a good map of Central Asia. HRH desires me to 'write regularly' to him from Egypt.

Haig travelled out to Egypt via Paris, Rome and Naples, where he caught the Orient Line's ship *Ormuz*. He complained that the customs in Paris had been 'most inquisitive' about his luggage. The Italians were almost as bad.

### Letter to Henrietta 2 February 1898. About 100 miles from Port Said:

There are a good many passengers on board and almost half are bound for Egypt. There are several whom I knew before, such as General and Mrs McCalmont,[8] Ld Desart, a few other old generals and such like. I dine at the same table with the McCalmonts and niece (a friend of Bee's I am told! Her name is Miss Pollock, I think, though I did not quite catch it and have not since asked them) and 4 other people bound for Egypt. A fairly pleasant party . . . There are several gold miners or financiers, bound for Western Australia, who speak about Coolgardie and Menzies, Hannan's etc. as you might about the position of Bond St. and Piccadilly. I gather that Tasmania contains untold wealth in minerals. Gold, copper and silver! There is also a man on board who is going up Country to see some intractable ore which assays 80oz. to the ton! Even 100 tons of that would not be bad to bring home as heavy luggage and crush in England! But the mine is some 180 miles from the railway . . . .

Haig arrived in Egypt on 3 February 1898. He reported to the War Office in Cairo, informing them that he had paid his own passage out! No doubt this pleased them no end as the budget was as tight as ever. He wasted no time in getting himself kitted out.

In a letter to Henrietta, dated 6 February, from the Hotel Continental in Cairo, he wrote:

I went to see Gordon Bey, Director of Stores, who seems to make everything in the way of kit and furniture. He is a nice little chap, nephew of Gen. Gordon and quite young. He fitted me out with everything, which I had not brought from England. Then I went and bought 3 Tarbouches (or fezzes).* These I shall wear above the ordinary uniform I had in India except in the sun of course. This morning I finished my purchase of ponies. They are so dear that I thought it best to wire for the grey arab[9] from England. It only costs £20 to bring out.

*One of the fezzes can still be seen at Bemersyde.

He started to learn Arabic. So in no time at all Captain Douglas Haig 7 Q.O. Hussars had become Bimbashi Haig Bey, Egyptian Cavalry. He had signed on for two years, but had been assured that he could resign and go back to England at any time.

In the same letter to Henrietta he also commented:

> The longer I stay here the more lucky I seem to be in having got to this Egyptian Army [said after 3 days]. The crowd of fellows that have asked to be taken and refused is very great . . . . I hear the cavalry is full as regards regular officers . . . . Kitchener will only take the best now and picks and chooses from hundreds who are anxious to come.

He attributed his good fortune to the intervention of Sir Evelyn Wood, who had asked Haig to write to him. He expressed his gratitude, that he had been selected to come to Egypt, in at least one letter. He also said that he had never felt in better health. The climate, warm days, cool nights, suited him well. He travelled south by train and boat arriving at Kitchener's HQ at Wadi Halfa on 16 February. The boat journey was in two stages, firstly on Cook's Nile Steamer to Aswan and then by means of a stern wheeler, the *Ambigol*, to Halfa. He wrote to Henrietta on 11 February 1898:

> We are to arrive in Assuan tomorrow morning so I write this line to send back by the mail boat to tell you my doings since I last wrote. I left Cairo about 9.30 pm on Tuesday by train and reached Nagh Hamadi at about noon next day (Wednesday). The train being some two hours late. This was 'the mail' which leaves Cairo twice weekly on Tuesdays and Fridays, and in many respects resembles the old Belfast train about which one has heard so much. The present train was equally rough, equally slow, but far more dusty. There are Cars on it too, dignified by the adjective 'sleeping' and for which an extra 5/- is charged, but all the name means is the side of a first class carriage to oneself with a pillow of sorts and a blanket. However, I was able, thanks to the pillow and other accessories with which you provided me before I left, to pass a fairly good night and I breakfasted from the lunch basket on Wednesday.
> At Nagh Hamadi the train runs alongside the steamer. The latter, one of Cook's Nile Steamers, is a comfortable arrangement with cabins and bathrooms on the upper deck level with the top of the paddle boxes. Lunch was ready on board the boat and we got away about 2 pm and halted about 10 pm for the night at a place called Keneh on the East bank of the Nile. There was a bright moon and some of us got on donkeys

and rode round the town which is one of the largest in these parts, and famous for its being the starting point of many pilgrims for Mecca.

Next morning (Thursday) we had breakfast about 7 am and the steamer crossed over to the West Bank to Dundera where there is a famous old temple 2,000 years or more old. We rode out on donkeys to this place and got off again about 10 am. Then we reached Luxor (& Thebes) about 6 pm where we landed some of our passengers and took on some others. We only stayed an hour here so I had not time to see much of the temples. A halt was made as usual about 10 pm until 5 this morning, and shortly after 2 pm we got to Edfu where there is a magnificent temple said to be the best preserved of all ancient monuments . . . . You will have gathered that although I am travelling in the post boat our rate of progress is not very swift. We stop every night not because they can't navigate but simply because there are only 2 shifts of men, and a halt must be made for rest . . . . There are about 7 or 8 Germans out of the 32 passengers on board. At dinner one of them sent to have the cabin door shut. Some non-Germans insisted on its remaining open. The Germans at first retaliated, putting up their coat collars, and the lady sent for her jacket which she flung round her expansive shoulders! Many of us laughed and the Germans no doubt felt uncomfortable and got up en masse and left the table, like many petted children. No doubt, they felt as if they had withdrawn from the Concert of the Great Powers. So in due course they will receive a telegram from 'Wilhelm' to congratulate them on their spirited conduct in supporting his Kolonial Politik and 'Mailed Hand' theory on the banks of the Nile!

## Letter to Henrietta 14 February 1898 – On board the *Ambigol*

I posted a letter to you at Assuan where I arrived on Saturday morning last about 9 am. The first cataract is at Assuan, so I left Cook's steamer and, travelling round the rapids by railway, embarked on board a Govt. Stern Wheeler called the *Ambigol* , where I am now writing from. At Assuan I reported to the Egyptian Staff Officer (Pedley by name) for further orders about my journey Southwards. He was most kind and entertained me to lunch at their mess. There are 4 other officers at present in Assuan. Among them a Staff Officer for British Troops, a man called Friend of the RE whom I knew before, who offered to do anything I might want in the way of sending forward things for me . . . .The train left Assuan about 3 pm. It is a military railway for forwarding stores and troops and is about 7 miles long. The South end being at Shellal, where there are piles of stores at present waiting to be shipped southwards. Most of the transport is being used for railway plant at present, and only enough food sent forward for the troops which are actually at the front. I mean to say that no depots of stores for the use of the expeditionary Force are as yet formed. Of course the first thing is to get the railway finished to Berber. Once that is finished the work of collecting stores at the front can be begun. Journey takes 35 minutes. Embarked on board *Ambigol*. It is a very shaky old ship. I am the only officer on board. On one side we are towing a barge with stores and details of RE who are going forward to assist in making the railway, and on the other a large native boat full of rails. The latter is very deep in the water and consequently we ran aground three times yesterday. Once so badly that we had to leave the rail boat aground in mid-stream, take the barge to the bank, and then return and get the other off. It took some 3 hours before we were all 3 lashed together and under way again. However we managed to go further in the 24 hours than Cook's steamer did, because we go all through the night without tying up.

## Letter to Sir Evelyn Wood 14 February 1898 – on board the *Ambigol* between Korusko and Halfa.

You very kindly told me to write to you, so I am doing so. But at present I have nothing of real interest to tell you . . . . I won't weary you with an account of my journey to Cairo, for of course it was just like everyone else's . . . . At Cairo I luckily (tho' in truth it was by accident) went first to the British Hd. Qrs. And found à Court, with whom I used to have dealings when he was at the Intelligence Office. I discovered the question of whether officers go first to the Egyptian War Office or to the DAAG is not viewed in the office of the latter as at all a trivial matter. The Egyptian War Office seems to be run at present by one man and a boy; Col. Paine being the man, and one Jusb Bailey, the boy. In fact there seems nothing doing there and all they did for me was to order me to leave by the mail on Tues. 8th Feb., but they could not tell me to what branch of the Egyptian Army I am to belong. This I shall learn on reaching Halfa. I found them most kind, however, in making arrangements for sending on my horses, and in advising me as to kit.

I found it most difficult to pick up a couple of horses in condition. Thanks to some friends I have in the 21st Lancers (Fowle and others) I was able to buy a couple of good arabs, and they also gave me a good syce. The latter is an important item at present, because I hear that 6 horses died from chill and one fell overboard among the last batch of horses sent to the front. The 21st Lancers, as well as Sir F.Grenfell, spoke most highly of the work done by their Arab troopers. I gathered that the Walers (of which they said they had 70 or 80) were past their age averaging 14 yrs. of age. The Hungarians too are no match for the small Arabs . . . .

Whilst at Assuan I had a good look round and from what I saw, the Staff have a hardish time of it with Cairo on the one hand and the Hd. Qrs. at the front on the other. There seem to be too many Staff Officers at the latter place, because they rather make work. However, thanks to the officers at Assuan getting on so well together (a regular happy family), things go on as smoothly as you could wish for. Their only care is the number of unnecessary telegrams which come (frequently to the same effect) from different sources, and all letters they get are 'very urgent'. One regiment at the front indented for 600 helmets 'very urgent' . . . Does the CO fear a short supply of these articles at Cairo or what? We were well warned at the Staff College about the use of 'urgent'. It is a pity that some copies of notes on the subject are not to be had in the desert! . . .

The Sirdar has asked for a reserve of 3,000 rations to be sent up. This can be easily done, for the transport has been busy with material for the railway, and as a sufficient supply of the latter is now forward, boats are available for food. I mention these little details just to let you see how things strike an outsider though I feel sure you know better than I can tell you what the real conditions of things are here . . . . Please forgive this stupid letter. I merely sent it to let you know what has happened to me and that I am ever mindful of how much I am indebted to you. With most respectful remembrances.

Wadi Halfa 4pm 15/2/98. just arrived. Boat very late as we lost 8 hrs. thro running aground! Have seen the Sirdar. He was very pleasant, but cannot say yet what I am to do. He goes to Berber to-night and will wire. Probably I go to Dongola and take over a squadron there. But in any case I am delighted to be here, thanks to you.

He organized his life very well, as he told Henrietta on 17 Feb.

. . . I am allowed feeding by Govt. for 2 horses and 1 camel. I shall have more than that and can always get grub somewhere for surplus. At present I have 2 horses which I got at Cairo but when Hurreed Jheet (the grey) arrives and the 2 from India (Sir Pratap Singh[10] was sending them) there will be 5 horses. I have now bought 2 camels. One at Assuan and one here. I must have two to carry my plates, cooking pots and supplies. Then as to servants, I have engaged a cook at £3 a month and the black fellow Suleiman . . . as body servant. Then a syce for every 2 horses and a camel boy. So you see I have already got quite a retinue.

He goes on to ask Henrietta for supplies, specifying very carefully the size and shape of the containers.

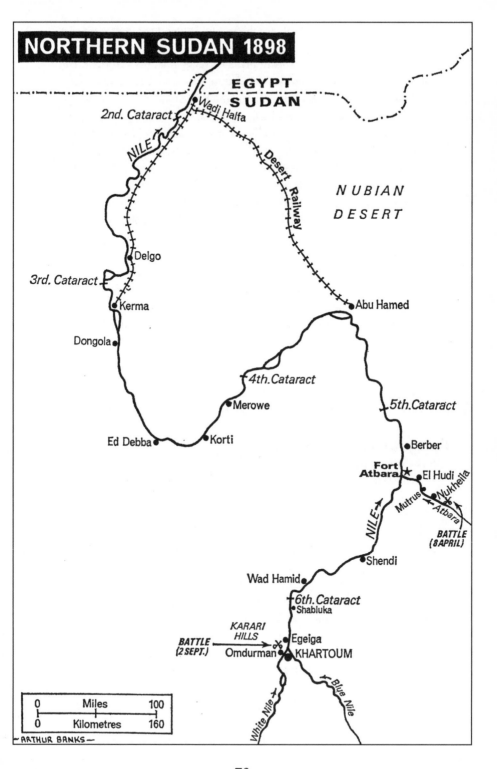

# NORTHERN SUDAN 1898

**EGYPT**
**SUDAN**

2nd. Cataract
Wadi Halfa

NILE

Desert Railway

*NUBIAN DESERT*

Delgo

3rd. Cataract

Kerma

Abu Hamed

Dongola

4th. Cataract

Merowe

5th. Cataract

Ed Debba
Korti

Berber

Fort Atbara
El Hudi
Nukheila
Mutrus
Atbara

**BATTLE (8 APRIL)**

NILE

Shendi

Wad Hamid

6th. Cataract
Shabluka

*KARARI HILLS*

**BATTLE (2 SEPT.)**
Omdurman
Egeiga
KHARTOUM

White Nile

Blue Nile

| 0 | Miles | 100 |
| 0 | Kilometres | 160 |

— ARTHUR BANKS —

73

The sort of things I would like would be jam, tinned fruit, cocoa, vegetables, haddocks in tin, tongue, biscuits, some hock and a bottle or two of brandy or any other sort of drink. Whisky I get here all right. But you know better than I do what sort of things to send. Spend whatever you like on the things, £50 or more [some £3,000 in today's money, but, judging by what was sent, she spent considerably less], which please get from the Royal Bank Leven. Kindly order a list of things to be put on the top of each box, and divide the stuff between the boxes so that in order to reach a particular thing one need not open the whole lot. That is, each box to contain a little of most things, except the drink which would be best in a box or boxes by itself. Send out through Cook & Co. addressed to Wadi Halfa, and they will forward them on. I don't expect them before August and can get on well enough with the supplies I can buy here, but things come better from England. Put a little soap (shaving) in and a few odds and ends and by the way a small mincing machine would be useful for the meat is usually very tough . . . . We live in good strong mud brick houses here. At present the nights are very cold and fine crisp mornings with a bright sun. During the day a wind gets up and blows the dust about. But I wear all my thick things just as when I left England.

Supplies seem to have taken about fourteen days on average to go from Britain to Berber via Thomas Cook, a remarkably efficient system. How long would it take now? – much longer, one imagines.

### To Henrietta 20 February 1898

Just a line to tell you that the Sirdar wired today for me to go to Berber, and that I leave this tomorrow (Monday) afternoon for Abu Hamed and railhead which latter is now 66 miles from Berber. I don't know at all what he wants me to do, but presume that the original idea of sending me to Debbeh has been changed . . . .I am taking 5 or 6 boxes of stores with me from this tomorrow – though the Suakim – Berber route is open to caravans and consequently stores should be arriving via Suakim. I think it best to be certain and I can get transport to carry it ! As I am going to Berber, please delay till I next write as to the best route by which to send the stores, which I asked for in my last letter.

By 28 February Haig had reached Berber. He then wrote to Henrietta on 2 March 1898 from Deckha, a suburb of Berber.

I wrote to you on leaving Halfa, and got here after a week's travelling. I'll send Hugo an account of the journey as it will amuse him no doubt and will save writing the story twice. For I am full of business today getting ready for the Atbara tomorrow. The present idea is that the Dervishes are advancing northwards from Shendi – under a young Emir called Mahmoud. Hence great efforts have been made by the Sirdar and his Staff to concentrate the British Brigade with all available troops at the junction of the Atbara and the Nile. The difficulty consists in feeding them. Before this reaches you, you will have heard by wire whether the Dervishes have come on or not. It would be great luck if they did come on, because then they would bring the whole matter to a conclusion at once. For if they gave fight and are beaten we could probably pursue them right on to Khartoum. Certainly over 150 miles from Atbara but no doubt the tribes on the flanks of the Dervishes would rise and assist in annihilating them as they fled.

Here we are living in great luxury! I have a fine big room – it is said to have been a mosque. The other officers have 2 or more rooms but small. We also have a mess and plenty of stores. The poor British Bde. are much less fortunate. They arrived near here this morning very foot sore and many quite done up. Some of the officers' feet all blood from the hot sand, and many of the men without boots, and unable to walk at all. I just preceded the British, but managed to bring up all my kit and 2 big boxes of stores – 7 camel loads in all! The poor British officer is limited to 30lbs of kit. You see transport is so scarce and there are a great many of them. Well we fed 17 or more at breakfast. Many more at lunch and there are a heap coming to dinner. One poor lad who was asked to have another bottle of beer – big Pilsener bottles, said, 'Are you sure you have ample, because I like water very much'. Poor wretches. Cold water has been a luxury for some weeks, and none of the men has been allowed beer since they got to railhead. It was quite a treat to see them feed and drink. They did themselves right well. We have 6 champagne for tonight . . .

My property in horse flesh is all over Egypt. 2 horses still at Assuan yesterday! 2 camels left Halfa marching yesterday! So I had to buy another horse here, a donkey £12 – a grand fellow – and a camel – £20 – terrible high prices, but one must have them.

Written at Es Sueiktab eleven miles south of Berber, half way between there and the Atbara 14 March 1898.

We had a pleasant time up the Atbara. Hot during the day but cold at night. We crossed to the S. side of the river but saw nothing but a wide expanse of stony desert. About the river itself there is plenty of shade. The water is beautifully clear and any amount of great big fish. About a mile on each side of the river there is a thick scrub jungle with clearings here and there. For in June the river comes down in flood and spreads over parts of the country; these have evidently been cultivated. There are many deserted villages too, and one of straw huts made by the Dervishes. The latter evidently abandoned in a hurry, because there were many 'augareebs' (native beds like the Indian charpoy) lying about and earthern jars etc. We saw nothing of the enemy however, though there are all sorts of rumours about them advancing. Two deserters came to Dakhila Camp the night we were there and said the enemy were afraid and would not come on. I thought they spoke truth, but others thought they were spies! Yesterday we heard that Osman Digna and Mahmoud advanced 15 miles on Friday from Shendi – ie they should be 75 m. from Atbara now. Whether induced by these reports or whether it is part of the general plan, we hear today that another Brigade and the Sirdar come from Berber tonight and halt in a village about 2 or 3 miles S. of this.

## Es Sueiktab 15 March 1898

I was called away yesterday as 3 squadrons of Cav. arrived from Berber and stayed with us here last night. They went on this morning to a place some 5 miles S. of this where the Sirdar is to camp tonight and take up his Hd. Qrs. for the next week or so. Thus all the cavalry (8 squadrons) is concentrated between this and the Atbara ready to advance at a moment's notice . . . .Your telegram says that you are attending to my orders. Many thanks.

Perhaps it will help you in ordering stores if I tell you what our arrangements are. First, our method of living varies according to whether we are settled, as here at Berber for instance. Then we have a mess of our own or live with some regt. Here I am messing with the 14th Sudanese (Hamilton is in the Corps) – and they do us very well. On the other hand, we may be detached on some reconnoitring or patrol duty and must then carry all with us. When settled down for a week or so we can get meat and bread and Rosbach water, claret etc. and are really living in luxury. For instance, we breakfast about 8 or 8.30 and usually commence with that crushed oatmeal porridge (which I asked you to send me in my last letter) and milk – the latter excellent from the goat. Then we have eggs from the hens which regts. carry with them. Bacon (in tins) and sausage. Sometimes fish from the Nile – rather good, and finish up with jam or marmalade. We lunch about 1o'c. and everyone does himself well. Soup, 2 meats, puddings etc. with tinned fruits. Dinner about 7.30. So you see we are very well off at present. We can get most things in Berber, tho' of course the tins from home are fresher. The 3 best things to send would be some fruits, jams, some light claret to drink with water, and that crushed oatmeal which one can't buy here. Hamilton gets his things from the A&N Stores.

Then when on patrol, I found tinned sausages good for breakfast in the early morning. The lunch during the day I had to carry on my saddle, so small tins of potted stuff (but not salt) and biscuits – for drink, Valentine's meat juice in bottles mixed in water was easily carried and is good to drink in the sun. Brand's Essence also useful. For dinner we can get most tinned things here, but 'minced collops', 'curry' and some tin soups are good. Tea and sugar we can get all right here. Things look as if we are going to move on soon, so use your own judgment when you get this as to whether to send me out things or not. Two days ago I saw a Reuter about the Russians occupying Talkin Wan and Port Arthur, so I daresay the Govt. will be anxious to have this show finished without delay.

Blair came here from Berber last Thursday and stayed the night. He is in the 9th Sudanese. Friday is observed as a holiday in this army – Capper is also here, and Sandbach[11] is at Halfa. So you see you have plenty of friends in the Sudan. The climate seems very healthy. Cool nights (2 blankets always, your rug and the one Hugo gave me from the Cabruch with Jaeger sheets is the bedding!) and the days hot, but the breeze off the desert seems pure.

## Letter to Sir Evelyn Wood 15 March 1898, written half way between Berber and the Atbara.

First I will briefly tell you what I have been about, myself, so that you may know what opportunities I have had of forming an opinion upon the subjects about which I propose to write. I left Halfa on 21st February, passed through Abu Dis where the British Camp then was, and where I spent a day (23rd) and got to Berber on Monday morning 28th.two days ahead of the British Brigade.

On the 3rd March I accompanied the squadron of Cavalry which protected the advance of the British Brigade from Berber to the Camp at Dakhila (1/2 mile from here). Since then I have been with a squadron of Cavalry and a Coy. of Camel Corps reconnoitring the line of the Atbara and a little South of it. We went from Dakhila, the entrenched camp at junction of Atbara and Nile to a point some 40 odd miles up the river, and then returned across the desert to this place.

Upon odd days I have watched the Sudanese and Egyptian Infantry manoeuvring in Brigade in the morning, and busied myself with Arabic during the day – And now I will say something about the march of the British. You will of course have had a full description of it in official language, so I won't describe it, but will merely give you the distances as they appeared to me after going over the ground and after checking them by the map and by the miles on the track prepared for the railway. I did so because I have asked many fellows in the Brigade from the General downwards what distances they covered and without exception the distances stated to have been marched seemed to me to be overestimated. Now for the sake of learning something, I think it best to keep to facts. Moreover, even according to my distances the march is a remarkable one. Abu Dis to Shereikh is 24 miles. The troops were detrained about 6 miles from the latter place, and then marched; but as they had done a route march in morning of the day they started, let us say they did 24 miles on the first day –

| | | |
|---|---|---|
| then Shereik to Bustanab | | 11 miles |
| on to | Diareea | 11 |
| | Wadi Homer | 11 |
| | Gininetti | 10 |
| | El Hassan | 16 |
| | Berber | 7 |
| | Dabeika | 10 |
| | | 24 first day |
| | | —— |
| | Total | 100 miles |

The route march was made on Thursday and Dabeika was reached at 9 pm on the next Thursday. Wednesday was a halt day. So we have 6 march days giving an average of 16 2/3 miles a day – a good performance; especially so, when we remember the heat of the sun by day, and the fact that there was no shade to enable the men to rest. The march began usually at 4.30 pm daily and ended about 8 or 9 am next day, with a long halt of 2 hours about midnight.

When the Brigade got to El Hassan (7 miles from Berber) the majority were very weary, and the feet of some officers and men were sore and bloody. So, without knowing the reason for such forced marching, I very much question whether, if it had been necessary actually to oppose the enemy on the Atbara, these men could have fought effectively. I mean that my conclusion is – do average marches and have the bulk of the command fit for battle and any emergency.

Our mess at Berber was close to the landing place, so we were able to entertain the officers of the unfortunates who were brought in by boat. You will be tired of hearing about the boots; but there seems no doubt that they were not strong enough to withstand the dry climate. The British are now in comfortable houses in Darmali Village, 2 miles South of this. For a week they were bivouacked on cotton soil at Dabeika ½ mile North of this and as there is a sand storm most days, their condition seemed the acme of discomfort. All seem very happy and cheery now.

## Letter to Sir Evelyn Wood 26 March 1898 from Hudi Bivouac on the Atbara.

Since I last wrote to you the Cavalry have been fairly busy, so perhaps a brief account of what has been done may interest you. Last Sunday (March 20th) the whole force which had concentrated some 3 or 4 days previously at Kunur Village on the Nile, marched for the Atbara . The bulk of the cavalry marched with the infantry at 11.30 am but 2 squadrons went off at daybreak, and reconnoitred to some 4 miles beyond the Atbara. I went with one of the latter. We did not find an enemy, and on receipt of our report the army marched. I mention this because the hour of march (11.30 am) may seem strange to you. The day, however, was favourable for marching as a strong North wind was blowing, and the sun was obscured by dust.

On the 21st we got away about 4.30 am, marched to Abadar (some 12m) where is a Jaalin post holding a block house. Here the whole halted except 2 squadrons – one under Le Gallais[12] and accompanied by me as a sort of odd man, was ordered to reconnoitre Umbadia from the right bank – Another squadron (accompanied by Mahon[13]) reconnoitred the left bank up to a point opposite Umbadia. Le Gallais and I proceeded for some 7 or 8 miles. He halted the mass of the squadron about a mile clear of the scrub and then he and I went on with a small patrol.

When just North of the scrub near Mutrus we saw a single Dervish scout but only for a second as he vanished at once. We went after him a short way, but as we had already proceeded farther than ordered, we returned through the scrub and the deserted villages along the river bank. We got back to Abadar about 1.45 pm. I had watered my horse and was still in the river bed when I heard the order to turn out as the Dervishes were on us! Briefly what had happened was this: The single scout had collected some hundred or more mounted men and followed Le Gallais and myself back to the halting place. They were met by a patrol from the outposts which they raced back and reached the picket simultaneously. The picket was dismounted; several men composing it were shot or speared; the leaders of the Dervishes were then close to the main body! This was fairly alert and prepared, having watered only by troops. One squadron which was ready saddled up was ordered forward, and in a short time, probably 3 minutes at most, 4 others were in support.

The leading squadron was commanded by Persse (Queen's Bays). He was ordered to clear the scrub, for as yet only some half dozen Dervishes had shown themselves to the main body. Having advanced into the scrub his pace was reduced to a trot or walk owing to the broken ground and bushes which are thick here. There he was met by some 50 or more mounted enemy. Under the circumstances he thought he could not go on so tried to draw off. At this moment he lost 7 or 8 men, shot from behind trees mostly.

A number of Dervishes tried also to work along the river bank, but the squadron returning from the left bank frightened them off. We pursued to near Mutrus and located the enemy (merely Cavalry) at Nakheila. It was 11.30 when we got back to bivouac. Our losses were 8 killed and 10 wounded (2 of the latter died on way to Camp) and 13 horses. The enemy lost some 6 or 7 only, and we got 4 horses. My comment on this action is –

1. The Outpost service tho' theoretically right, was carelessly done. When I passed the picket in question, many were lying down apparently asleep.
2. The eyesight of the Egyptian vedette can't be relied on. For the Dervishes passed the front of the line of vedettes!
3. The pluck of the Egyptian Cavalryman is right enough in my opinion.
4. The Horse Artillery against enemy of this sort and in scrub is no use. We felt the want of machine guns when working along outside of scrub for searching some of the tracks.

On Tuesday 22nd 2 Battn., and 1 squadron were sent at dawn to Abadar. Firing was soon heard, so the whole Cavalry turned out. This day we had 2 machine guns. The enemy (still Cavalry) disappeared as soon as we approached. He was supposed to halt at Umbadia and Native spies at night said he was there.

On Wed. 23rd a whole Infantry Bde. and 1 squadron was sent to Abadar as it was expected enemy would come on in force. As he did not appear by 9 am I was sent off at 10 am to reconnoitre Umbadia from the left bank. I crossed at Abadar, took 2 native trackers (one a sheik of the Jaalin and one the Bishareen) and a native officer to interpret. We went out into desert and came to river near Menawi. Here I met Dervish patrol as I was going through scrub to river bank. The enemy must have thought us stronger for he made off up stream.

I was able there to see well into Umbadia and the bend of river about Mutrus. My report was that no force of enemy was North of Nakeila – not at all agreeable to the Commanders of this Army who rely more on spies than on their Cavalry and wished the enemy to be in Umbadia. Thursday and Friday we have done the usual reconnaissance to Umbadia and I went for 15 miles (with my pal the sheik) NE from Abadar to see if enemy had moved on Berber. Not a sign of him.

I have enjoyed my reconnaissance work very much, but it is slow for the infantry sitting in camp doing nothing, for the days are hot and the officers of the British have only what they stand in and a blanket. Yesterday I was asked to do Staff Officer for this Cavalry Brigade, and I have been busy today arranging to carry 3 days supply in the hopes of our having to pursue. We have the Camel Corps Cos. attached to us, and we have got that body to carry the stuff with 15 led camels – I fear this is rather a badly put together epistle, but possibly it may be better than what the newspapers publish, as none of the correspondents comes with the cavalry and their reports are mere camp gossip.

Neither do any of the Hd. Qr. Staff come out, tho' they anticipate a battle on the ground over which we work daily! This bivouac is v.dusty (no method in its arrangement at all). Scarcely the place for writing, so kindly make allowances for shortcomings.

## Letter to Henrietta. 1 April 1898 from Hudi Camp on the Atbara River

... We get on fairly well in the way of stores here. We sit down 12 or 13 as a rule to dinner and Teck looks after the messing. He takes after his family and is fond of his grub! We drink Rosbach water with claret or Graves – also Pilsener beer when we can get it. But it is unusual having so large a mess, and when we go out on any expedition it is impossible to cater for so large a mess – then we mess 2 or 3 together. Although we (the Egyptian Army) live in comparative luxury, with our baths, cooking pots, beds, etc, the British Brigade (ie General Gatacre's lot)[14] live in the greatest discomfort. In fact the officers only have what they stand up in! and a blanket. The nights were so cold when we first came here to the Atbara that I lent my big fur rug to some of the Seaforth Highlanders who were so kind to me at Aldershot – I had three others for myself you know, and the Jaeger sheets (viz. the rug you gave me, Hugo's cabrach one and the Austrian leather one which I carry on my saddle always). It is quite unnecessary in my opinion that the English should be in such discomfort. For the last 2 or 3 months they all, stout elderly parties of Majors and Colonels, have gone to sleep in the dust with one rug apiece rolled round them. I felt sorry for them with their ration of bully beef and maybe a sardine tin as a luxury.

Besides Gatacre is an awful fidget and has them out for all kinds of parades. Even here, at a distance of 18 miles from the enemy's camp he has his whole Bde on duty in 2 hour reliefs all night thro' fear of a night attack. This must be rather fatiguing as the days are hot and the men can't rest then. Besides quite unnecessary as the men are all lying down on the ground close to the thorn zeriba (or fence which is made round this bivouac) and can easily man it on the slightest alarm. The infantry have a

81

bad time of it for they have little to interest them. We Cavalry on the other hand are out every day and get plenty of fun chasing Dervish horsemen who won't face us at all in the open now, but make off at once into the bush and scrub near the river.

Last Tuesday we left here (the whole Cavalry Brigade, 8 squadrons, 1 Horse Art. Batty., 2 Maxim Batts., 1 Company Camel Corps all under Broadwood[15] I being Chief Staff Officer of the Brigade) to reconnoitre the enemy's position. We halted about 10m.from here the first afternoon, and went off before 5 am on Wednesday. We found his 'dem' (dame pronounced) or camp strongly made with deep ditches. Tho' our guns fired 29 shells at it at 1,000yds. range and the maxims over 2,000 rounds, the Dervishes stayed in their trenches and took not the slightest notice!

Some of us were able to get up within 500yds. and we had a good look at the place. We got back again here in the evening. I forgot to say that we saw 4 to 500 Cav. or more but they would not face us at all and their patrols chased ours and ours their patrols, much after the fashion of an Aldershot Field Day.

I see that you imagine that I am with the Sirdar. He is a man that does everything himself and, in fact, has no Hd. Qr. Staff at all! Indeed General Hunter[16] who has come to command the troops in the field cannot get the Sirdar to tell him what his position in the Army is! In addition the Sirdar is most silent, and no one has ever the slightest notion what is going to be done until he gives his orders! He has 2 aides-de-camp who have a hardish time, but beyond that he employs no staff at all.

Sometimes it might be better for the comfort of the troops if he had a staff, but on the whole things get along pretty well and we cavalry get a pretty free hand. Broadwood (12th Lancers) is a very good fellow and quite understands what the enemy and his own troops are worth. By all means show my letters to anyone you like. I have really a good deal to do and it is difficult to write in the open air with wind and dust. The climate is very healthy I think and I really feel very well indeed . . . .

Please send me out (by parcel post) a big white umbrella lined, with spike to stick in the ground.

Following the reconnaissance described in the letter to Henrietta dated 1 April it was clear that the force of Dervishes was a large one and that it was under the command of Mahmoud, one of the Khalifa's most trusted lieutenants. Its aims had presumably been to harass Kitchener into making a mistake and to re-capture Berber. Mahmoud, however, made no attempt to attack the Sirdar's army and simply

82

remained inactive in the Dervishes' well dug defensive position on the Atbara River some miles upstream from where it joins the Nile. Clearly this gave Kitchener the opportunity to destroy a significant part of the Khalifa's overall strength. It also gave Haig his first opportunity to test himself in battle, in this case a reconnaissance in strength which led a few days later to the battle of the Atbara.

## Diary for 5 April 1898

Brigade with 2 Maxim Batteries attached, Gen. Hunter (O.C. Egyptian forces), Sir H. Rawlinson[17] (one of K's two ADCs, his only Staff Officers) and sundry other 'hangers on' left camp at 5.10 a.m. to reconnoitre Dervish camp and position . . . On approaching Dervish 'Dem' about 8.30 a.m., guns opened fire . . . upon which Dervish horsemen seen moving in 2 columns Eastwards, partly in hollow and partly on spur. Some men knocked over, and this body of the enemy fell back. The guns then moved (nearer to the Dem) and opened fire again. A shot from Big Gun in Enemy's dem now fell near Bde. HQ. It was well aimed to enfilade our Battery, but trajectory was high and curved, so passed harmlessly over it. Having driven enemy into dem on his right, our 'sketchers' were able to locate his right flank. Bde then fell back North Eastwards with the object of seeing enemy's left clearly.

The Brigade had scarcely retired 400 to 500 yds before infantry was seen rushing out of the camp, the cavalry some 500 (strong) also came on again and a second body (of equal strength) down stream also pressed forward . . . I was engaged in getting 2 squadrons to cover the right flank of the guns as they retired. The left rear squadron was then attacked in force . . . I galloped to ask what orders he (Broadwood) wished to issue. He told me to get squadrons to protect flanks of guns and he himself advanced to the attack with 1st Squadron.

I went to Le Gallais to tell him to see to west flank of guns, found him already moving to attack the cavalry, which had moved downstream and round his flank. I advanced with his squadrons, dervish horsemen fell back and a few were stuck or shot. Meantime I noticed (another) squadron was in difficulties and galloped to Mahon. I told him I had no orders for him, but stated that the 1st squadron was attacking and asked him what he would do so that I might get the rest of the Bde to cooperate. The dust was so thick, that he could not see what had happened, so he asked me;'What do you suggest?' I replied at once; 'Put one

83

squadron on right of guns and attack with the other 2: I will bring Baring and the remaining 2 squadrons to your support on the left flank.'

He did this and his resolute advance checked the enemy for a moment, tho' one of his squadrons faltered. Meantime I went to Baring[18] to bring him up. I placed the 7th squadron (detailed to escort the guns) under Baring and galloped on to join Mahon. I met 2 squadrons coming back at a sharp canter. I yelled 'Ashkeen' (or walk) and brandished my sword, . . .

The situation looked nasty. So I galloped to the guns, which were still retiring at a good trot. I could not find the O.C. Artillery (Young) so gave an order direct to Maxim batteries to halt and come into action at once and that I would bring the cavalry back towards their flanks so as not to mask their fire. The gunner officers responded nobly and I galloped towards the enemy, met Broadwood on the way, who approved of what I had done and led the squadrons as I had suggested. All this time the Dervish infantry were pouring in a hot fire and their cavalry had quite cut off our line of retreat.

The Maxims did good work and the enemy was checked for a bit. As the 9th and 10th squadrons were falling back, one wounded N.C.O. of the 9th squadron was somehow ridden over and left lying in rear. I managed to get him on to my horse and brought him in to the guns where we had some led horses. I put him on the front of my saddle. We got back to camp about 5 p.m. having lost:

|          | Men | Horses |
|----------|-----|--------|
| Missing  | 8   | 10     |
| Dead     | –   | 8      |
| Wounded  | 18  | 13     |

| Guns fired | 22 common shells |
|------------|------------------|
|            | 35 shrapnel      |
| 2 Maxims   | 5,500 rounds     |

## Letter to Henrietta dated 12 April from Berber

Wednesday April 6th. We changed camp to Umbadia and about 11 o'clock I went on with a couple of squadrons to escort General Hunter to find a halting place for the Infantry near Mutrus where they might rest on the way to attack the enemy's position next day. Thursday April 7th. Infantry marched at 6 pm but cavalry waited till 2 am Friday and caught up the Infantry columns on the march. The attack on the position was on this day. You will be able to read about it in the papers better than I can describe it. We Cavalry were on the left of attack and drove back enemy's horsemen to the river bank, but as we were not allowed to cross until late in the day, they naturally got away. We picked up a good many prisoners, poor wretches; many had terrible wounds. It was 9 pm before we got back to Umbadia, a long day.

On Saturday 9th we left at 3.30 pm to return and got as far as Abadar that night. Sunday we got to Kunur and yesterday came in here. Tomorrow the Sirdar is to make a triumphal entry into Berber – a sort of Roman triumph, with Mahmoud (captured in the battle) tied to his horse's tail I suppose. The order is to decorate Berber. A lot of mud walls and dust and only palms available for the job!! Well, I have given you a good long story. We Cav. have had very hard work and I have kept very fit indeed. The sun very hot and we lost several horses daily from sunstroke.

PS You need not send enclosed all round the family, as there is too much about my own doings in it and they talk such a lot. Show it to Hugo. You can also tell him that when the squadrons were returning just before the Maxims came into action, I was able to pick up a poor devil of an Egyptian who was wounded in the shoulder and had given himself up for lost and put him in the front of my saddle and carried him to the guns where we had some spare horses and the Dr. This is quite the gymkhana style of things which you used to see in India!! In doing this I did not incur the slightest danger tho' there is no doubt that had I not taken this man the Dervishes would have got him. Indeed I saw two other poor chaps collared by them while a rescue party was being organized!

If you see Colonel French you might show him this letter confidentially, for the Gyppie Cavalry is really better in some respects than he thinks. I am very lucky to have acted as Broadwood's C. Staff Officer, because, as a rule, new arrivals in this army are allowed to do nothing, and are thought to know nothing till the climate has fossilized their brains somewhat!

Although Haig made light of the rescue of the Egyptian sergeant, saying that pulling the man up onto his horse was only the sort of thing they used to do in the gymkhanas in India, [but presumably not under fire], his brother officers in the 7 Hussars were sufficiently impressed to commission a picture of the event. This used to hang in the Field Marshal's dressing-room at Bemersyde and is now in the collection at Huntly House, Edinburgh. It has been said that, had the soldier been British rather than Egyptian, Haig might possibly have won a V.C.

**Diary for 13 April**

Triumphal entry of Sirdar at 7 a.m. 5 Sqns. of cavalry met him on w. side of town and Guard of honour of 100 men . . . .Sirdar arrived with cavalry escort. The latter fell back and 1st Bde. preceeded by dervish prisoners headed by Mahmoud followed Sirdar through Berber. In front of Mahmoud was a Calico screen with inscription; THIS IS MAHMOUD, THE COMMANDER OF THE ARMY WHICH SAID IT WAS GOING TO RE-CAPTURE BERBER.

After 1st Bde followed artillery, then cavalry. The natives lined the route and cheered. Finally Sirdar halted under dais in market place and saw troops pass. Cavalry were back at camp by 8 a.m.

It is clear that Haig thought the whole occasion ridiculous. A fuller description of the battle of the Atbara was given to Sir Evelyn Wood in the following letter.

**Letter to Sir Evelyn Wood dated 29 April 1898**

We have just received the London papers of 9th April with accounts of the Battle on the Atbara. What rubbish the British Public likes to read! The exaggeration of some of the reports almost makes a good day's work appear ridiculous. The headings of the 'DT' are so overdrawn that instinctively one says 'Waterloo Eclipsed'. But the story of Mahmoud the C-in-C being taken 'under his bed' rather gives the show away! As a matter of fact he was taken in a kind of 'reduit' with a gallery. Here his bodyguard fought hard and were all killed except one. The latter, I am told, came out shouting 'Don't shoot. Here is Mahmoud'. So he got off with his life. The 11th Sudanese came across this sort of keep after entering the Dem, and had the best part of a Company shot down opposite it. Their casualties were over 100 on this account.

You must not think that I am trying to find points to criticize. (I'll tell you much more when I get back). But as I owe my presence here to your kindness, it pleases me to write to and tell you of any odd event which may not otherwise reach you, except with the accompaniment of an official colouring. I am very busy with my squadron now, which oddly enough is the 7th. Most of the men are recruits. I am glad of this, for the saying is 'It is ill teaching old dogs new tricks'.

My chief difficulty is with the horses. Many have sore backs and all are very poor. Still I get 80 out for troop drills every morning. I work solely with the object of meeting Dervishes and go in for individual riding, circling round bushes and round lances put in the ground (bushes are square) to get the men to ride their horses. I have also dummies on the ground and balls on posts, which I make the men thrust at. The men are all very keen about it and some in the other squadrons come and look on in the mornings; for they are resting now! And the usual training hitherto has been the regimental turns and circles in the open manege.

The weather is still pleasant, though the therm. is said to reach 112 each day. We have not heard yet what effect the news of the fight has had on the Khalifa. The general opinion is that Mahmoud's force came from Darfour and Kerdofan. Its defeat won't make much odds. Indeed Mahmoud's numbers seem to me greatly exaggerated. I thought 7 to 800 not more were present.

## Letter to Henrietta 29 April 1898. from Berber

I heard today that poor Jameson in the Seaforths is very ill with congestion of the liver and is suffering much pain. I met him at dinner with little Johnnie (nephew) in Cairo. He is to leave by steamer on route for Cairo and England. I also saw 'The Duke'[19] today (Egerton) looking quite ill, but still able to talk! The terrible worry and discomfort to which Gatacre has subjected his brigade seems to be beginning to tell. For here (Berber) everyone looks very well indeed. For myself they all say I look far better than I ever did in England. The days are hot, but the nights are cold. That is to say that from 6 pm to 6 am the climate is excellent.

I have the Squadron to play with in the mornings and 3 days a week play polo. At present we have not got our fizzy water yet, and the soda water machine has broken down. Still, the Nile water is excellent at this date. We filter it and cool it. This with some claret is excellent. I see Spain and the Yanks are fighting.

## 29 May 1898 from Berber

The mail leaves Thursdays and Sundays at 6 pm and should arrive on Tuesdays and Saturdays, but there are one or two mails stopped on the road somewhere owing to a breakdown on the railway. So I have not any letter to acknowledge since yours 2nd May. The railway reached here 4 or 5 days ago, but no plant came forward till today owing to the breakdown. This morning, however, 2 trains arrived so they will be able to lay some 3 miles of rails.

It is wonderful the way the railway is put down. There are about a couple of thousand men in the railway Battalion. Great strong fellows who never tire. I saw one of them running with 2 heavy wooden sleepers on his shoulder, and 10 of them carry a rail at a swinging trot. The sleepers are brought up, another lot of men arrange them on the embankment as they arrive at the right distances, then the rails arrive, and each lot of men drop their rail first as far as their knees and then (on a word of command) drop it on to the sleepers within an inch or two of its right place. The rails are then spiked down, gauged, belted together and all without a hitch. The engine with the material train keeps creeping on every moment as the line is laid. It's really a strange sight; and how the different groups of men don't get in each other's way surprises me.

I play Hurreed Jheet at polo 3 days a week. I forget if I told you that Sir Pratap sent me 2 excellent horses.

## 10 June 1898 from Berber

The British Infantry Officers have all, as many as can be spared, been sent to Cairo. The 'Duke' amongst them. I saw him pass here. He looked quite poorly. Every week too the British send a sick convoy North, of some 50 or 60 men and officers. The moment anyone gets seedy they pack him North it seems, hence there are not a large number of British left – well under 3,000 all told. The 'Duke' is wrong to say that many British were wounded by Sudanese in their rear. . . . all 3 Brigades converged on the enemy's Dem; the British had the farthest to go and so were in rear when the firing commenced, so that a delay occurred to allow the British to come up in line. Then the nature of the enemy's position caused both of the attackers' flanks to converge. However, many at any rate some, of these in both flanks Bdes. were wounded by friendly bullets.

But this must always happen more or less I expect. On the other hand Major Napier of the Camerons (recently dead) was wounded early in the action by one of his own men – and Brooke (7th H.) showed me the hole in his breeches right along his thigh of a Lee Metford bullet which some man let off carelessly in his vicinity – But accidents must happen, especially amongst men who are excited and possibly too closely crowded. As to his statement that there were not enough Drs., one hears contradictory stories. The difficulty in organizing a Medical service for an expedition of this sort, is to correctly estimate beforehand the probable number of sick and wounded and one must guard against converting the operating force into a train of stretcher carriers!

The Sirdar certainly successfully avoided the latter error, for there was not one carrier in the whole force I believe! But he used all the Egyptian Battalions after the fight for this purpose, and right well they did it, poor creatures. Many were so fatigued that they slept as they stood at every short halt during the night, on the return march with the wounded. The Egyptians carried the Blacks' wounded as well as the British. But in criticizing the medical arrangements you must remember that the Sirdar never calculated on having to fight some 40 miles or more from his line of camps, the Nile. Hence it is a pity to be too severe on what could not well have been foreseen, viz. Mahmoud taking part on the middle Atbara.

## Letter to Sir Evelyn Wood 25 June 1898 from Berber

Broadwood, Tullibardine[20] (attached to my squadron) and self are the only Cavalry officers here. We are all in bed at 9 pm and up at daylight. The old Anglo-Egyptians keep fashionable hours and dine at 8.15 pm! May was a hot month but the weather tho' hot is healthy I think. Anyhow the time passes very quickly. Again best thanks for your kindly letter.

## Letter to Henrietta 21 July 1898 from Berber

We expect to leave this by the end of this month. The idea is for us Cavalry to cross the river here, and march up the left bank to a point within 60 miles of Omdurman. All the force will assemble there — that is if the Khalifa does not go off before . . . . I am glad to know all about where the fight is to be, because I very much doubt if the Khalifa himself knows where he will fight!! . . . .The Khalifa was collecting his forces in a Hegva (training camp) 2½ to 3 miles west of Omdurman. Whether he is training for battle or for running, no one is able to say. If he does run I daresay that the Sirdar will be able to arrange to occupy the place with some 'friendly' Arabs so as to give the Guards a bit of a fight. The Durweesh and the friendly are quite the same to look at, so no would be much the wiser.

## 30 July from Atbara Fort, opposite Dakhila

I crossed my squadron last Monday at Berber in 2 sailing boats. We got 17 into one, and 20 into the other each time. Fortunately there was a good north wind and in spite of the current we got back very quickly without having to tack. The river is about a mile wide at Berber store depot where we crossed and we made the trip there and back, loaded and unloaded in 45 minutes average per boat. We began at 10 am and I had finished by 3 pm. 142 troop horses, 4 mules, my 3 camels, 5 horses and 1 donkey and my baggage!

On Tuesday and Wednesday it blew hard from the south, so that we had to be given a steamer to get the other squadron over. This actually took over 2 hours to cross on the Wednesday morning and when it got to my side it had to wait some hours before it could cross back. However we got all finished by lunchtime on Wednesday and marched at 3 pm that day. We continued till 6.30 pm and then halted for the night. We had a grand dinner that night off your stores (These were the ones which left in April!) We were Le Gallais and myself and Lewis (the vet. a very good fellow who used to be at Poona), Broadwood and the others were on leave and only joined us here yesterday.

On Thursday we got our camels off at 4.45 am and were ourselves on the road at 5. (The sun does not rise till after that hour now). It was about 10 when we got here. Friday (yesterday) the box you sent by J. Vaughan[21] arrived here; a grand one and I have unpacked it. The quails are bad I am sorry to say. One can always tell a bad tin by its bulging out at the end instead of being flat. So I made a man open it (at a safe distance) to be sure; there was no doubt about it, so we had to throw them into the river. The box is to be used on the march to carry our daily supply of food in. You have no idea how difficult it was to get boxes in Berber to pack up our mess stores in. So this box is quite a god-send! I am well equipped for this trip! Everything I required has turned up. Actually your red night-cap arrived as we were marching and I wore it on the first night on the march when a beastly dust storm came on at about 1 am. I just drew the cap on over my eyes as far as the tip of my nose, and can then sleep thro' any duststorm!

Last night we had a burra-khana here! 15 to dinner. The turkeys I have been fattening for a month (they came from lower-Egypt) was the reason. But I must tell you of my turkeys. When I left Berber we broke up the mess, and the mess corporal was to come up by boat with the 2 'dindies' as they call them here. In the hurry of packing up, the turkeys were lost sight of. However, it was considered probable that the ladies of the 10th Sudanese (who had lines about 1 mile from ours) might have carried them off. Accordingly the OC 10th Sudanese was applied to and sure enough they were in the ladies lines. They then started in the boat. We got a steamer to tow it up here, or rather to Dakhila (opposite) where all supplies were landed under El Sirdar's eyes . . . . The water transport officer was duly notified and as the ships arrived (each tug tows 4 or more) he called out to another steamer to bring our boat across here at once '2 dindies for the Cavalry mess must be delivered at once' . . . .But alas, one dindy only arrived . . . . The other they said would insist on drinking the Nile water and fell overboard! 'Of course you could not expect me to jump overboard' says the boy in charge. However 1 dindy did us well. I opened the big box of apricots too. They were so fresh and good and much appreciated – better than the box by parcel post which the sun had melted a little. It is almost dark ¼ to 7 pm so I must stop. The Nile is very high now. Yesterday the Atbara came down in great flood. We start from here on 4th August and reach Metemmeh in 5 marches (100 miles). Then 40 miles farther brings us to Wad Hadeshi where the army concentrates. We have a good mess house (sun dried bricks) but live in tents here.

## 3 August 1898. Opposite Atbara Fort

I got 6 new shirts from Bowring 2 days ago. So I am starting with a regular new outfit throughout. The shirts are beauties and are a treat after the old ones which had shrunk as much they barely fitted a small Jaalin boy who insists on accompanying my establishment to Khartoum. The establishment is as follows:

Servants

| | |
|---|---|
| 1. | Mahdi (soldier) a copt, a sort of prehistoric looking man. Head of the household. |
| 2. | Moosa (a Hadendown arab from Suakim) an excellent valet and cook. |
| 3. and 4. | Ali and Achmed, two Berberi syces from near Korosko. |
| 5. | Salim (a soldier) Camel man. |
| 6. | The small Jaalin boy (his people all killed by the Dervishes last year). He looks after my clothes, ponies or donkeys as required |

The above look after me, 5 horses, 3 camels and a donkey and a goat for milk. One camel carries store, another my tent and some champagne, the third my clothes – while the donkey who trots like a pony (cost £12) is loaded with luncheon basket and a few things required on first arrival in camp. This will show you that we travel in greater luxury than the poor Duke and the English did. And Wauchope[22] was here today. I am going to let him have a pony when we get to Wad Habeshi as I have more than I want.

## 14 August 1898. At North end of Sableega Cataract (about fifty miles North of Omdurman)

This is rather a nice camp, and just upstream there are numbers of islands covered with trees and grass which is pleasant after the Berber desert. We have our mess established in a palm grove so we have plenty of shade during the day. There is always a good wind blowing from the South and the climate feels much cooler than Berber. It is not certain how long we remain here, as this depends on the time it takes to concentrate the troops here. Probably till the end of the month; for both the current and the wind is against the steamers coming from Dakhila. All the food supplies are ready. Once we start from here it won't take us long to reach Omdurman. Possibly 8 days marching as the troops fresh from the North will be out of training, not having marched a yard in this country – so if this big force averages 7 miles a day it will be well. The dervishes had a camp about 8 miles from this but left it about 3 weeks ago.

## 16 August

I have not been able to get my letter of 14th off to you as there has been no steamer going north. There may be one tomorrow. I found the metal boxes for the wallets most useful. I used them nearly every day, either during a march or immediately on arrival. I had a fire lighted and made some soup. The tins of liquid soup too which you sent me have come in very handy either before marching (as soup is more easily taken at 3 am than sausages and cocoa) or sometimes I have drunk the soup during the march when the halt was not long enough to make a fire. I carry a tin on my 2nd horse in the wallet, and the heat of the sun has been quite enough to keep the soup thoroughly liquid.

## 22 August 1898 Wad Hamed

I have just heard that the steamer which leaves in 20 minutes will be our last chance of posting letters until after Khartoum! All the steamers will be wanted here to carry the force forward.

Tomorrow the Sirdar has a big Field Day for the whole force here. On 24th General Hunter and the Sudanese and Egyptian troops march to Wad Bishara and next day to south side of Shabluka Cataract near Jebel Royan. I cover the advance with my squadron. On 25th the British troops covered by 1 British squadron follow, and on 26th the remainder of Cavalry follow, doing 2 marches in one day. All sorts of people are turning up at the last moment. It is a sort of picnic for them now! Many are still North of Atbara, so will be late for the show I imagine . . . The weather is nice and cool now. This morning quite fresh.

Now don't worry yourself if you don't hear from me for a time, because the Sirdar's post is very irregular, and now that he is within measurable reach of his goal, he won't think of sending letters back, as all transport is needed here. There is little danger in this kind of warfare so don't imagine things.

P.S. The 21st Lancers have not arrived yet. We hope they may come tomorrow. The Sirdar said yesterday 'They have mismanaged their march'. But I thought it would be hard for fresh troops!!

By 30 August the 21 Lancers had arrived and all was now ready for the final show-down with the Khalifa.

## Diary for 1 September (see sketch map of reconnaissance)

About 1a.m. a terrific storm of rain and wind broke over the camp, and lasted till 9o'clock in a moderate form. The force marched at 5.30 in spite of the wet. The cavalry pushed on ahead; the 21st Lancers kept near the river, working independently of us, and (I thought) somewhat recklessly, knowing, from what I saw on the Atbara, what a foxlike enemy the dervish is. The Egyptian cavalry and horse (artillery) batteries and four maxims reached the west end of Kerreri ridge about 7 o'clock. From the top of the ridge, Omdurman was visible some five or six miles off, with the Mahdi's tomb standing high above every other building. To the west of the city is a vast plain, and those with binoculars saw something which looked like a column of people leaving the city and moving south west. As I carried a strong telescope on my saddle, Broadwood sent and asked me to go up and have a look. There was no doubt that there were a lot of horses grazing with their riders beside them about five miles off, and still further south cattle and things which looked like tents or camel coverings in which women travel. We at once advanced SW towards a round topped hill some five miles from Kerreri hill and the same from Omdurman.

On the way thither we crossed the Khor Shambat, at present very boggy in places, and pools of water standing here and there. Our approach had evidently been perceived, because on reaching the round hill a most wonderful sight presented itself to me. A huge force of men with flags, drums and bugles was being assembled to the west of the city; the troops formed up on a front some three miles long, and as each body or 'roob' was complete, it commenced to move northwards. With my glass I saw they were moving very fast indeed. To my mind we were wasting time where we were, seeing that we were to camp on the south side of Kerreri; if we waited, we would have to make a detour to reach it.

There were some 30,000 men extending across the plain, and all in movement before we left the round hill. I acted as rear guard with my squadron to five companies of camel corps and two machine guns. The cavalry preceded us in the retirement – a faulty disposition: the more mobile arm (cavalry) should have been in the rear of the slow moving camelry. I suggested to O.C. Camel Corps that he would have to push on at his best pace to get across the enemy's front without being caught; he quite agreed. The ground being open, I kept all my squadron together except for three small groups which I left out towards our right rear. Some dervish horsemen galloped forward and engaged these – two dervishes were disabled; my fellows were still all right and full of pluck. I was now in the heavy ground (with the squadron) about the Shambat Khor. The dervish infantry were coming on in lines, running and shouting and beating drums; it seemed to me still a race, though of course we could always pass to the north of the Kerreri hill if cut off from passing south of it.

After passing the Shambat Khor, Le Gallais galloped back to me and said he saw one of my horses riderless, and the man pursued on foot by dervishes. I said it could not be one of my men, for all my detached parties were complete – I could see them. There was no doubt about the riderless horse, for I saw that between us and the advancing dervishes. The man I could not see; however, Le Gallais showed me where he had last seen him. I accordingly at once ordered my first troop (which was then second in rear of my squadron) to wheel to the right, fell out two or three weak horses, dismounted one man (so as to have a spare horse for the man we were to rescue) and galloped out towards the dervishes. We went about 700 or 800 yards and were within 250 yds. or less of the enemy's advancing line; they commenced firing briskly, but, as usual, high. I saw that there was no man to be rescued, and galloped back.

We caught the horse, and found that it belonged to the maxim battery. This little episode delayed the advance of our column, and the enemy had gained on us – some of their cavalry were coming uncomfortably near. Our column now had to cross a slight rise, and then the ground fell towards the river. As soon as my squadron reached the hill I dismounted a few men behind it, and (taking a carbine myself) fired as rapidly as possible at those of the enemy nearest to us. We disabled several, and they delayed for those following to join them; then they opened a hot fire against the ridge, evidently thinking it was our main position. By the time they discovered their error, we were well on our way to camp. The enemy halted for the night along the Khor Shambat. We camped at place shown on the sketch map.

### Diary for 2 September (see sketch map of battle)

There was an alarm about 1a.m. and the troops stood to arms. But two friendlies arrived, and stated that the enemy was still quiet on the Khor Shambat, so the camp settled down again. Had the enemy really attacked in the same determined manner as he did later in the day, he must have broken in, because our front was much extended (about two men deep throughout) with no zariba to check a rush. About 5 a.m. Baring went out with his squadron to reconnoitre, and the whole force moved out at 5.30 a.m. – Egyptian cavalry nine squadrons, Camel Corps six

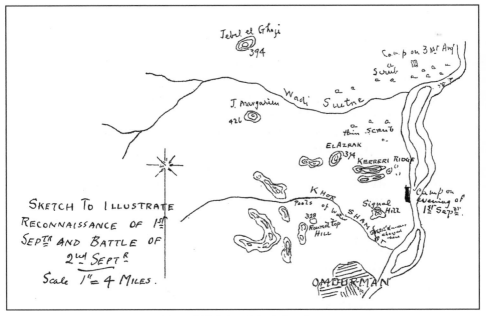

One of Haig's original sketches

companies, four maxim and horse artillery batteries moved to Kerreri Ridge, the 21st Lancers to Signal Hill, and the infantry paraded by brigades in front of the camp.

The Sirdar ordered a movement on Omdurman in echelon of brigades from the left. By a quarter to six a.m. Baring reported in person to the Sirdar that the whole dervish army was in movement northwards, its right two miles from the river; ie it would probably touch the shoulder of Signal Hill.

By this hour I had my squadron deployed as an advanced guard for the infantry between Signal and Kerreri Hills. I had my first and second troops (each in four groups) extended, and third and fourth together as support. Going forward to my advanced parties I could see the vast masses of the enemy going for the Kerreri Hills (that is northwards) and not moving east. I got orders to clear the front in good time in order to allow the Artillery to open fire. Before retiring I led my support (troops) along the col between Signal and Kerreri Hills southwards to make the enemy think our force was behind the former (Signal) Hill and then getting into the dip towards the Nile retired to the right of our infantry and then rejoined the cavalry behind Kerreri Hill. I found the squadrons in mass behind the horse artillery batteries and maxims and camel corps, all of which were in action on the southernmost ridge and drawing the enemy's fire. This, in rear of guns in action, I thought no place for cavalry to wait in, so I kept my squadron further off to the left rear and went forward to see what orders there might be for me.

The dervishes were climbing the hill at a great pace. The fire of the horse battery was of not the slightest effect (9lb. Krupp) in checking them, and by the Sirdar's orders the maxims were now sent to the infantry, who had taken up a defensive position at the camp. The horse battery took up a second position on the second ridge (the more northerly one) of the Kerreri Hill. The cavalry still stood supporting the camel corps still in action on the southmost ridge. By this time the dervishes had crossed the westerly part of the southerly ridge, and a hot fire now fell upon the squadrons. The camelmen mounted, and together with the squadrons fell back over the stony ground behind the second or more northerly ridge. The distance was about 600 yards, and the enemy who had crossed the south ridge poured in a very hot fire. Our losses were severe, during this short retirement.

Again the cavalry was halted behind the guns, which were in action. I said I thought the position unsuitable for us. I had scarcely made the remark before my trumpeter was shot above the right temple, the bullet remaining embedded at the back of his head (he was still quite cheerful); his horse was also wounded. My leading troop leader standing next was hit, and the guide behind him was hit in the thigh – 2 other horses were also hit – all in less time than it takes to write.

The cavalry retired northwards with the artillery batteries; 2 guns of which had to be abandoned – (I would have left them all on the first ridge, as they were more harm to us than good, and merely hampered our movements). The Camel Corps got off to the river and got protection from a gun-boat, the 'Melik'. They lost many camels and one British officer wounded, i.e. 70 casualties.

The enemy followed us with a very hot fire, and large parties, moving further from the river, tried to get round our flank. We halted about 8 o'clock about Wadi Suetue, some three to four miles north of Kerreri Ridge. We now saw that the enemy had discovered his mistake (viz. that he had attacked en l'air) and that he was moving back over the west portion of the Kerreri Ridge very fast. We then trotted south and rejoined the infantry (on the right of Macdonald's Brigade) at the moment the dervish second attack was being prepared.

Kitchener had seen what was happening and sent Rawlinson, one of his two staff officers, to tell the cavalry to withdraw into the zeriba surrounding the camp. Had this been done the Anglo/Egyptian army would have put themselves into a dangerous position, outflanked on their right by a large dervish force. The order was ignored and the cavalry drew the enemy northwards so that, as Haig says, they attacked an enemy which was not there. Rawlinson recorded his meeting with Haig on the battlefield:

At length we could see our contact squadrons under Douglas Haig gradually withdrawing as the Dervishes advanced . . . I rode out to him over the ground which an hour later was heaped with dead and wounded Dervishes. When I reached him he was within about 600 yards of the enemy's long line, and I noticed that his confident bearing seemed to have inspired his fellaheen, who were watching the Dervish advance quite calmly.

Haig summed up:

. . . roughly what then happened was:

1. First our infantry occupied a defensive position at the camp. A small portion of the dervish army attacked but never pushed home, being beaten back by artillery and infantry fire at long ranges (say beyond 800 yards).

2. Then the Sirdar ordered a move on Omdurman in echelon of brigades as shown on the sketch map. Macdonald's[23] Bde had not reached its position in this formation when he had to repel a strong attack from the westward. This was preceded by a charge of some 100 or more horsemen, who charged boldly till all were shot down – the last about 40 yards or less from the line. Mass upon mass of dervish footmen then attacked; they were beaten back at 300 yards about.

3. Now Macdonald had to face to the right to meet an attack of some 10,000 men who had already been launched upon us. Again some 100 or more horsemen launched themselves on the infantry and almost reached the line. The big green flag (that of the Khalif's son) was seen behind a small rise about 800 yards off, and many other flags. The enemy seemed to me to come on in countless numbers and in rank after rank. Their order and

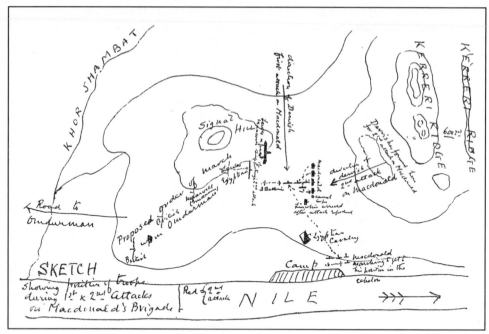

One of Haig's original sketches

manoeuvring power was wonderful. There was little or no firing
– indeed I thought that this was the safest place I had been in all
day! Macdonald's Bde was supported by the Camel Corps on his
right, and after the action was over by the Lincolns; on his left
was an Egyptian battalion of Lewis'[24] Bde and a Sudanese
battalion from Maxwell.

The effect of the infantry fire was poor and not in accordance
with the teachings of the theorists who design modern
breechloaders! The dervishes rushed on heedless of the hail of
bullets – many were killed about 100 yards from the firing line.

After some 20 minutes the dervishes began to draw off, seeing
Macdonald being reinforced with more troops. The Sirdar seems
to have become anxious and sent back a British Bde, tho' he
replied to Broadwood's message, that '10,000 unbeaten
dervishes were on his right' that 'he intended to march on
Omdurman not withstanding'.

The Egyptian cavalry now galloped out in pursuit towards the
round topped hill. We crossed the front of the infantry. Many
wounded men still rose up and fired at us as we approached, and
spearmen tried to hurl a spear. As we proceeded westwards,
many little groups of men dropped down on their knees in

submission, though some firmly resisted till killed by our lances. I saw men beg for pardon and then, when we had passed, treacherously assault some unsuspecting trooper from the rear. My squadron was on the left of the line and I directed the line; bearing first west and then SW to take the round topped hill where we were yesterday.

Arrived here, we came under a hot fire from thick crowd of fugitives still further SW of us. The going had been heavy; some men had stopped to pick up loot and others escorted prisoners. My squadron was fairly intact, about 100 horses still, and two other squadrons joined me shortly. It was clear the enemy tho' flying was not routed.

I dismounted my squadron and fired volleys by troops, waiting for the other squadrons to come up. We could not charge towards Omdurman; there were too many resolute men intervening. So it was decided to charge about E. by south, towards the mouth of the Shambat Khor. We commenced our gallop; my squadron on the left, the centre one directing and a third squadron on the right. The fire increased as we advanced, and men on my left who had flung down their arms in submission picked them up again – so that we were enveloped with a cross fire from all directions. The squadron on my right passed in rear of mine to the left, and the right hand one did likewise, its leader galloping right across my front. My men seemed to bend their heads to the right as one does to escape a storm of rain. I had seen eight horses go down in my front rank, and being unsupported on my right flank, I too brought up my right and moved now directly on Signal Hill. It was a ridiculous idea for three squadrons to attack some 10 or more thousands of resolute and armed men all scattered across the plain.

I lost only five men wounded, but 19 horses. Our horses were dead beat and we moved to the Nile after dressing our wounded. We reached the Nile at about 3 o'clock – at the mouth of the Khor Shambat.

About 5 pm we were ordered to move towards Omdurman 2 m. distant, but city about 7miles long. We understood we were going into camp, so no trouble was taken about filling water bottles.

We marched round the west side of the city until about S.W. of the Mahdi's tomb. Here we saw vast multitudes leaving the town far away to the South – camels, donkeys, horsemen, footmen, men, women and children and armed fugitives.

Some came out from the city to surrender. When opposite the West gate Slatin[25] galloped from the city very excited and said Khalifa had just escaped after beating his big war drum in vain; for only 50 of his Mulazimin had rallied to him. Our orders were to pursue at once!! It was then about 7 pm almost dark. We got two guides (Kababish) mounted on camels of the Camel Corps and we went into the dark – horses dead beat, biscuit till tomorrow morning in the men's haversacks and feeds for horses till noon. A steamer was to bring up further supplies. We could not take the river road; too many armed men on it for safety in the dark, so we struck south towards some hills. The going soon became very soft, and our horses floundered occasionally up to the knees in the wet sand. At 11 o'clock we could go no farther, and drew off to as dry a spot as we could find. Here we halted for the night. Horses were watered from shallow muddy pools and we all had to drink the same water.

## Diary for Saturday, 3 September 1898

All night we heard firing. At 3 am we moved on, there being a good moon, and at 7 o'clock we saw steamer close to the river bank. On reaching her we found she was 300 yards from the shore and stores could not be landed. We watered and fed our horses, and then moved on up river hoping to find a place where the stores could land. Again the going became very boggy and wet. By 2 o'clock we had gone about seven more miles and though we saw the steamer's flag we could not get to the bank. So we watered and gave the last of our feed to the horses and halted till 3 pm.

Having now no feed for man nor beast, and returning fugitives told us the Khalifa had pushed on all night, we decided to return and camp where we had struck the river in the morning. We got there about six o'clock and spent another night on the desert. The Camel Corps gave us a few pounds of dhurra for the horses and a little biscuit for the men. They also gave us officers some soup and MacConaghie's rations for dinner. This seemed to us a most luxurious dinner, for we had not had a proper meal since dinner on 1st September. The fatigue of the horses was extreme. Several had to be shot. Anticipating this we had taken three led horses per squadron.

**Diary for Sunday, 4 September 1898**

We marched at 5 a.m. and coming by the river road reached the S. end of Omdurman by 8 o'clock. We were still seven miles from our camp at the north of the town. A most unpleasant ride through the town on an empty stomach. Many unburied corpses, dead donkeys etc strewed the road. We passed some truculent-looking people returning to the town, but for the most part the people seemed friendly enough.

We passed the mosque (Mahdi's tomb) – much battered with shells, and the Khalifa's house which the 32nd Fd. Battery shelled by some mistake in the evening of the battle nearly killing the Sirdar and HQ Staff.

Camp was reached about 10 o'clock and right glad were we all to have a wash and sleep!

Haig points out with some amusement that there was a memorial service in Omdurman that morning at which the English parson with the British Division refused to take part because General Gordon, whose memory was included in the service, was a Presbyterian! The Sirdar told him that he would be sent home immediately in disgrace if he didn't behave himself. 'The parson managed to overcome his scruples to read the Lord's prayer.' In contrast the Roman Catholic priest: 'Father Brindle then made a fine prayer of his own composition, which was the feature of the ceremony.'

**Diary for Tuesday, 6 September 1898**

21st Lancers leave for North marching at 3 p.m. We entertained them all to lunch before starting and the Sirdar came to see them off – just 200 out of 480, which left Cairo just one month ago! [The Commanding Officer, Colonel Martin, had already been relieved of his command for the folly of their famous charge at Omdurman.]

**Letter to Henrietta 6 September 1898 from Omdurman**

My squadron lost five men, and 19 horses killed and wounded in the fight, while we had to shoot several others, dead tired. I started 114 in the ranks and ended here with 40. Our Cavalry lost heavily from the dervish fire; seventy casualties when standing behind the ridge which the enemy attacked. The 21st Lancers lost many good officers and men. You will see about their charge in the papers . . .

## Letter to Henrietta 7 September 1898 from Omdurman.

Young Churchill is going north by steamer today, so I'll get him to post this for me, with the leaves of my diary. Half the British are already gone, but we know nothing yet as to what changes will be made in the Egyptian Army.

I got a letter from Sir E Wood dated 26th July saying that he would like to get me a job at the Horse Guards – so as these appointments rest with him, I suppose I'll get one; but when, I don't of course know, for he does not say.

## Letter to Sir Evelyn Wood 7 September 1898

You will hear a lot of the charge made by the 21st Lancers. It took place at 9 am south of Signal Hill, into an arm of the Khor Shambat. The Sirdar was then meditating an advance on Omdurman and the 21st were to precede the infantry.

The regiment seems to have advanced without any patrols in front. Seeing a few men in front, the colonel thought it a good moment to charge. He seems to have marched parallel to the enemy in columns of troops, then wheeled into line to the right and charged. While in column of troops they were under a hot fire, so his suspicions ought to have been aroused, especially as Slatin before had told him of the nullah.* Away the regiment went, four squadrons in line, and came down in this nullah filled with rifle and spearmen. The result was scarcely as bad as might have been anticipated, for the two flank squadrons suffered little. Two troops of the centre squadrons were, however, practically wiped out. A rally with their backs to the river followed, the enemy meantime going on to join the attack on Macdonald. The loss inflicted on the enemy (judging by the corpses) was trifling, 14 or 15 at most . . .

We onlookers in the Egyptian Cavalry have feared this all along, for the regiment was keen to do something and meant to charge something before the show was over. They got their charge, but at what a cost? I trust for the sake of the British Cavalry that more tactical knowledge exists in the higher ranks of the average regiment than we have seen displayed in this one. Yet this Commanding Officer had had his command extended. I wonder why. Is he a tactician? No. Is he a good

*[Haig's sketch maps show the nullah between the Khor Shambat and Signal Hill (Jebel-Surgham). It evidently branched out from the Khor Shambat, the Dervishes' main forming up line before their attack. This would explain why there were so many dervish troops there at that time. Some of the letters to Henrietta refer to sending what Haig called 'loot' back to various family members in Britain. Loot seems also to have been sent back to the Royal family.]

disciplinarian? No. Is he a stud groom? His predecessor Hickman was, but alas the latter's mantle has not fallen on this man. Really I cannot think that the Promotion Board fully appreciates the responsibility which rests with them when they put duffers in command of regiments.

I am writing to you just what I think, and now one word on the Battle as a whole. I had ample time to 'appreciate' the situation on the 1st and 2nd morning. The enemy, halting as he did on the upper pools of the Khor Shambat on night 1–2 September, abandoned the key of the position, Signal Hill (Jebel Surkam), to the Sirdar. The latter hill has long sloping shoulders, and to my mind should have been occupied on evening of 1st. Why should the enemy not have taken it? And what losses would we not have suffered in turning him out? Lastly, occupied and used as a pivot, and keeping our army concealed to the east of it with gunboats and heavy guns in position protecting the flanks, we could anticipate any move of the enemy. Then on morning of 2nd when the enemy had divided his forces, the Sirdar's left should have been thrown forward to this hill, and gradually drawing in his right and extending his left south-westwards, he might have cut the enemy off from Omdurman and really annihilated the thousands and thousands of Dervishes.

In place of this, altho' in possession of full information, and able to see with his own eyes the whole field, he spreads out his force, thereby risking the destruction of a Brigade. He seems to have had no plan, or tactical idea, for beating the enemy beyond allowing the latter to attack the camp. This the Dervishes would not do in force, having a wholesome fear of gunboat fire. Having six Brigades, is it tactics to fight a very superior enemy with one of them and to keep the others beyond supporting distance? To me it seems truly fortunate that the flower of the Dervish army exhausted itself first in an attack and pursuit of the cavalry. Indeed the prisoners say, 'You would never have defeated us had you not deceived us . . .

Again thanking you most sincerely for your kind letter, and hoping that you won't think me forward in criticizing this successful General.

## He wrote as follows to Henrietta from Omdurman on 15 September:

. . . The town (Omdurman) was well looted before we (Cavalry) got back from our pursuit, and indeed before our troops entered the city. I saw a lot of rubbish which is going to Her Majesty, and some to the Prince of Wales. You ask if I write to the latter! Yes. I sent him 2 letters and got back very civil replies from Sir F. Knollys.[26] I also wrote to him after this fight, but I don't suppose he understands half what I write, if, indeed he reads it! What Tum [The Prince of Wales] likes is gossip. Now I am not in the way of hearing gossip, and if I did I have not the time to write it . . .

There are some examples of the loot sent back from the Sudan at Bemersyde. There is a conical bronze helmet, a suit of chain mail, both obviously worn by Dervish horsemen, some fearsome spears and two tunics, known as 'jubbas'. The tunics are beautifully made and were clearly worn by leaders. They are white with large coloured patches and a pocket embroidered with emblems, which may indicate rank and unit. The pocket was also used for a quotation from the Koran. The Dervish community were Sufis and wore ragged robes with patches to indicate their contempt for worldly and material things. The patches on the jubbas at Bemersyde are clearly symbolic, rather than practical. The Dervishes were meant to be a society in which everyone was equal, but evidently the owners of the Bemersyde jubbas were more equal than others! Or maybe they both belonged to the Emir Mahmoud. Haig thought they had been Mahmoud's – he bought them from some of the Sudanese who had captured him.

### Letter to Sir Evelyn Wood 21 September 1898 from the steamer *Ambigol* between Halfa and Shellal.

It was on this boat that I started to write my first letter to you from the Sudan – and this will be the last letter from these parts, for the present at least. Five days ago we officers in the EA were asked whether we wished to continue in the Khedive's service or not. Many sat on the wall (metaphorically speaking) and are still sitting there, uncertain what to do. Some fear that premature departure will cost them a decoration, others wait on, hoping so-and-so will go and they will be selected for promotion to Bey, etc.etc. To me there were no such fancies.

I have got all I want out of this place in that I have seen a lot and (in a small way) done a lot, which all means experience. For all this I feel I have only you to thank, hence this little line – for fear after the last volume I sent you that you will scarcely care to embark on another pamphlet. What really decided me to resign was partly because the nature of the country to SE and West of Omdurman is unsuited for Cavalry action, and partly because the Cavalry (Egyptian) was ordered 60 miles north of Omdurman for 'grazing'. That is no work for an officer who cares about his work, so here I am on my way to England.

What a heap of nonsense has appeared in the papers about the battle. The cause of the ignorance of the correspondents and of the Sirdar as to what really happened is due to their being down in a hole by the river from which they could only imagine what was going on. The attack on the camp was (as I wrote to you) nothing of importance, and was made, Slatin now tells me, by what he calls 'some Kassala boys under no Emir of any note'.

As to the numbers said to have been killed, 10,000 odd, I can only say that the first count made the figure 14,000 odd, but as Gatacre thought some had been counted twice, 4,000 odd was knocked off the total. To my mind, another 3 or 4,000 might have been just as well deducted, and the result would have been nearer the correct figure. But I'll tell you all about the show when I get to London. I shall come and pay my respects the first thing, meantime I sincerely thank you for getting me out here.

As he said in the above letter, Haig felt it was time to go home. There was no real role for cavalry in the south of Sudan. He arrived home on 5 October. He went back to the 7 Hussars as squadron commander. He was gazetted brevet major on 16 November, in recognition of his excellent performance in the Sudan.

Douglas Haig found the Sudan campaign stimulating and enjoyable. He clearly did well as a trainer of troops; Egyptian fellaheen would not be one's first choice of raw material, but he was proud of their performance at the Atbara and particularly at Omdurman. He obviously led them well and was able to demonstrate a bravery and indeed fearlessness, which stood out in battle. One interesting feature of his command was that he regularly dismounted his squadron in order to fire their carbines at the enemy. He clearly considered this to be normal cavalry practice and was obviously not entirely an *armes blanches* man. There were several occasions in which he found himself having to take command in a critical situation, although strictly speaking it might not have been his job to do so.

His observation of Kitchener's method of command, direct to Battalion commanders without the use of staff officers or indeed the brigade commanders, probably struck him as a good way of causing confusion and was an object lesson in how not to do it. He was also critical of Kitchener's tactical ability. On the other hand he clearly recognized that Kitchener's genius was in organization and logistics. The latter was what won the campaign and was a lesson, which Haig must have taken to heart. Perhaps he realized that warfare would never be the same again. A year later he was successfully meeting the challenge of a very different war in South Africa. As General Sir Neville Lyttleton,[27] who commanded the second British Brigade at Omdurman, said:

Few people have seen two battles in succession in such startling contrast as Omdurman and Colenso. In the first, 50,000 fanatics streamed across the open regardless of cover to certain death, while at Colenso I never saw a Boer all day till the battle was over and it was our men who were the victims.

The correspondence between Douglas Haig and Evelyn Wood ends with the letter of 21 September quoted above. Sir Evelyn sent all the letters to Lady Haig in 1916, after he had been ill and feared his life was coming to an end. (In fact he lived until 1919). The following is the covering letter with which the letters were returned.

**Letter from Sir Evelyn Wood to Lady Haig, 14 April 1916**
Douglas wrote to me some interesting letters 18 or 20 years ago. It is undesirable that anyone but you should see them, so I am now, before I get ill again – and on 13th March I did not for a few hours care to live – sending them to you. I do not think that many women would care to read them, however devoted they might be to the writer, but I believe you will find them interesting. Anyhow you might sample one or two. I am sending by rail some military books which Douglas allowed me to take away. I suggest you should not undo the parcel. I congratulate you not only on Douglas's safety but also on the honour he has shed on our Army.

The Sudan campaign was the last of its type, perhaps until Iraq in 1991, where once again technological superiority proved to be infinitely more important than numbers and there was a huge disparity in the casualties of the two armies. Haig took a light-hearted, but nonetheless highly professional, approach to the campaign. Sudan was an important step in his career.

Notes
1. Mohammed Ahmed ibn Seyyid Abdullah was the self proclaimed Mahdi or 'he who is guided aright', somewhat akin to the Messiah. He was one of several Arabs to claim the title.
2. General Charles George Gordon CB (1833–85) was Governor General of Southern Sudan. This appointment followed a spectacular career in China and Africa – he was known as 'Chinese Gordon'. He had been in Egypt since 1874.
3. Field Marshal Viscount Garnet Joseph Wolseley (1833–1913) served in the Crimea, Canada, India, China, Ashanti, the Zulu War, the 1882 War in Egypt and became C.-in-C. of the Army after the retirement of the Duke of Cambridge in 1895.
4. Field Marshal Earl Horatio Herbert Kitchener (1850–1916) was commissioned into the Royal Engineers in 1868. Having become Sirdar

or Commander-in-Chief of the Egyptian Army in 1892 he set about the reconquest of Sudan with great skill. He became Field Marshal in 1909, Earl in 1914 and Secretary of State for War. He died in the cruiser *Hampshire* which was taking him to Russia in 1916 and which hit a mine off Scapa Flow.

5. Princess Victoria (1868–1935), who never married, became a personal friend of the Haigs and was godmother to their second daughter, Victoria (Doria).

6. General Sir Richard Harrison GCB, CMG was commissioned into the Royal Engineers in 1855 and eventually became their Colonel Commandant. He retired in 1904.

7. Lord Claud Hamilton (1843–1925), son of the 1st Duke of Abercorn was ADC to Queen Victoria 1887–97. He was a captain in the Grenadier Guards.

8. Major General Sir Hugh McCalmont KCB, CVO was born in 1845 and commissioned into the 7 Hussars. He became a major general in 1896 and retired in 1906. He was Colonel of the 7 Hussars.

9. Hurreed Jheet was a favourite polo pony, the gift of Sir Pratap Singh. She may be the pony Haig is shown riding in South Africa. There is a photograph of her in very old age in India, being held by Secrett, Haig's soldier servant.

10. Lieutenant General Sir Pratap Singh GCB,GCSI (1845- 1922), Maharajah of Idar, Regent of Jodhpore, was a friend of Haig's from his first time in India. He commanded the Indian Corps in France in 1914–15. As a cavalryman he found the static war hard to understand. He used to ask Haig 'Sahib, when does the charging begin?' He was godfather to Haig's son.

11. Colonel Arthur Edmund Sandbach CB, DSO, Royal Engineers, was born in 1859 and commissioned in 1879. He served in Bengal, India and South Africa, becoming Chief Engineer Irish Command in 1910.

12. Lieutenant Colonel PWJ Le Gallais, 8 Hussars, was killed at Bethulie in 1900.

13. Lieutenant General Sir Bryan Thomas Mahon KCB, KCVO, DSO was born in 1862 and commissioned into the 8 Hussars in 1883. He transferred into the 12 Lancers in 1900. After service with the Egyptian Army he became a respected Mobile Column Commander in South Africa. His Column relieved Mafeking. He returned to Egypt in 1901 and from there to India, where he commanded a Division. He commanded the 10th (Irish) Division in the First World War in Gallipoli and Salonika. He was C.-in-C. Ireland from November 1916–18. He retired in 1921 and died in 1930.

14. Major General Sir William Gatacre (1843–1906) was known to his troops as 'Back Acher'. Something of the unnecessary burdens he put on his troops comes out in Haig's diary for Sudan, where Gatacre commanded the 1 British Brigade. He did well enough against the

Dervishes, but his career came to an abrupt end in South Africa, where he mis-handled the Battle of Stormberg in December 1899.

15. Lieutenant General Robert George Broadwood CB was born in 1862 and commissioned into the 12 Lancers in 1881. He became a lieutenant general in 1912 and was Colonel of the 12th from 1909–1917. He retired from the Army in 1913. His career was damaged by a misfortune in South Africa. He rejoined the army in 1914 and was killed in action in 1917.

16. General Sir Archibald Hunter GCB, GCVO, DSO, was born in 1856 and commissioned into the Royal Lancashire Regiment in 1874. He was a Divisional Commander in the Egyptian Army from 1884 until 1899. The appointment also included being Governor of a large part of Sudan. He was Chief of Staff in South Africa, subsequently commanding a Division. At the start of the First World War he commanded a Corps., but only briefly. He became a Member of Parliament after the war. He died in 1936.

17. Field Marshal Henry Seymour Baron Rawlinson GCB, GCSI, GCVO, KCMG (1864–1925) was also a baronet. He was commissioned into the KRRC in 1884 and transferred into the Coldstream Guards in 1892. He did a number of staff jobs (ADC, Brig. Major, DAAG and AAG) before becoming Commandant of the Staff College in 1903. After commanding a Division at the start of the First World War, he was given command of 4th Corps, then of 4th Army. In 1920 he was appointed C.-in-C. India, where he died five years later.

18. Brigadier General The Hon. Everard Baring CVO CBE was born in 1865 and commissioned into the 10 Hussars. He commanded a brigade between 1916–18. He died in 1932.

19. 'The Duke' was Captain The Hon. Arthur Fred5erick Egerton DSO, son of the Earl of Ellesmere and grandson of the Duke of Sutherland. He was born in 1866 and commissioned into the Cameron Highlanders, but attached to the Seaforth for the Sudan campaign. He served in South Africa and the First World War. He was honorary Lt. Col of the 2/9 Royal Scots. He died in 1942.

20. The Marquis of Tullibardine MVO, DSO was the son of the Duke of Atholl. He was born in 1871 and commissioned into the Royal Horse Guards in 1892. He served in Sudan, South Africa and the First World War. He succeeded to the dukedom in 1917. He died in 1942.

21. Major General John Vaughan was born in 1871 and commissioned into the 7 Hussars in 1891. He became a close friend of Haig and his sister Henrietta Jameson. He transferred into the 10 Hussars in 1900, commanded his new regiment in 1908, became a full colonel in 1911, when he became Commandant of the Cavalry School. He was a GSO 1 in 1914, then commanded a Cavalry Brigade and finally 3rd Cavalry Division from 1915–1918. He died in 1956, having written an amusing book of memoirs.

22. Major General Andrew Gilbert Wauchope (1846–99) was commissioned into the 42 Foot in 1865. They became the 1 Royal Highlanders. He served in Ashanti, Egypt, Sudan twice and South Africa, where he was killed commanding the Highland Brigade at Magersfontein on 11 December 1899. He was blamed by Methuen for the failure of the attack.
23. Major General Sir Hector Macdonald KCB, DSO (1853–1903) was the son of a Black Isle crofter and rose from the ranks. His brigade of Egyptian and Sudanese infantry fought with great distinction at Omdurman and arguably saved the day. He fought in both Boer Wars. His final appointment as C.-in-C. Ceylon ended in disaster. He was accused of being involved in a homosexual affair in the island. This appeared in the papers and was picked up by a Paris newspaper, where Macdonald was on leave. He shot himself in the hotel in Paris where he was staying. The homosexual allegations were almost certainly untrue.
24. Lieutenant Colonel David Francis Lewis CB born 1863, commissioned in 1885, became a brevet colonel in 1898 and retired in 1905. He commanded 3 Brigade of Egyptian and Sudanese troops at Omdurman.
25. Sir Rudolf Carl Von Slatin GCVO, KCMG (1857–1932) was an Austrian. He was invited to Sudan by Gordon and became Governor General of Darfur. After Hicks Pasha's defeat he surrendered to the Mahdi in December 1883. He was a prisoner of the Dervishes until he escaped in 1895. He was a fluent Arabic speaker and was thoroughly knowledgeable about Sudan and its politics. He was an invaluable adviser to Kitchener.
26. Sir Francis Knollys GCB, GCVO, KCMG (1837–1924) was Private Secretary to King Edward VII and subsequently to King George V. He was created 1st Viscount Knollys in 1902
27. General The Hon. Sir Neville Gerald Lyttelton GCB, GCVO (1845–1931) entered the Rifle Brigade in 1865. He served in Canada, Ireland, India, the War Office, Gibraltar and the Sudan, in command of the 2 British Brigade. Subsequently he commanded an infantry brigade at Aldershot, then a Division in the 2nd Boer War. He was C.-in-C. South Africa from 1902–4, Chief of the General Staff from 1904-08, then C.-in-C. Ireland from 1908–12. He retired in 1912 and became Governor of the Royal Hospital, Chelsea.

# Chapter 5

# 7 Hussars again, Aldershot and South Africa

## 1899

By January 1899 Douglas Haig was back with his regiment in Norwich as a squadron commander. His diary entries for January and February give glimpses of the day-to-day life of a major in a cavalry regiment in peacetime. The routine described here could have applied to life in peacetime for a regimental officer at any time from the eighteenth to the twenty-first century, quite boring routine interspersed with leisure activities, in Haig's case hunting and shooting. The first three entries in January give an idea of just how boring everyday life had become.

There is no further mention of the possibility of a Staff job at the Horse Guards. Presumably this was overtaken by events, with Haig going to Aldershot in April as Brigade Major for the Cavalry Brigade commanded by French, which led to his very active participation in the Boer War of 1899–1902.

**1 January 1899**
At Norwich Barracks. Took stock of grocery bar and canteen. J. Vaughan and Johnstone assisted.

**2 January.**
Arranged with Brown of Fish Market to supply fish to Regimental Institute at contract prices – 3d a lb. for cleaned smoked haddocks – a stone; bloaters at 6d a dozen."

**3 January.**
Most of the officers went to shoot with Johnstone at shooting, which he has hired about 7 miles from Norwich – Carew,

Dalgety, Cole, J.Vaughan, Johnstone and self formed the party. Commenced suppers tonight in supper room of Regimental Institute. Charges are 3d. per plate of meat, 1d. for cup of tea or coffee, 4d. for potatoes or bread.

The following are extracts from letters to Henrietta.

### 8 April from Norwich

I stayed in the flat Wednesday night and came down here early on Thursday morning to be in time for our Pt. To Pt. Races. The day was fine and they went off very well. General Grant[1] comes to inspect us on the 20th April and stays till Saturday 22nd. I enjoyed the Staff Tour. Your copying machine is very useful, as I have several little schemes for the Squadron which I am busy at just now.

### 19 April from Norwich

My name was in the 'Times' on Friday as having been appointed to Aldershot. French wrote to me that I shall have to be at Aldershot on 30th April. The regiment leaves here on Monday week for Colchester. I am sorry to be leaving now as the life here is pleasanter than with strange regiments at Aldershot. The inspection went off as well as could be expected considering the number of recruits which we have; in fact General Grant said things were better than he had expected. Babbington[2] was also here. He has this Cavalry Brigade with Hd. Qrs. at Colchester. I think he is a good man, and I am glad he has got the command instead of some of the useless old busters who are now grousing at being passed over.

### 25 April from Norwich

We march from here on Monday 1st May for Colchester, camping on the road for 2 nights. I have written to French to say that I'll join at Aldershot after I have taken my squadron to Colchester. The marches are long (nearly 30 miles daily) and with saddles in marching order, sore backs are likely to occur. So it is better that I should be in command and take the blame if anything is amiss. They want me to play polo for the regiment in the Tournament at Hurlingham.

The following are diary entries:

### 4 May

Travelled from Colchester to Aldershot and took over keys etc. from Frith (Brigade Major Cav. Bde. Aldershot). Returned to Colchester.

**6 May**

> Arrived at Aldershot 1 o'clock from Colchester and took over duties as Brigade Major.

In May 1899 there was nearly a disaster, which would have finished French's career with immeasurable consequences not only for the forthcoming Boer War. John French had evidently made some unwise and speculative investments in South African mining shares and his creditors were closing in, with the prospect that French would become bankrupt. Obviously this would have meant that he would have to resign from the army. Desperate, he swallowed his pride and asked his newly appointed Brigade Major, Douglas Haig, for a loan. They had been friends for about eight years and French knew Haig was well off.

Haig's lawyer, Boxall from Chancery Lane, wrote to Haig as follows on 15 May 1899.

> I think unless we are able to divide about £800 among some of the most troublesome of the Creditors they will withdraw tomorrow from the deed. With that amount I think I can hold the others in check for 10 days or so but the whole affair is, of course, extremely urgent or Genl. French would not, I am sure, have allowed you to be worried. I cannot say for certain that the further £1200 will secure everyone but I am disposed to think it will. In any case it is most distinctly understood that that is the limit of your generosity towards Genl. French – and as I gather you prefer some plan of guaranteeing money rather than paying it in cash I am trying to arrange that sort of plan for the £1200 part of the affair altho' from my experience I have always found it far better to provide the money when helping a friend.
>
> If you like to send me a wire tomorrow morning to say the £800 is coming in a day or two I will go on paying tomorrow morning but you must understand quite precisely from me that altho' I will shew you with pleasure how the money you send is applied I have absolutely nothing whatever to do with it as a matter of business for of course there is nothing practical to rely on but the General's word and in short nothing of 'business' in the transaction so far as you are concerned.

Haig's comment in a letter of 16 May 1899 to Henrietta Jameson was:

See enclosed from Boxall. I have wired that I'll produce the £800. It would be a terrible thing if French was made a Bankrupt – such a loss to the Army as well as to me personally. For of course we can do a lot here together towards improving things.

By September it was obvious that there was an emergency in South Africa and that Brigadier General John French and his Brigade Major, Douglas Haig would be required for duty there.

### Diary for 14 September
Dining with 12th Lancers when telegram brought to me ordering General French to embark on 23rd to command Cavalry in Natal.

### 20 September (Wednesday)
Received telegram informing me that I have been appointed DAAG for Cavalry, Natal, and to be ready to embark Saturday.

The War Office gave the newly promoted commander of the Cavalry in Natal, Major General John French, exactly nine days and his DAAG, Major Douglas Haig, a mere three days to wind up both their personal and official business in the UK and hand over their duties. They embarked on SS *Norman* on Saturday, 23 September 1899.

They were required to take part in what was arguably Britain's most unnecessary war. It lasted from 11 October 1899 to 31 May 1902 and cost Britain over £200million and more than 22,000 lives, over half from disease. The Boers lost 25,000 and the Africans about 12,000 lives (Thomas Pakenham's figures). The War Office grossly underestimated the size of the forces required and by mid-October 1899, militarily the most critical period of the war, had with difficulty only managed to put together a force of some 15,000 troops to meet the Boer armies from the Transvaal and Orange Free State, which numbered some 54,000 men. Eventually some 400,000 British Regulars, Militia, Imperial Volunteers, locally-raised Volunteers and 10,000 Blacks served at one time or another in South Africa and managed to 'win' the war.

The tragic rivalry between the British in South Africa, who saw the Cape as an essential element in their Imperial strategy and the Dutch settlers, who had been there since the seventeenth century, had waxed and waned from the turn of the eighteenth and nineteenth century onwards. To get away from British rule, some Dutch settlers moved across the Orange River and into what became the Transvaal in 1835–37 and there established two independent republics – the

113

Transvaal and the Orange Free State. Nevertheless the majority of the Dutch stayed in the British Cape Colony and outnumbered the British settlers, particularly in the farming areas, to a considerable degree.

This remained true at the time of the 1899–1902 Boer War and caused at least one notable difficulty. This was that any Cape Boers taking up arms against Britain were committing treason and were liable to be executed. Indeed, for example, two Boer Commando leaders, Lotter and Scheepers, were executed on these grounds. Captured Boers from elsewhere were treated as prisoners of war.

Ironically, whilst Boers were the majority in the British Cape, Uitlanders, including many British, outnumbered the Boers in the independent Republic of Transvaal. This followed the discovery of gold in the Johannesburg area in 1886. The enormous wealth from the exploitation of the gold in the Rand turned the Transvaal into one of the richest states in the world, per capita, and enabled the Boer Government to buy arms, artillery from Creusot and Krupps and rifles from Mauser, in both cases superior to anything with which the British were equipped.

The Uitlanders also provided the British, notably Sir Alfred Milner,[3] Governor of the Cape and High Commissioner for South Africa, plus Wernher[4] and Beit,[5] two of the biggest 'gold bugs' in the Rand, with the opportunity to exploit the so-called grievances of an underprivileged majority, in that they were not entitled to the same democratic rights as the Boers. What it amounted to was that they had to become Transvaal citizens and then wait until they had been at the Rand for fifteen years before they got the vote. As the Uitlanders were there to make their fortunes from the gold, it is hard to believe that the vote was top of their agenda in importance. Nevertheless the Gold Bugs and their British supporters clamoured for the voting quali-fication period to be reduced to five years. The Uitlanders' relative indifference became clear when a coup d'etat, in the form of the Jameson Raid, was attempted in 1895. In any case the 'end game' of turning the Transvaal into a British Colony was not attractive to the non-British Uitlanders. In consequence there was no rising in Johannesburg in support of Jameson and the raid was a fiasco.

In May-June 1899 a conference took place in Bloemfontein to try to settle the question of the rights of the Uitlanders. With the benefit of hindsight one can see that the negotiations between Milner and the Boer governments, the latter advised by a brilliant young Cambridge lawyer called Jan Smuts,[6] were not intended by the British to succeed, despite very great concessions on the part of the

Boers, including a move towards a franchise giving the Uitlanders the vote after five years. Milner, supported by his Rand allies, and with a nod and a wink from Joe Chamberlain,[7] the Secretary of State for the Colonies, wished to precipitate a war in which the British would conquer the Boer Republics by force of arms in the name of St Jingo! This would further promote the British policy of dominating Africa from Cape to Cairo. Milner was taking an enormous risk; he must surely have known that the British forces in South Africa were weak and outnumbered.

The Bloemfontein Conference broke down on 5 June. Little wonder that Paul Kruger,[8] President of the Transvaal, said to Milner: 'It is our country you want.' Alas, this was only too true. War, it seemed, was now inevitable. From the British point of view the question was a military one in relation to the number of troops needed to defend Cape Colony and Natal against greatly superior Boer strength and then to invade Orange Free State and the Transvaal successfully. From the Boer point of view it was more a question of timing. In June the veld was burnt dry and could not provide adequate fodder for the Boers' horses. But by September or October, the spring rains would be starting; that would be the time to start a war! In the meantime negotiations continued, with Chamberlain pulling in the direction of a settlement and Milner pulling in the direction of war.

In July the British Government thought they had reached a settlement with the Transvaal Government, but somehow the fleeting opportunity passed unseized and stalemate ensued. This was broken by pressure being applied by the pro-war group, including some of the papers, notably the *Times* and *Morning Post*, and the Gold Bugs, who purported to fear that the uncertainty in South Africa would affect the prices of their companies' shares. The British Government was being urged to send troops to South Africa to strike fear into the Boer hearts and make them concede everything being demanded. But the Boers had, in effect, conceded all the important issues, with only two provisos remaining, these being intended to preserve their independence. The announcement of reinforcements for South Africa was more likely to provoke, than encourage a climb down by Kruger and his Government.

In September the War Office managed to scrape together enough men to make good their promise of a total of 10,000 reinforcements for the defence of Natal (1,000 had already been sent in August). This number was considered to be enough to meet the expected Boer invasion. It was decided by the Cabinet on 22 September that a second force was to be sent out as soon as possible, in this case an Army Corps under the command of Sir Redvers Buller, with the aim of occupying the Boer Republics. Unbelievably the defence of Natal – the short term problem – was to be entrusted to Sir George White,[9] 'too old and doddery' in the opinion of Joe Chamberlain.

The reinforcements were accompanied by an ultimatum demanding that the Boers 'climb down' immediately. The Boer response was to issue their own ultimatum that there would be war unless the British withdrew their troops from the borders of the two Dutch Republics and returned to Britain all troops, who had arrived after 1 June 1899. They mobilized their forces at the end of September.

Throughout the period leading up to the war the British had under-estimated the military effectiveness of the Boers. They regarded them as armed farmers, with very limited military knowledge, whereas they were well trained in rifle shooting, were highly mobile with their ponies, had excellent skills in fieldcraft and concealment and were better armed than the British, all of which became only too clear before the end of 1899. Their military organization was similar to the modern Swiss Army or the medieval Scottish Army in that all males of military age kept their personal weapon at home. They attended a 'wappenschaw' ('wapinschaw' in medieval Scotland) once a year, at which they 'showed their weapons' and fired them. Their Army could be mobilized in forty-eight hours and, like the Scots who carried a fortnights' ration of oats with them, the Boers were able to exist in the field on 'biltong', which they carried with them. They had not been beaten since Sir Harry Smith defeated them at Boomplatz in 1848. Since then they had learned much and had fought a series of small wars against Africans as well as defeating a small British force under General Colley[10] at Laing's Nek and Majuba in 1881.

Had the Boers acted in early September before the British rein-forcements arrived, there would have been little to stop them sweeping into both Natal and the Cape Colony with the possibility even of capturing Durban and perhaps annexing some of the northern part of the Cape. But they left it too late and at least some of the British reinforcements had arrived before they took the field. In the mean-time General French and Major Haig were on the high seas in the SS *Norman*.

**Diary, 23 September**

Left London 11.40 by Union SS Co. train and embarked at Southampton on SS *Norman*. Henrietta and John Vaughan accompanied me, but left about 4 p.m. The steamer sailed at 4.30. The weather was windy and looked threatening, but kept

116

fine down channel. There were a large number of passengers on board, Uitlanders, Boers represented by 2 of Kruger's nephews, newspaper correspondents and some 20 or 30 soldiers. At dinner a party of 12 soldiers. General French, Milbanke,[11] Laycock,[12] Colonel Downing RA and his staff, Captain Russel, 2 officers of the 9th Lancers, Grant RE, map maker of Natal border, and an officer of the 18th H and 2 of 5th DG.

Haig had arrived on board to find that he had not been allocated a cabin. Initially he was shown into something the size of a 'broom cupboard', but fortunately his boss, General French, came to the rescue and he was able to share French's cabin. There was also a mix-up with his luggage.

## Letter to Henrietta dated 26 September from SS *Norman*

We expect to reach Madeira at daybreak tomorrow, so I must write you a line to go back with the next mail to England. I hope you got back all safe to London and that John Vaughan took proper care of you. You and I always seem to be saying 'Goodbye' to each other, and yet practice in this does not seem to make the process easier but rather more trying. However, you must not allow yourself to feel low-spirited, but arrange to enjoy yourself in a quiet sort of way. I have not a great deal to record so far. The weather has been fine, and the ship has been steady. We are very comfortable on board, and all seem to do their best to make us so. On the first day I had no clothes! The tickets got rubbed off my bag and mule trunk, which I had intended for 'use on the voyage' so they were put in the Hold. However they got them for me on Sunday morning. Our cabin in the upper deck is very nice; the Captain lets us use his bathroom and as the W.O. sent both the General and me a pile of confidential books before leaving, it is useful to be out of the way and have peace and quiet in which to read and study them. The Captain seems a pleasant fellow and looks after the wants of his passengers. His Officers too are a nice lot. We have the 2nd Officer's cabin you know, and when the General expressed the hope to him that he (the 2nd O.) was not much inconvenienced thereby, he said 'not at all, he was proud to give up his cabin for he felt he was doing something for the good of his country'! Now there is useful patronage for you! There are some 20 odd (Army) officers on board. There are 12 at our table. The General and I drank your Port and enjoyed it greatly. I drank to you of course. We finished it last night. The ship's Port is good, and so is the Brandy on board. So we are all right. I am writing this on the upper deck. But there is a fine library with writing table and paper, pens etc. for the passengers, but so many people are

117

writing now that it is better up here. The breeze is still fresh and cool tho' awnings were put up yesterday. Our run today is 378 miles, and the average is about 15½ knots an hour. I found a great pile of telegrams on board when we started; 17 or 18. This means a heap of letters! One was from Sir Evelyn Wood saying that he would suggest Vaughan for buying mules and so get him out. This was kind of the old man to think of it. Another from Lady Londonderry[13] and her daughter.

**Diary for 27 September (Wednesday)**

Arrive Funchal (Madeira) 7.30 a.m. Land and breakfast at Reid's Hotel – a comfortable Inn with fine gardens. We go to Gosart and Gordon's and sample his Madeira and malmsey. The ship sails again at 11 o'clock.

Warmer. On 2nd October (Monday) we cross the line. The S.E. Trade winds are blowing strong – off the African Coast the weather was hot and several get fever through sleeping on deck. Numerous amusements take place, concerts, dances, fancy dress ball, newspaper published and the editors tried by the judge and jury.

On Tuesday morning 10th October the *Norman* reaches Cape Town. Great excitement as to what the news is. *The Cape Times* published a little leaflet with epitome of last week's news. From this we learn that Reserves have been called out, and situation appears very warlike. I land with General French and go to Post Office to find out how the mails are going to Natal. The Transvaal route being now unsafe, they are being sent to East London by train. But when the trains would start they did not know! We then went on to the Head Quarter Office in 'the castle' an old Dutch Fort on the sea coast. Found Du Cane here D.A.A.G. He was at Staff College with me. He telephoned to Union Castle Line Offices to find out if any ship going from East London to Durban – 'Nothing before the *Norman*'. So there seems nothing for it but to wait in patience and go round in the *Norman*. I see copies of telegrams received from War Office and among them find one 'to be shown to Sir George White on arrival'. This directs him to form the troops in Natal into a Division of Infantry and a Cavalry Brigade. Any troops over to be used for Line of Communications. Colonel Brocklehurst is appointed Brigadier of the Cavalry with Wyndham as Brigade Major. Under these conditions it seems questionable whether it is necessary for General French and me to go round to Natal! Du Cane accordingly wired to Secretary of State for War to ask

118

whether we should go to Natal or remain in Cape Colony. General Sir Forestier Walker commanding troops in Cape is absent looking round posts on the Orange River. We then went to Government House and called on Sir Alfred Milner. He was very busy but saw the General for a few moments. He said that he expected the Boers might begin fighting tomorrow. There is a report in papers that Boers have sent in an ultimatum calling for the withdrawal of our troops from their frontiers. Probably Sir M. refers to this! Engaged rooms at Mount Nelson Hotel. A nice clean place on the hill about 1½ miles from the main street (Alderley St.). House very full and only 2 vacant rooms which the General and I take. We lunch at the City Club. Like the Hotel, quite recently built. We see several of the Bond party at lunch; Hofmeyr and others. Most of the inhabitants of Cape Town live in the suburbs and use the Club for lunch. So there was a great crowd.

### 11 October (Wednesday)
The comfort of a bed and a long bath of fresh water very enjoyable after so many days on board a crowded ship. Coffee and fresh milk excellent at Hotel. Telegraph to Knox 18th Hussars for 2 horses each to be ready on arrival. General and I spend most of the day hanging about the Staff Office waiting for a reply from London. It was about 6 p.m before it came. It was 'General French and Officers with him to go to Natal as soon as possible for the present'. This taken with what Buller said to French before leaving England seems to indicate that we will return and join the Cavalry Division which will advance from Cape Colony across the Orange River into the Free State as soon as the Army comes out. The Boers ultimatum published in a second edition of the *Cape Times* today. It is generally agreed that even Lord Sailsbury cannot knuckle under to this last piece of Boer swagger and that consequently hostilities may be expected to begin at 5 p.m. today. The Cape Colony Border near the Orange River is very unprotected and I gather the Authorities are very anxious as to what may take place in that quarter. The inhabitants are very anti-British in these parts.

### 12 October (Thursday)
General French and I go to look at a pony which is for sale at Newlands, about ½ an hour by train towards Rondebosch – Rhodes' place. The pony tho' well bred lacked a rib; price also

too high – £30 apiece. We can also get a waler from some of the regiments which have come from India. This seems better than buying a pony here with the risks and trouble of taking him by sea to Durban. We find many rumours flying about. After lunch the General and I take the electric train out to Sea Point and walk from there along the Kloof road. The sea and rocks are very fine. The air seemed so bracing and the sun bright and cheerful. We had tea at one of the little Hotels along the road and got back in time to entertain Du Cane and Birkbeck (who arrived last week as Officer in charge of Remounts) at dinner. (City Club) I saw Dunbar and others off for Mafeking at 9 p.m. by rail. Milner issues a proclamation stating War exists between Dutch Republic and Great Britain and informing colonists of penalties for treason.

### 13 October (Friday)

General Sir Forestier Walker having asked for General French's views on employing the 9th Lancers, who are expected tomorrow, I got up at 6 a.m. and wrote a memo on the question. The following is an outline of it.

(1). After providing for the protection of the frontier the chief object to keep in view is so employ the squadrons as to have as many horses as possible in the ranks, fit and in hard condition, when the moment for the general advance arrives. With this object the horses should be allowed if possible at least a fortnight to recover from the voyage.
(2). Their disposition on the frontier will then depend on the existing situation and on the intentions of the G.O.C. Cape Colony. With the troops at present on the frontier only a passive defence seems at present possible. The following sketch shows existing dispositions on Orange River.
(3). Three methods of Disposing the Cavalry seem possible: (a) On the River – (That is to say at *Orange River Bridge*, because there are not sufficient troops available to hold the other crossings over the river; in fact these are already in possession of the enemy). (b) Mid-way between the river and the line occupied (De Aar – Stormberg) so as to reconnoitre up to the passages across the river. (c) As outpost Cavalry at the posts now held as shown on sketch.
   The advantages of (a) seem to be (1) that, provided with a sufficient number of light troops and guns be available to co-

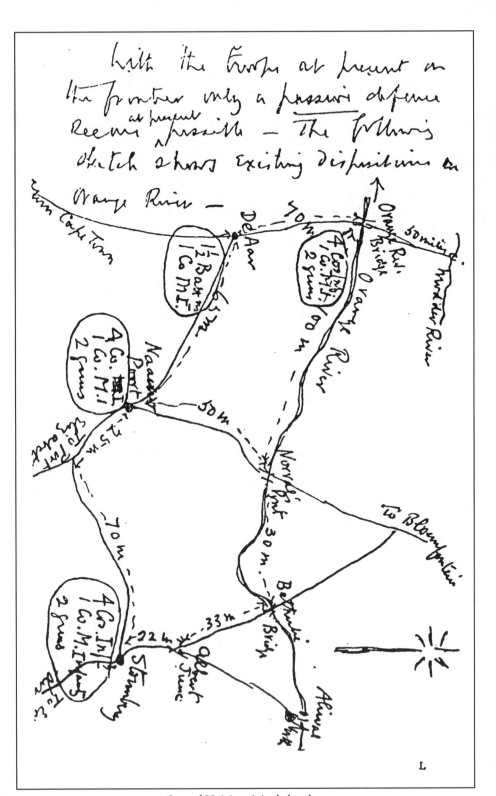

One of Haig's original sketches

operate with the Cavalry, incursions can be made into the Free State which would require them to detach in order to preserve their communications to Bethulie etc. (2) The diversions of a movable column from Orange River Bridge would probably mislead the enemy as to our intentions (viz. To make our main line of advance via Bethulie). (3) The communications with Kimberley are strengthened, and a helping hand could be given to detachment at Modder River Bridge if circumstances required it.

The chief objection or rather difficulty is the choice of a commander for this moveable column . An incapable man might suffer a check which would at this moment be of far reaching consequences. As regards (b) it seems probable (1) that full information of the enemy's movements on South side of Bridges can be gained through local sources, without detaching squadrons. That squadrons thus detached in the midst of a hostile population seem to invite attack, and consequently the means of security thereby rendered necessary will be wearing out for Cavalry men and horses. (c) The employment of the Cavalry Regiment as Outpost Cavalry – say 2 squadrons at Naauw Poort and one at Stormberg (or vice versa) would be less fatiguing for horses, while this disposition does not preclude the possibility of circulating thro' the country in order to check revolt. Moreover the direction of the railway lines enables the British to concentrate at 4 points on the river, while the Free State can only use the line to Bethulie and Norval's Pont.

The conclusion seems to be that having regard the few troops in Cape Colony and the political situation, the best disposition to adopt is (c) and to direct at the same time that squadrons be ready to concentrate on the flank and rear of the enemy should he cross to the South Bank of the River and attack either of the 3 positions, i.e. De Aar, Naauw Poort or Stormberg.

The General has appointment with Sir F.W. at 11 a.m. and gives him my memo. We hear that one steamer with 9th Lancers (one squadron) on board lost 12 officers' horses, 71 troop horses and 10 mules and out back to Durban. A very severe loss. Heard also of loss of armoured train just S. (about 35 miles) of Mafeking. Colonel Baden Powell[14] commands at Mafeking with only local levies. Dine at Club, but go on board *Norman* to sleep.

## 14 October (Saturday)

*Norman* left Cape Town about 10.30 a.m. Steamer again very full owing to Cape Parliament being broken up, and refugees and others going to coast ports. Weather fine.

## 15 October (Sunday)

Reached Mossel Bay about 6 a.m. but sailed again at 7.30 a.m. Arrived at Port Elizabeth about 9 p.m. Sea quite smooth, a very unusual occurrence in this part!

## 18 October (Wednesday)

Arrived at East London early in the morning. Sea rough and had to land in basket. Wire from Cape Customs to stop *Norman* until 5 packages booked to Durban for Transvaal are out on the shore. As well hunt for a needle in a haystack as for 5 packages amongst the cargo in a big ship like *Norman*. But this so like all action of Government officials – i.e. general want of foresight all round! E.g. deficiency of troops in South Africa!! By luck 4 packages were found labelled 'stationary' for Oom Paul. The Captain of *Norman* decided to sail with customs officers on board. At last moment permission to sail was signalled and we got off about 6 pm.

## 19 October (Thursday) 1899

Arrived Durban 2 pm. Left by 5.40 train. Some fear of Boers breaking line. However I slept soundly thro' all.

## 20 October (Eland's Laagte)

Arrived Ladysmith 5.40 am. No-one knew where Staff Office is. Finally get to Head Quarters about 7 am and breakfast there with Brooke, 7th Hussars, before Sir George White gets back. The Boers having stopped a train and broken railway near Eland's Laagte, General French is ordered to move out in that direction to reconnoitre. Go back to station and change in railway carriage. Get horses from 5th Lancers and start at 11 am. The Force consists of 5th Lancers about 6 squadrons of Natal Mounted Rifles and Carabiniers, and a Brigade of Infantry. More than 4 miles from Ladysmith get touch with Boers but Eland's Laagte being held by 200 of them, the reconnaissance is not pushed home. Dine with Sir George White. Wet night. At 9 pm receive orders to start at 4 am tomorrow to occupy Eland's Laagte and repair line.

## Operations of 21 October

In accordance with orders the Imperial Light Horse 5 Squadrons, and Natal Field Battery with detachment for working telephone, left Ladysmith under the command of Major General French at 4 am of Friday 21st October. Rain was falling, and the ground was heavy so that the progress made by the guns and ammunition waggons was slow. The advance was covered by one squadron of the Natal Light Horse. At 5.30 am a halt for ¼ hour was made near Spruit about 7 miles distant. At about 6½ am when near Modder Spruit (where horses were watered etc.) information was received from the advanced Squadron that Eland's Laagte Station was reported by natives to be still occupied, but no hostile patrol had been yet met.

The advanced patrols soon after sent back word that parties of the Boers were on the hill which overlooks Elands Laagte Station from the West. – The guns preceded by one squadron were pushed forward along the road which makes a bend to

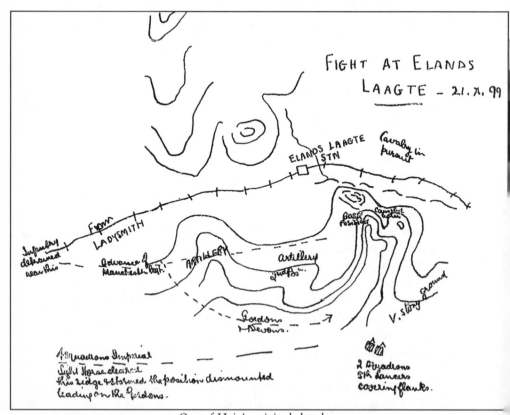

One of Haig's original sketches

S.E. before reaching the hill just referred to, and the remaining squadrons were sent direct across the country. The guns opened fire on the station buildings from which numbers of Boers were seen retiring Northwards. The range was about 1800 yards. A squadron had meantime been detached to threaten the place from the N.W. The Natal Battery had fired some 4 or 5 rounds when the enemy posted on a hill about ½ mile S.E. of the station dropped a shell over our position. Another shell fell in front, and several more in and around the Battery and ammunition waggons. The wheel of one of the latter was broken by a shell but the ammunition did not explode. The fire of the Natal Batt. was now directed against the enemy's guns of which there appeared to be 2 or 3. It was soon evident our guns (7lbs) could not carry as far as the position held by the enemy. It was therefore decided to withdraw the battery. – The armoured train, followed by another, was seen approaching: it was now about 7.45 a.m. The guns were directed to retire on hill no. 3180 (1" map) and an officer was sent to stop the trains and direct Infantry (½ Battn. of Manchester Regt.) to occupy a defensive position near the guns. Meantime the squadron manoeuvred to cover the retirement of the Battery. – A telephone message was now (about 8.30 a.m.) sent to C.S.O. Ladysmith explaining situation and requesting reinforcements as it was hoped the enemy would attack. Some of the enemy's shells began to burst in front of the position now held. A party of about 50 Boers was at the same time reported working round in the hills above and commanding our left flank. The enemy's shells had also dropped close to the position on Modder Spruit. Information was received from Head Quarters that the remaining ½ Battalion of the Manchester Regiment with Battery FA one squadron 5th Lancers, one squadron D.G. were ordered to join. The two forces united on the Modder Spruit position about noon. Major General French then explained to the CSO Ladysmith by means of telephone the situation: viz that the enemy occupied a very strong position with a line of entrenchments overlooking the railway, that his strength was about 1,000 with 2 or 3 long range guns. The Cavalry Force, which had been out all morning, were much fatigued and wanted food. If it was intended to attack enemy's position, the best line of advance would be by ridge running from SW to position. The necessary Force for this purpose would be:

GERMAN

SOUTH WEST

AFRICA

TRANSVAAL

Vrieskraal
Elandsrivierpoort
• Onderste Poort    Dullstroom •
Mafeking •        • Pretoria                    • Berge
        Vlakfontein                      Geluk •      • Van Wyk
Gruisfontein      Quaggafontein    Kleinfontein
Hartebeestefontein    • Witklip          Bothwell
        Johannesburg                         Umpe
• Tweebosch    • Geduld          • Nooitgedachte    L. Chrissie
                    Brakpan • Cyferfontein         • Onverwac
                        Gatsrand    Zuikerbosch
Wolmaransstad              Parys       Spruit
                    • Vredefort
                ORANGE            Paardekop
                            Zandspruit        Roi K
        Honing Spruit                    • Ingogo
    FREE            Armstrong Drift
                    • Fanny's Home
            Zand R.    Tiger Kloof
        Grootvallei    Spruit • Groenkop      Blood R.
Bothashoek        Moolman's
    • Klippan      Biddulph's    Spruit • Elandsfontein    Buffalo R.
                Berg                    Scheepe
• Bosjespan    • Leeuwkop    STATE            Nek
        • Glen        Brandwater    • Ladysmith
• Rooidam            Basin
        Bloemfontein    Springhaan's            ZU
                • Nek                    LA

                BASUTOLAND        NATAL
                                    Du
                                    • Nottingham Rd
    Smithfield •    • Koesberg

                            BRITISH

                        BECHUANALA

ATLANTIC            Orange River

    OCEAN        NAMAQUA

            LAND                    Orange Rive

                    De Aar J

            Camarvon •

        CALVINIA        Victoria We
        • Calvinia        Victoria Rd
                    C A P
        • Kordemoersfontein    • Fraserbugh
LAMBERT'S
    BAY    • Clanwilliam
                • Sutherland

                            Willov

Cape Town    • Stellenbosch

Cape of Good Hope

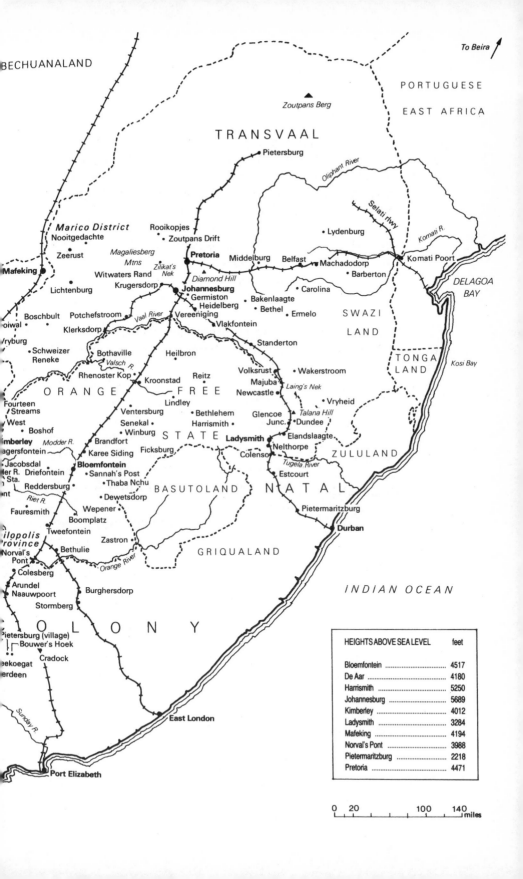

BECHUANALAND

PORTUGUESE
EAST AFRICA

▲ *Zoutpans Berg*

TRANSVAAL

• Pietersburg

*Oliphant River*

• Lydenburg

*Selati rlwy*

*Komati R.*

*Marico District*
Nooitgedachte
Rooikopjes
• Zoutpans Drift

Zeerust
*Magaliesberg Mtns*
• **Pretoria**   Middelburg •   Belfast •   • Machadodorp
Komati Poort
*Zilikat's Nek*
• Barberton

**Mafeking** •
Witwaters Rand
*Diamond Hill*
• Carolina
DELAGOA
BAY

Lichtenburg
Krugersdorp •
**Johannesburg**
Germiston •
• Heidelberg
• Bakenlaagte

• Boschbult
Potchefstroom
*Vaal River*
Vereeniging •
• Bethel   • Ermelo
SWAZI

oiwal •
Klerksdorp •
• Vlakfontein
LAND

Vryburg
• Schweizer
Reneke
Bothaville •
Heilbron
• Standerton

TONGA
LAND
*Kosi Bay*

*Valsch R.*
Reitz •
Volksrust •   • Wakerstroom

Rhenoster Kop •   Kroonstad •
Majuba ▲   *Laing's Nek*

Fourteen
Streams
Lindley •
Newcastle •

West
Ventersburg •
• Bethlehem
Glencoe •
• Vryheid

ORANGE      FREE      STATE

• Boshof
Senekal •
Harrismith •
Junc. •Dundee
*Talana Hill*

mberley
*Modder R.*
• Winburg
Brandfort
**Ladysmith**
• Elandslaagte

agersfontein
Karee Siding •
Ficksburg •
• Nelthorpe
ZULULAND

Jacobsdal
**Bloemfontein**
Colenso •

ler R. Driefontein
• Sannah's Post
*Tugela River*

Sta.
• Thaba Nchu
Estcourt •

Redddersburg •
• Dewetsdorp
BASUTOLAND
NATAL

nt
*Riet R.*
Wepener •

Fauresmith
Boomplatz •
• Pietermaritzburg

ilopolis
rovince
Tweefontein •
Zastron •
GRIQUALAND

Norval's
Pont
Bethulie •

• Colesberg
*Orange River*
INDIAN OCEAN

▲ Arundel
Naauwpoort
Burghersdorp •

Stormberg •

OLONY

Pietersburg (village)
Bouwer's Hoek
• **Durban**

eekoegat
Cradock ▲

erdeen

*Sunday R.*

**East London**

**Port Elizabeth**

| HEIGHTS ABOVE SEA LEVEL | feet |
|---|---|
| Bloemfontein | 4517 |
| De Aar | 4180 |
| Harrismith | 5250 |
| Johannesburg | 5689 |
| Kimberley | 4012 |
| Ladysmith | 3284 |
| Mafeking | 4194 |
| Norval's Pont | 3988 |
| Pietermaritzburg | 2218 |
| Pretoria | 4471 |

To Beira ↗

0   20        100      140
└─┴─┘              miles

3 or 4 Battalions of Infantry
2 Batteries RFA
Some fresh Squadrons

A reply was received about 1 o'clock that 2 fresh Battalions of Infantry, another Battery RFA, 1 Squadron 5th Lancers, 2 Squadrons Natal Mounted Rifles would join as soon as possible and General French was ordered to engage the enemy. The Force advanced at 1.20 in accordance with the following order:

March order by Major General French.
Coms. Detached Force
Modder Spruit 1 p.m.
21.10.99.

1. The enemy estimated at about 800 holds a position about 1 mile S.E. of Elands Laagte Station. Reinforcements are expected at once.

Reconnoitring Cavalry
Squadron      5th
D.G.
    "      5th Lancers

Mainbody

Squadron I.L Horse
Batt.R.F. Art
"      N.F. Art.
Impl. Light H. (less
I Squadron)

2. The detached force will advance forthwith in the order as per margin, except the Infantry which will proceed by train, moving abreast of the column as far as hill 3600 where the men will detrain – The direction of the advance will be over hill 3700 in a westerly direction.

3. The Infantry arriving by train will detrain at same place and be Brigaded under Colonel Hamilton C.B.[15] etc.

4. The G.O.C. will march at head of the mainbody where reports will be sent.

By Order, etc

Special instructions were issued to the Reconnoitring Cavalry. By these the 5th D.G. squadron reconnoitred a front of 2 miles on right of railway. – The advance began at 7.20 and soon it was seen that the 5th Lancers squadron on the right of the railway could not get onto the ridge which overlooks the valley along which the railway runs. The 4 Squadrons of the I.L.H were at once sent to reinforce this squadron, and drove the Boers along the ridge, acting dismounted. The Infantry was then detrained

128

and the reinforcements coming up, the 3 Battalions were formed in line 2 Quarter Columns on the right of the railway line – One Battalion then was extended in column of Companies at wide intervals and covered the advance. About this time our Cavalry on the left of the line was checked and suffered some loss from Boers on the ridges above. The F.A. Battery accordingly moved to the support and by fire drove off the enemy in this direction. The reinforcements by road now joined. – The Batteries crossed the railway and opened fire on the enemy's guns which were already in position and knew the range. The I.L.H. with 1 squadron 5th Lancers covered the right flank of the Infantry attack, and acting dismounted, pushed forward in line with the Gordon Highlanders. – After bombarding the position for half an hour, the Infantry pushed forward one Battn. against the front, and 2 along the ridge against the enemy's left flank. All available cavalry was concentrated upon the left and occupied Elands Laagte Station at 4.45 p.m. and from there threatened the enemy's right and rear. As the enemy began to leave the position, a squadron of Lancers and one of Dragoons charged through the fugitives, killing many and capturing 40 prisoners. The position was captured about 6 p.m. Night put an end to the pursuit. – The Infantry slept on the Battlefield – as many squadrons could be reached before pursuit began were ordered before night-fall to concentrate at Elands Laagte when they fell back. The guns rallied there also. – A telephone message was sent at about 8 o'clock telling Sir G. White of the result of the fight and a message came back stating that 'Sir G. W. wishes the force now at Elands Laagte to return to Ladysmith as soon as possible, the repairing of the line to be discontinued' – 'The hospital train to come in with wounded at the earliest moment possible'.

### 22 October (Sunday)

Acting on these instructions the Artillery and all the Cavalry excepting Squadron 5th D.G. and detachment I.L.H. left at 3 a.m. by road. The Devonshire regiment was sent off about 5 a.m. The hospital train was sent off at 3 and arrived back at 4.45 and returned to Ladysmith at 7 a.m. and 11 a.m. – Some difficulty was experienced in shunting the trains as the sidings were short, and a train which had been captured by the Boers was in the siding.

## 23 October (Monday)

Report from Kaffirs indicated that Force of Boers had passed through DRIEFONTEIN moving Eastwards.- Sent Squadron 5th D.G. to clear the situation. Sergt. and 26 men 18th Hussars arrived Glencoe (i.e. Dundee Column) very fatigued and worn out. They stated that they had been cut off and had been 48 hours on the road here. No Boers at Elands Laagte, but some on heights nearer here – probably hill marked Intintanyoni – Instructions received re. Flying Column about 11 p.m.

## 24 October (Tuesday)

The whole force moved out today to engage Boers on Intintanyoni and prevent them moving against Dundee column which is on its march via Beith and Sundays River. Assembled about 3 miles out at 5 a.m. – 7 days supplies carried in supply column: 2 days food by Regts. in Regimental supply carts and 1 days forage. – XIXth Hrs. pushed on to junction of Newcastle and Glencoe Roads. From there the 5th Lancers watched the left flank and connected with Ladysmith. The Imp. Light Horse remained as Reserve with General French. Infantry and guns follow. About 9 am XIXth.H. report enemy in force, and they lose 1 man killed, 2 wounded. Shortly after gun from high hill opens on ILH. V. good shooting, but as enemy used percussion shell and ground was soft no harm done, altho' the 2nd shell fell into the interval between 3rd and 4th troops of the 2nd Squadron. We trotted round the shoulder of the spur near Modder Spruit and were out of sight. The enemy next turned their fire on our Infantry and guns and column of route. Their shooting was excellent but fortunately the shells did not burst.

Our guns opened fire. Soon the Boers withdrew their guns but their horsemen moved down towards us and tried to outflank our Infantry. The 5th Lancers, by holding a Kopje, prevented their movements being successful because when the Boers came forward their left flank became exposed to the Lancers' fire. The Gloucestershire Regt. lost their Colonel, 10 men killed and 52 wounded through some mistake on the part of Head Quarter Staff. The Battn. having received indefinite orders, but expecting that the GOC intended to attack, got too far in advance and was fired on by the Boers with fixed sights (ie 500 yards range).

About 4 pm Infantry withdrew covered by Cavalry. It was a

130

matter of some difficulty to get the 5th Lancers away without serious loss. They managed it well however and only had 2 men wounded. The ILH had 5 horses killed in the forenoon when going to a spruit to water.

The Force reached Ladysmith at dark. The evening set in very wet and rained all night. The ILH had one Squadron on Outpost duty all night. – Total Cavalry Casualties as follows amongst Officers & men.

|  | |
| ---: | --- |
| 2 | killed |
| 29 | wounded and |
| about 15 | horses |

## 25 October (Wednesday)

Messages received about 2 a.m. from Outpost Squadrons that enemy have not yet moved Eastwards, but reports received – induced the belief that he intended moving today. – O.C. XIXth H. warned about 4 a.m. to turn out his Regt. to support the I.L.H. squadron. His object was directed to be (1) to retain enemy in his position of yesterday if possible; and (2) If the enemy had already moved, to hang upon him, so as to prevent him establishing himself on the Ladysmith-Helpmakaar Road, thereby intercepting General Yule's column. – At 7 a.m. 5th Lancers forming part of a mixed force under Col. Croxhead R.A. moved out via Lombard Kop to Bell's Spruit to hold the Nek for General Yule's column. – At 7 p.m. XOXth H. returned; very wet night – Rain fell in torrents.

## 26 October (Thursday)

All the force ready to turn out at 3.30 a.m. this morning in case the Boers attempted an attack on General Yule's Column. – About 7 a.m. the head of the Dundee Column began to arrive. The Boers had not molested their march in the slightest way. – This is generally attributed to the moral effect of the Victory at Eland's Laagte. – The Dundee column arrived quite worn out. They marched at 6 p.m. last night and arrived here between 7 and 9 a.m. Everything they possessed was left in camp – Officers and men marched off merely with what they stood up in! –

4 officers who came out on the *Norman* managed to slip away from Cape Town on a Gun Boat arrived here in time to reach Dundee before the line was cut. All have lost their fine kits which they brought with them from India: one was killed one wounded! The other 2 say that they have not slept for a week.

The mention of General Yule's Column, (the Dundee Column) refers to the former garrison of Dundee, some forty miles north-east of Ladysmith. Dundee had become impossible to defend despite General Symons's[16] Pyrrhic victory at Talana near to the town on October 20th. Yule had been Symons's second-in-command and had taken over after Symons was mortally wounded in the battle. Casualties had been high and Symons had succeeded in losing most of his cavalry, the 18th Hussars, who had become surrounded and surrendered. In any case Dundee, at the end of a railway line, with the Biggarsberg Mountains between it and Ladysmith could not have been supplied even if Ladysmith itself had not come under siege shortly afterwards.

Military advice, supported by Sir Redvers Buller, was that defence of Natal should be based on positions south of Tugela River, some 12 miles south of Ladysmith, which like Dundee should have been abandoned. The Governor of Natal, Sir Walter Hely – Hutchinson, considered this to be highly undesirable for political reasons. The consequences was that most of the British troops in Natal were holed up in Ladysmith and the way was clear for the Boers to move into Natal with little to stop them reaching Pietermaritzburg, the capital of the Colony, or even Durban. The arrival of Buller's army did at least prevent this happening.

### Extracts from a letter to Henrietta on 26 October 1899 Ladysmith

I am sending you this by mail a grand budget of a Diary which should keep you busy reading for a long time! You will see how busy French and I have been since we got here. I have not had much sleep, but the climate here is so good that I feel very fit indeed. Plenty of rain at times, but the climate is cool and fresh like England. We were very lucky to have the fight at Eland's Laagte. General French in command and self Chief Staff Officer. The Boers fought till the end with extraordinary courage. This is accounted for by the fact that the command was composed of high class Boers, who had more or less organized the present revolt and so must sink or swim by the result of the campaign. The Imperial Light Horse fought well. After the Battle I had a busy night examining prisoners and preparing for the return of the troops and wounded to Ladysmith. We had prisoners of all kinds. Boers, Germans, Hollanders, American-Irish, British Naturalized Boers, etc. etc. All the leaders were either shot down or taken prisoners; none escaped. The Boers say that they never thought the British could have taken their position. They abandoned their tents, waggons, everything in fact, and took to flight. Some 1815 Brandy was found in one of the waggons. They are wild at the way the fugitives were killed with the lance! They say it is butchery not war. But as they use express rifles bullets, I don't quite see where the difference comes in. Joubert[17] wires today that 'General Symons is dead and wants to know how long this sort of thing is going on'! The Dundee Column came in this morning; a draggled and worn out crowd. You will see that we have been doing all we could to help them in. – As to news; I fancy the *Daily Telegraph* and *Daily Mail* (i.e. Bennet Burleigh and Stevens) will give you the best accounts. I must tell you how useful the boxes of stores have been. You must please send me out the bill for them so that our mess accounts may be squared; because I handed over everything into the common stock. We have a nice little house here; when we are at Ladysmith! but most days we are out of course. I was delighted to get your first letter to me yesterday since I left . . . . Best Love, and hoping that you are not anxious; for if I am meant to be shot no amount of care will prevent it.

## Diary 27 October (Friday)

At 1.15 a.m. information received that at 4 p.m. yesterday a large force of the enemy were about 16 miles off on the Helpmakaar Road. General French was ordered to start at 4 a.m. with XIXth Hussars and 200 of Colonel Royston's Volunteer Cavalry to ascertain situation. This Force leaves Ladysmith at 4 a.m. and occupies Lombard's Kop at about 5.30 a.m. By 8.20 a.m. a squadron of XIXth Hussars was established at farm about 2½ miles East of Modder Spruit. Enemy was met by patrols about 2 miles further on. Two officer patrols were pushed round enemy's flanks and the Reconnaissance Squadron reinforced its detachments in front. This effectually drew the enemy, his men dismounted and line the Kopie in our front while his guns (2 or 3) came into action. We had also reported a movement on the part of the enemy Southwards on Pieter's Station. The C.S.O. now sent out 5th Lancers and the 5th D.Gs. to assist in delaying any turning movement enemy might attempt. Then reinforcements were directed by General French to Klip river drift about 3 miles North of Pieters Station. The result of the morning's reconnaissance was reported to H.Qrs. in the following messages at 10.5 a.m. 'The situation now appears to be (1) A laager of about 2,000 Boers near X roads about 2 miles West of letter R. in R. Matuzan (on map 4). (2) Very large laager, with transport waggons, tents and oxen, one mile S.E. of Modder Spruit culvert on Dundee railway. (3) About 5 or 6 bodies each of about 800 men moving along the front of the Intinanyoni position held by Boers last Tuesday (in avr. say 4 to 500) (4) At

133

10 a.m. a body of about 1,000 was seen moving down from Western end of position referred to in (3) to Pepnoorthis Farm. (5) Nothing further from Pieter's Station: have diverted 5th D.G., 5th L. and Natal Volunteer detachment here to that point. Will follow thither as soon as General Hamilton's Infantry Column arrives here (Lombard's Nek). – Enemy was found not to have reached Klip river. About 4.30 p.m. General French returned to Lombard's Nek with all the Cavalry except about 100 men of the Natal Cavalry Volunteers who were left to protect Pieter's Station. Sir George White was at Lombard's Nek and handed over all the troops there to General French with orders to attack the enemy and defeat him next morning. The force consisted of 5 Battns. of Infantry under General Ian Hamilton, 24 guns, 9 squadrons of Cavalry. Orders of the attack of the enemy's position were issued at 8 p.m. The Force was ordered to march at 2 a.m. to a position of readiness from which one Battalion was to go forward in the grey twilight before dawn and clear the enemy's position with the bayonet. The country facilitated this movement. The main road led up to a farm (distant about 2½ miles); from this point open meadow land extended for 1500 yards to the enemy's first position. The moon rose about 1 o'c. Lastly, as the enemy had their backs to the East, their figures would show up against the sky line as the Dawn approached. All these detailed plans came to nothing. At 11 p.m. an order was received from the Chief of the Staff stating that Sir Geo. White wished the troops to return to Ladysmith, marching at 3 a.m. Baggage was ordered to be packed at once. Some difficulty experienced in unparking the waggons owing to O.C. Transport having parked them in some fancy way! The Force had 7 days food and 3 days forage with it – involving a large number of waggons! Modder Spruit lay immediately behind the Bivouac – Numerous and deep ruts and ditches lay around the drift. It was a matter of some difficulty to get so many waggons over in the dark. By 3.40 a.m. all the Baggage was over, and the troops were directed to follow. Some Cavalry and the Artillery were sent on first to hold Lombard's Nek. The Infantry column then passed through the Nek, while a couple of squadrons remained behind on the outpost line keeping touch with the enemy. Numerous fires were lighted in the Bivouac before marching off to make the enemy imagine that we were still there. Our retirement seems to have been unperceived. At any rate the enemy made no attempt to follow the retreating columns.

## 28 October (Saturday)

7 a.m. Infantry reached Ladysmith; the baggage having already come in. The Cavalry left detachments to observe the enemy, and reached camp about 9 a.m. – 9.30 p.m. Order received for Cavalry to reconnoitre tomorrow in order to discover (a) whether enemy occupied a position on both sides of the Newcastle road, and (b) how the commandoes to the East of Modder Spruit were situated. – Orders sent out to 18th and 19th Hussars at 10 p.m.

## 29 October (Sunday)

4 a.m. 18th and 19th Hussars left Ladysmith and marched along the Helpmakaar road. Occupied Lombard's Kop and Nek and pushed squadron Northwards to ridge which runs in continuation of Limit Hill. 8.30 a.m. Information received embodied in following messages to C.S.O

(1). Large Force (possibly 4 to 500) holds long flat hill on West side of Newcastle Road about 1½ miles West of Height 3600. (Kaffir kraal hill). 2 or 3 guns are visible on this ridge. A large laager with tents is visible about 2 miles to N.W. of this position of the enemy.

(2) Height 3600 a long hill on S. side of Newcastle Road, and just S. of Kaffir Kraals is occupied by enemy – 2 or 3 guns, one of which is a maxim, are seen in the position. Enemy's reserves are on the East side of this hill. Gun emplacement is being dug.

The above information (1) and (2) is confirmed by squadron sent in direction of Kaffir Kraal Hill.

(3) Laager reported by me on 27th Oct. as being 2 miles S.E. of Modder Spruit railway culvert, is not visible today. – Squadron 18th H. now detached to verify this.

(4) Two Laagers are visible East of Lombard's Kop – One laager of the two is situated about 2 miles S.W. of letter R in R. Matuzan. The second is about 2 miles S. of the first; possibly on road to Pieter's Station.

About 11 a.m. I went in to Ladysmith to explain situation to Sir George White and to request him to send out an Artillery Officer to reconnoitre for suitable position for the Artillery. Sir George explained to me his plan of attack for tomorrow and directed Colonel Pickwood to accompany me back with his Range takers. I took the Gunner officer to a Kaffir Kraal lying to the North of Lombard's Kop and about 2 miles S. of Farquhar's House. From this point he was able to get accurate ranges to this part of the enemy's position. (Unfortunately the enemy abandoned this hill after dark so that the range was of little use!) – Orders for tomorrow's attack were issued at 9 p.m. – These were briefly as follows.–

(a) 2 Battns (Gloucesters & Irish Fusrs.) With Med. Batt. were to march at 11 p.m. up Bell's Spruit and take up a position near Walker's Nek to protect left flank of the main Force.

(b) The bulk of the force was to take up a position at Limit Hill about 4 a.m.

(c) A Brigade of Infantry supported by Artillery was to attack the enemy's position on the S. of Newcastle Road.

(d) General French's Cavalry was to observe the right flank and retard the approach of Lucas Meyer's Commando from the East should he try to intervene.

### 30 October (Monday)

2.45 a.m. 5th L., 19th Hrs. and Col. Royston's Cavalry marched for Kaffir Kraal at N. end of Lombard's Kop. This was reached about 4 a.m. Owing to straggling of some of the volunteer squadrons, about half the column loses the road! For about ½ hour some anxiety was felt. They were however found and put into position before light came. About 5 a.m. guns began shelling enemy's position. The spur on S. side of road was seen to have been abandoned by enemy in night. General French moved his command Eastwards towards Modders Spruit in order to work round enemy's left flank. About 7 a.m. the head of the column came under a hot fire from low hill East of Hill occupied by enemy on 29th. Another commando is reported coming from East; probably under Lucas Meyer. The line of Kopies on right bank of Modder Spruit is at once occupied by the Cavalry. The right flank is gradually extended to connect with Royston's men holding Lombard's Neck, and the left is drawn in as Infantry come up.

About 10 a.m. Boers attack Kopie (see sketch) in force. It was

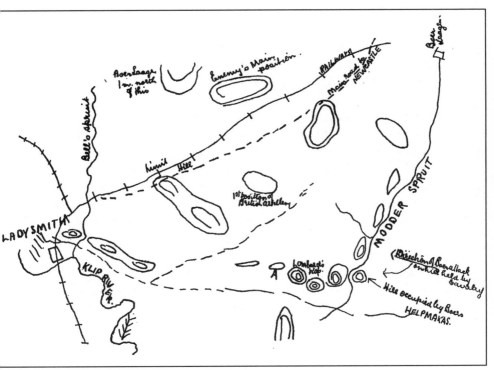

One of Haig's original sketches

held by dismounted Cavalry. The enemy could make no way against the hot fire of dismounted men and extended to their left to occupy a black hill to South of our position and from which they could enfilade it. This hill was occupied by a squadron. The Boers drove them back. A report was now received that the Infantry on our left were retiring. The situation was critical. We could not retire without losing many horses, for the enemy from his position on the Black hill would pick off our horses the moment they moved out from the shoulder of the hill. The order was given to hold on, and a request sent to O.C.R. Artillery asking for a Battery. The 5th D.Gs. and 18th Hussars were brought up from Limit Hill. The Battery came up shortly after 11, and firing over the heads of some of our men effectually drove the Boers behind the Black Hill. The enemy again attacked the Kopies on the Modder Spruit in front, but failed to make any impression. About 1 o'clock a general retirement was ordered. The position held by Cavalry was a very strong one. Indeed when the retirement was ordered the Boers had fallen back from before it. Our Artillery in the plain seemed to have suffered severly. One gun and limber had to be abandoned. Ladysmith was reached about 2.15 p.m. The main force on the left about Limit Hill seems merely to have held the enemy and not to have attacked his position. About 9 p.m. report received that Boers had occupied the positions vacated by the Cavalry.

## 31 October (Tuesday)

Usual patrols went out at 4 a.m. Reports indicate that enemy is moving guns on to Bulwen Mountain. The 5th D.G. are sent out to clear up the situation. The result of the reconnaissance shows that Boers are closing in upon the East and North. Information came to H.Qrs. last night by 2 of our Infantry men under a flag of truce, that the Gloucester Regt. and R. Irish Fusrs. had been surrounded yesterday about 2 p.m. and forced to surrender. Their ammunition is stated to have run out owing to the ammunition mules having being stampeded by Boers throwing stones down the mountain side into the gorge through which the detachment was marching. Among the prisoners is Major Adye of the H.Qr. Staff and Chief Intell. Officer of this Field Force. It should be noticed that this detachment moved without any Cavalry at all. As well let a blind man out without a dog, as Infantry without some horsemen to attend and reconnoitre for it! Heavy dust storm about 6 p.m. New Camps for the Cavalry were marked out by me today, owing to the enemy's shells bursting yesterday amongst the tents and horses left in.

## 2 November (Thursday)

All the Cavalry (except 19th Hussars and Imperial Light Horse) marched at 3 a.m. By 5 a.m. the Nek above Becter's Farm was occupied. The farm was found unoccupied and at the same time a laagar of the enemy was seen about 3 miles farther southwards. Reconnaissances were pushed to West and South to discover a good line of approach. Royston's Cavalry with 2 guns were left to hold the Nek above Becter's and to hold a line of Kopies on the left line of advance which was directed parallel with the Colenso road. About 8 a.m. the remaining 4 guns came into action at 4,200 yards against the enemy's laager. The Boers seemed to be at breakfast! Crowds of ponies, waggons and tents were visible. At the first burst of the shells there was a regular stampede. The camp was bombarded for about quarter of an hour. There were probably some 2,000 men in this laager.

The order to cease firing had scarcely been given before the

Boers opened upon us from a hill above their camp. The guns seem to have been directed upon Colenso; hence the delay in bringing them round to bear on us. The enemy's fire was erratic. One man was hit with a fragment of a shell on the back of the head. The Cavalry returned to Ladysmith at 11 o'clock leaving a squadron to keep touch and report enemy's movements. General French went to Head Quarters to report the result of the morning's reconnaissance. He received a telegram of which the following is a copy:

From General Chief – Cape Town

3.45 p.m. 1.11.99
    French should take command of Cavalry Divn. on the way from Home, and it is my wish particularly that he and Haig should come here if you can spare them possibly.

We left at 1 o'clock. The train consisted of an engine, two trucks and the guard's van, at the end of which there was a first class compartment. The General, self and two A.D.Cs. travelled in first class compartment. Seven servants and the guard in the guard's van. 9 horses in one of the trucks and our baggage in the other. No passengers went with this train. The train which started at 10 a.m. had been fired upon, and the railway authorities doubted our getting through. About half an hour after leaving, the train came under a heavy fire from both sides of the railway. We heard shells bursting and bullets hit the carriages. We all lay down on the seats and floor! Not a very dignified position for the Cavalry Division Staff to assume – but discretion is some times the better part of valour! Pieter's Station was reached about 1.30. The train halted. A British post was found here. As we went again, and about 3 miles beyond, the train was again fired upon. At about 2 p.m. Colenso Station was reached. The Dublin Fusiliers and N.Fd. Batty. were encamped here. An examination of our train showed that the iron truck containing some of our baggage had been pierced by a 2" or 2½" shell – my mule trunk which was behind the opening had its top and strap cut out, evidently by the projective. An armoured train followed us at about a mile distance. This was the last train to get through before the Boers broke the line. Had the shell hit the engine or a wheel we should have been on our way to Pretoria instead of to Durban! or indeed if the Boers had torn up a rail, the engine driver would not have seen it, because the moment the Boers began shooting, he lay down amongst the coal!

## 3 November (Friday)

Arrived at Durban about 6.30 a.m. Stayed at the Club. Mr Alstin the Agent of the U.S.S.Co entertained General French and self to lunch with the city magnates! Many very weak-kneed amongst them! In fact great anxiety prevails at Durban that Boers are marching on that port. Hoped to sail at 5 p.m. in *Arab* but she did not arrive till 9 p.m.

## 4 November (Saturday)

Left in tug for jetty at 8 a.m. *Arab* (U.S.S. Co.) sailed at 11 a.m. A considerable sea was breaking on the bar. The *Arab* does not usually carry passengers. The Union Co. kindly agreed to send her to Cape Town direct on account of General French and Staff wishing to go quickly. The same Co's. steamer *Mexican* was to leave at 3 p.m. but is only due at Cape Town on Wednesday week. Sea rather rough.

## 7 November (Tuesday)

Anchored at Mossel Bay about 6.30 a.m. Weather moderated and began to take in cargo about 8 a.m. 3 p.m. transhipped to *Tintagel Castle* (Capt. Harris) as the *Arab* has to await cargo. Sea very rough; we transhipped in barge which broke adrift from small tug. *Tintagel* very full with 1000 refugees from Delagoa Bay.

## 8 November (Wednesday)

Arrived Cape Town after lunch about 2 p.m. Steamer obliged to anchor outside harbour as Government had reserved berths in docks for transports which are expected to arrive tomorrow and following days. Landed in tug with General French – called at the Castle and then went on to Sir R. Buller who has rented a house in 55 Grave Street. Cavalry Division is to concentrate near Cape Town (camped at Maitland 3 miles out). Then will probably move to De Aar. The offices of the Hd. Qrs. Staff are in Main Barracks. A great many Staff Officers, all apparently anxious to do something. No troops have yet arrived. We got rooms with difficulty at Mount Nelson Hotel. I share one with General French. Major Du Cane and Birkbeck dine with us.

## 9 November (Thursday)

Called on Sir R. Buller with the General at about 10 a.m. and take my Staff Diary. He wanted information on Country from

Colenso to Ladysmith, and discussed best line of advance for a relieving force moving up from Estcourt. Asked me to let him have copies of certain maps which I had made, and sent me off to use his office in the main Barracks. Difficult to get proper paper etc.

## Question of organizing force to relieve Ladysmith
Sir C.F. Clery[18] going on at once to Durban with his Division and General Hildyard's brigade of the 1st Division is to be added to the Command. – As to Cavalry, we recommended organizing local force of volunteers on Cape horses. For this purpose these are the following troops already formed:

One squadron Imperial Light Horse at Estcourt.

Bethune's[19] Natal Mounted Infantry. Cape Mounted Rifles to be sent from Cape Colony. Recommended Walter 7th H. (who arrived here with mules) to go as C.O. or 2nd in command of this force. He should know the Ladysmith country.

The U.S.S. *Moor* arrived this morning with mail, having on board the Divisional Staffs.

General  Clery
     "    Gatacre
     "    Methuen.[20]

## 10 November (Friday)
Busy completing maps for Sir Redvers. General Clery came to see me on situation in Natal. Stayed over 2 hours in my room. As regards future operations after relief of Ladysmith, my opinion is not to take the offensive in Natal until force advancing from the Orange River causes the Free State Boers to withdraw from Van Reenan. The force at Ladysmith might then make Harrismith 100 miles to Standerton, or repair railway via Botha's Pass and move via Vreda to Standerton, thus turning the Lang's Nek position. – Colonel Hamilton, General Clery's A.A.G. also came to see me and took copies of extracts from my Staff Diary on Natal. Also Gogarty A.D.C. – Took my maps etc. to Colonel Stopford[21] Sir R. Buller's secretary about 5 p.m.

## Extracts from letter to Henrietta. 15 November 1899. Cape Town
The mail came in yesterday (28 Oct) with Brab and a crowd of officers wanting appointments. The Post Office here is by the way of stopping our letters for Natal, but somehow mine have not been caught for yours of the 24th Sept. is the one and only letter I have received since I arrived in

141

S.Africa! Your telegram in reply to mine from Durban took 3 days to get here. I suppose you will know now to address *'Cavalry Division, Cape Colony'* and stop addressing to Natal. I am at present acting as Chief Staff Officer of the Cavalry Division which is to be formed here before moving up country. Colonel Gough is the A.A.G. but General French has told Buller that he does not want him and insists on my being appointed. Buller knows and had (before we arrived) sent him off to an out of the way station called 'Orange River' Bridge. There he sat still and knew nothing of what the enemy was doing within 5 miles of him, so he got an order from here to go and reconnoitre. He did so in what is considered here an idiotic way and lost 2 officers killed of the Mounted Infantry and others wounded. They say too that if the Boers had been at all enterprising he would have lost his guns and many more of his men. Mounted Infantry are not intended to reconnoitre and are not trained for it. The officer killed (Keith Falconer) came home from Egypt with me last year, and was a very able and promising fellow. His wife is now in this hotel. They had only been married 3 months. None of our Cavalry regiments has arrived yet. The 12th Lancers are 3 days overdue. I hear from an old sea Captain here that the Admiralty are the laughing stock of the Mercantile Marine for the way they have hired transports. Certainly the Cavalry seem to have been sent out in the slowest old tubs when of all the troops it was essential to have the horses here first to let them get over the voyage before moving. I send my diary for the last week – not much in it, but I have been pretty busy all the same making arrangements for the arrival of our Division. I am sending my Staff Diary to Sir E. Wood today. It contains all the orders received and messages sent by us during the days General French was in command of the Cavalry in Natal, and an outline of each day's operations. I am asking him to send it on to you when he is done with it, for safe keeping. Best love, and hoping to hear soon from you and that you are keeping fit and well.

### Diary 16 November (Thursday)
City of Vienna with 1st Cavalry Brigade Staff and Sqr. 12th Lancers arrived in Bay.

### 18 November (Saturday)
Went out to Maitland Camp to arrange details. On return found order from Sir R. Buller ordering General French to proceed at once to De Aar with the object of occupying Naauwpoort and then Colesburg where 2,000 Boers are reported to be. Left by train at 9 p.m. taking 2 A.D.Cs.- Capt. Lawrence D.A.A.G. for Intelligence – Mr. Little from Free State (but native of Markinch

N.B.) as assistant to Intelligence Officer. Dr Hathaway Surgeon Major.

## 19 November (Sunday)

Telegram received about 1 a.m. that Boers had blown up railway bridge near Naauwpoort. Luckily charge had been badly placed so bridge would be repaired at 9 a.m.! It was however arranged to expedite journey and special was arranged for at Beaufort West – there was no spare engine nearer. That place was reached at 5 p.m. and De Aar at 10.45 p.m. Met by Commandant (Major Haking who was at Staff College with me) who handed us list of troops and explained situation in district generally. Lord Methuen at Orange River ready to advance to relieve Kimberley. General Wauchope commanding line of Communications from Kimberley to Beaufort West. Detachment of Boers 2 to 400 strong reported to have left Colesberg for Philipstown. Methuen had ordered detachments of Mounted Infantry to watch line from De Aar to Orange River – some 75 to 80 miles. The true defence of this line seems to be to defeat enemy at Colesberg and no patrols and detachments will be necessary! Haking had not been to bed for 2 nights owing to troops passing through going to join Methuen.

## 20 November (Monday)

Arrived Naauwpoort at 5 p.m. Major McCracken Comdt. of place and O.C. ½ Battn. Rl. Berks regiment met us. Garrison consists of 2 half Battalions, some 60 men S.Wales Lancers and 25 police with 2 9 lb guns. Stay in train all night. Gave strict orders to Comdt. to allow no one in or out without a pass – or to go thro in train without a pass.

## 21 November (Tuesday)

Sent detachment off at 3 a.m. consisting of 25 Austn. Lancers and 3 police to reconnoitre along railway as far as broken culvert about 9½ miles distant. Train left about 5.30 a.m. No signs of enemy. Train advanced to broken culvert – detrained horses by means of platform made of sleepers. Posted infantry on hill to guard train, and disposed detachment of N.S.W. Lancers as Outposts to give warning if enemy appeared. General French and staff advanced Northwards with a troop composed of 5th Lancers and 18th Hussars, men who had been at remount depot at Stellenbosch – more farmers than soldiers therefore! – in all

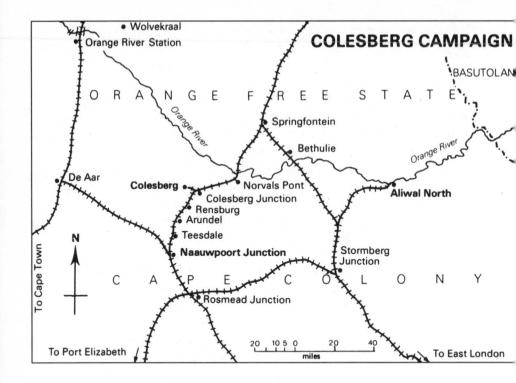

about 20 men and 4 policemen. This is the only Cavalry here!! The N.S.W. Lancers can scarcely be called *efficient* cavalry. – This morning on General French approaching a post of the latter Corps, the 2 men on look out at once left their post and came down to meet him – No doubt out of thoughtfulness for the General, to spare him trouble in climbing the hill – But what about the enemy? He would naturally wait in his advance till the men on the lookout got back to their posts! Reached Arundel Stn. about noon. Sent officer and 3 men forward to Kopje about 5 miles distant commanding view of country towards Colesberg. He arrived within 8 miles of that town but saw nothing of the enemy. Surrounded farm of a Dutchman called Rensburg near Arundel Station. It was stated that he had received Boer uniform and was about to leave for Colesberg. We took him back as prisoner to N'poort. A Kaffir was taken with letter riding from one farm to another; (about 20 miles apart)- He stated that one of his Master's brothers had already left to join Boers, and two others of the family were to leave shortly. Returned to N'poort about 4 p.m. Thanks to use of train, a reconnaissance of 28 miles was made i.e. 56 miles at least, if horses alone had been used.

144

## 22 November (Wednesday)

Train with detachment to repair line left at 4.45 a.m. The two broken culverts were repaired by 11 a.m. Sent patrol to Rensburg's farm to tell his family that he was well and happy but his house was found shut up. Train returned with covering troops about 5 p.m. Issued orders for defence of Naauwpoort. The place is now well nigh impregnable. A detachment of N.S.W. Lancers left at 3 a.m. for Jackelsfontein to arrest people referred to in letter taken from native yesterday. 2 Vanderwalts were brought in and 7 horses. The latter we sent back at once with a letter to the owner (who was ill in bed) explaining why his sons were taken.

## 23 November (Thursday)

Intended reconnoitring right up to Colesberg today. The detachment of M.I. sent on accordingly at 3 a.m. to make good the ground for about 10 miles along railway. Train left at 5 a.m. – with one Co. Black Watch; a detachment of 30 picked riders of Mdt. Infy. and a troop of Cavalry. On reaching party which marched out, the M.I. were detrained and ordered to reconnoitre to Arundel Kopje and 3 miles N. of it. Train waited for an hour and orders were issued to 3 officers patrols which we intended to detrain at point about 10 miles from Colesberg – (& 25 miles from N'poort) – The officers were Lts. Vaughan & Milbanke A.D.Cs. and an officer of 5th Lancers at present attached to N.S.W. Lancers – (There are no Cavalry officers in this Station and *no cavalry*!) About 8 a.m. train advanced slowly and report was received that country was clear up to Arundel Kopje. About 10 minutes after receipt of this firing was observed from Arundel Hill. The M.I. were seen falling back across the plain, and a party of Boers (about 80 or 90) were observed galloping round our left flank evidently to reach the Kopje in our rear and cut us off from N'poort. M.I. were at once ordered to Kopje, and the troop of Cavalry was detrained and sent under J.Vaughan at gallop against flank of the Boers in the open. – The latter at sight of Cavalry at once drew off tho' more numerous than our wretched troop – Train then fell back unmolested and the force reached N'poort with loss of 3 men wounded. One was a policemen who was shot thro' thigh but rode home 15 miles, not knowing for some time that he was wounded. The other two were advanced scouts of M. Infantry. One man was walking up Arundel leading his horse when he was shot by enemy in hand. He then turned to come down, and was shot twice in the back, and again in other wrist. He is doing well and will recover. The 3rd man was shot in arm; not serious. The M.I. evidently know nothing of this kind of reconnaissance work. Moreover they cannot ride. The lot we used today were 30 men especially picked out of 250 men of Colonel Tadway's Mounted Infantry Battalion. That officer tells me that those of his men who have been trained as M.I before have been taught in all kinds of ways and on different systems; in many cases 2 years have elapsed since they rode; others have never been taught to ride before; some have been grooms to Infantry Officers and are thought therefore not only to know about horses, but also to be able to ride them! It is murder to send such men in their present condition out to meet the Boers. They fall off, if the pace is faster than a trot, while they cannot get their horses to a position which possibly their Comg. Officer may have indicated to them. This class of M.I. is useless. It would be better to call up all reservists of the Cavalry and send them out here to ride horses of the country.- In any case, the Sec. Of State for War must be strongly condemned for not sending out ample Cavalry in fast ships to this country. An engine & carriage was telegraphed for by us from point near Arundel to go out under Red Cross and bring in the man who was so severely wounded close to the enemy's position. The train came out very quickly but there was no red cross flag in N'poort! We therefore tore down a white blind at Tweeddale Station and cut up the red signal flag of the guard's into 4 strips which we sewed on to the blind with Drs. medical needles and thread. This did well when fastened to funnel of engine. Dr Hathaway R.A.M.C. went with this train. He was met by Asst. Commandant Goblaar in command at Colesberg. This worthy took off his hat after the style of the musketeers, and most politely told Hathaway he could have the wounded man. He said we had several other wounded lying over the country, but would not let Hathaway go and see! His statement was a lie of course.

### 26 November (Sunday)
All went to parade service at 7.30 a.m. this morning except 12th Lancers who took horses to exercise in view of possible move early this week. Parson kept us too long with 12 minutes sermon on Hamlet and such whom soldiers don't know much about. He is parson at Colesberg, and we gave him the job of parson to troops in Colesberg district until we recaptured that town!

146

Telegram from Orange River asking for ½ Battn. Black Watch from here, as Methuen had gone forward and asked for Battn. from Orange River to guard his communications. We are not strong enough here yet to enable us to advance. On other hand half a Battn. won't render this place unsafe, while the addition of it to Orange River will enable Methuen to go forward in safety. So decide to send forward ½ Battn at once tomorrow morning as asked for.

### Extract from letter to Henrietta. 26 November 1899. Naauwpoort.

I enclose the diary to date, which will show you what we have been doing. The one thing required here is 'Cavalry'! I think the Country ought to be alive now to the fact (which we have always pointed out) that we don't keep up enough of the arm in peace time! This Mounted Infantry craze is now I trust exploded. So far, they have proved useless and are not likely to be of use *until they learn to ride*! You had better not give these views to Sir Evelyn, for both he and Lord Wolseley are the parents of the Mounted Infantry. I am very sorry for the latter for they are the best of men and officers, but they are no use and can't get about on their ponies. I am Chief Staff Officer here. We are waiting for reinforcements to enable us to take Colesberg. I am to be appointed A.A.G. Cavalry Division with local rank of Lieut. Colonel. Best love. P.S. Our mess is good here. We live in a nice house too – and this place is healthy.

### Diary 27 November (Monday)

Half Battn. Black Watch sent off today to Orange River to hold Methuen's Communications near there. Patrol sent to Volschfontein Farm brought in bandolier filled with ammunition (Martini). Owner Nineabar is in jail here. – General Buller wires from Natal 'Tell French to maintain an active defence, not running any risks'. – Gatacre at Queenstown in reply to telegram sent from here about situation states that he understands that telegraph wires are being tapped between us.

Arrivals 'O' R.H.A.
Ammunition Column of 2nd Cavalry Brigade
Army Ordnance Officer and 6 men.

### 1 December (Friday)

Squadron of 12th Lancers reconnoitred Northwards. No sign of enemy. Sent 150 Mounted Infantry to Rosemead and hold Talfelburg Bridge on railway. Reinforced with one squadron, the squadron of 12th Lancers now out reconnoitring, and ordered the two to bivouac to Hartebeestfontein Farm with the object of pressing the reconnaissance northwards next morning at daylight. Sent supplies out by train. – 1st Battn. Suffolk Regiment arrived. A 2nd Lieutenant, a photographer, sent to join us to photograph positions. We get everything except fighting men. – ½ Battalion Black Watch sent from here to re-inforce Methuen. 10 p.m. telegram from Chief of Staff ordering 12th Lancers to join Methuen at Modder River and adds 'General Buller suggests a policy of worry without risks'. Instead of suggesting, he should send troops!!

## 2 December (Saturday)

4 a.m. Order 12th Lancers to abandon reconnaissance and return without delay, and proceed to Modder River by rail. Mounted Infantry to watch Arundel till sunset. Annoying to have to cancel plans which have already been postponed twice! Only 2 squadrons 12th Lancers could leave today; no rolling stock. – Report from Rosemead that about 100 Boers within 1,000 yards of station, and attempt on Tafelberg Bridge only frustrated by our timely dispatch of Mounted Troops. Some firing reported on grazing parties near this camp. Sent some police to warn farmers in vicinity that if any firing by small parties on our men takes place they will be held responsible. – Wired to Cape Town 'There being now *no reliable Mounted troops* here, General French considers that at least one squadron of Cavalry be sent here soon to enable reconnoitre Colesberg. Enemy might leave any day without our discovering it'.

## 3 December (Sunday)

Church Parade: After last Sunday's experience, I directed Chaplain to confine his service to 20 minutes.

## 4 December (Monday)

Reconnoitred North with New Zealanders – A sensible lot of men dressed like Boers. They are not armed with swords-a pity-so General made them fix bayonets in their Carbines and practise using them as lances. They worked all right!

## 5 December (Tuesday)

Whole force marched out today. Any amount of transport, Hospitals, Bearer Co. and Ammunition Columns, but only 1½ Battalions of fighting men. When force out, returned to camp,

148

and sounded the 'Alarm'. The 'Railway C's R.E.' very slow in leaving their work in line, and manning works. – 3 p.m. Force returned. Many of the Suffolk's fell out, though the march was only 6½ miles out, to a stream of water, and the same distance back. – Colonel Porter and 3 squadrons Carabiniers arrived.

## 7 December (Thursday)

6 a.m. New Zealanders left with waggons of Mounted Troops. 8 a.m. N.Venter arrived as prisoner – Party of Albert's Volunteer Guarde left Rosmead by train about 10 p.m. last night. Went along Steynsburg line as far as Thebar, where Bridge is broken – detrained; marched 3 miles, arrived at Groots Vlei Farm (some 40 miles from Rosmead) and arrested the owner in bed at 1 a.m. – all doors locked, and had to be broken open. – Noon – Three trains left with Carabiniers, 200 Mounted Infantry Detachment, Telegraph section for Hartebeestfontein. Troops under Colonel Porter detrained covered by New Zealand Contingent, and marched to Arundel. – Drove a few Boers away, and occupied a position on the Kopje. Railway Bridge at Arundel has been broken up by Boers. Telegram from Chief of Staff that 'Boers had cut line & Telegraph near Gras Pan, and garrison at Enselin cut off'.

## 10 December (Sunday)

Church Parade at 7.30 a.m. Issued orders placing Naauwpoort and Arundel under Colonel Watson and Colonel Porter respectively for defence so that General French is free to move about the district. 2 squadrons Enniskillings arrived and sent to Arundel at once. – 6 p.m. Telegraph in cipher from Chief of Staff that 'Gatacre attacked Boers early this morning at Stormberg – suffered reverse – falling back and *endeavouring to concentrate* at Queenstown. No further particulars received.' This sounds bad. There was no necessity for an immediate advance. Time all in our favour and we knew Stormberg a very strong position. The Boers will now attack our line to Port Elizabeth.

## 11 December (Monday)

General French & Staff left for Arundel 5 a.m. Patrols reported Boers had extended their right to Vaal Kop & Knitfontein Farm. Sent out detachment of Cavalry and 2 guns – bombarded farm killing a man and wounding several. Boers fell back in great hurry leaving ammunition. Some bullets were found to be hollow explosive ones. Not very sure why enemy should occupy a position so far (13 miles) from Colesberg and not covering it directly. Looks as if he intended to hold out hand to force from East, say Groblaar from Burghersdorp, or to work round our right flanks upon the line of rails. – Sent wire to Officer Commanding Tweeddale, telling him to reconnoitre widely to Eastwards. Colonel Porter also warned, and the advantage pointed out of catching Groblaar, should he attempt to march to join Boers in position S.E. of Colesberg. His ponies must be well tired out and in the open plain between Kopies must fall an easy prey to our Cavalry and Horse Artillery. A vigorous offensive also enjoined should Boers attempt to march round his flank upon Naauwpoort.

## Extracts from letter to Henrietta. 12 December 1899. Naauwpoort

I am really very busy; so many things to arrange – We have the line of communications from Port Elizabeth to control as well as this place and the enemy (some 5,000) to retain at Colesberg. The Civilians get excited and we are flooded with telegrams from magistrates and those who think the seaside is the only safe place – Others again get fits and get ill in divers ways of which must be duly informed! So we have information of all sorts to deal with and so many questions to ask. We administer Martial Law of course rough and ready. Then again on one hand we have Gatacre defeated at Stormberg, on Sunday morning, and tonight we hear that Methuen has been checked on the Modder River. – While in our front are some 4 to 5,000 Boers about 13 miles this side of Colesberg. Our task is to bluff them with the few Cavalry we have. So far we have been successful in hemming them in, altho' today they got a reinforcement from the East (friend Groblaar from Burghersdorp). If we only had sufficient Cavalry with fit horses, we could do anything we liked with the Boers.

## 25/12/99. Arundel about 20 miles from Naauwpoort

Tomorrow being Sunday, and the next day being Xmas, the English Mail is to close today – in half an hour. So I can only send you a short line to wish you a merry Xmas and many of them. The *Daily Telegraph* correspondent came to us yesterday to get a telegram from us for our relations and friends in England – so no doubt you will see it. I have given up keeping the diary which I will send you until we start moving again. I keep a Staff Diary similar to the one which I sent to you through Sir E. Wood and gum into it telegrams and orders sent and received (if important). At present we only carry out small reconnaissances round the enemy's flanks and do our best to induce the enemy to keep quiet so as to rest our horses as much as possible. We heard yesterday that Buller's Staff had left Cape Town yesterday afternoon to join him in Natal. But you will get all this sort of news more fully in the papers than I can give you. Our usual day's work is to go out about 4.30 a.m. to one or other flank of the Boer's position and have a look to see if they are going on all right! For this we take out usually some dozen or so men as escort to the General and to look out when we halt. There is a large plain on 3 sides of the enemy's position, so we feel quite safe as the Boers won't venture into the open with us near them. It is very satisfactory to have kept so many (about 5,000) of the enemy to their positions near Colesberg. We have, all told, about 2,000 men here, and half that number at Naauwpoort. But our Cavalry only joined in billets and the horses could not stand much work. General French had to come out here last Saturday because those in command here did not understand that, if we are able to hold the Boers and prevent them coming S., it is essential to bluff them in this part and carry on an active defence. Certainly I was surprised to find many officers here in a fit of the funks and the whole garrison standing to their horses at 3 a.m. expecting an attack – when a Boer patrol of some 20 or 30 men went out for an afternoon's ride, those on outpost duty reported an advance in Force, and the whole of our troops turned out! Of course horses cannot be got fit under those conditions! Since we came there have been no alarms, and troops except on duty for outposts don't get up till 5 a.m. I have been interrupted in my writing and the clerk has just come to say that the orderly is due to go to the post. I'll send you a better letter next week. This is a grand climate and all are very well – only 1 per cent sick in the force here! Best love and hope you are looking after yourself and that you will have a good Xmas.

The diary entries for 30 and 31 October 1899 give details of the engagements referred in the records as 'Mournful Monday', or the battles of Modderspruit and Nicholson's Nek, although they were hardly full-scale battles. Nevertheless they demonstrate that the Boer Generals, in this case Joubert, were skilled tacticians and could take advantage of an opportunity, when it presented itself.

Neither the diary nor the letters to Henrietta Jameson deal with the more serious reverses suffered by Methuen at the Modder River on 28 November 1899 and Magersfontein on 11 December 1899, although the former is mentioned in passing. Buller's defeat at Colenso on 15 December 1899 is not mentioned, although Gatacre's defeat at Stormberg on 10 December, far closer to Haig at Naauwpoort, comes in for a somewhat incredulous comment that 'there was no necessity for an advance'.

Methuen's campaign was intended to relieve Kimberley and Buller's to relieve Ladysmith. French had been ordered to transfer half a Battalion of Black Watch to Methuen and complied with some reluctance. His total force was reduced to about 2,000 men, on paper quite insufficient to control the 5,000 or so Boers in front of them. This considerable achievement is referred to in the letters of 12 and 25 December 1899.

Stormberg had brought Gatacre's career to an end. Colenso resulted in Buller losing his Commander-in-Chief role. The British press seized on the mess made by Hart's Brigade in trying to cross the Tugela River against Boer rifle and artillery fire from three sides and above all on the death in action of Freddy Roberts, the Field Marshal's only son. Although the overall casualties at Colenso were only about 5 per cent, Lansdowne, Secretary of State for War, used the defeat as his opportunity to replace Buller with Roberts as C.-in-C. and Kitchener as his Chief of Staff. They arrived in Cape Town on 10 January 1900. Buller remained as the Army Commander in Natal.

Haig's diary continued to record his activities in detail until January 1900, when he became responsible for the Cavalry Division's Staff Diary. After this his personal diary entries became briefer and more military in content. But he continued to write at length to Henrietta. There is an obvious sense of joie de vivre in the diary and letters; Haig obviously preferred action to supervising the Wet Canteen at Norwich!

Notes
1.  General Sir Henry Fane Grant GCVO, KCB, born 1848, commissioned into the 4 Hussars in 1869, served in Egypt (1884–5 campaign), Bengal, India as I.G. of Cavalry, then I.G of Cavalry in Great Britain and Ireland (in 1898–1903), commanded a Division, then Governor of Malta, followed by being appointed Lieutenant of the Tower of London. He retired in 1912.
2.  Major General Sir James Melville Babbington GCMG, CB was born in 1853 and commissioned into the 16 Lancers in 1873. Before South Africa he had commanded his regiment and at one stage had been Sir Evelyn Wood's ADC. In South Africa he commanded 1 Cavalry Brigade, but was relieved of his command by Roberts. He then commanded a mobile column in the Western Transvaal. He was C.-in-C. New Zealand forces from 1902-07. His ranking as a general was honorary. He retired in 1906 and died in 1936.
3.  Alfred Viscount Milner KG, GCB, GCMG, (1854–1925), called to the bar in 1881, appointed Under-Secretary of Finance in Egypt in 1889,

152

Inland Revenue 1892–7, High Commissioner for Southern Africa and Governor of Cape Colony from 1897, peerage in 1901, established the system of government in Transvaal and Orange River Colony, Chairman Rio Tinto 1909–11, War Cabinet 1916, Secretary of State for War 1918–19, retired 1921, died of sleeping sickness.

4. Sir Julius Wernher Bt. (1850–1912), born in Germany, worked with Jules Porges in Paris, who sent him to Kimberley. One of the founders of De Beers, he bought Luton Hoo. He was created a baronet in 1905.

5. Alfred Beit (1853–1906). Like Wernher, worked under Jules Porges. He went to Kimberley in 1875. With Wernher formed Wernher, Beit and Co. in 1884. Rhodes's efforts to amalgamate the diamond mines resulted in the founding of De Beers, with Beit becoming a life governor.

6. Dr Jan Christian Smuts (1870–1950), born in Malmesbury, Cape Colony, educated at Cambridge, outstanding guerrilla leader during Second Boer War, negotiator of Vereeniging Peace Treaty, commanded First World War campaign in East Africa, joined Imperial War Cabinet 1917, delegate to Versailles peace conference, Prime Minister in South Africa 1919–24, Deputy Prime Minister 1933–9, Prime Minister 1939–48, close advisor to Winston Churchill in Second World War and signatory of the peace treaty. Honorary Field Marshal.

7. Joseph Chamberlain (1836–1914) born in Islington, he was sent by his father to Birmingham in 1854 to run a screw manufacturing company belonging to the Nettlefold family. He joined the Birmingham City Council in 1869 and was Mayor from 1873–6. He became a Member of Parliament in 1876 and was President of the Board of Trade from 1880–85. He resigned over Irish Home Rule, but became Secretary of State for the Colonies in the Conservative governments of Salisbury and Balfour from 1895 to 1903.

8. Paul Kruger (1825–1904) born near Colesberg he took part in the Great Trek at the age of ten. After the annexation of the Transvaal in 1877 Kruger was one of the leaders of the Boers in the First Boer War, culminating in the Boer victory of Majuba Hill. As President of Transvaal he was responsible for the negotiations with the British over the Uitlander issue. He left Pretoria shortly before Roberts arrived and fled to Europe. He died in Switzerland in 1904. Brought up as a strict Dutch Calvinist it is generally believed that he thought the world was flat!

9. Field Marshal Sir George Stuart White VC, KCB, OM (1835–1912) was born in Northern Ireland and commissioned into the Inniskillings in 1853, with whom he served during the Indian Mutiny. He transferred into the Gordon Highlanders and was their second in command in the Afghan War (1878–80), where he won his VC. He was C.-in-C. India, then QMG of the British Army. He was in command of the British forces in Natal at the start of the war and succeeded in getting himself bottled up in Ladysmith in a siege, which lasted 119 days. He was Governor of

Gibraltar from 1900-04 and in 1905 became Governor of Chelsea Hospital.

10. Major General Sir George Pomeroy Colley (1835–1881) was born in Ireland and commissioned into the 2nd Queen's Regiment in 1852. He served in South Africa and China before going to the War Office to assist in the Cardwell reforms. In 1871 he was an instructor at the Staff College before further service in India and then South Africa. His small force was defeated by the Boers at Laing's Nek and he was killed at Majuba Hill in February 1881.

11. Major Sir John Penniston Milbanke Bt. VC, 10 Hussars, born 1872, commissioned 1892, retired 1911.

12. Brigadier General Sir Joseph Frederick Laycock KCMG, DSO, Royal Horse Guards.

13. Theresa Susey Helen, daughter of the 19th Earl of Shrewsbury, married the 6th Marquess of Londonderry in 1875. She died in 1919. The daughter, Helen Mary Theresa, was born in 1876 and married the 6th Earl of Ilchester in 1902.

14. Robert Stephenson Smyth, 1st Baron Baden-Powell GCMG, GCVO, KCB (1857–1941) was commissioned into the 13 Hussars in 1872. He served in India, South Africa, Ashanti and Matabeleland before his remarkable defence of Mafeking in the Second Boer War. He became a lieutenant general in 1908 and retired in 1910. He founded the Boy Scouts in 1908 and the Girl Guides in 1910.

15. General Sir Ian Standish Monteith Hamilton GCB, DSO, (1853–1947) was commissioned into the 12 Foot in 1872, before transferring into the Gordon Highlanders, the regiment with which he is usually associated, in 1873. He had an amazing career, mainly in India until 1898. He was brought back to England to command the School of Musketry at Hythe in 1898 and was there until September 1899. He commanded the 7 Brigade at Elandslaagte and subsequently a mounted infantry division, which had been specially created for him. He was Chief of Staff in South Africa in 1901-02. His subsequent appointments were QMG, GOC.-in-C. Southern Command, Adjutant General and GOC.-in-C., Mediterranean. With the start of the First World War he was responsible for mobilizing and training the Territorial forces. Today he is chiefly remembered for his disastrous Gallipoli campaign of 1915.

16. Major General Sir Penn Symons KCB, born in1843, commanded the Natal field force at the start of the war. Unwisely he pushed a brigade forward to Dundee, near the Natal border, thus weakening his garrison in Ladysmith. He fought Lucus Meyer's Commando at Talana Hill on 20 October 1899. Although he captured the hill it was at the expense of his own life and some 250 British casualties.

17. Petrus Jacobus Joubert (1834–1900) was of Huguenot origin. He farmed near Laing's Nek and became a member of the Volksraad. He was Commandant General of the Boer forces in the First Boer War. He stood

unsuccessfully three times against Kruger for the Presidency of Transvaal. In the Second Boer War he was again in command of the Boer forces, but most of the operations were delegated to others. He died in Pretoria in March 1900.

18. Lieutenant General Sir Cornelius Francis Clery KCB, KCMG, (1838–1926) was commissioned into the 32 Foot in 1858. He was an instructor at Sandhurst in 1871–2 and, after serving in Ireland, Aldershot and Egypt, went to South Africa for the Zulu Wars, where he survived Isandhlwana. He returned to South Africa in 1899 as a divisional commander under Buller, who evidently admired his fighting qualities. At that stage he was sixty-one years old, with whiskers dyed blue and varicose veins! He 'retired' in 1901.

19. Lieutenant General Sir Edward Cecil Bethune KCB, CVO was born in 1855 and commissioned into the Gordon Highlanders in 1875. He transferred to the 6 Dragoon Guards and then to the 16 Lancers. Before coming to South Africa he served in India. In the Second Boer War he was one of the most successful of the mobile column commanders. He became Director General Territorial Forces in 1912 and died in 1930.

20. Field Marshal Paul Sanford, 3rd Baron Methuen GCB, GCMG, GCVO, (1845–1932) was commissioned into the Scots Fusilier Guards in 1867. He served in Ireland, was Military Attaché in Berlin, was in South Africa in 1888–9, became a major general in 1890 and lieutenant general in South Africa in 1899–1902. He won some minor battles but lost the major opportunity of defeating the Boers at Magersfontein in December 1899, which would have opened the way to Kimberley. He was captured at Tweebosch in March 1902, after his raw troops had fled. He was C.-in-C. South Africa from 1908–12, Governor of Malta from 1915 until he retired in 1919. He became Constable of the Tower in 1919.

21. Lieutenant General The Hon. Sir Frederick William Stopford KCMG, KCVO, CB (1854–1929) was the son of the 4th Earl of Courtown. He was commissioned into the Grenadier Guards in 1871. He served in Egypt, Cyprus, Aldershot, Ashanti and came to South Africa as Military Secretary to Sir Redvers Buller. In 1904 he became Director of Military Training, then the Major General (London District). He was appointed Lieutenant of the Tower in 1912.

# Chapter 6

# South Africa

## 1900

In November 1899 Major General French was ordered by Sir Redvers Buller, still Commander-in-Chief, to go to De Aar in the Cape Colony with the object of occupying Naauwpoort and then Colesberg where a force of some 2,000 Boers was reported to be. The Cavalry Division was still arriving in South Africa and would eventually find its way to the De Aar – Colesberg area. In the meantime a small force of infantry, mounted infantry and a few cavalry was placed under French's command. Apart from the instruction to occupy Colesberg, which was heavily defended by the Boers, French was made responsible for the railway line from De Aar to Durban.

The previous chapter finished with Haig's Christmas letter to his sister rather than at the end of December. This is because operations against Colesberg started on 29 December and continued into January without a break.

### Diary 29 December 1899 – Operations against Colesberg

H.Qrs. Cavalry Division at Arundel. Boers reported vacating their positions on ridges North of Arundel. No doubt owing to the many threats of Cavalry and Horse Artillery against both their flanks and towards their rear. 2 Squadrons Cavalry sent to keep contact and follow enemy up.

### 30 December (Saturday)

Colonel Porter sent on at 3 a.m. with Carbs., N.Zealand Md. Rifles and Batt. R.H.A. to clear up situation towards Colesberg. General French and Staff left Arundel at 5 a.m. Established advanced post 3 m. S.E. of Colesberg and pushed patrols round enemy's flanks. Enemy's guns opened fire and disclosed his position. Returned to Rensburg to which point Cav. Div. Hd.

Quarters was moved this afternoon. Half Battn. Berks. Regt. Remaining H.A. Batty. as well as Col. Porter's Brigade camped at Rensburg.

### 31 December (Sunday)

Visited advanced post 5 a.m. and reconnoitred ground between Koles Kop and Colesberg town. Left Porter's[1] Brigade at Rensburg to hold enemy in front and threaten his left (on East) flank. At 5 p.m. left Rensburg with 10th Hussars. 2 Sqrs. 6 Dgns. 2 Batteries R.H.A. Half Battn. Infantry in waggons 1 Co. M.I., ½ Bearer Co., Detc.Md.R.E., 2 days supply in Regimental Supply waggons. Arrived Maeder's Farm about 9 p.m. Halted till 1.30 a.m. Marched with Infantry and M.I. leading over ground reconnoitred in morning. About 3.30 a.m. (still dark) reached kopje, clue to S.West entrance to Colesberg town. Boers picket surprised. Sentry ran back yelling 'Roinches' and fired wildly. McCracken and his 4 Companies occupied Kopje without opposition, enemy completely surprised. Guns get into position to open fire when suitable target visible. Cavalry pushed farther round enemy's flank to North. About 4.15 a.m. Boers guns opened a very hot fire from Maxim Vicker's quick fires (called '10 a penny' because it fires ten shots 1 lb. shells like a repeating rifle). Two 15 lbrs. also fired from heights (one a British gun taken from Gatacre at Stormberg). Boer fire very accurate, but our gunners fired as if at a field day! Strange to say only 2 of our gunners were wounded; one of the escort was killed. Boers reinforced their men on hill between Berks and town. General sent order to Berks to retire, but it was soon countermanded as it was obvious Major McCracken,[2] Comg. Berks. Det., could easily hold his position. About 10 o'clock Boer guns ceased firing. Pushed our Cavalry right round enemy's right, on to plain North of Colesberg. Situation at night – McCracken still holds his hill. Cavalry post on hills North of him. Enemy's communications by Colesberg road Bridge cut. H. Qrs. Cav. Div. bivouacked at advanced post, called 'Porter's Hill'. R.H.A. Batty. Retired there at sunset.

### 2 January (Tuesday)

General French and Staff moved to Kole Kop shortly after 3 a.m. If enemy attacked in force General had decided to retire. But it was apparent a retirement could not be made in daylight, without incurring great loss. Boers fired briskly. General and I walked half way up Koles Kop to look at situation of enemy; it was arranged to postpone issue of orders for withdrawal. After first hour or two enemy limited his action to sniping. Report received from Rensburg that train with 3 days' supplies had broken away in night and dashed into broken culvert near enemy's lines. Dutch Ganger suspected of having released the brakes. H.Qrs. Cavalry Division at Rensburg tonight.

### 3 January (Wednesday)
Reinforced McCracken with 6 Co. Suffolk Regt. They camp at Kole Kloof where some water was found. Boer deserters state that General Schwemann had tried to turn our right on Monday, but was checked by the detachments sent from Porter's Brigade in view of such movement on his part.

### 4 January (Thursday)
General French left Rensburg about 4 a.m. for Kloof Camp. When at Porter's Hill very heavy firing heard towards Suffolk's Hill. Wired at once to O.C. troops Madders Farm to turn out all his force at once to support Suffolks. Half Sqr. and 2 guns R.H.A. sent from Porter's Hill to support. It was found that during night the Boers had occupied some Kopjes close to Inniskilling Squadron whose duty it was to patrol during night and protect their flanks. The squadron was at breakfast when the Boers opened fire! Luckily a sensible young gunner officer was at hand with his 2 guns R.H.A. and at once opened fire on Kopjes occupied by Boers. A second section R.H.A. joined him and the Boer movement was checked. The Cavalry and another section R.H.A was sent to attack enemy on his right flank from the Westwards; this settled the Boers and many retired. About 2 p.m. the Kopje occupied by Boers was attacked by our M.I. and taken without a single casualty. 19 prisoners were found on it and many dead and wounded. Some 50 horses were also taken.

### 5 January (Friday)
General French and Staff went to top of Koles Kop – about 1,000 feet above plain and very steep and rocky – it affords fine view for many miles round. Boers quiet today. We fired a few shells today to keep down sniping. Issued orders at 6 p.m. at Rensburg for the troops about Kloof camp to shell 'grassy' hill at daylight tomorrow. Porter's Brigade to hold enemy on his South, and South East front and make him fear an attack in those quarters.

158

8 p.m. Colonel Eustace[3] Comg. R.H.A. who had been to Kloof Camp to arrange details about guns for tomorrow's action brought urgent request from Colonel Watson, Comg. Suffolks, to be allowed to occupy 'Grassy' Hill during the night. He (Col. Watson) said he had personally reconnoitred the ground; the matter was easy of accomplishment and he hoped the G.O.C. would rely on him for once as he felt confident of success. I telegraphed between 8 and 9 p.m. to Colonel Watson giving him a free hand 'if he found he had a good chance of success'.

## 6 January (Saturday)

At 1 a.m. woken up by report from outposts that a battery has been cut up by enemy! Truth was that some horses in a limber had bolted from Porter's Hill! General French and Staff left Rensburg 2.30 a.m. On arriving at Porter's Hill heard heavy firing near Suffolk's Hill. It was then 3.10 a.m. We went on quickly to Kole Kop. It was then getting light. From top of Kole Kop groups of our men could be seen surrounded by 110 Boers! What happened was as follows; Watson left about 12.30 at night. Occupied hill in question which was only 1,000 yards from his outposts. About 3 a.m. he assembled his officers to give directions; the Boers, from a lower part of the hill, fired rapidly and shot and wounded most of the officers. The 4 companies Suffolks in close column had bayonets fixed but magazines not charged. There was no one to give orders . . . .At this moment a cry of 'retire' was raised. The rear companies ran away back to the pickets. Those in front did what they could, but surrendered after losing

| | | | | | |
|---|---|---|---|---|---|
| 4 officers and | 23 other ranks | killed |
| 1 " " | 20 " " | wounded |
| 6 " " | 107 " " | missing |

I sent orders at once for Essex to replace Suffolks at Kloof Camp. This move was carried out by 10 p.m. Suffolks sent to line of communications.

On 24 January 1900 Buller suffered yet another reverse, this time at Spion Kop, where 243 British troops were killed as the result of astonishing military incompetence, with a series of failures of command and finally of nerve. Buller blamed Warren[4] the Divisional Commander, in the same way as he had blamed Hart, the Brigade Commander and Long,[5] in charge of the Artillery ('I

159

was sold by a damned gunner') for the fiasco at Colenso. Spion Kop could have been a British victory had someone, Buller himself for instance, taken a grip of the battle at the crucial time. Instead he seems simply to have stood watching, whilst chaos reigned, without intervening.

The further defeat at Vaal Kranz in early February brought once again to an ignominious end yet another attempt by Buller to relieve Ladysmith. Haig makes no mention of these events in

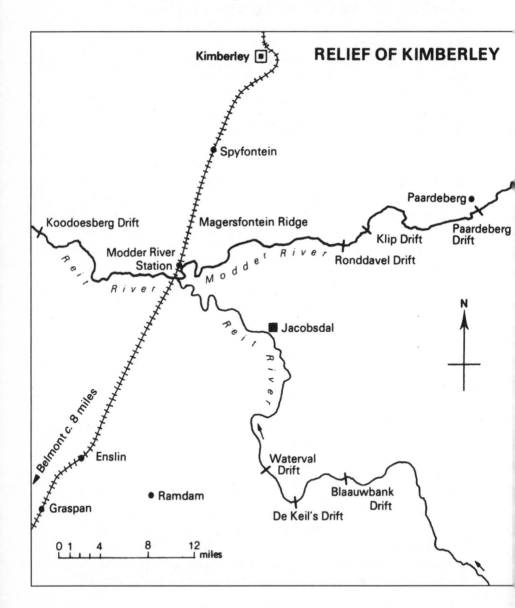

his diary or his letters, because no doubt he was fully occupied with events around Colesberg, more than 350 miles away.

On 10 January 1900 Field Marshal Roberts and General Kitchener arrived in Cape Town as Commander-in-Chief and Chief of Staff respectively. Henceforward the campaign became a much more business-like affair. Roberts' force consisted of three Infantry divisions and the Cavalry division, compared with Buller's five Brigades at Colenso and Methuen's two at Magersfontein.

The Cavalry Division's thrilling dash to relieve Kimberley is described in detail by Douglas Haig in the following extracts from his letters to his sister Henrietta Jameson and to Colonel Lonsdale Hale, a friend and noted military historian.

Kimberley was relieved on 15 February 1900; three days later Roberts fought the Battle of Paardeberg; Cronje[6] surrendered on 27 February at Paardeberg; Buller relieved Ladysmith on 28 February; the Battles of Poplar Grove and Driefontein and the capture of Bloemfontein took place in March; Roberts occupied Kroonstad and captured Johannesburg in May; and Mafeking was relieved on 17 May. By September it looked as if the war was 'practically over'; Buller went home in October, followed by Roberts in December. The latter would have gone home two months earlier, but his daughter was suffering from typhoid fever and he waited until she was well enough to travel. Kitchener took over as Commander-in-Chief and found that the war, far from being practically over, had become a guerrilla campaign. Peace was not declared until June 1902.

### Letter to Henrietta 4 February 1900 from Nelson Hotel, Cape Town

I arrived here yesterday and return to Rensburg tomorrow. You will see from the enclosed telegrams the ostensible reason for my visit is to confer with the Director of Mil. Intelligence!

### Telegram General French to Chief of Staff, Cape Town

May I point out that appointment as AAG to Cavalry Division was promised by Sir Redvers Buller to Major Haig with local rank of Lieut. Colonel stop I was officially asked to recommend officer to fill his place as DAAG stop I earnestly beg that Field Marshal will be pleased to confirm this stop He has acted in this capacity under my command in 3 general engagements and many smaller fights stop I have several times mentioned him in my despatches stop His services have been invaluable. General French

### Telegram, Chief of Staff to General French

FM C-in-C fully realizes the very excellent services rendered by Major Haig and much regrets not being able to meet your views as regards his taking position of AAG of the Cavalry Division. That position however the Field Marshal thinks must be filled by the appointment of a senior officer and he feels sure you will find in Colonel the Earl of Erroll[7] an efficient officer.

### Telegram to GOC, Rensburg

Major Haig, DAAG, is directed to come at once to Cape Town to confer with DMI. He is to remain as long as you can spare him. Intelligence Army HQ Cape Town.

### Telegram to General French.

From Chief begins; I think there will have to be a change in Broadwood's Command. Can you spare Haig, if I want him? It would be a good thing for him and I could send you Broadwood if you like.

The short-lived appointment of Colonel the Earl of Erroll as AAG of the Cavalry Division was seen as a set-back for Douglas Haig. He himself took it in good part, realizing that, with his growing reputation as a soldier, there would be plenty of other opportunities, sooner rather than later. Presumably Roberts had already promised the appointment to Erroll before either of them had left England. Roberts was always keen to have officers with titles on his staff; some said Lady Roberts's influence could be detected in these appointments. Two of his ADCs were the sons of Dukes; both were amongst relatively few officers in South Africa awarded the DSO, giving rise to the comment that DSO must stand for Dukes' Sons Only!

The following letter to Lady Haig was written in 1929 after her husband had died, when she was collecting material for a book about Douglas Haig's life. The book eventually appeared in 1936 as *The Man I Knew*. The letter was not included in the book. Joe Laycock was one of French's ADCs. By 1929 he had become Brigadier General Sir Joseph Laycock KCMG, DSO, TD. He was the father of Major General Sir Robert Laycock KCMG, CB, DSO, Chief of Combined Operations from 1943–47.

DEAR LADY HAIG,

I wonder how I can be any help in your writing of Douglas' life. You probably have the details of our start on R.M.S. *Norman* and our arrival in S.Africa; one point I might bring light on was when Lord Erroll was sent to go over Douglas' head before our advance to relief of Kimberley. This was a set back to Douglas and of course didn't work and Douglas took it wonderfully correctly and I remember all so well . . . .It is a long time ago and I have no notes to help my not very retentive memory. As far as I can remember, I was in Cape Town when Lord Roberts and Lord Kitchener arrived to take over command in South Africa. I found out then that Lord Erroll (then a full Colonel in the Army) was to supersede Douglas. I went back at once to where General French was at Rensburg Siding outside Colesberg and told him. He sent me back to Cape Town immediately with the definite instructions that I had somehow or other to get the matter put right. I saw Lord Roberts who was very pleasant took the trouble to explain to me that Douglas Haig was then only a Major in the Army and was too junior in rank to act as senior staff officer to the division about to be formed for the relief of Kimberley, also that Lord Erroll had been definitely sent out by the War Office to take up his post. I pointed out that it would be impossible for any officer coming fresh to the command and not knowing either the country or the regiments composing the division to be able to succeed, that Douglas Haig had worked continuously with General French, that he intimately knew all the commanding and squadron officers and made out the best common sense case I could. On the third time of making my appeal to Lord Roberts and apologizing very humbly for doing so, I was so seriously shut up that it was impossible to carry the matter further and I returned to Colesberg. Naturally General French and Douglas were very annoyed. Soon after that Lord Erroll arrived. Douglas handed over the necessary papers and it was soon perfectly obvious that Lord Erroll, even with the best intentions, was unable to carry out the work, and it had to be done as best it could. Douglas was all the time, of course, maintaining a most correct attitude. After the capture of Cronje, I saw Colonel Hamilton, who was senior officer to Lord Kitchener, and told him that the position was definitely harmful. He asked me to see Lord Kitchener, which I did, and explained the situation to him. Next day Lord Erroll was given command of the troops which were to form the escort to Cronje and the Boer prisoners and

Douglas resumed his position and all went well . . . We were a very happy family there and you know how we all worshipped Douglas. The thing that struck one most was his extraordinary ability to express in concise form capable of being copied into a notebook on the field important orders for the movement and disposition of troops. In this he was an absolute master. (Signed) J.F. Laycock.

## Extracts from letter to Colonel Lonsdale Hale. 2 March 1900 Hd. Qrs. Cav. Div., Koedoes Rand Farm

I was delighted to get your letter the day before we left Modder River, and enjoyed reading it very much indeed. Would have written to thank you for it before, but as you will have seen from the papers, we have been continually on the move. – And even now I have not got a sheet of paper worthy of you on which to write! This being torn from the end of a diary. But I daresay you won't mind. You will have seen many accounts in the papers of how the Cavalry relieved Kimberley, and then moved to head Cronje, and enabled the Infantry to come up: but possibly a line from me on the subject may please you, and enable you to correct the gossiping tales that are sure to result from the hearsay evidence of the correspondents: for not one really rode all the way with us. We left Modder River on Sunday 11th Feb., rather a scratch pack! Not a single Brigadier for the 3 Brigades. Gordon joined after we marched – Broadwood at Ramdam about 10 p.m. – Porter (after we had forced the Modder) not till 14th! All the Brigade staffs were also new. – We marched at 3 a.m., and having taken the precaution of sending our baggage and supply column beyond the outposts (Methuen) on the previous evening, we got all away southwards out of sight of Boer position of Magersfontein before daylight. – We halted at Ramdam Sunday night. At this point we had 2,564 Cavalry which we brought from Modder and 7 Batteries R.H.A. We now were joined by 550 Roberts' Horse. 155 K's Horse and 562 M.I. under Alderson. – We had been told that we would have 8,500 horsemen on this night! Kitchener at Modder impressed me with the importance of our mission, said 'if it failed neither he nor the P.M. could tell what the result on the "Empire" might be!' – There was no good waiting, so French decided to push on next morning as all depended on 'surprise'. We marched at 2 a.m. on. Monday 12th as long as there was a moon. Luck and the ground enabled us to get our many odds and ends away from camp in 3 groups without a hitch. When the moon went down we halted till morning, then pushed on to the Reit River. We threatened it in 3 places and got across at De Kiel's drift with the loss of a few men and poor Majendie. Had a very hot day and it was about 3 p.m. before we got firmly established. We left our baggage at Ramdam till we knew whereabouts we could cross the Reit. Tucker's Division also camped at Ramdam. He marched about 7 a.m. and brought on all his bullock transport, passing it in front of ours. So that at 8 a.m., when I sent for our transport, it could not move, and did not get away till 5 p.m – Tucker arrived at the Drift (a very steep and bad one) at De Kiels. We had arranged to keep well back for waggons from the river bank so as to let waggons have a clear run: but Tucker's people coming up jostled and crowded till the drift got into an indescribable state of block! I mention this to show you the want of a Commander in Chief when there are 2 independent Divisions. Our supplies got up next day (Tuesday 13th) in time to enable us to fill our nose bags and start at 10.30 a.m. We took no waggons except 4 ambulances with us and a cable cart. The country was open and we advanced in line of Brigade masses, and then opened out to Sqre. Coln. more or less – for we were sniped at from positions in our flanks, and had to detach squadrons to turn them. – This was again a very hot day, and several heath fires sprung up and burnt our cable! About 2 o'clock about 1000 to 2000 Boers occupied a farm and hill on our right flank, and gave us some little trouble, but we took them in satisfactorily! – We left the 1st Brigade to play with the Boers and pushed the other 2 quickly for the Drifts which were about 8 miles off . . . The Cavalry arrived alone at the drifts, the R.H.A. could not keep up. The 12th Lancers attacked Klip Drift, dismounted and pushed across and held the kopjes beyond, which formed a sort of natural bridgehead. – The Boers were completely surprised. We got all their supplies, hot bread and peaches and fruit sent up by the friends of the Boers in Magersfontein. – On Wednesday 14th we halted for we had no supplies except what we carried in our wallets. The Transport arrived about 2 a.m. on Thursday 15th. We handed over our positions to Kelly-Kenny's Division and marched at 9.30 a.m. carrying 2 days' supplies on the horses: leaving behind the ammunition columns and using the spare horses to horse the Batteries. – Porter had now joined us and our strength all told including R.H.A. was 4,890 horses – some what short of the promised 8,500! However, we Cavalry must not complain, for Kitchener had backed us up well, and is really the working man of the Obercommando! We had not gone 3 miles from Klip Drift Northwards before our Advanced Squadrons were heavily fired on from some hills in their front – at the same time some Boer guns opened on us from a hill to our left (i.e. N.W.). The situation seemed to me to be that our friends of 2 days ago were holding the hills in our front to stop us going towards Bloemfontein, while Cronje from Magersfontein had extended his left to prevent us out-flanking him . . . . There was an open plain towards Abon Dam between the 2 parties of the enemy. The ground rose from the river, so we could not see whether there were wire fences or not, but there seemed to be only a few Boers at the end of the rise. – There seemed only one thing to be done if we were to get to Kimberley before the Boers barred our path, namely charge through the gap between the 2 positions. Half our guns were ordered to keep down the fire from the kopjes in our front (which would be on the right flank of the charging cavalry) and half engaged the enemy's guns. The 9th and 16th Lancers were then ordered to charge followed by Broadwood's Brigade in support. For a minute it looked in the dust as if some of our men were coming back, but they were only extending towards a flank. Porter's Brigade followed with the M.I. and brought on the guns. Our lancers caught several Boers and rode down many others in the open plain, and really suffered little from the very hot rifle fire – about 20 casualties I fancy and we passed within 1000 yards of the Boer position! – We got to Kimberley about 6 p.m. The garrison made not the slightest attempt to assist us. Alone we cleared all the Boers investing positions in the south and took 2 laagers. The people in Kimberley looked fat and well. It was the relieving force which needed food!! For in the gallop many nosebags were lost and 7 lbs tins of bully beef is an unsuitable adjunct to one's saddle in a charge. On Friday 16th we left Kimberley at 5 a.m. with Gordon and Porter's Brigades and M.I. moved N.E. and cut Boers' communications with Boshof. Then pivoting on left, moved N.W. passed North of the Dronfield ridge. A large force of Boers held hill at Macfarlane Station (12 miles north of Kimberley). The two Brigades turned each flank and the M.I. and guns connected them in centre. The Boers retired, but we lost a dozen or more casualties. We had now command of the country to the Vaal (5 miles). A large covoy of Boers at least 5000 with many waggons was seen moving towards the drift. (Boshof had been its first destination.) Our arrival again caused an alteration of direction – more towards Barkly West. The day was very hot and our horses had had no water or forage: it was impossible to push on against the convoy. There was also a laager between us and Kimberley (Dronfield). We held the position at Macfarlanes to Kimberley, bombarding the laager as we retired. This surrendered next morning; many escaped in night leaving a gun. – Saturday 17th. We marched with Broadwood's Brigade and part of 1st Brigade (namely Household Cavalry, 10th Hussars, 12th Lancers and 2 squadrons Carabiniers) 12 guns at 3.30 a.m. for Koedoes Rand Drift on receipt of information that Cronje was retreating up the right bank of Modder. About 10 a.m. we saw his dust, and shortly after 11 we headed him completely and opened fire on the head of the convoy. The surprise was complete. But the Boers tried to turn our right: our left rested on the river. All day and all night we held on. The confusion in the convoy is indescribable: many waggons caught fire from our shells. The Boers too brought 4 guns and fired hotly in spite of some of their waggons with ammunition exploding. It was not till 8 a.m. the next day (Sunday 18th) that the troops under Kelly Kenny put in an appearance. And then oh tacticians! Piece meal and frontal-attacks took place: each one beaten back in turn without inflicting on Cronje any real damage. More Infantry came up, and as far as we could see no attempt was made to surround Cronje in the river bed. – Next morning (Monday 19th) we were called upon to send 'a Brigade' to support the infantry on left bank! But we scarcely had a Brigade to send! However, we sent all we could.

### Entries in Staff Diary.

**1 March** Heard at noon that Ladysmith was relieved yesterday. **13 March** About 11 a.m. the chief citizens of Bloemfontein came and surrendered to F.M. Lord Roberts. About 1 p.m. the Field Marshal entered at the head of 3rd Cavalry Brigade.

### Extracts of letters to Henrietta 7 April 1900. Bloemfontein

You will have seen of the disaster which happened to Broadwood. 7 guns, 32 officers and 525 other ranks killed, wounded or missing. You will remember I told you of our going to Thabanchu and we thought it a mistake to engage on a secondary operation in that direction instead of making good our Comns, and pressing the enemy at a decisive point (viz towards Brandfort and Winburg) that is Northwards. At Thabanchu many poor creatures brought in their guns and swore an oath not to fight against us again. Then we withdrew our troops and the Transvaalers burn all the farms!! Such conduct merely brings us into contempt, altho' Roberts no doubt expected to gain popularity with the British Public by being generous & merciful to the 'conquered'.

General French and I left Thabanchu on the 26th March and got back here next day. We had hoped to have a few quiet days in which to refit the Division, but we only had one night in Bloemfontein and were ordered off at once Northwards on the 28th. On the 29th we fought near Karee Siding and drove the Boers back on Brandfort – a 40 mile march.

We got back here on 30th and 31st had to march out to support Broadwood. So you see we are continually on the move and our horses are quite done up. Whenever there is an alarm Lord R at once orders out French and the Cavalry. I don't know what we'll do for horses; only wretched beasts of Argentine ponies are arriving and very few of them. There will be 900 here by the next few days. One Brigade alone wants

167

that number. All this delays our further advance. You ask where we sleep! Out of doors, of course, unless there is a farm handy which is not often . . . .

## Letter of 14 April 1900 from Bloemfontein.

We have had a fairly quiet time this last week as far as marching goes, but are full of work refitting. Our great trouble is to find horses; only underbred Argentine ponies are arriving here, and few of them even are in condition for hard work. I think this omission to provide us with good remounts reflects little credit on the home Authorities.

Of course we must make the best of what we have got, but the most ignorant must have foreseen that horses which are worked in an almost waterless country such as that over which we rode to the relief of Kimberley and afterwards, soon give out. Moreover (as I have told you) there was no grazing in that district, even if we had had time to graze, and often only 6 or 7 lbs. of mealies per horse. We want about 2500 horses to make our 3 Brigades up to strength again. I think there are some 12 or 1500 ponies available

The Division consists now of 4 Brigades each of 3 regiments. The Mounted Infantry have been formed into a Division by themselves, and are no longer under French. We don't regret this, for the MI are a useless lot, and seem as soon as mounted to cease to be good infantry. You will have seen of a force of Infantry and MI being surrounded at Reddersberg & surrendering! Has ever anyone heard of mounted troops being surrounded? Cavalry never suffer themselves to be surrounded. [Haig had obviously forgotten Lieutenant Colonel Moeller's disastrous performance at Talana, where he and a large part of the 18th Hussars were indeed surrounded and did surrender.]

Broadwood has got off v. cheaply. One almost thinks Lord Roberts likes losing guns, judging by the way he received B on his return. But you get enough of war news in the papers!

Rumour says that HM the Queen has signified her disapproval of so many ladies being in Cape Town. The old lady is right. They ought all to be ordered to England. Three arrived here, and were ordered out next morning. They declined to go! Lord R then wrote one of them a letter (they were ladies of title Lady C Bentinck and others I believe) and they have gone off.

No one is allowed to pass Norvals Pont without a pass! One old woman had not got a pass, but insisted on coming on. No amount of entreaties would move her! She sat still. The Station Staff Officer, Commandant etc.etc. & minor officials could do nothing with her. They

168

could not drag an old woman out by force, so the carriage was unhooked, and the old woman remained victor; alone on a siding!

## Letter to Henrietta dated 14 May 1900 from HQ Cav. Division near Jordain Siding 6 miles N. of Kroonstad.

We are now only 84 miles from the Vaal and a march like the one we made last week would bring us to Johannesburg (120 odd miles from here – we did over 130 miles in 4 days last week).

Neil Haig [cousin)]was taken prisoner on the 10th and some say he was wounded. Had his wound been a severe one, the Boers would not have taken him with them. So I hope there is not much the matter with him.

I hear from several sources that the infantry are quite jealous of the success of the Cavalry. The poor creatures only carry their guns without a chance of loosing off! In fact they simply wear out their boots to no purpose!! All the same, but for the Cavalry having turned this last position South of Kroonstad, many of them would be now below the ground – for the position was a stronger one & more difficult to turn than Magersfontein.

The Field Marshal was in a bad temper yesterday and opened upon French because so many men were missing! But what can you expect to happen if horses stop from exhaustion & one covers 60 or more miles in 2 days. The missing men gradually drop in, so it is quite unnecessary to report their names home by telegraph until one is quite sure that the men are taken prisoner, or killed and so won't return. Kitchener also has a baddish time with Roberts' temper. You will see in the diary how the Landrost of Kroonstad came out to surrender the town to French, but we packed him off into the town again to wait for the Field Marshal! The latter meantime had helio'd that no patrols were to enter the town. We came on here with the Cavalry and Roberts marched in at the head of the Infantry! I am afraid he is a silly old man & scarcely fit to be C-in-C of this show . . . .

## 8 June 1900. Pretoria

We came into Pretoria two days ago after releasing the prisoners at Waterval (about 10 miles N. of the town). I tried to send you a telegram yesterday, but the wires is so taken up that no private wires are read for delivery at present. We have just received orders to start off again to day to the Eastwards.

## 17 June 1900 Pretoria

Some 60 tons of mails for the troops are said to be near Kroonstad, and rumour says that De Wet captured a convoy with mails and burnt the letters. However the railway is expected to be here in 3 or 4 days and should bring up some letters I think . . . . . We left here again last Sunday and returned Friday, so on arrival here I sent you a telegram by runner to the nearest telegraph office open for private wires. There is only one wire at present working from here, and the C. in C. and Military telegrams more than employ its capacity. This is quite a nice town with plenty of trees and running water. We are still occupying a state school but move this afternoon into the Dutch Club. Last week we took over the house of one Van Althen, the Postmaster General of the S.A. Republic who is absent with Kruger still. When we returned on Friday we found Mrs. Van A. had arrived so we came back here temporarily. So we chose another house which curiously belongs to the Head of the Telegraphs – really a very nice house with gardens and fountains, electric light and hot-water bath! I personally had too much to do to go house-hunting so some of the others went. The lady was living in the house and an order to quit was duly presented to her. She is quite young – about 25 or 30 (Milbanke says). The old telegraphist (who is with Kruger) is in the sixties! Well, the poor thing was much upset at the idea of leaving her nice house. To make a long story short, it is now arranged that we take over the Dutch Club, also a good house, and perhaps more suitably furnished for our requirements than the lady's one! The Dutch Consul and others have now produced books on international Law and have protested. This won't have much effect, and we now have a guard over the building. I believe it is a regular meeting place of the disaffected and some arms were discovered in the house. It is hard to know exactly how long this war will go on. We took some interesting telegrams in the office here which had been passed between Kruger, De Wet, Botha and others. All complain that Burghers had gone home in large numbers. Botha blames Kruger for taking all the money from Pretoria as he cannot keep his men in the field without the means of feeding them. De Wet is told to destroy communications in the Free State or Orange River Colony as we call it now. This he is doing with much success . . . You will see by referring to the map what long distances we have covered in quite a short time. The mules and horses have suffered a good deal of course.

### 3 July 1900. Pretoria

Old Brab is here with Valentine and a complete staff, but with absolutely nothing to do! So they are grumbling. I think it would be much better for all concerned, and cheaper too for the country, to send all such people to England at once. I like old Brab, but you know he is no chicken. Lord Edmund Talbot[8] left us today. He is to call on you and tell you how I am getting on out here. He was my assistant Staff Officer, or D.A.A.G as they call it. A very good fellow and I am sorry he has gone; but he goes to command the 11th Hussars. His brother (the Duke of Norfolk) went with him. I admire the Duke of Norfolk.[9] He came out here and insisted on doing the work of an ordinary subaltern in Tab Brassey's Coy. of Yeomanry.[10] There is not much going on here, except trying to get together some horses, men and saddles! We started polo yesterday. So things seem gradually quieting down, tho' Botha is still close by – and De Wet is still able to defy some 70,000 odd of British troops with possibly 2,000 men at most! P.S. I asked Joe Laycock and Guy[11] to call on you. They left here a week ago.

## 9 July 1900. Pretoria

We are just off in a great hurry. The Field Marshal sent for French at 7.30 a.m. and told him to start as soon as he could with a Brigade to support the troops now operating South East of this under General Hutton.[12] The latter asked for more mounted troops, so French is going to take command. We will be off by 11 a.m. I have a good many things to do before starting, especially as the move is so unexpected. We did not expect to go till the end of the week . . . . You must not imagine that I run unnecessary risks; this is not the case. I am always most careful where I go.

## 15 July 1900. Pretoria

We are starting again tomorrow for the N.E., but hope to return here tomorrow night in order to leave early on Tuesday for the right wing of the Army which is in the S.E. about 40 miles from here. Since I last wrote, French was hurried back to assist in the defence of Pretoria! When we arrived the funk had subsided. We hear that all the Hospital Orderlies were armed and that the policemen were turned out to the West of the town. I hope that this movement, which really begins tomorrow, will end the war in about 3 weeks. The policy of treating the Boers with leniency has not paid so far; they surrender their arms and take an oath of allegiance, but on the first favourable chance they go out on commando again! I have not received a mail since I wrote you last week. It is due tomorrow. I fancy the mails have been delayed at Kroonstad owing to the movement of troops on the railway. The C. in C. thinks they have got round De Wet at last!

## Letter to Henrietta dated 15 August 1900 from Middleburg

I enclose three letters from old Stodger.[13] I did all I could for him at Pretoria, but as I had not seen him recently and the evidence of eyewitnesses was so damning the Field Marshal sent him home. Stodger's letters are also rather queer: not those I send so much as the earlier ones which contained little rhymes! If you see S as you are sure to do, please tell him not to excite himself too much over the shortcomings of the military, but in a quiet way to have his case thoroughly enquired into.

I also enclose the diary up to date. You will see that we have opened communications with Buller and are likely to move on shortly.

It is impossible to say whether the Boers will continue fighting after we occupy Machadodorp. Spring is now coming on, and the sun gets warmer daily so that life in the bush veldt and lower valleys will soon be unbearable, and unhealthy. So I expect a good many will try to get back to their farms. I am therefore inclined to believe a report that the war will be practically over by the time you get this, (beginning of September).

Sir E. Wood wrote a letter to French about me & suggesting he should take steps to make me 2nd in command of a regiment with a view to putting me shortly in command. F wrote back to him, that instead of promotion such an act would be to reduce me. I might have command of a Cavalry Brigade here any day were it not that my duties as Chief Staff Officer of the Cavalry are more important & French would rather not change his CSO at the 11th hour of the campaign.

The diary will show you what I am about. Remember of course it is quite confidential and that you should neither quote it as your authority or show it to all and sundry. The original goes to the War Office and, I am told, is carefully read by the Sec.of State.

I am sorry to hear from you that Lipton[14] is so changed, for I remember you rather liked the man. Is Willie, notwithstanding this, still going to sail the boat? I can't help thinking from what we read about these Yankees that they are not real friends of England, but only pretend to be friendly when the situation requires it . . . .

## 2 September 1900. Machadodorp

I sent you a telegram the other day as I was not able to get a letter written and I found a telegraph office in Buller's Camp for private wires. This part of the country is very mountainous, but pretty. The railways run down a deep gorge; it is so steep that there is no road from here down to the low country except by a wide detour, and down terrible slopes. Our Cavalry has done very well: dismounting and running up these steep hills, miles in front of any Infantry support. We have had hard work with the transport over bad roads and steep hills. Buller is now close to Lydenburg, and we start for Carolina and Barberton tomorrow. Algy Lennox is now with us as an extra galloper. He is very cheery and pleasant, and anxious to do any odd job. I am glad Joe Laycock, Lord E. Talbot and the boy 'Guy' have been to see you. They will tell you I am very well.

172

## 17 September 1900. Barberton

I have an opportunity of sending back a letter by some Dutchman whom we have released from prison here; they had taken the oath of neutrality and been subsequently apprehended by the Boers and imprisoned here. The railway is not yet open and some of these men are going back to railhead (Godwaan) so I send this with one of them. Burleigh of the D.T. is the only correspondent who has been with us, so you will no doubt see a full account of our recent doings, more or less accurate probably. We left Carolina on Sunday 9th, had a fight that day for a high pass into Buffelspring. Tuesday 11th we crossed the Komatie river by the Natal road at Hlomehlom store. Wednesday 12th we had a fight for the 'Nelshoogte' pass about 15 miles N.E. of it. The enemy were strongly posted. Hills very high and steep. The road rises 500 feet in last 800 yards of the pass. We turned the enemy out however by sending the Cavalry about 4 a.m. to turn the place by a cattle track to the East, while we threatened the pass from the front with guns and Battalions of Infantry. If the Boers had any fight left in them they must have given us a heap of trouble there. But our coming this route quite took them by surprise. We said we were going to Ermelo and Standerton, meaning of course that the rumour should reach them and it has! For we find telegrams here to that effect. On Thursday morning the General with 4 regiments of Cavalry left the Nelshoogt pass and occupied this place. We could bring no guns or vehicles of any kind, but crossed the mountains by a bad footpath. We had to walk most of the way on foot in single file. We got here quite unexpectedly, the head man tells us 'Sunday at soonest' was the day we were expected. So we made a good haul, 44 engines alone! £10,000 from one man alone who was trying to escape (the landrost of Vreilhead), any amount of supplies, etc. etc. Our march was about 25 miles but by the road it would have been 40 miles. We left our waggons at the pass and working day and night they finished getting them up on Saturday forenoon. Three spans have to be put into each. This is a pretty country but quite a different climate to the veldt, being quite hot. I sent you a wire on the 15th.

## 19 September 1900. Barberton

We had a terrible country to pass thro' from Carolina here. It is amusing now to see how all the other columns which were (on the date we got here) exactly in the same position as when we left them. They are now hurrying on and jostling one another to reach Komatie Poort. As a matter of fact the Boers cleared from the low country which lies to the East of this, the moment we got in here, and those who have horses are moving back to the high veldt North of the railway. A few dismounted men were near

Komatie Poort ready to cross into Portugese Territory on the first shell being fired. I hope we won't go to the low country as Horse sickness is very bad there. We have now to feed the Infantry columns with our supplies from here. We gave Pole Carew[15] 5 days and today we are sending a week's supply for 5,000 men to Ian Hamilton in our trains which we captured here! Altogether we got over 105 engines – Crewe Station is not in it with our engine yard and siding here!! Fine heavy engines most of them are: from Orange Free State and Transvaal Mail services. We have plenty of food except for horses.

## 29 October 1900. Heidelberg

Since we left Machadodorp we have had a hard march and had a large number of casualties. What is wanted now is to form detachments all about the country to protect supplies so that moveable columns can sweep the country without having to take waggons with them.

One column by itself does no good. The Boers merely move out of the road until it has passed, sending out a few snipers to worry its flanks and rear. We leave this tomorrow for Pretoria and shall arrive there on Friday. I should think that the Cavalry Division must be broken up as a Division, and the regiments spread about with various columns and posts. There is now no enemy in formed bodies to be dealt with but merely a lot of brands of marauders numbering 30 to 200 men each. But as yet we know nothing of what Roberts' scheme may be! P.S. We have a good deal of rain now and the mackintosh comes in useful which you sent me last June.

## 30 October 1900. Springs

I sent you a telegram from here, because in your letter of 28th Sept. you said you had not had a letter from me for a week or two. Of course when one is on the march there is no means of posting letters! The Field Marshal came over here today and reviewed the remains of the Cavalry Division. We have 2 Brigades with us. 1575 horses exactly. Tomorrow we march towards Pretoria and should arrive there Saturday. The Cavalry Division is then to be broken up, but General French (and his Staff) is to go to Johannesburg to command the J'burg District. This appointment according to the Field Marshal will probably last about 3 months. I suppose Johannesburg is quite the best part of this country to stay in, so we can't complain. The poor Field Marshal was in very low spirits about his daughter, who has got enteric fever. He had intended going home in 10 days time, but has now decided to remain out here in consequence – probably for 6 weeks or longer till she is better. Prince Christian Victor[16] died of enteric as you will have heard. I'll be able to tell you all about the

mines around Johannesburg! By the way, I forgot to tell you that we
marked out a lot of claims on the Barberton gold fields! I don't know if
they will be valid, but Brinsley Fitzgerald did it for General French and
Staff: it did not cost anything really and might be worth a lot later on.
Yesterday morning we passed the Nigel gold mine. So you see we are in
the midst of your fancies . . . . This is just a line to let you know what we
are going to do. We have sent in to Pretoria today to select a house for us
to live in. It might be worth your while, being a restless 'old body' to take a
trip out to this county before I come home. I just mention this, so that
you may let me know in good time before you arrive. Houses are very dear
in J'burg, but of course we don't pay any rent yet!

## 14 November 1900. Natal line of Steamers. S.S. *Untalia*

I told you in my last letter that General French had been appointed to
command J'burg District. I expect he will have moved to J'burg by the
time I get back. The District is subdivided into smaller commands so that
there won't be a great deal of active work to be done by General French
and his staff. At present all is at a standstill waiting for Lord Roberts'
daughter to get well and his departure!! Lord Kitchener will then take up
the command and no doubt will quiet the Country very soon. Lord K.
lunched with us at Pretoria the day before I left. He said he would like to
go to India very much but was afraid that he would not be allowed to do
so as they wanted him at home.

Personally I have been quite fit strange to say. I suppose thanks to
plain fare and early hours on the veldt. I saw Lord Chesham in Pretoria.
He was in hospital with a bad throat. K. offered to put him in command
of all the Yeomanry. I fancy he will arrange to take the appointment.

## 18 November 1900. Mount Nelson Hotel, Cape Town

John Vaughan and I got here on Wednesday night but did not land till
Thursday morning. I sent you a letter by the mail which we just caught on
Wednesday night. We are leaving tonight for Johannesburg, having
enjoyed our few days here very much. We got phot'd and I have ordered 3
copies of each one to be sent to you, and one of each to Hugo. I also left a
Kruger plain sovereign to be engraved with 'a Merry Xmas' on it and sent
to you. I mention this so that you may know what it is! It is one of those
we got at Barbertong from the Landrost of Vrieheid, whom we captured
you will remember. I also sent you several others from Durban by
registered letter and '1900' stamped sovereigns. I see one of the Cape
Town papers says that 'seven of the oldest, if not the boldest of the
Generals sailed for England on Wednesday'. Poor old Brab is amongst
that lot. Pole Carew had his passage booked by that steamer but is waiting

till next week in order that the public may not associate his name with the oldies.

## 30 November 1900. Johannesburg

I sent you a line by John Vaughan last Saturday. Since then I have received your letter of Nov. 1st and a plum pudding!! So the Xmas dinner will be all right! I remember the last one was at Arundel, and your plum pudding was its main feature. Brinsley Fitzgerald left us on Wednesday and is to call and see you, so you should have full details regarding me and the surroundings from him and John Vaughan. The latter is to wire you from Madeira so that you may know when he arrives, and can arrange to see him if in London. This is a grand house on the top of a hill overlooking Johannesburg. Two bathrooms with hot and cold water, so that we are living in luxury now. I play polo 3 days a week. French is down the line towards Pehfstroom and my work is to look after the remainder of the District and see to their requirements. There is considerable excitement in the Orange River Colony, and we have just received orders to send some troops from here. So I have a certain amount of work to do. The post leaves here at noon today, and I have been interrupted by 4 or 5 people since I began this letter, so it is difficult to get off a coherent epistle to you. I see you mention an 'escape' I had from 16 Boers near Barberton. The officer with me was John Vaughan and an incident (not so terrifying as you imagine) happened near Carolina on our march to Barberton. John will tell you all about it, but we had not far to gallop as were just in front of our Outposts. But keep your mind easy now I am in quite a safe place!! The Field Marshal left here yesterday for Natal. Before leaving, he wired to War Office recommending me for a Cavalry Regiment. It is a good thing to command a regiment, but at present there is only the 11th Hussars without a C.O. The 11th are in Cairo on their way home, so it would suit me well to command them, except that it is rather expensive to command a corps like them I fancy. I sent you six spoons made of Kruger's money. The only thing made here are present!!

## 7 December 1900. Johannesburg

J.V. should reach S'hampton about Dec. 21st I think. So no doubt you will have seen him before this reaches you. There seems to be considerable alarm at Head Quarters and at Cape Town that De Wet and his friends are about to invade the Colony. We have sent a good many troops to the North of the Colony from here, and now the General and his Staff ordered South at once. We leave tomorrow morning for Bloemfontein. How long we are to be away I don't know, nor do we yet

nily group at Cameron House, Fife. The baby is Douglas Haig. John (with beard) and chel Haig are seated towards the left of the picture. Henrietta is the young girl sitting the ground to the right of Douglas. *Bemersyde*

uglas Haig, aged about three, clearly ious at having been photographed in a ss but allowed to carry his favourite tol. *Bemersyde*

3. Douglas aged about five. *Bemersyde*

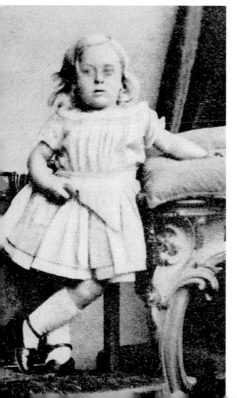

4. Haig's mother, Rachel Veitch. *Bemersyde*

5. Haig on his American visit in 1879 so
after leaving Clifton. *Bemersyde*

6. Bullingdon Club, Oxford, 1883. *Museum of Edinburgh*

Haig's Sandhurst intake forming a Square. It is surprising that this was still being taught in 1884. *Museum of Edinburgh*

Douglas and Henrietta Haig at Bad Schwalbach in 1887. *Bemersyde*

9. Lieutenant Douglas Haig, 7 Hussars. *Bemersyde*

10. 7 Hussars officers at Secunderabad c.1890. Haig, third row second from right has 'Stodger' Carew on his right. *Haig papers in The National Library of Scotland*

11. The Staff College course relaxing in 1896-7. *Haig collection at Museum of Edinburgh*

ield Marshal Sir Evelyn Wood
879. *National Portrait Gallery*

13. John French as Colonel of 19 Hussars,
1912. *Museum of Edinburgh*

Iaig with the Egyptian Cavalry after the Battle of Omdurman.
*Museum of Edinburgh*

RANK DADD, R.I.
FROM A SKETCH BY OUR SPECIAL ARTIST, W

ay to Omdurman during a patrol from the camp, Captain Haig, with some troopers of the Egyptian cavalry, came in touch with two bodies of Baggara cavalry. The latter retired without firing
up bustires as a warning to the Dervishes in the rear of our advance

15. Haig rescuing anEgyptian NCO at the Atbara. The drawing was commissioned by officers of the 7 Hussars and was taken from an illustration in the Graphic magazine.
*Museum of Edinburgh*

16. One of the two Dervish 'jub-bas' at Bemersyde. Haig thought they came 'out of Mahmoud's wardrobe'.
*Countess Haig*

17. Arthur Blair, KOSB, as BGS in Egypt in 1918.
*Imperial War Museum*

Cavalry Division Officers at Geluk in the Transvaal in August 1900. L to R: Lieutenant Colonel the Hon. Cecil Bingham, Colonel Lord Algernon Gordon-Lennox, Lieutenant Colonel Douglas Haig and Captain Brinsley Fitzgerald. *Museum of Edinburgh*

'A General Group', South African War. L to R: Colonel Plumer, General Hunter, General MacDonald, General Buller, General Baden-Powell, Lord Roberts (seated), General Dundonald, Lord Kitchener, General Pole-Carew, Sir George White (seated), General French (seated), Sir Frederick Carrington.
*Haig papers in The National Library of Scotland*

20. 17 Lancers' Polo team, winners of the Inter-Regimental Tournament 1903.
    *Haig collection at Museum of Edinburgh*

21. General Haig's sitting room in Simla, with furniture from Princes Gate.
    *National Library of Scotland*

2. General Haig's gharry with one of Headquarters' staff, Captain MacAndrew.
*Haig papers in The National Library of Scotland*

3. General Haig's railway carriage. He used this carriage for travelling all over India, both as Inspector General of Cavalry and Chief of Staff.
*Haig papers in The National Library of Scotland*

24. Secrettwith Haig's favourite 'Waler' mare, India c. 1904.
*Haig papers in The National Library of Scotland*

25. The Kadir Cup, Meerut, March 1905. A line of elephants, used as beaters.
*Haig papers in The National Library of Scotland*

26. Douglas Haig and Dorothy Vivian married in the private chapel at Buckingham Palace on 11 July 1905. The bride and groom are shown here with Queen Alexandra.

27. Haig's friend, General Sir Pratap Singh c. 1914. *Museum of Edinburgh*

28. Vice-Regal Lodge, Simla.

29. Amateur theatricals at Vice-Regal Lodge. Lady Eileen Elliot (Viceroy's
    daughter) and Lord Francis Scott (ADC) in The Truth by Clyde Fitch.
    *Tweedie Collection*

30. Lord and Lady Minto, Viceroy and Vicereine 1905 - 1910, in Calcutta. Lady Eileen Elliot, their daughter, and Lord Francis Scott, their future son-in-law (back row on right), are in the picture with members of the staff. The Mintos always had Dandy Dinmont dogs. *Tweedie Collection*

31. Lord Hardinge of Penshurst, Viceroy of India 1910 - 1916.

32. Haig with King George V in Aldershot, 1912. *Haig collection at Museum of Edinburgh*

33. The visit of King George V and Queen Mary to Aldershot in 1912. The group was photographed at the Royal Pavilion. *Haig collection at Museum of Edinburgh*

34. Aldershot 1912. L to R: Prince Alexander of Teck (the Earl of Athlone),
Douglas Haig, a Siamese prince. Aircraft of the RFC in the background.
*Haig collection at Museum of Edinburgh*

35. Haig and his staff at Aldershot c. 1913. Baird, Charteris and Haig himself
were described as the 'Hindoo invasion' when they arrived in 1912. Haig
had served many years in India; Baird and Charteris were both Indian Army
officers. Robb was i/c Administration; Davies was BGS. Photograph from
*Field Marshal Haig* by Brigadier General Charteris published by Cassell
in 1929

CAPTAIN BAIRD,   GENERAL ROBB,   SIR DOUGLAS HAIG,   GENERAL DAVIES,   CAPTAIN CHARTERIS

36. Dorothy (Doris)
    Haig c. 1912.
    *Bemersyde*

37. Haig's two eldest
    daughters, Doria
    and Xandra in
    1914. *Bemersyde*

know what the General is really to command when he does get South. We are keeping on this house, and leaving most of our belongings here with one Staff Officer to look after ordinary details. With De Wet in the S.E. corner of the Free State and the Orange and Caledon rivers in flood, I think he ought to be caught at last. Moreover, there seems to me little fear of a rising in the Colony even if he did get onto it. Last year when the situation there was much more favourable for a rising the Dutch kept quiet. Why then should they rise now/ the climate here is rather pleasant at present, though it rains every other night very heavily. The mornings are bright and fresh. We have pretty well cleared this district of inhabitants, and carried off most of the supplies, but there are still in parts mealies and forage hidden. So the idea is ridiculous to think that the Boers can be starved into submission when they have such a vast area from which they can draw supplies of a kind. This will reach you about New Year so I wish you and Willie a very Happy one and best of Good Fortune in 1901. P.S. This is not much of a letter, but so many people come in and out, and wires by the score at a time, that one has not a chance of collecting one's thoughts about one's own affairs. I hear that the 11th Hussars have been given to an officer in the regiment.

## 14 December 1900. Johannesburg

I told you last week how busy we had been sending troops to O.R. Colony and that we had a special ready to take General and Staff right away to Stormberg in Cape Colony. As you will know by this time De Wet was headed off. Now an ass of a General called Clements gets a hiding and loses some of our best officers (including Capt. Macbean whom Jenty knows) some 20 miles north of Krugersdorp. He is not exactly under General French, but when he comes to Krugersdorp he is, and he gets his supplies from there – that place being in this District. Now we hear that he has retired North towards Rustenberg and that the Boers are coming to attack Krugersdorp which is now uncovered. So we have to give up the system on which the General has been acting for clearing this District and concentrate the few troops now available (they are few owing to the Cape Colony excitement) for the defence of Krugersdorp. I am rather busy in consequence and telegrams are flying about in the most profuse manner! So I am sorry that this epistle is not better put together. I note what you say regarding Evelyn Wood. Of course it is a necessary thing to command a regiment and I should like to do so if I was given command of a good one in a good station. French is only too anxious to help me on, but I think in remaining on as his Chief Staff Officer I did the best for the Cavalry Division, for him and for myself. One did not foresee this war lasting so long, otherwise I might have taken some scallywag corps or

other! So don't make a fuss about my being now in the position as I
started in! Recollect also many have gone lower down! And as to rewards,
if you only knew what duffers will get and do get H.M.'s decorations and
are promoted, you would realize how little I value them. Everything
comes in time, and decorations come in abundance with declining years
and imbecility! No one yet on this staff, unfortunately, has got a
decoration of any kind, otherwise we might have achieved disaster like the
other decores!!

## 18 December 1900. Johannesburg

I am writing to you today because we are off this afternoon on the trek
again, and I may not have a chance of writing by this next mail if I delay.
You will have read of Clements defeat before this reaches you. He seems
to have allowed himself to be surprised in the early morning. The District
which he commanded has now been added to French's command. You
will see from my letter to Hugo what a very large district is now under
him. We go by train this afternoon to Krugersdorp and then march
towards Rustenberg to clear the country in that Direction. French was at
Pretoria yesterday and from what he tells me I gather that Kitchener is
not in the best of spirits about the outlook. Chesham is here having been
appointed Imp. General of Yeomanry in South Africa. I picked him a
fine house about half a mile from here. He seems quite fit again and full
of keenness about his yeomen. Most of the troops are rather stale, having
been so continuously employed for so many months. But notwithstanding
this, every day shows a little progress and brings us nearer the end. Now
goodbye, I won't forget to telegraph to you about Jan 8th regarding the
situation here at that date.

## 26 December 1900. Johannesburg

Your letter of Nov. 29th reached me last night. I also got your wire
addressed to General French and sent off on 14th Dec. saying that you
will be ready to start on Jan 26th. I am afraid that the country is so
disturbed that I shall have to wire to ask you to delay. We are starting off
again today to conduct some operations against Vendersdun. They should
be over by Sunday and I can see what the situation is like then. We
captured a Commandant Krause the other day – a very superior man and
evidently quite in the inner councils of the Boers. He says they are all
'waiting' for something to happen, and if it does not take place, then the
whole opposition may collapse at once all round. I presume the Boers
were placing their hopes on a rising in the Colony. This has quite failed;
in fact the Colonial Boers won't have any dealings with the 1600 who
entered the Colony and are now near Britstown (West of De Aar). We

178

had a cheery Xmas dinner last night. Excellent plum pudding thank you. And I drank your health. We are starting in a short time so I must be off now.

## Notes

1. Brigadier General Thomas Cole Porter was born in 1851 and commissioned into the 6 Dragoon Guards in 1873. He was one of the three brigade commanders in the Cavalry Division in South Africa, the others being Broadwood and Gordon. He went onto half-pay in 1901 and retired in 1904. He died in 1938.
2. Brigadier General Frederick William Nicholas McCracken CB, DSO, was born in 1859, commissioned into the Berkshire Regiment in 1879, and served in the West Indies and India as well as South Africa. Commanded 7 Brigade in 1912.
3. Major General Sir Francis John William Eustace KCB, born 1849, commissioned into the Royal Artillery 1870, major general. 1904, retired 1909.
4. General Sir Charles Warren GCMG, KCB, born 1840, commissioned into the Royal Engineers in 1857, commanded the 5th Division in South Africa, retired in 1905. He died in 1927.
5. Colonel Charles James Long born 1849, commissioned into the Royal Artillery in 1870, retired 1906.
6. General Piet Arnoldus Cronje (1840?–1911) made his reputation in the First Boer War when he was responsible for the failure of the Jameson Raid in 1893. In the Second Boer War he besieged Kimberley and Mafeking and was defeated by Roberts at Paardeberg, where he surrendered with some 4,000 of his troops. He was imprisoned on St Helena until peace was declared in 1902.
7. Colonel Charles Gore Hay 20th Earl of Erroll KT, CB, (1852–1927) commissioned into the Royal Horse Guards in 1869, retired in 1907.
8. Colonel Edmund Bernard Talbot 1st Viscount FitzAlan of Derwent KG, GCVO, DSO (1855–1947) was the second son of the 14th Duke of Norfolk. He was Member of Parliament for Chichester 1894–1921 and was private, then assistant, secretary to the Secretary of State for War 1896–1903. He held a number of other junior government posts before becoming Lord Lieutenant of Ireland in 1921–22. He commanded the 11 Hussars in the Second Boer War.
9. Henry 15th Duke of Norfolk KG, GCVO (1847–1917), Edmund Talbot's elder brother. He was a lieutenant colonel and honorary colonel 4th Battalion Royal Sussex Regiment for forty-two years, retiring in 1913. He must have been easily the oldest subaltern in South Africa!
10. Colonel the Hon. Albert Brassey (1844–1918) was Colonel of Queen's Own Oxfordshire Hussars, having previously been a lieutenant in the 14 Hussars.
11. Leopold Guy Francis Maynard 6th Earl of Warwick CMG, MVO

179

(1882–1943) was a captain in the Life Guards. He became ADC to Viscount Milner 1901–2. He was an honorary lieutenant colonel in the Territorial Artillery Regiment.

12. Lieutenant General Sir Edward Thomas Henry Hutton KCB, KCMG, born 1848, commissioned into the King's Royal Rifle Corps in 1867, became the first C.-in-C. of the Australian Army after Federation in 1901. He was responsible for the selection of the famous Rising Sun badge used by the Australian Imperial Forces in both World Wars and is still used today. The Gordon mentioned in the letter to Sir Lonsdale Hale (2 March 1900) was Hutton's close friend Brigadier General Joseph Maria Gordon CB, who became Chief of the General Staff of the new Australian Army. He gave Hutton the 'Trophy of Arms', consisting of swords and bayonets arranged in a semi-circle around the Crown, which inspired the Rising Sun badge. Hutton died in 1923.

13. 'Old Stodger' was Major G.A.L. Carew, one of the 7 Hussars polo team. See Chapter 2 note 2.

14. Sir Thomas Lipton (1850–1931) ran away to America, stowing away on a ship aged fourteen. Having been a grocery clerk in New York he opened a grocery store in his native Glasgow. This soon expanded into a major grocery business, with one of their strongest lines being teabags, invented by Lipton. The connection with Willie and Henrietta Jameson was that Willie, the largest shareholder in the Jameson whiskey business, backed Lipton's bid to win the America's Cup. Willie was in charge of sailing *Shamrock* and the row with Lipton was the latter's assertion that Willie had had too many women and non-effective people on the yacht, as a result of which he lost the crucial race.

15. Lieutenant General Sir Reginald Pole-Carew (1849–1924) was commissioned into the Coldstream Guards in 1869. He became a major general in 1899. In South Africa he commanded firstly the 9 Brigade, which had a difficult time at the Modder River Battle, then the 11th Division. His main achievement was, with General Tucker, the capture of Komati Port, forcing some 3,000 Boers to take refuge in Mozambique. He became Member of Parliament for Bodmin from 1910–16.

16. HRH Prince Christian Victor GCB, GCVO, (1860–1900) was Queen Victoria's grandson through her daughter Princess Helena, and brother to Princess Marie Louise, who Haig met in Berlin.. He was commissioned into the KRRC in 1888 and was a major from 1896. He served in Sudan in 1898 and had come out to South Africa in 1899.

# Chapter 7

# South Africa

## 1901 – 1902

By early 1901 Field Marshal Lord Roberts, having decided that the war was 'practically over', had returned home to take over from Lord Wolseley at the War Office as Commander-in-Chief. Kitchener, his successor as Commander-in-Chief in South Africa, was faced with mopping up the remnants of the Boer Armies. This turned out to be a mammoth task as Boer Commandoes carried out hit and run attacks throughout South Africa. They continued to be considerably more mobile than the British and succeeded time after time in eluding the British Columns attempting to round them up.

Kitchener's response in this guerrilla war, conducted over an enormous area was to build a network of blockhouses, manned with troops, within rifle shot of each other and linked by barbed wire. Eventually there were some 8,000 blockhouses made from corrugated steel sheets and concrete. Their garrisons were alternately British troops and Blacks, known to the Army as the 'Black Watch'. Woe betide any British troops going near the 'Black Watch' blockhouses at night. Their garrisons loosed off at the least sound and movement and no doubt many unsuspecting animals were as a result slaughtered!

The network of blockhouses was used in conjunction with a policy of burning Boer farms and removing the women and children into what history has called 'concentration camps', where there was much death from disease and much suffering. Britain's reputation also suffered, with considerable justification. It was one thing for the camps to be created, but quite another that many of them were appallingly badly run. Nearly 154,000 Boer and African women and children were sent to the camps. Of these over 32,000 died from disease; typhoid and measles being the most common causes.

The logic behind Kitchener's ruthless policy was that, before the blockhouse policy started, the Army had been reducing the number of Boers in the Commandoes by 1,000 or so a month. As the estimate of the number of Boers still under arms in early 1901 was about 20,000, it would take twenty months or so to finish the war. Kitchener's aim was to reduce this time quite considerably, but actually it took eighteen more months, from January 1901 to June 1902, to finish the war even with the blockhouses, scorched earth and concentration camps. The army had increased in size to some 250,000 men by 1901, with the British government becoming increasingly anxious about the enormous cost.

By early 1901 the Cavalry Division had been split up and Douglas Haig had an independent command of three mobile columns, rising to six, with as many as seven reporting to him for particular operations, with the task of rounding up any Boer Commandoes in the north-west of Cape Colony. In addition he was appointed to command the 17th Lancers. A newspaper comment of the time reads as follows:

> The selection of Lieut. Colonel Haig, 7th Hussars, for the command of the 17th Lancers, became almost a foregone conclusion directly the decision was come to that the promotion should be given outside. Colonel Haig not only has done admirably in South Africa, but had established a reputation before he left England. Sir John French has a high opinion of him, and so, too, has Sir George Luck, and he has fully justified the confidence of these two cavalry leaders by his performance during the war. Colonel Haig has not been particularly fortunate for one of his standing and experience, but doubtless he will now make the headway he deserves to make, for the pushing on of men of his stamp is in every way advantageous to the Service.

The above news-cutting is included in the Haig papers in the National Library of Scotland, but the name of the publication which carried it has been lost. It is interesting that the writer had noted that Douglas Haig's career had progressed only slowly despite the high regard of all under whom or with whom he had served. He had been promoted to brevet major (carrying the rank, but paid as a captain!) at the end of the Sudan Campaign, on Kitchener's recommendation. At this stage, in 1898, he was aged thirty-seven. He was a lieutenant colonel in 1901, having been appointed to command the 17th Lancers, by which time he was forty – hardly very fast advancement. As will be seen below the breakthrough came with his appointment as Inspector

General of Cavalry in India with the rank of major general in 1903, when he was forty-two and was said to be the youngest major general in the British Army at that date. His promotions came as the result of his performance on the battlefield, firstly in the Sudan and then in South Africa. In 1899 he was a major; in 1903 he was a (local) major general in India. The following extracts from letters show him thoroughly stimulated by the task of chasing and cornering the remaining Boer Commandoes, particularly Smuts's. He had the opportunity to go home with French in January 1902; French intending that Haig would command a Cavalry Brigade at Aldershot. He declined and was determined to see the South African War out to the end. In any case he wanted to be an effective, full time commander of the 17th Lancers rather than a part time one combining his appointment with responsibility for clearing the Boers out of a very large tract of the Cape Colony's area.

**Extracts from letters to Henrietta.**
**20 January 1901. Willowmore, Cape. Colony**

I have been so much on the move since the beginning of the year that I think I have only sent you one letter. We are having a tremendous hunt after these wretches – there are about 6 or 700 of them at the outside, but each one has two and some three horses. Lord Kitchener is evidently afraid of a rising, but from all I see, the well to-do Dutch farmers quite realize they have everything to lose by a rising. On the other hand, they assist the enemy with food and information, and do their best to put us off the track by sending in false news. However, we are beginning to know the Boer and his ways, and have so far managed not to be misled. I thought we had the Boers caught in the mountains near Bethesda (North of Graaf Reinet) on Sunday the 6th, but owing to one individual waiting for his waggons instead of pushing on to the posts ordered by me, the enemy was allowed to slip away thro' the hills across the front of his advanced Squadrons. I'll send you a copy of my report on the operations. This letter is merely to let you know generally what I have been doing. When the enemy slipped away, I sent Grenfell[1] with some Brabant's Horse to stick as close as he could to him, and with Byng[2] and South African Lt. Horse, moved to head him at Murraysburg. These two columns arrived in Murraysburg when the Boers were just 2 miles off the place, but on the other side of a mountain. The enemy at once separated into small detachments and reunited two days later. I have now got another Column up (Col. Williams) with about 400 M.I. and 2 guns. The Boers spread all kinds of rumours of their intentions; they were going to Aberdeen, to Nelspoort on railway (N. of Beaufort West) and 500 were said to be near Richmond. From my own scouts and spies I thought the enemy would make for this place; so I struck west from Murraysburg to avoid a nasty Nek at which I heard the Boers had prepared a surprise for us, then turned south and actually got to within 4 miles of them last Tuesday night. Since then we raced them South and got in here on Friday. Over 130 miles in 4 days. The town guard took us for the Boers and opened fire on our advanced troops. I thought the men moving up the hills did not look like Boers so I ordered 2 shots from our guns to be fired towards a flank – The enemy have no guns, so the local guard was encouraged and sent out a man to see who we were. Yesterday we got all the horses we could and I was able to continue the pursuit with Williams' Column by midday: he had not one man left dismounted – This is very satisfactory. We are getting into a very mountainous country, much like the mountains North of Graaf Reinet. It seems to me a most fortunate thing that the Colony did not rise last year, for we come across many passes in which 20 determined men could defy 2,000. The 7th D.G. with 2 guns R.H.A are also under my command. When I saw Boers moving south I sent them by rail to Prince Albert and thence to Klaarstroom to block the Meirings Pass – a defile 10 miles long N.E. of Oudshoorn while I have another Column on the East near Steytlersville to flank the enemy as it were; much in the way you drive the partridges! I have the sea as stop or guns in front, and with positions East and West held, and a column in close pursuit from the North, I think we ought to arrive at some conclusion in a fortnight. This is quite a big business to have in hand, and I came from Johannesburg without any staff at all, but have been most fortunate in picking up fellows to assist. If you will look at the map you will see the great area over which troops under my control are operating. The question of feeding and keeping in communication with the several parts of the column is at times difficult, while, at the same time, I have had to assist in the administration of the districts thro' which I passed. All the magistrates nearly are disloyal and ¾ of the population; indeed I may say all farmers are Dutch. However, I enjoy myself very well. This is a nice change to have a show of one's own. All, too, with whom I have dealings in a military way assist me to the utmost. Old Inigo Jones[3] is General at Naauwpoort and Settle at Beaufort West, and then I have dealings with Supply people at Port Elizabeth and Cape Town. So you see at last I have got quite a nice command, much more interesting than a Cavalry Brigade because I can get no orders from anyone but merely move as I think best in pursuit of the enemy. I have also to report to the C. in C. at Pretoria direct, to General Hunter at Bloemfontein and to Cape Town as well as to the 2 Generals named above. I have a spare moment today as the main telegraph wire is cut, and

I am using the railway line telephone. So in order not to delay trains I have limited the hours for transmitting messages.

## Wire from Lord Kitchener to Col. Haig. Klipplaat. Clear the line. Feb. 8

You seem to be getting at them well stop A little more and they will be done stop Tell all troops under your command I am very pleased at their exertions and hope they will soon finish with raiders.

*Extracts from letters to Henrietta:*

## 10 March 1901. Edenburg. O.R.C.

I arrived here on the afternoon of the 8th. I send copy of my report to General Lyttelton since leaving Victoria West until I crossed the Orange River at Norvals Pont. Since then I have been to Phillippolis and away N.W. towards Luckhoff then back in this direction passing South of Fauresmith and Jagersfontein. The latter is a diamond mine! We ought to have quite smashed up De Wet's force had my column been detrained all at Colesberg, instead of only part there and 2/3rds at Hanover Road. The intention uppermost in Lyttleton's mind seems to have been to prevent him getting South into the Colony again. However we have picked up a certain number of prisoners who all say that the worst thing De Wet ever did was to enter Cape Colony, so I don't expect that he will try it again for some time. They crossed the Orange River in a regular panic. The water was breast deep and they crossed at a place where there is no regular drift but a good hard bottom (an easy bank on the landing side). They led their horses across, 20 of them were drowned crossing. While the crossing was going on a small patrol of a dozen men (Nesbit's Horse) came up and fired for all they were worth. The Boers left their clothes and half cooked food and made for the other bank. Several arrived at Phillippolis with not even a shirt on! I saw the old Dutch Parson there by name Fraser. His father from Inverness (sent out in 1838) and he was educated there, with a very Scotch wife. I left the old parties your papers all about the Queen's death. They had not seen a paper for months, and were immensely pleased and sent me all kinds of fruits and milk etc. Fraser is Steyn's father in-law. Steyn had passed thro' just the day before I got there and is apparently as convinced as ever that we will get tired of the war and give them back their country. The Free State is looking quite pretty at this season – all green after the rain and plenty of fine fruit, grapes, peaches etc. growing in the deserted farms. I don't know where I'll go next. They seem to have allowed Kritzinger to get back South again since I left off hunting him!

## 20 March 1901. Thabanchu

The Orange River Colony has been divided into 4 districts. I am in Lyttleton's command which extends from this (Thabanchu) line to the Orange River. He has also General Bruce Hamilton and Colonel Hickman. I have more troops however under my command than any of them, having 3 columns under me in all 2,700 men while B. Hamilton, tho' a general has only some 2,300 and Hickman has only 850. so they have done me well. I would rather be in this part of the Colony too than north of Bloemfontein. Lyttelton too is a nice fellow to work with. Bennet Burleigh turned up today. I last saw him at Barberton in September when he and all said the War was over! He is still confident that the Boers cannot go much longer. We have had a good deal of rain lately and this weather is colder than this time last year. By the way I must tell you about the fate of the fur lining which you bought me at Wiesbaden or Schwalbach before I came out here. You will remember, I told you that I had it changed into a short Khakee coloured jacket (made in Cape Town) which I carried on my saddle. Well, the other day near Luckhoff I wanted to send a sort of intelligence agent or spy with a message to the railway – A man Distin by name. There were a good many Boers about so he wanted some kind of khakee coloured jacket uniform in case he were captured. He was afraid that if caught in plain clothes he would be shot. Well, the only spare coat I had with me was this fur jacket which I gave him. Yesterday I had a telegram from Kimberley to say that he had arrived there safely but had been stripped of everything by the Boers including the old coat! The coat at any rate had served its turn. We march towards Bloemfontein tomorrow.

## 23 March 1901. Camp 3 miles east of Bloemfontein

We arrived here yesterday afternoon. General Lyttelton came out to see we were all right here yesterday afternoon. He is a very nice fellow to work with. He thinks of giving me one side of the railway to clear, and General Hamilton the other. My part would then be bounded on the North by a line Bloemfontein-Petersburg to the Kimberley railway, on South by the Orange river and East by the Norval's Pont – Bloemfontein railway. Quite a big country! Before clearing the country (which is unpleasant work) we must first hunt down any odd commandos in the District and also take steps to prevent any other fellow like De Wet breaking South into the Colony. During the last week my columns have been driven on over 120,000 head of stock! Some grand cattle! They would look fine in your domain! I have a couple of beautiful cows which come along with the Camp now for my own use. So we are well supplied with milk when moving slowly. I am keeping very fit thank you – getting 'stout and heavy' like the rest of the family! You ask about Miles (soldier servant). I think he is very well indeed. He spent Xmas Day in jail at Johannesburg. He was caught by the picquet out in the streets after 9 p.m. more or less drunk with some other men, so I left him in the jail for his Xmas dinner. This did him a lot of good, for he knows that if he misbehaves he will be sent to some regiment here and left on the country. I have two other excellent men, one a 16th Lancer and another (my orderly[4]) from 8th Hussars so I am quite independent of Miles. We have had very wet weather for last week.

### 3 April 1901. Near Bethulie on Caledon River

We had scarcely got to Bloemfontein when word came that our old friend Kritzinger was trying to cross the Orange. So off we marched at once to Smithfield and Comminie Bridge over the Caledon, and now I am covering a front about 40 miles with my commando and am ready to follow him should he come our way. We are gradually clearing the country so that in 2 months time I expect the Boers won't have much to live upon in the district. The weather has been very wet, but is now gradually getting colder so I hope the rainy season will soon be past.

### 11 April 1901. Naauwpoort. C.C.

Since writing to you I got an urgent order on the 7th April when East of Smithfield O.R.C. to go to Cape Colony at once to take command of certain columns. So I left for Edenburg at once and arrived there yesterday morning and came on here by train arriving about midnight last night. I got a telegram on arrival here from Lord K. telling me to 'take command of all columns now operating in the Midland area of Cape Colony. Act vigorously with the object of clearing Cape Colony of the enemy as soon as possible'. He also told me to 'Consult with General Jones and Settle'.[5] – Old Inigo Bones is the man meant. He is here and has been here for the last 5 or 6 months living in a railway carriage. He is a nice old man and feels quite sure that 'things will be all right once General Settle is sent back to De Aar'. I am practically relieving Settle who is at Graaf Reinet and seems to have commanded merely by writing long telegrams. Old Jones can't give me much information as to where the parts of my army are, or what they consist of! So I am off at once to Graaf Reinet to see Settle. Since I went to Victoria West with my columns to be ready to hunt De Wet, those left to hunt Kritzinger have

187

pretty well let him and his commandos do as they like! The moment an officer commanding a column gets a correspondent and half a day ahead of another column, he seems to feel quite satisfied and forgets about the enemy. So you see the evil of correspondents and the value of the rubbish which is published in the papers. It is more difficult hunting Boers in this Colony when all farmers are secretly their friends, and the Government almost seems to assist the invader, than in the Free State when one can treat everyone as an enemy. However it is very satisfactory to be again chosen for this job when things have got into a mess. I was very sorry to leave my old columns as we all got on very well and I knew what each commander could do best. I must be off now to lunch with your dear old friend 'Bones' and take the train for Graaf Reinet.

## 19 April 1901. Graaf Reinet C.C.

I sent you a line from Nauuwpoort and also a telegram on my way here. I also wired you today to tell you that the wine etc. had reached me, and that 'everything is excellent'. The champagne, claret and port could not be better and all are much appreciated. Please see that it is all charged to me! My mess consists of myself and 2 others, but in as much as I am in command and invite people to dinner at my mess, I of course like to pay more of the expenses. I like the change of work down here to what I had in the Orange River Colony – there we merely cleared farms and made raids on them at night. But here, the situation is different. Some people say it is the most difficult operation of the War and causes a certain amount of anxiety. You will remember how I was called away last February from hunting Kritzinger, Scheepers[6] and Malan[7] and held in readiness to hunt De Wet should he turn towards Cape Town. Since then Kritzinger seems to have been allowed to run loose, while Malan has wrecked trains just as he liked! Now the local farmers have begun to join in and the situation is much more serious than when I was here before. Added to this there were some Yeomanry captured near Aberdeen which has greatly elated the Boer party. Some of the troops too in this part are not quite the thing. I have quite an Army at present, and I expect the quality of it will soon be improved because I have told Lord K. some are only fit for clearing farms. He wires me that he will do his best to send me good men. At present I have 5 columns[8]

Gorringe

Crewe

Henniker

Scobell

Cape Md. Rifles

and they are sending me the Tasmanian Contingent and some Victorians so I should have quite a menagerie. I am off to Pearston tomorrow and so to Cradock. It is late now and I start at daybreak. You would be surprised at the number of telegrams I receive and send daily! P.S. General Lyttleton goes home on Saturday for 3 months leave and then comes out again to command in Chief. So I suppose Lord K. hopes to get away home by August.

## 4 May 1901. Cradock. Cape Colony

I am very glad indeed to hear that Hugo is so well. He seems to be having great times making Wills! There will soon be quite a library of them. I think I last wrote you from Graaf Reinet. I left there on 20th April and came by Pearston and over the mountains here. I arrived here on 25th. Since then I have been out westwards seeing the Commanders of the other columns in order to ensure combined action against the Commandos. I have 4 columns in this part commanded by Heneker, Scobell, Lukin,[9] and MacAndrew besides some Tasmanians who have recently arrived. In addition to these I have Crewe's and Gorringe's columns between Steynsburg and the Orange River. So you see my operations cover a wide area. My orders are 'to command all columns operating in the Midland District' so that I have a pretty free hand, and report to Lord. K. direct. The latter has at last arranged that all rebels are to be tried by military courts instead of by the courts of this Colony which consist of rebels at heart really. This will have a good effect. My chief difficulty now is to find horses for the 6 columns under my command independently of the Remount Department. This is a difficult matter as the country has been pretty well cleared already. So I have people all over the Colony commandeering what horses they can find. Last Sunday I had all the horses in this town paraded and we got over 70. I am having the inmates of each farm house registered and a ticket pasted on the front door giving a description of each man. Then our patrols pay surprise visits at night and arrest anyone not on the list and note the absentees as rebels. We have already caught several (5) in this way although I have only been at it about a fortnight. I have also arranged that no house is to have more than a month's supply of food for its inmates, calculated at the rates allowed to refugee camps. This will cut the supplies of the commandos. Some of the Colonial (South African) Corps have required weeding out. Many men did not care to be shot at, and instead of pushing on, were satisfied at shooting off their rifles at 2,000 yds. This sort of thing will never end the War, so I have got quit of a good many, both officers and men. Besides all thro' I have been asked to reorganize the Intelligence Services in this Country by the Director of Military

Intelligence, and am now busy with it. So you see I have a good many things to think about and arrange at present. But the time passes quickly and pleasantly, though of course there are anxious moments, and the loyal people in the colony get the funks the moment a Boer appears. The new General at Cape Town too keeps writing to let me know how few troops he has South of Somerset East and Aberdeen! The climate is very fine at present; cold frosty nights and bright sun by day.

I have a nice fellow as orderly, but unfortunately he has fever and I had to leave him at Graaf Reinet in hospital. His name is Secrett, 8th Hussars.

## 10 June 1901. Middleburg (Cape)

A considerable number of the enemy crossed into the colony and so I have been moving about a good deal and not able to write to you last mail – at least I found I had missed it when I got near the line. I have managed to drive the Boers back into the corner near Lady Grey, away to the N.E. of the Colony. Lord K. reinforced me with a good many troops, and now General French has been sent to command all the troops in Cape Colony but I practically have the same command as before. You seem to be having a busy time assisting Hugo to make his will! It almost seems to me to be an advantage not to possess these properties if the disposal of them at death is a matter of such difficulty. I am very sorry to hear such a bad account of the new yacht, but possibly with practice, and getting to know the boat she may turn out better than at first trial. I see too the American boat is equally unfortunate in the matter of breaking spars. I have the 17th Lancers in my command now. I only saw them for a day but there seem to be a lot of nice young fellows. I was quite fortunate in my first operation with them, as they caught 22 prisoners 3 nights ago!

## 16 June 1901. Stormberg. Cape Colony

We have given Kritzinger and those with him a real good hustling. It is now 3 weeks since they left the Zuurberg 1,500 strong. Kritzinger has now only 250 men with him; and another 200 are under a Commandant separated from Kritzinger; all their horses are much done up and many of the Boers are on foot. We chased the enemy from the Zuurberg nearly to Tarkastad and Queenstown then away N.E. past Jamestown. They entered the latter town as the guard was asleep on one hill, possibly by design! At any rate the Boers were able to cut the wire entanglement round the Fort and shot four of the town guard when slumbering! The garrison merely consisted of local celebrities, the head storekeeper being commandant. The Boers fired on the fat fellow in his trench for half an hour, his old fat wife looking on and imploring him to surrender, which

190

he at once did. From Jamestown (which is really only a village of 10 houses and 3 stores) the Boers were driven East to Lady Grey and Barkley East narrowly escaping Cape Town one night. Then doubling back thro' our columns, they came back S.W. some scattering towards Maraisberg and others being still East of the Moltens line. I hear the authorities at Pretoria are quite pleased with the way events are going and think October should see all more or less settled.

## 1 July 1901. Steynsburg

I took over command of the 17th Lancers last Thursday as I thought it best to identify myself with the regiment as soon as possible having been appointed their Commanding Officer. I have them here with me, and find I can easily look after the regiment in addition to directing the other columns. I know the country so well now that it does not bother me much to make up my mind where to send the latter to hunt the enemy. Besides I am giving the squadron commanders a chance of having a little show occasionally on their own account. There is nothing so good as responsibility for making good officers. So I have one squadron and Head Quarters of the regiment here, and keep 2 squadrons out on the trek. I hope thus to be able to give officers, men and horses occasional rest which does them all good. Today we have a little race meeting here, and we played polo 2 days last week. Meantime Van Reenen's[10] commando is being hunted up this way so that my commando will be able to go for him fresh and fit and keen instead of being stale like many of the troops are now. I have hired a little house here for those of the officers who are here to mess in when they come off the trek. I have still my own mess and a separate house, for, of course, I have to move about a good deal to supervise the operations of my other commandos. I have two other officers with me in my mess Farquhar[11] (whom I have already told you about) and Captain Legard[12] 17th Lancers my signalling officer – and I expect Greenly[13] 12th Lancers to arrive in a day or two as my chief Staff Officer. He is now at Durban waiting for a steamer to East London. I enclose a copy of my despatch and enclose the receipt now.

## 28 July 1901. Steynsburg. Cape Colony

Many thanks for the 'Subaltern's letters to his wife'. I believe it is written by Rankin's brother (7th Hrs.). He seems clever and a good observer, but my eye just caught that passage about scallywag troops (I think he calls them irregulars) versus regular soldiers, and I think he knows nothing about either! As I think I told you Brabant's Horse (or Brabandetti as I call them) and several other corps of Colonial fame have been in my commando so that I know a great deal about these rascally bandits. All they enlist for is 5/ – a day and they are much annoyed if one makes them go out to fight. Few of them really fight! They are expensive luxuries too to keep up. Since French took over the direction of affairs in the North of the Colony, K. has reinforced him with lots of troops including 4 Cavalry regiments. The 10th, 12th and 5th Lancers arrived during the last week. So that we ought soon to make an impression on this vast country. French came to see me for an hour the other day, and then away again in a hurry by train towards De Aar. Kitchener came to see me at Middleburg, evidently fearing that De Wet and other celebrities were about to visit us here again. I think always that it is a pity they don't let them come, and then we could get behind them and drive them into the sea, or at any rate give them a long way to come back on foot, because we have collected most of the horses now. But I fancy the politicians are at the bottom of all our troubles, and they are afraid of losing their houses or that their property might be damaged if brother Boer was allowed to get near to Cape Town or P.E. as they call Port Elizabeth. I act 2nd in command to French and direct the operations in the Midland and Eastern Districts still. There is a big move on soon in which French has certain columns under him and I some others on his Eastern Flank. He spoke to me about Oliver the other day as he can take him on now as A.D.C. Milbanke having been made a D.A.A.G. but Kitchener won't apply for any officer with less than 5 years service! I have not much in the way of news. Five of our officers got 34 Buck near here on Friday, and some Koraan (a big bird of the Buster type, rather good eating) so that there is amusement of sorts going on. It has been rather cold again for the last week, and snow fell here yesterday while I hear by telegraph that there has been a heavy fall in the district North of Dordrecht where I have 3 columns operating against Fonches commando. I am anxious to hear how the ship gets on in America. You should get a snapshot man to do Willie several times daily, just to be able to hand down to posterity how an Englishman can be worried in the New World. I have not much you see in the way of news and I don't think narrating military movements would amuse you, besides you will see my report later when things are completed. P.S. The mail comes most irregularly now; the bundles of papers which you send me arrive all right, so possibly the address on the mail wrapper might be changed omitting D.A.A.G. Cavalry Division, which I ceased to be in Feb. 1900!! Kimberley time.

## 4 August 1901. Cradock

I am living in a railway saloon here as I shall only be here for a day or two. It has a kitchen in it and I just attach it to the armoured train with horse box and truck for my camp, and go wherever I think it necessary.

This is more comfortable than going to a Hotel in these South African Doops which is usually of a second rate stamp where one cannot dine after 6.30 p.m. and not at all on Sundays! Only high tea! I have only Legard (17th Lcrs) with me here as my C.S.O Greenly fell out of a Cape cart.

One day. I don't think I told you. I was driving from Steynsburg to Schoombie with him and Legard to see a new column that was being formed at the latter place. Greenly was driving in front seat. The road was a bit rough, and suddenly he was shot right out of the cart and the wheel went over him. Luckily we had a biggish stone in front on the foot board to balance the cart. This fell out too and the cart in going over it seems to have missed crushing Greenly's leg. Only one of his knees was bruised and one of his fingers very much cut, so poor fellow he was not able to come with me on this trip. He is alright nearly tho' now. When he fell out the horses made off, but luckily I was able to catch the reins before they fell out and pulled up the horses. Old Farquhar (my Lord Chesterfield of perfect manners) who usually does my Intelligence work got something the matter with his brain I thought – too many telegrams – and he used to open his eyes very wide, so I sent him to see French's Dr. who prescribed rest. So as it was mental rest, and not physical, which he wanted, I sent him off to Gorringe's column, and I think he is all right again. I feel sure it is quite a dangerous thing for people who have not been accustomed to work their brains suddenly to be obliged to do so. The unaccustomed exercises no doubt stiffens the brain, and produces much the same effect as riding does on you when you have not been taking horse exercise for some time! Gorringe had quite a success yesterday morning. He has been following some 300 Boers in the Barkley East District for the 6 or 7 days. At last he drove them West over the Burghendorp railway north of Stormberg on Saturday evening. – He started again by moonlight; so did the Boers. The latter halted before dawn, and Gorringe surprised and captured several men. This was N. of Kromhoogt about 10 miles East of Steynsburg. You will see what a hunt he had; fully 150 miles . . . . Wishing you the best of luck in the States and with best love.

## 25 August 1901. Steynsburg

In any case I cannot tell whether I shall be able to hunt at Radway or not this coming winter. Every day the situation here improves and I fancy this last proclamation forfeiting all property of men in arms after 15th Sept. will have a good effect. Also our recent operations resulting in driving Kritzinger from the Colony has done much to discourage the enemy, especially as Kritzinger was the 'Hoof Commandant' or C. in C. of the

Boer Commanders in Cape Colony and had written orders (which we captured) from Steyn and De Wet on no account to leave Cape Colony until he was ordered to do so by them. We have had a very successful 3 weeks operations as I said above. I left here on 30th July by train via Middleburg (where I saw General French) and went to Cradock. The idea was to get all the troops we could to the South of the Boer commandos and then drive them North against a line of blockhouses which had recently been made along the De Aar Stormberg railway. I had a number of local mounted troops in addition to 5 columns and commanded the Eastern half of the operations while French personally directed the columns on the West. By August 1st I had a line of 'stops' from a point West of Mariasburg, past Tarkastad, then South to Pringles Kop and Westwards to Witmoes (on the Cradock railway) and on to the Koetzoesberg (half way between Cradock and Graaf Reinet). (About 200 miles long.) Kritzinger and some other commanders tried to break through my line of stops but they were checked in the passes and retired Northwards. This was near Pringles Kop. I followed them up at once and fairly hunted them back and fore but always getting them northwards. Then on the 9th August I really had Kritzinger and his men surrounded, but somehow he managed to slip thro': but I had Crabbe's column handy and making him leave his guns we raced Kritzinger for about 30 miles as hard as we could go up to the Thebus railway. I told old Crabbe to kill every horse if necessary but he must gallop. The Boers took up a position about 14 miles north of Maraisburg, but we soon had them out of it, and continued the chase until quite dark. Those in the blockhouses said the enemy could not get north of their line! I questioned this rather, and moved a column (Gorringe's) north to be ready to head the enemy when he had crossed the railway. I remained at Maraisburg whither I went in one forenoon from Cradock (48 miles). On the 11th I heard of parties being north of the line, so I moved troops at once. On the 13th Gorringe was all ready for them. First about 200 spare and tired horses came along, the enemy thinking the only danger they had to fear was from South or West, and had their rear guard and main body in that direction. I had posted Gorringe so as to stop them going Eastwards. At noon the Boers off saddled having done their morning march! Gorringe attacked about 1 o'clock. One Comdt. (Cachet[14]) was killed: a very bitter anti Britisher – and another Comdt. (Erasmus[15]) was captured besides several others. I had ridden here (Steynsburg) from Maraisburg and was off again by 5 a.m. next day bringing on three columns. Kritzinger was joined by some more commandos north of this and we raced the lot across Orange River at a point about 10 miles N.W. of Venterstad (early on 15th August). If you look at the map you will see it was a good hunt. I went

194

myself from Cradock to the river in 3 marches. These distances coupled
with the rides I had to take from one column to another to ensure co-
operation meant a lot of riding. I tried to send you a telegram to wish you
and Willie success in America and a safe return but could not get it
through in time to reach you, so you must just take the will for the deed.
No newspapers have reached me for several mails.

## 7 September 1901. Steynsburg

It is quite impossible to tell for certain if there is a 'possibility' of my
getting home for a hunt. Of course there is a possibility. The war I hear is
practically over in the Transvaal, and many more troops have been sent
South into O.R. Colony, and more into this Colony. A whole commando
over a hundred strong was caught by Scobell three nights ago S.W. of
Cradock. This all tends to clear this Colony. Tomorrow I am leaving for
Stormberg to conduct operations in the North East. Some few Boers
crossed into the Colony near Herschell last week, and must be driven out
again. I shall have about 5 columns to employ in that direction, but still
continue to command troops in the Colesburg district as far West as the
Sea Cow River. On the whole things look better in this part of the
Colony. Indeed since we hunted Kritzinger North from S.E. of Cradock
and drove him across the Orange River, this (the centre) part has been
clear of commandos. So on the whole there is a possibility of my going to
England, but you can understand that as long as I am fit and strong I
have no inclination to leave here until the war is ended. I have plenty of
troops to command, and lots to think about and keep me employed. I am
quite happy to remain out here. I cannot understand men calling
themselves soldiers loafing in England when there is lots of work for
them out here. General French was here yesterday. I returned here from
Colesberg the day before and passed Lord Milner on the way, but during
the night so did not see him. The General however went to Naauwpoort
to see him. Milner apparently was afraid of having his train held up by the
Boers because he came by sea from Cape Town to East London, and then
by train past here to Naauwpoort, when he joined his Staff who had come
by train from Cape Town. I hear he is inclined to divide the country into
three commands and merely have a nominal C. in C. so I expect he will
have his way and Lord K. will go to England shortly, or at any rate in a
couple of months or so. Lord K. seems to meddle rather, and does not
give French quite a free hand. Personally when I was in command directly
under K. I did not find this the case. Indeed, I did just whatever I thought
fit, and never asked him what he wanted but merely told him what I had
done and the situation from day to day. Periodically he used to get a fit of
the funks and think De Wet was going to invade the Colony. But from

my point of view nothing would have pleased me and my column better than a good hunt after De Wet! But I have only once been after him and then only for 4 days really. The next best fox is Kritzinger. But I doubt if he will be in a hurry to come back. We gave him such a doing last time and shot his best Commandant (Cachet). The Authorities are all for blood now I hear! This will have a good effect. There were 3 men shot at Colesburg when I was there. I did not care to go and see the spectacle but all the local Dutch magnates had to attend and a roll was called to see that they were present. – I am told the sight was most impressive and everything went off well.

## 22 September 1901. Cradock

I have not received this week's mail yet owing to having been on the march, but in any case I don't expect a letter from you this week as you would have been on the sea on the way to New York when the mail left. You will have heard ere this of the terrible losses C. squadron 17th Lancers sustained on Tuesday last. I trained the regiment from Stormberg to Tarkastad to head Smuts' Commando which had broken S.W. from near Dordrecht. The Squadron in question under a most capable officer (Sandeman) was holding a position about 14 miles from Tarkastad to prevent the enemy coming south. I was out with the squadron on the previous day. (Monday) when it marched from Tarkastad. The weather for several days had been terribly wet. However it cleared for an hour about 3 o'clock and Sandeman lunched with me (off some of those nice tin things you sent me from Cobbett) on the fatal kopjie on which next day so many poor fellows were killed. I got back to Tarkastad at 9 p.m. Next morning was v. foggy. However his patrols reconnoitred the two passes at the exits of which Sandeman had his camp. All was reported clear, but about noon message was sent to Sandeman that Boers were advancing to attack his camp. A troop moved out at once. The officer in charge of it saw some men in khakee whom he took to be some of Gorringe's column which was expected N. of the post. These men levelled their rifles at him when about 200 yards distant. He shouted to them 'Don't fire. We are 17th Lancers' (these irregular corps often fire at one another by mistake). The Boers, as such they proved to be, opened fire at once and emptied several saddles. Before the troop got back to camp the enemy had worked up a donga to the rear of the camp. Again their khakee dress assisted them. They were now between Sandeman's squadron and another squadron which was about 3 miles distant. Seeing khakee dressed men in rear of camp they were allowed to approach quite close before fire was opened on them. Our men held the position to the last and not a man surrendered. Out of 130 men, 29 were killed and 41 wounded. The other men were still fighting when the next squadron came up to their support and the enemy made off. All the officers were either killed or wounded. Such nice fellows too. Three officers killed and 2 wounded of 17th Lancers, one other (a gunner) has since died making 4 killed. It made one feel very miserable to see what had taken place. The wounds were terrible. The brutes used explosive bullets. I was in Tarkastad when the news reached me about 4.30 p.m. I was just starting out to see one of the other columns. I at once galloped to the scene of action but was too late to come up with the enemy. I got to the place at 5.45 p.m. It was about a 15 mile ride and the going terribly wet and heavy owing to the rain. I stayed that night at Eland's River Bridge and we have been pursuing these ruffians hard till yesterday when I came in here. We have a good many columns round them now. I am afraid this is a rather dismal letter for today.

## 30 September 1901. Cookhouse. Cape Colony

Since writing to you last week we have hunted Smuts' commando a long way! I left Cradock last Tuesday and have been to Bedford and Adelaide and then back here. My columns all the time close on the enemy's tail. I don't think the latter's horses can go much longer. He has dropped a good many and we have picked up some prisoners. Those taken in khakee we shot at once. One was taken actually riding with our scouts and wearing the uniform of Nesbitt's Horse. The fellow's movements seemed suspicious and he was arrested for identification: his uniform was complete, all except the badge N.H. which he pretended he had only just lost! Finally he confessed that he was a Boer and was promptly shot. This shows you the difficulty of operating against those who wear one's uniform and of course rather than risk firing on one's own people our troops often miss a good chance.

## 20 October 1901. Cradock

I arrived here from the south on Friday and received four letters from you . . . . Many thanks for them all and for all your news. You certainly are having an experience if not exactly 'a right nice time'! I am very sorry that you did not manage to bring back the cup. However, I suppose you will keep on trying till the cup is captured? I wonder when you will be back in England. You will see from my letters that I have been moving about a good deal lately – Jansenville, then Pearston, Zwager's hock and on here. I have been pursuing Smuts' Commando with several columns. He used to be chief judge of the Transvaal and has come down here for a change, I suppose! We have given him a good chase and, but for the people called 'District Mounted Troops', most of his commando would be walking now. The D.M.T. are local volunteers. Many are Dutchmen by parentage and also at heart. Last week 187 of these creatures surrendered to the enemy without making a fight or suffering a single casualty! This surrender took place in a fortified position which 30 men could have held against all the Boers in this Colony until starved out. Luckily I sent an old fellow (Captain Thornton), a Captain in the Cape Police, to look after these D.M.T. of Somerset East District, because they had been doing such stupid things and I could never get at the truth of what was going on. In his report before a committee of enquiry he tells a strange tale of cowardice or treachery. I enclose the telegrams which I received from him while the affair was going on. I am sure John Vaughan and Lonsdale Hale would like to see them. I have lots of other strange ones about the D.M.T. but I daresay this lot will be enough for you at one time. The reason for employing such people is to be found in the political state of this Colony. It has been ruined by their politicians just as the politicians in England are going far towards ruining the Empire. The Cape Town Government think that by enlisting numbers they will drive out the Boers. What is wanted is quality, as well as quantity in troops. They are also anxious, or at any rate certain Colonial soldiers (amateur) who are really politicians by trade, and their pals want to get command of a district in Cape Colony as soon as there are fewer Boers about. However, things seem slowly to be improving. The Colony is now clear of horses so that it is merely a question of time and energy on the part of our columns when the enemy are reduced to walking. This is just a line to catch the post today as I am afraid I did not get a letter off to you by last mail. You see I was away from railways and there was really no means of sending letters this week.

## 26 October 1901. Steynsburg (Cape)
## Telegram from General French. 25th Oct.

I wish you to start at once and take three weeks rest at Cape Town stop You were not looking well when I saw you and I am told you are looking worse and tired stop You can take all or any of your staff with you stop I must insist on your doing this at once stop You must not delay one hour as I can just spare you now but may want you badly in three weeks time now don't argue but go stop.

## Continuation of letter 26 October 1901

We are taking some horses and will have a ride with some hounds which hunt near Cape Town. There will be 5 of us, so I think we shall have quite a jolly time. You will have heard that General French has been appointed to the Aldershot Command and will take it up as soon as the situation in

198

South Africa will allow him to go home. I am glad that the Authorities removed Buller because he was going on in a most unsoldierlike and undignified way. If discipline is not maintained in the senior ranks of the Army, how can it be hoped to keep it up amongst the rank and file?

## 6 November 1901. Mount Nelson Hotel, Cape Town

Your letter dated 8th Oct. from Waldorf Astoria, New York, arrived yesterday morning! It came in the *Norman* the same steamer which I came out in 2 years ago. Many thanks for it and the newspaper cutting telling me of Willie's misdeeds. These American newspapers seem a regular scourge. The telegram which you say you sent me telling of your departure from N.Y. has not yet reached me, nor the congratulations! (Haig had been awarded the CB.)However I thank you very much for the latter which seem really to be the best part of the honour. I have received a large number of letters on the subject! We are having a capital time here. 'We' consists of the following

| | | |
|---|---|---|
| Captn. Greenly | 12th Lancers | (my C.S.O) |
| " | Legard 17th " | (signalling officer) |
| " | Farquhar Roberts' Horse | (Intelligence) |
| " | Skeffington 17th Lancers | (Adjutant) |

Lt. Thompson " " who has not been very well, and I brought him here for a change. Also Oliver and Hugo De Pree. We all dine at the same table and have quite a cheery party. Today we are driving round the mountain in a coach of sorts and take our lunch as it is an affair of 8 hours. On Monday I lunched with the Governor (Sir Healy Hutchinson). He is very like Donoughmore in appearance, and so kind and hospitable. I am glad Willie has got safely away from N.Y. without being jailed up in the jail for his misdemeanours. Lipton's goings on read as if he were a very zweite klasse individual. I wonder how you can put up with such (apparently) an odious wretch.

## 10 December 1901. Matjiesfontein

I went with General French by train to Piquetberg Road 3 days ago to arrange our movements with General Stevenson and returned here next day. You will have seen that General Wynne has been sent home from Cape Town. He leaves by this mail boat. He came out as Buller's Chief of Staff and latterly as Major General commanded the Cape Colony District while French commanded all the Mobile columns in Cape Colony. So of course there was friction and Wynne had to go. The Chief came to see French at Naauwpoort last week and the whole thing was settled at once and Wynne ordered home! I fancy Wynne, with overwork, had become a little difficult to get on with, and irritable. Want of work sometimes has the same effect on some you will say. I see Hugo has changed his plans. You must not allow yourself to be hustled off to Egypt! Many thanks for advising me a long rest and a trip to England. You would at once think I had been 'stellenbosched' as they call it, if I were to arrive home now! But I am very fit. There is really no anxiety at present moment as we have driven the enemy away North and we have a house and a fine Court house here as an office. But I expect soon we may be off in the wilds of North of this. There is a very rich part about 100 to 200 miles North of Sutherland called Tantelbosch Kalk – simply a sea of grain. I sent a strong column there last week to relieve a garrison which had been besieged since Nov. 28th and is still holding out.

## 16 December 1901. Matjiesfontein (Cape)

I shall probably be back in Orange River Colony by the beginning of the year. Poor Broadwood, I am sorry that he should not have done what was required; but in most cases of this sort in which fault is found, the sin is usually one of omission and not commission. Several column commanders don't like risking a check, and prefer to sit still and do nothing. I'll let you know the moment I get orders to go North. I have just moved the headquarters of the 17th here from Steynsburg. If I go, I suppose it will be to Kroonstad so that you will have to get out another set of maps! You ought to be quite an expert in the geography of South Africa by the time this War is over. The country about here is terribly stony and mountainous, yet we managed to find a flattish piece of ground and have made a polo ground which we played on on Saturday for the first time. All this place and many miles along the railway belong to Logan of cricketing fame. He came from Berwickshire as a lad and was message boy and then Stationmaster at Tomos River 25 miles from here. He now owns half a million and has spent over £180,000 he tells me on this place alone. There is a Hotel here with lots of water and gardens and some 30 houses or so. It is intended to be a health resort! But I pity any poor invalid sent here. The air may be splendid but the district is so dry and barren. We have a depot for tired horses here with about 1200 horses in it – also 200 donkey-waggons each with 14 donkeys plying with supplies between here and Sutherland – so you can understand there is lots of dust at times! In fact at present I should think this was the worst place for any consumptive to stay at. The 7th are to go to Stellenbosch for a month to fit out and rest their horses. As Hammy (the Mil. Sec.) wires me 'little beginnings sometimes have great endings'! Stellenbosch is really a nice place with lots of trees and grass. I see Lord Downe is being sent out here to take charge of remount operations. I think that it is unfair on Birkbeck sending such a man out here at this time of day! No one in the Army could have done this remount work as well even as Birkbeck has. He has had difficulties on every side to contend with and has done right well. The fault lies in those who buy the horses, and in not sending out sufficient to admit of a Reserve being kept in hand. Moreover, most of the horses sent out are raw, untrained animals, good enough perhaps for going in a van but not to catch Boers! I think the local ponies are marvellous. I have never ridden anything else since the beginning of the war.

## 6 January 1902. Matjiesfontein

Enclosed I send you a letter from Carew giving an account of how the horses of the 7th stampeded on New Year's Eve! I am really very sorry for them all starting with such an unfortunate piece of bad luck. We had a most successful day on the New Year here. The sports went off very well. My hangers on were most successful. What is know as 'Colonel Haig's Staff' won the 'tug of war' and 'wrestling on horseback'. This is good because they were competing against many yeomanry and artillery men (v. big men) who had come in for the day. The 17th Lancers won 'tug of war on horseback'. There is a small detachment of the regiment here with headquarters. Besides these events for teams we had a lot of individual competitions as well. At night there were fireworks and another concert given by the men. Some rather good songs. You ask the names of my column commanders. At present I have Lund – Callwell – Doran[16] and Wormald. But sometimes I have others put under me for some operation of a special nature. My chief occupation at present is putting supplies into Sutherland (82 miles North of this) with a view to further operations. As I think I told you we have great difficulty in getting convoys forward on account of want of water. I have 2 parties boring with diamond drills, and already have been most successful. I get these boring parties from the Cape Government (Public Works Dept.) Abe Bailey[17] has been of great assistance to me, not only in getting these people out of the Govt., but in helping me to get men for Intelligence work ever since I came to this Colony a year ago. He went up to Johannesburg today to reopen his office there. I gather from him that things are booming.

## 27 January 1902. Clanwilliam, Cape

I wrote you last Monday from Cape Town. I left that night for Piquetberg Road where I left some horses. On Tuesday I caught up my camp and on Thursday arrived here. The distance is about 96 miles and one passes through some of the nicest country in this colony. The road crosses the Grey's Pass and then comes into the Oliphant's River which (unlike most S. African Rivers) has a splendid flow of clear water in it. The grapes are now ripe, and at every farm we stayed at large quantities were bought. So we quite enjoyed the ride out here! Calvinia is another 100 miles on, but I find that there are not enough waggons here to keep more than a few troops supplied out there, so I have delayed my further move until we can collect some more supplies. We have about 300 waggons working between this and the railway, but what with garrisons, columns and blockhouse a lot of stuff is wanted. Meantime there are quite a number of Boers near to keep us busy. In fact I think the enemy has been allowed to do what he likes in these parts! Clanwilliam lies in a valley running off the Oliphant's River and is only about 400 yards above sea level so the days are pretty hot but nights cool. We have taken the Dutch Parson's house; quite a fine mansion with high rooms and wide verandahs, so we are quite comfortable! There are large meadows in front, with grass and trees which is a pleasing sight for this country. I have Kavanagh's and Wyndham's columns in this vicinity at present; that is to say the bulk of the 10th Hussars and 16th Lancers. Kavanagh is a first rate fellow and has done the 10th a lot of good. I am surprised at the large number of officers in that regiment who have gone home to take up Yeomanry Adjutancies! I hear Colonel Alexander who was sent home on leave to get him out of the way is on his way to South Africa! I do not know what they will do with him but he is not going to have his former command which Kavanagh now holds. Colonel Atherton of the 12th Lancers went home in a similar way and is also on his way back. I think it would have been much kinder to have told them in the first instance not to come back, than to allow them to return and then say that they are not to command their regiments in the field. However this was not my doing as I had nothing to do with their columns at the time these two officers were in command.

## 22 February 1902 Pakhuis Pass N.E. of Clanwilliam C.C.

I moved my headquarters from Clanwilliam to a farm near the head of this pass, about 2,500 feet above the village. The latter stands very low about 240 feet only and was extraordinary hot. (112 degrees on the verandah one day). The Boers call Clanwilliam 'little Hell'. But I had good quarters there as we occupied most of the rooms and the kitchen in the Dutch parson's house. They always have the best houses! . . . I have the telegraph here, and we are building a line of blockhouses across the Pass to Calvinia and thence on to Williston and Carnarvon and Victoria West. Quite a big undertaking, and v. difficult to supply with food and water. There are about 1800 natives and some 400 non combatant whites in Calvinia. It is a difficult matter to supply our troops in that district, so I am bringing these people all away and establishing them near the railway to save transport. I hear about 400 Boers managed to cross the line at 3 a.m. yesterday at a place between Beaufort West and Victoria Road and are now in the Midlands again! I thought that they would like to get back there because there is more food and water in those parts!! Here there is little or no grazing for horses. I have Wyndham's and Kavanagh's columns with me near here i.e. the 16th Lancers and 10th Hussars and a column of the Cape Police between the range of mountains and the sea in what is known as the Sand Veldt. I think it is the worst ground in S. Africa! Little else but sand and a few low bushes; it is difficult to ride through the country except by certain tracks because the ground is honeycombed with holes so that every few yards one's horse disappears up to the girths. Water too is very scarce. There was a road between Lambert's Bay and Clanwilliam, and we land some supplies and stores at the former place. But the numerous convoys which pass along the road have broken the top crust entirely away so that there is nothing left but sand! This is most trying on the oxen and wears them out very quickly. We are getting the great bulk of our supplies in mule waggons now from Piquetberg to which point the railway runs. So you see that it is no easy matter to feed our men and horses.

## 1 March 1902. Achtertein. 30 miles E.N.E. of Clanwilliam

This is just a line to go in to Clanwilliam by a runner who is leaving to catch the mail cart from there on Monday morning. We have rather more Boers round in the Van Rhynsdorp district and General Smuts is there, but there is very little food and not much water so they cannot remain concentrated for long. On the 25th they captured a post of the Cape Police about 15 miles South of Van Rhynsdrop and rumour has it that Smuts is determined to go as far South as he can even to Stellenbosch!! And they are bent on destroying the Hex River Tunnel. I sent a convoy to Calvinia on the 24th escorted by Wyndham's column in which are some squadrons of the 16th Lancers. I arranged for some 150 Bushmanland Borderers (yellow coloured troops) to meet the convoy about 25 miles out. The latter mistook Wyndham's scouts for Boers and seem to have chased them and finally opened fire and hit an officer and 1 man. The officer is called Fowler (Lieut. in the 16th) and was hit in the thigh. I heard today that the Dr. had to amputate the limb and that poor fellow never rallied from the shock. It is sad to lose one's life in such a stupid way. Both detachments knew that they were to meet the other, yet this stupid mistake occurred. The news seems very good from the O.R.C. I had a wire yesterday that over 400 were caught on 'Majuba Day' and Lord K. sitting on a hill (as a sort of grand stand) seeing the country 'black with captured cattle and prisoners'!!

## 9 March 1902. Pakhuis Pass, near Clanwilliam (Cape)

I am still busy in this Western country and command columns operating
between Williston and the sea. I have the line of Blockhouses which is
being erected in that area also under me. (Col. Parke C.B. late 3rd D.Gs.
quite an old boy, commands the Blockhouses, but is under my orders). I
have 4 columns – really more than I can feed. It will take 300 waggons
to feed 2 columns at Calvinia. This will show you the difficulties of
carrying on war in this country where there are no railways. I see Brodrick
says the war West of the De Aar railways is 'merely a matter of Police
Work'! I suppose somebody told him this. Still the numbers of the enemy
are well over 1400, and in a rugged country of this sort with bad roads
and no supplies and little water all is in favour of the defender who can
live scattered about on the farms of his friends, and merely concentrate
when a good chance offers of attacking some detachment carelessly
guarded convoy. My Western point on the coast is at Lambert's Bay where
the Navy have sent a gunboat to assist in holding the place. It is about 40
miles only from Clanwilliam, but the road is quite broken up and now
nothing but sand, so that we bring all our supplies from Piquetberg where
is the railway. I have my headqrs. in the Pakhuis Pass about 2000 ft.
above Clanwilliam as the latter is very hot and close being in valley of the
Oliphant River. There is capital water where I am and I have a cottage
sheltered by some kind of fir trees where we do our writing and have our
meals. I always sleep in a tent as it is cooler. This is a bad part of the
country for horses. I have lost 2 since I came. The old friend which I have
ridden ever since Bloemfontein (March 1900). Another horse (which
one of my servants rode) ate some kind of poisonous bush when we were
near Calvinia last month, and died in about 4 hours.

## 30 March 1902. Pakhuis Pass (near Clanwilliam)

I have not much in the way of news to give you. We go slowly forward
with the blockhouse line towards Calvinia, and my columns hunt back
strong parties of Boers . . . Holdsworth's brother-in-law (Eynstie) has
made an ass of himself. He has had a column of yellow (Bastard's men)
for some time near Ookiep in the N.W. corner of Cape Colony, covering
some copper mines. On the 16th he came south to Garies where he has a
garrison, enticed south by some liberated men of the Cape Police whom
Boers sent to Garies, no doubt meaning Col. White to come South for
them! – Meantime a commando or two slip in between White at Garies
and Ookiep. He can't now get back North as the country is so difficult
without risk of capture or defeat, and he sends to me to send him food.
He has supplies for 6 weeks. But there is no water for a stretch of 55
miles between Van Rhynsdorp and Garies so that it will be a difficulty to

help from this side. I heard from Carew yesterday. He and the 7th
Hussars are near Heidelberg in the Transvaal. Lawley has got 'Ghazi'
Hamilton's[18] column. The latter is brother to the Hammy you know and
who is Lord K's Mil. Sec. and who always sends you such kind messages
when he writes to me, and looks forward to a glass of Port at Radway with
you again. That reminds me of your poor old Coldfoot. But why is he not
a Yeomanry Colonel and a C.B. like Sir — Howard? he ought to come
out here instead of letting 2nd Lieuts. of Cavalry regiments become
Majors, and Captains be promoted to Colonels like Blanford for instance
– a case of the blind leading the blind and to think that Lord Chesham[19]
is at the head of the lot! – I have noticed it repeatedly that whenever the
Boers hear of a column of Yeomanry being by itself, it is like a View hollo
to the pack and they all rush in to have a worry at it – and in many cases
their recklessness has been justified by results.

## 5 April 1902. Karamoe (Cape) about 40 miles from Calvinia

General French wired me in a message today that John Vaughan had been
wounded in the knee, but he believed not seriously. He was acting as
Intelligence Officer to Lawley so it was not part of his duty to go out
scouting. But I do not know yet what he was doing. I left Pakhuis Pass
last Monday where I have a sort of Swiss Chalet amongst the fir trees as
my highland home! . . . a chalet of the most cottage-like dimensions viz.
3 rooms so that I always sleep in a tent, but the house is convenient for
the mess and for writing in. I moved up to the Pass when Clanwilliam
(which is only 240 feet above the sea) was so hot. I am now about 55
miles from Clanwilliam on the same high plateau which Calvinia stands
on, 3000 to 4000 feet above the sea.

## 20 April 1902. Clanwilliam

I have been writing letters to 'General Smuts' enclosing instructions for
him from the 'Commandant General Louis Botha' to proceed to the
nearest railway station on receipt, in order to be present at a 'meeting of
the people' on the 15th May at Vereeniging. – Smuts is about 250 miles
North of this, so I sent out 3 copies – One by steamer to Port Nolloth to
try and catch him from the North and the others from this side. I wonder
who will compose 'the people' and whether they will vote for surrender! I
suppose the 'leaders' must have come to some agreement with our
Government before this meeting (to ratify some agreement apparently)
could have been summoned. But I hope that there is no question of giving
terms to these rebels. It would be much better to go on fighting for 10
years than give way in anything to them. I suppose I'll have Smuts here
shortly, as I have to arrange for his safe conduct to Vereeniging. He was

State Attorney at Pretoria and was at Cambridge University. It is very nice of you to think of collecting and sending out things for 17th. I have wired to Matjiesfontein to find out how our supplies stand. Until recently they were particularly well off for 'comforts' of that sort – while if the negotiations come to anything I expect some of the troops will be put under cover in a short time and won't feel the cold so much as if on the trek. If we want anything I'll wire to you at once. When the regiment came abroad a fund was started. I do not know exactly what the state of it is now, but if I wire that we want certain things you should send a line to Major Ricardo (who is now in command of the Depot at Dundalk) and he will tell you exactly what to do. He is a grand manager and will save you all trouble about getting the things together and despatched to South Africa. Poor Ricardo bears me no malice tho' I stated in my Corps report about him that I did not consider him fit to command a Cavalry regiment in War. It was his one ambition in life to command the 17th. I am sure that you would like the poor creature, as he will gamble in a mild way and play Bridge and lose his money on the Stock Exchange and knows everything that goes on and writes to the King! So you will have lots of mutual acquaintances!

## 26 April 1902. near Van Rhynsdorp (Cape)

I came here 3 days ago to organize a column to go to Garies with supplies, ammunition, etc. etc. for Col. White who I told you had come away South leaving the Port Nolloth – Oskiep railway unprotected. Our plan for assisting him was to send him the means of drawing supplies etc. from Houdeklip Bay which is about 50 miles from Garies. The Navy however say they cannot land anything there at this season of the year! Any ship they send would have to lie 4 miles off the shore and they won't undertake the risk. You will remember a gunboat was lost off Lambert's Bay this time last year, and so the sailors are a bit careful now. We have therefore to draw all our supplies from Cape Town tho' only some 30 miles here from the coast. I am now about 50 miles from Clanwilliam and still over 100 miles from Garies. The chief difficulty in getting supplies forward to White is the want of water for the transport animals and horses along the road. Luckily it rained 2 days ago which has simplified things greatly. Had it not rained then there was a march of over 50 miles without water. The nights are cold now and animals don't want so much water, but even so it is a big undertaking to take about 2000 animals such a distance without drink. I have Rankin 7th Hussars with me here. He is a local Major and commands the W.P.M.R. (Western Province Mtd. Rifles). Quite a smart well disciplined corps of irregulars. They do him credit as the men are only enlisted for 3 months. A good many irregular corps have been disbanded during the last 3 or 4 months so he has picked up some of their men who wished to continue on. We have not yet heard from 'General' Smuts in reply to Botha's communication which I sent him. But I scarcely expected to hear yet because Smuts is near Oskiep (200 miles at least from here). I enclose an interesting letter which I got from Stodger the other day and will show you what he is doing. Our blockhouse line here seems a more complicated obstacle to cross than theirs in the Transvaal as we start with an obstacle between the houses of a dozen or more strands of barbed wire and then keep the garrison of the blockhouses busy every day strengthening it with ditches and spring guns etc. I gather Dick Lawley is rather feeble and asks everyone's advice. They say the betting is 100 to 1 on peace in J'burg and 50 to 1 in Pretoria. I hear that Ex. Prest. Steyn has paralysis and cannot live. This seems to me the best sign of all which makes for peace. The farmers in this district have scarcely felt the pinch of War yet! I think they are beginning to get a bit hungry now! The farmer here (Aties) got first prize for raisins at the 'London Show' they tell me. I presume the Colonial Exhibition. He is a real rebel and thoroughly deceitful.

## 29 May 1902. Calvinia (Cape)

I received a wire from Lawley on 27th saying that he has no objection to Oliver joining my Staff so I have sent in an application to Army Headquarters asking for him to be appointed 'signalling officer' instead of Legard who has enteric fever and will have to go to England for change after it. I arrived here last Sunday from Clanwilliam. I wrote you before leaving there and have not got another letter of course since I wrote. Cobbett's parcel has come safely by parcel post. Many thanks. If you happen to be passing tell them not to send any of those 'Belgravia Pies'. I think they are cat's meat! Everything else is excellent especially the whole chickens in tins. This is rather a nice little village. We have it pretty well all to ourselves, because I cleared all the inhabitants nearly out of it last Jan. some 800 souls white and coloured including the magistrate and other rotters of the Cape Official class. No one comes up now without a pass from my Staff Officer. We occupy the Mayor's house! He is in Cape Town and is now very loyal! The village stands in a wide flat valley with high mountains on North and South. It is over 4000 feet above sea level and the climate seems just like England.; lots of clouds and rain at present, which no doubt will soon become snow. The blockhouses from Lamberts Bay were finished yesterday, and the line from Victoria Road will be completed to the East edge of the mountain North of this tomorrow. The Duke of Montrose[20] is in command of the latter and will be in charge of my most Easterly section from here to the Fish River. He came in to see me here two days ago. A nice cheery fellow, v. like Brassford I thought. His Battalion of Militia is very strong – they are called Argyll & Sutherland Highlanders. The Boers from Oskiep, Garies and the N.W. have come S.E. to the Bushmanland (about 80 miles North of this) and are apparently waiting to see the result of the Peace Conference. There must be almost 2000 of them because we have gradually pressed them back into this sort of 'promised land' from the rest of the Colony. Bushmanland is very cold in winter and there is very little water. It rains there in summer and the grass is very fine for stock. (We have winter rains in this part as you know.) I don't think the Boers can live in Bushmanland after the end of June on account of the want of food and the cold. They say that the very animals unless herded will trek back of their own accord to the lower and warmer valleys westwards in Namaqualand or Southwards. I suppose that you must have a thorough knowledge of the Cape Colony map now! Please buy marriage presents for the nieces who are getting married. Spend whatever you think right (but don't give them rubbish!!) on my behalf.

## 5 June 1902. Calvinia

Yours of 9th May reached me last night – I can imagine Daisy Fingall[21] chattering rubbish just to amuse you! – That's all right as long as you don't believe half you hear! I got your telegram regarding the 'joyful news' and at once replied thanking you for it, and answering your question 'when I would be home' viz. probably after Cape Colony has been pacified! The question of course is when will that be? The London folk must know that! I have been sending out messages to the different commanders from the 'ex-attorney Smuts' who now calls himself 'General' S! directing them to abstain from any hostile act until he has seen them. I have also let them know that they must not come South of a certain line or my troops will drive them back until I have seen this Smuts. General French wired me last night that he (Smuts) will be round here next week, and directing me to meet Smuts at Clanwilliam and to make arrangements 'to bring him up from the station' as they call it at Clanwilliam when one sends 108 miles to Piquetberg road station 'to meet the train'! I have today got the gist of the proclamation regarding the rebels viz letting all the rank and file off with disfranchisement for life and stating that the leaders will be punished. Of course the real leaders are in Cape Town or in Europe. Moreover very few of the rank and file have ever had the franchise – so all the loyal men about here are much disgusted with the terms given to the rebels. But of course they have suffered from the enemy because they were loyal, while the farms of the disloyal have not been touched by us to any extent. All the same their chief reason for objecting to the rank and file getting off light is because I fancy they are rather vindictive and would like to grind their opponents to powder. My own opinion is that the proclamation is right enough provided Martial Law is maintained in this Cape Colony for another 3 years. The Cape Government consists of a lot of nonentities quite unfit to rule anybody or anything. Van de Venter[22] (also a 'General') is coming here tonight. He is quite a good fellow judging by his behaviour on many occasions so I'll be glad to see him. I'll keep you informed by wire how we progress and will tell you as soon as I have the slightest idea when I am likely to get away. We have made a grand polo ground here and had our first game today on it. I sent a party of an Officer, 3 N.C.Os. and 7 men off at moment's notice to represent the 17th Lancers at the coronation! I hope they get to Cape Town in time for the steamer (the *Bavarian*) which sails on the 7th.

## 12 June 1902. Calvinia (Cape)

I am busy here trying to get these Boer Commandants to concentrate their Commandos at suitable places for General Smuts to see them and arrange for them to lay down their arms. The difficulty is due to the absence of food in the District as we have cleared the country as thoroughly as possible outside our Blockhouse line, and I decline to allow them to come South of that line until they have laid down their arms, we have Van de Venter in hospital here. He seems a good honest fellow and led their attacks in all their small successes. At present he is suffering from a bad throat, the result of a wound and can hardly speak. General French hopes to sail on the 25th for England and kindly asked me to go with him. But as I also command the 17th Lancers, I feel it my duty to rejoin them as soon as I have finished my work here, in order to look after their welfare. Squadrons have been so much detached that many matters require attention, in addition to the numerous changes which become necessary on passing from a war to a peace footing. However I expect that a month or two should see me on the way to England. As you enjoy letters relating to things concerning me. I enclose one I got from General French the other day, thanking me for my assistance which (as a matter of fact) has not really amounted to a great deal. You seem to have done wonders in sending out warm things for the regiment. I hear that the things are greatly appreciated, as also your kind thought in the matter. It is very cold here now. Hard frost every night, and all the water frozen in the morning. I am going tomorrow to Oovlogshloof to meet Smuts, and hope to have all the surrenders arranged in time to enable me to go to Cape Town by 23rd to see General French before he sails. With best love and hoping you are having great times at the Coronation!

## 25 June 1902. Mount Nelson Hotel, Cape Town

It will be a great treat to get back again. I wired to you last Monday after I
saw General French off, to tell you that I hope to be home shortly. The
General has kindly said that he is going to insist on my being appointed
to command the Aldershot Cavalry Brigade. But of course he may fail in
getting his way. In any case I could not well have left Cape Colony at this
moment. General Settle now commands here (you will remember that I
took over the columns from him in April 1901 when he was sent home!)
A nice old fellow and may do this job now very satisfactorily. At the same
time he does not know the vast country which lies to the West of the main
line from here to De Aar – and yesterday I spent a long time with him.
He has been left few troops really for finishing the job in hand. I hear
from several friends and secret agents that the rebels have hidden horses,
stock, waggons, etc., also arms and ammunition so that the country must
be thoroughly searched during the next two months. I do not anticipate
any real trouble but merely police work. My knowledge of the country will
be of use to old Sir Settle and he asked me for proposals regarding the
disposition of the troops West of the line. So you see I have still some
work to do. But in any case I hope to take some leave in October say for
6 months whether General French manages to get me brought home or
not. The 17th told off as part of the garrison of Cape Colony so will no
doubt be here for a year or two yet. This is terrible bad news about the
King's illness. I hope the poor fellow will recover. This is just a line to
catch the mail boat. The General will tell you I am very well – broad as I
am long thanks to breathing pure air. The little man was almost in tears
bidding Goodbye and I was sorry to part with him. We lunched with the
Mayor. He (F) had a much warmer welcome from the people and soldiers
on the ship than Lord K. F. is most popular. By the way, when I come
home there must be no nonsense – meet me just as you sent me away; no
crowd of relations – just yourself and a friend. I'll try and come by a
mailboat. These transports are so slow, and soldiers are out of place on
board a ship. Best love to you and looking forward to seeing you very
soon (but don't postpone your American trip on my account). I dine with
the Government tonight. All are very kind to me here.

## 29 June 1902. Porterville Road (Cape)

I enclose a map which will show you the huge tract of country which I
have been given to command. It is a triangle of about 600 miles each
side, and includes the main line from Cape Town to Kimberley. General
Settle, as you know, commands the whole of Cape Colony District, and
my arm of command will be known as the Western Sub-District. He has
recommended that I be given the local rank of Brigadier General. As I

think I told you last week. General French went home with the intention of asking for me to be given the command of the Aldershot Brigade. If he succeeds I would have the rank of Major General, but if he does not I have a fine command out here. At present there are a large number of troops in the command waiting for transports; it will take 6 months to work them all off. Then when they go, I shall have 5 Battns. of Infantry, 1 Cav. Regt., 2 Battns. M.I. and Battery and odds and ends of pompoms, volunteers etc. etc., so that I am lucky to have got such a command for peace time. It is a busy time getting all settled. All the administration of Martial Law is also in my hands. We are keeping on the administrators for the present, but will gradually let them go as we can dispense with their services. I am moving my headquarters to Victoria West, but of course will have a good deal of moving about to see how things are going on. All the magistrates are at present under me. Many are disloyal and will want careful looking after, or removing altogether. But of course our chief trouble will be the so-called Cape Government, for it consists of a lot of feeble individuals unable to exercise control over anything; and they have to be considered as rulers. They have no police at all in my area of command and don't seem able to find money to pay for raising a corps.

## 13 July 1902. Mount Nelson Hotel, Cape Town

Everyone seems passing through here on the road home . . . . I expect in 3 months time very many of them will be on what J. Vaughan calls their 'kneel downs' at the War Office asking for a job. But at present they were all delighted at getting off. Personally I am quite happy! I question whether the Government in England know the real state of feeling in this Colony, and I am certain that the Government of Cape Colony know very little about the feeling in the Districts. I have had several interviews with Graham who is acting Premier in the absence of 'Field Marshal' Sprigg at the coronation. The Government here seem like a lot of schoolboys, quite happy and thoughtless of the future. Martial Law will soon be a dead letter but they have no police in sufficient numbers to keep order, and I fear the loyalist and those who have helped us, will have a bad time. However we are doing all we can to arrange to keep troops in the Districts in order to let the Dutch see that British Rule is still in existence. If the constitution is not suspended the Bond party will be stronger than ever.

## 5 August 1902. Stellenbosch (Cape)

French wires from the *Octava* that Lord Kitchener is anxious for me to go to India as Inspector General of Cavalry when the present man's time is up i.e. in a year and a half's time, but he (French) wishes me to get the

Cavalry Brigade at Aldershot at once, I have written to him that I would prefer the Aldershot Brigade of course, but the other is a fine appointment too, and one only has work in the winter time in India, with great opportunities of keeping one's hand in in handling mounted troops. In England I fancy these politicians will let everything slide in the same way as they did before the war. However I don't much mind which appointment I am given. I see you say I must 'bring home some trophies of the War'. But what trophies do you expect me to have? I can send you a tin mug and table or chair or two! Or would you like a Blockhouse or two and some barbed wire? Really there are no trophies worth having. At least I have never had the chance of collecting and carrying things of historical value. Tho' the papers say officers do have pianos and ranges I am told! I have been travelling about inspecting troops on the railway during the last week. De Aar, Victoria Road, Beaufort West, Worcester and then here. I saw one of the last yeomanry regiments here today (Kemps Regt). They are mounted on Russian ponies and really look very workmanlike. These ponies are extremely hardy; stand heat equally as well as cold and keep their condition on very little food. The local people are all very anxious to buy Russians at the sales, but at present we are clearing out the rubbish from the Remount depots.

## 11 August 1902. Victoria West. (Cape)

I returned here this morning from Cape Town. I arrived there last Wednesday after visiting Malmesburg and other stations, and got your welcome letter and papers which the Post Office retained for me all safely. I don't think I told you that the 17th Lancers are now under orders for England as the Greys have been told off to replace them in this Colony. In reply to a wire from me asking the probable date of embarkation, I received a telegram from Pretoria saying that the regiment would sail probably about the end on November, but not before that date.

Poor old Sir Settle took to his bed on arrival at Cape Town as the result of the hard work he had 'on tour'! and they said I had galloped him too fast and too far. The old fellow has almost as bad a seat in a Cape Cart as on the horse; and he nearly fell out of the cart going to (not from) dinner with the 17th Lancers at Victoria Road! The thing is that he is never accustomed to take any exercise. The latter together with slight cold obliged him to lay up. There are many colds going about, but I personally keep wonderfully free from them. I have got little Blair the order of appointment on Settle's Staff. The old man's staff have been in that office at the Castle of Cape Town pretty nearly all the war and are stale; and so I think the poor General has more work thrown on him than he ought to have, and like the willing horses he does his best to get

212

through it instead of throwing the papers at the heads of his S. Officers! I think Blair ought to be able to assist him, and at the same time he will get a good deal of experience in office work as Cape Town is a large military centre.

## 25 August 1902. Victoria West
Many thanks for yours of July 30th and finished on Sat morning 2nd August. I am glad you met General Johnny Hamilton. He is a nice fellow. I see General French told you that I could have either the Aldershot Cav. Bde. or the Inspector Generalship Cavalry in India which one I preferred! He did not write that to me, but said that Lord K. wished me to become the latter and French the former. However, I have already told you all my views on those matters, but I fancy the excellent house at Aldershot in which the General Officer commanding Cav. Bde. lives will oblige Lord Roberts to select the husband of dear Mrs so and so because the nursery rooms will exactly suit the family! – and I'll be given the Indian appointment. General Settle sent me a copy of a cablegram received from the C. in C. London stating with reference to the organization of the commands in this Colony that 'the Chief did not approve of Colonel Haig's appointment. He is to rejoin the 17th Lancers and remain in command.' As a matter of fact I *am* in command of the regiment now and look after everything.

## 31 August 1902. Victoria West. (Cape)
Longford and his Irish Yeomen passed thro' here this morning on his way to Cape Town to embark. But only those are being sent home who agree to take their discharge on arrival in England. I believe some on reaching England insisted on being paid for a whole year, stating that they were enlisted to serve one year, or to the end of the War! Hence the order to delay the yeomen out here until they sign this new agreement.

## 8 September 1902. Victoria Road. (Cape)
I came over here from 'the village' as they call Victoria West, last Wednesday and am now living in the Mess of the 17th Lancers. It is quite a pleasure to be back at Cavalry work proper again, and to do whatever one thinks right in the way of training the squadrons. Troops go out, each under its own officer, every morning except Thursday which we keep as a sort of holiday after Indian fashion. But on that day we have sports for the men, tent-pegging, line cutting, etc. etc. though indeed almost every afternoon there is something going on for the men, either football or shooting at bottles (6d. a break 1d. a shot)! or something or other. Sandeman looks after their amusements and he has arranged the

213

'Institute' very well. We have 3 marquees fitted up with tables etc. where they can write, play cards, etc. and read the papers; here they get coffee or tea. There is also a wet and dry canteen in a tin shanty adjoining which we had erected for them so the men are having quite a comfortable time now. We officers play polo, course hares, etc. and I find the time passes pleasantly enough. As I told you last week I hope to get away towards the end of the month, but I have not yet heard about the sailings of the transports. The regiment is not down amongst the first troops for home, but I expect it will get away in Nov.

## 17 September 1902. Cape Town

We (the 17th Lancers) are to embark on the 23rd on the S.S. *German* – I expect she will sail next morning. You will recollect it was the 23rd Sept. 1899 that I embarked on the *Norman* – just 3 years ago. The *German* is a fair ship about 6,700 tons but slow. She is what the Union Castle Co. class as an 'intermediate steamer' and takes 21 days to do the passage, so we should arrive about October 15th. At first we had orders to embark on the *Johannesburg* – a small trading vessel, scarcely large enough to make the voyage in safety! But the owners would not carry out the requirements of the Military, and so the contract was cancelled. We call at Las Palmas not Madeira. If you ask at the Union Castle Office they will tell you when to expect us exactly; but I trust you will not make any fuss, or put yourself or anyone else out in any way because of my arrival. The orders are for the regiment to go to Edinburgh . . . .

As soon as I get home and after I have got matters arranged, I shall ask for some leave – Up to date I have heard nothing officially about either going to Aldershot as G.O.C. Cavalry Brigade or to India as Inspector General. – so no doubt some of Roberts' pals (or Lady Roberts' pals) have been chosen for the former. I really don't mind, but I don't propose to go off to India without having a good spell of leave and a thorough change for a time. For 3 years straight away on active service against a well armed and active enemy like the Boers, entails a considerable amount of hard work upon all ranks, and much anxiety at times upon those responsible for giving and transmitting orders. So tho' very fit and well I am anxious to do something else as a change.

## Notes
1. Colonel Harold Maxwell Grenfell MVO, (1870–1929), Commissioned into the 1 Life Guards in 1892, transferred to 17 Lancers in 1903 (when they were commanded by Haig) and to the 3 Dragoon Guards in 1904. Special Service in South Africa, i.e. a Mobile Column, 1899–1901.
2. Field Marshal Julian Hedworth George Viscount Byng GCB, GCMG,

MVO (1862–1935) was commissioned into the 10 Hussars. Before South Africa he served in Sudan 1884. After commanding his regiment from 1902–4 he commanded the Cavalry School. He commanded a Cavalry Brigade 1907–9 and a division from 1910. He was commanding in Egypt when the First World War broke out. His commands in the war were a Cavalry Division, a Cavalry Corps, the Canadian troops and finally the 3rd Army. His troops captured Vimy Ridge in 1917. After the war he became Governor General of Canada 1921–26 and afterwards Chief Commissioner of the Metropolitan Police.

3.  Major General Inigo Jones took over from Major General Pole-Carew as commander of the Guards Brigade, when Pole-Carew was given command of 11th Division.. In the winter of 1901 he was put in charge of the Midlands District. Subsequently he was responsible for building blockhouses over 241 miles, which he achieved in fifteen days. He died in 1914; Haig went to his funeral in the Guards' Chapel.

4.  The orderly was Thomas Henry Secrett (1886–1942) from the 8 Hussars. He was with Haig for twenty-five years and marched behind his charger at Haig's State Funeral in 1928. He was an excellent groom. His book *Twenty-five years with Earl Haig* includes some fairly tall stories, but a shrewd assessment of Haig's character.

5.  Lieutenant General Sir Hubert Hamilton Settle KCB, DSO, was born in 1847 and commissioned in 1867. He became a lieutenant general in 1908 and retired in 1911.

6.  Commandant Gideon Jacobus Scheepers (1878–1902) was in de Wet's Commando and established a reputation as a scout, signaller (heliograph) and saboteur. He was captured by the British, tried for war crimes, found guilty and shot . He was thought to be a British subject, which may not have been correct.

7.  Commandant A.H. Malan worked with and under Kritzinger.

8.  Of the four Column Commanders listed Colonel Harry Scobell (later Major General Sir Henry, 1859–1912) was the most successful, with a reputation for speed of movement equal to the Boers. He captured Commandant Lotter and the survivors of his Commando in September 1901. As a resident of Cape Colony, and thus a British subject, Lotter was shot for treason. Brigadier General Sir Charles Preston Crewe KCMG, CB (1858–1936) became a member of the Cape Parliament and, after the war, a Member of the Council of Defence under Smuts. In 1916 he commanded a brigade in East Africa. George Frederick Gorringe (1868–1945) became a major general and commanded a Division from 1916–18. According to Gary Sheffield and John Bourne he was known to his troops as 'Blood Orange'!

9.  Major General Sir Henry Timpson Lukin KCMG, DSO, (1860–1925) was Inspector General of the South African Mounted Rifles after the war. He commanded a South African Brigade in 1915–16 and a Division from 1915–18.

10. Van Reenen was the leader of one of the small commandoes, following the splitting up of Kritzinger's force. He operated in the northern Cape Colony and Orange Free State. He survived the war.

11. Fitzroy James Wilberforce Farquhar (1858–1941) was in the 13 Hussars. He served in both the South African War and the First World War.

12. Major D'Arcy Legard , born 1873, commissioned into the 17 Lancers 1895, became a major in 1905.

13. Major General Sir Walter Howorth Greenly KCB, DSO (1875–1955) was commissioned into the 12 Lancers in 1895, but transferred into the 19 Hussars in 1912 in order to command them. He had been one of Haig's Staff Officers in South Africa. He was GSO1 of the 2nd Cavalry Division in 1914–15 and by 1916 had been given command of that Division. He invented the 'Greenly Field Boot', with straps down the side for easy and quick removal in the event of the wearer breaking his leg. Perhaps the mishap in the Cape cart alerted Greenly to the need for such an innovation! He collapsed from nervous exhaustion during the Kaiserschlacht of 1918. He died in 1955.

14. Commandant Calmon Lion Cachet was born in the North-Eastern Cape, the son of a professor of Dutch Jewish ancestry. The professor supported the view of the Prime Minister of the Cape, the Hon. W.P. Schreiner, that a rebellion by Cape Afrikaaners would be a disaster. It was a source of embarrassment to him that his son was an early recruit into a commando.

15. General Daniel Erasmus, known as 'Maroela' was one of the less effective commando leaders. He was demoted to commandant in 1900 because of 'lacklustre performance'. After capture he was sent to St Helena.

16. Brigadier General Beauchamp John Colclough Doran CB born 1860, commissioned into the Royal Irish Regiment in 1880, served in Bengal, Punjab and Tirah before coming to South Africa. He commanded the 8 Infantry Brigade from 1912 and went with it to France in 1914.

17. Sir Abe Bailey (1864–1940) South 485African financier and statesman became a friend of the Haig family. Haig's second daughter Lady Victoria (Doria) and her husband Colonel Andrew Montagu-Douglas-Scott DSO spent part of their honeymoon in South Africa staying with Sir Abe and Lady Bailey.

18. 'Ghazi' or Gha-C Hamilton was Lieutenant Colonel Gilbert Henry Claude Hamilton CB, born 1852 and commissioned into the 14 Hussars; he became a brevet colonel in 1900. He retired in 1906. He was 'Hammy's' brother.

19. Charles Compton William Cavendish 3rd Baron Chesham KCB (1850–1907) served in the Coldstream Guards, the 10 Hussars and the 16 Lancers. He became a major general in the Imperial Yeomanry in the Second Boer War. His eldest son was killed near Pretoria in 1900, whilst serving as a second lieutenant in the 17 Lancers.

20. Douglas Beresford Malise Ronald Graham 5th Duke of Montrose KT (1852–1940) served in the 5 Lancers and Coldstream Guards. He was in South Africa in command of the 3rd Battalion Argyll and Sutherland Highlanders.
21. Arthur James Francis Plunkett 11th Earl of Fingall (1859–1929) served in the Second Boer War in the 17th Battalion Imperial Yeomanry. His wife, Daisy, or more accurately Elizabeth Mary Margaret came from County Galway. She obviously had the Irish gift of the gab!
22. General Sir Jacob Louis 'Jaap' Van der Venter KCB, CMG (1874–1922) was a commando leader with Smuts. He led one of the four Commandos to invade the Cape in 1901 after capturing a blockhouse. He was wounded in the throat in January 1902. He commanded a South African Brigade against the Germans in East Africa and finally led the campaign until 1918. He was only forty-eight when he died of heart failure in 1922.

# Chapter 8

# The 17 Lancers
# and Return to India

## 1902 – 1905

Douglas Haig returned to Britain with the 17 Lancers on board the SS *German*. They arrived at Southampton on 19 October 1902. The ship also had on board part of the 2nd Battalion the Dorset Regiment. *The Times* reported their return as follows:

Union Castle Steamship *German* arrived at Southampton yesterday morning from the Cape, bringing home 14 officers and 527 men of the 17th Lancers under the command of Lieutenant Colonel D Haig CB, 17 officers and 200 men of the 2nd Battalion Dorset Regiment, and a few details. The 17th Lancers, who have seen considerable service in South Africa, were met on landing by Lieutenant General Sir DC Drury-Lowe,[1] the Colonel of the Regiment which he for many years commanded, and when the men were paraded in the embarkation shed he addressed a few words to them. He said he had come down to welcome them home after the fierce and arduous work which they had done in South Africa. They had upheld the tradition of the regiment and their splendid achievements in the field deserved well of their King and Country. As he saw the men before him it made him wish that he could once again don the jacket of the regiment, but he was too old. They were going to their homes and families, and he wished them all happiness and joy. Colonel Haig called for three cheers for Sir DC Drury-Lowe, and the men responded with enthusiasm. The general subsequently shook hands with several of the men who had served under him. Later the 17th Lancers entrained for Edinburgh and Glasgow, the men of the Dorset Regiment proceeding then to Portland.

The above news item observed that Haig had been awarded the CB. This occurred in August 1902, when he was also appointed ADC to the King. The royal appointment carried with it the rank of colonel, but as always the most the War Office would concede was a brevet colonel's rank! Haig had to wait until the end of October 1903 before he became a substantive colonel. This coincided with his arrival in Bombay as Inspector General of Cavalry in India – a major general's appointment.

It must have given Douglas Haig personally great pleasure to be based in Edinburgh, where he was born and where he would be close to many of his family. On the other hand he was less than enthusiastic, from the military point of view, to be based at Piershill Barracks with parts of the regiment on detachment at Portobello and in Glasgow. He had evidently written to French to try to get the station changed to York or Aldershot. 'Indeed'; he said, 'any place is better as a Cavalry station than Edinburgh.'

Before leaving South Africa he had received overtures about more senior commands. French, in command at Aldershot, wanted him to command a Cavalry Brigade there, whilst Kitchener, now Commander in Chief in India, wanted him as Inspector General of Cavalry there. He chose the latter, despite advice from others that the Indian appointment was something of a backwater. Maybe he also felt that he needed the next part of his career to be less closely tied to French. Before he left South Africa he had received a letter from his friend Dick Lawley (7 Hussars), advising strongly against the Inspector General post. It was written at Pretoria and is dated 15 August 1902.

My dear Douglas

Very many thanks yrs of the 9th – very interesting though not particularly satisfactory reading about the state of the Cape Colony. However it will be all the same 100 years hence, as I'm quite sure we will not keep S.A.; we've never done the right thing politically here yet, and I doubt if we are in a fair way to do it now. Next time however it will be a bigger business than this & we shan't fight: I have spoken!

Now about yourself; I do implore you not to think of I.G.C. in India; on two grounds I'm dead opposed to your going there; in the first place who ever hears of the I.G.C. in India? 'Out of sight is out of mind.' And if there is any question affecting Cavalry, the I.G.C. in India is much too far away to be consulted.

No, your place is at home, & with French to back you up they may take an intelligent interest in Cavalry.

Secondly as regards yourself, would you kindly tell me who you propose should succeed Grant as I.G.C. at home? All the 'coming' Cavalry men of 3 years ago have come to grief, & we have to come to the generation that is now commanding Regts. Take the pick; Rimington, Allenby, Scobell, Lowe, Garrett, Small; some of them A1 men I grant, but do you mean to tell me that they'd make any of them I.G.C. with you commanding the Cav. Bde. at Aldershot? Again I say no.

What you should do is go to Aldershot, and next spring move on to 41 Pall Mall. Of course one never knows what influences are brought to bear, and for all we know the lot may fall on such constellations in the firmament of cavalry leaders as Hemming or Ghazi Hamilton or Burn Murdoch; but I am supposing they want to try & run the show properly & put in the best man.

Have you formulated any ideas for Cavalry training in this country? I don't hear anything of a Cav. Col. on the Staff, or an I.G.C. in S.A. & we shall get everybody running his own show according to his own ideas, & some perhaps not running them at all. It can't tend to efficiency if there is no sort of uniformity of training and whatever there may be to be urged against 'working up for the inspection', I can't believe it's a sound system to let everybody run his show on his own.

I'm taking Dugald for a little shoot: we start at the end of this month & should be back end of October, so I fear we are not likely to meet just yet.

Yrs. ever

Richard Lawley

It is interesting that Douglas Haig kept this letter from his former brother officer and fellow member of the 7 Hussars' polo team. No doubt he considered the advice and decided against it. At the time he had had no firm offer of either appointment. All he knew was that for the time being he should keep his head down and concentrate on making the 17 Lancers the most efficient cavalry regiment in the army.

It is a truth universally acknowledged, as Jane Austin might have said, that an officer's most exciting and satisfying commands are his first platoon or troop and his battalion or regiment. No doubt this is how Douglas Haig felt when he was appointed to command the 17

Lancers. Having failed to persuade the authorities to move the regiment to either York or Aldershot, he made the best of his Scottish appointment despite its wide geographical spread, with a detachment in Portobello, a squadron in Glasgow and the remainder in Piershill Barracks, Edinburgh. Apparently the only available space in the vicinity large enough for cavalry drill was the beach at Portobello.

The old adage of 'half a day's pay for half a day's work' did not apply to the 17 Lancers under Douglas Haig. They worked hard for six days and on the Sabbath the Commanding Officer took several of his officers to play golf at Muirfield. Duff Cooper's description of life for the 17th at Piershill was as follows:

Throughout his career Haig attached the greatest importance to physical fitness. While he was at Edinburgh every day of the week was fully occupied and on Sundays a regular routine was observed. It began with a three-mile drive in a fly from the barracks to Waverley Station, a half-hour journey to Drem and then a four-mile walk to the golf course of Muirfield. During the walk there and back and the two rounds of golf that were played, each man carried his own clubs, for local sabbatarianism forbade the employment of caddies. On these expeditions Haig always insisted on paying all expenses and when occasionally the others protested he would say that all he asked of them was that they should do the same for their own junior officers when their turn came to command.

This intensity of work by the Commanding Officer was presumably only possible because he was not married. There was a different routine in the winter and also golf was obviously not allowed to conflict with polo. He himself still hunted with the Warwickshire, using Radway Grange as his base. In January 1902 he had a bad fall and dislocated his shoulder. The shoulder was put back in place in the hunting field and he hacked the 12 miles back to Radway! He recorded in his diary next day that the shoulder was somewhat stiff.

Haig's diary for 1902 records something like half-a-dozen Sunday golf expeditions, but polo was played at least once a week. Haig considered the skills required of a good polo player were highly appropriate to a cavalryman's training. There are references to the use of polo for training purposes in some of the diary entries and letters quoted above, both in the Sudan for the training of Egyptian cavalry and in South Africa. Polo was work, particularly for the polo team.

The Inter-Regimental Polo Tournament had lapsed during the South African War. Mainly through Haig's influence, supported for once by Roberts, the Commander-in-Chief, it was revived in 1903. Much to everyone's surprise, the 17 Lancers, dark horses from Scotland, turned out to be a thoroughly efficient side. They just managed to beat the Rifle Brigade (surprising to find an infantry regiment, who were good at polo) in the semi-final and met the Blues in the final. The 17th were considered to be the under-dogs, but won easily by five goals to one. Sadly the 7 Hussars, without Douglas Haig, came nowhere. A press item reporting the Tournament noted that since it started in 1878 the 7 Hussars had won the cup six times, including four times running from 1883 –86, then again in 1898. Douglas Haig had played in their winning team three times.

Haig's appointment was not without controversy. Many thought that one of the regiment's own officers should have become the new Commanding Officer. In the first place Major the Hon. Herbert Lawrence, one of the 17 Lancers' senior majors, was thought to have been passed over and in consequence resigned. In fact he did not resign until May 1903, when Haig had already been in the post for ten months. He was married to the Hon. Isabel Mills, daughter of the first Lord Hillingdon, MP and senior partner in the bank, Glynn, Mills, Currie and Co. He may have felt that, with doubts being cast on the future of the Lancer Regiments, following the Army Order dated 1 March 1903, which said that the Lancers and Dragoons would have their lances in future for ceremonial purposes only, it was time for him to pursue a career in the City and make some money. He evidently did not fall out with Douglas Haig, as his letter congratulating him on the success of the 17 Lancers' polo team shows. In 1918, as Lieutenant General Lawrence, he became Field Marshal Sir Douglas Haig's Chief of the General Staff. They worked together extremely successfully.

> Wilderness, Sevenoaks
> 12th July 1903

My dear Colonel,

A thousand congratulations on your brilliant victory. The whole Army owes you a debt for what you have done for polo. Without your influence the Tournament would have been a thing of the past, and without your coaching and example the regiment would never have won this brilliant victory. The Army owes you a great deal, and the regiment owes you still more. I am quite miserable I couldn't be there to see it and to congratulate you in person. That I wasn't there wasn't my fault but my misfortune. I hope I shall see you before you go East.

Yours very sincerely,

H.A. Lawrence

The other senior major, who was thought to have resigned from the army in pique when Haig became colonel of the 17 Lancers, was Harry Ricardo. He had more reason to be unhappy with Haig as was shown by Haig's letter to Henrietta dated 20 April 1902. He was in command of the depot at Dundalk and was clearly very efficient as an administrator. Haig, in his Corps report about him, had said that he should not be given command of a cavalry regiment in war. He refers again to Ricardo in a letter dated 11 May 1902, saying that he would recommend him for anything except the command of a Cavalry regiment in the field. Exasperated, he suggests several alternative futures for Ricardo, including becoming Equerry to the King (referred to as Tum). Ricardo did not become an equerry, but he did become a Gentleman at Arms. So he ended up as almost a courtier! Another alternative future was to marry an heiress, Miss Keyser. Maybe he did!

After the South African War a Commission was set up in October 1902 under the Chairmanship of Lord Elgin.[2] It examined the performance of the Army in the war, and discussed future needs to improve efficiency. Amongst the subjects on which evidence was taken were the future of cavalry in relation to mounted infantry and the arms with which the cavalry should be equipped. Ian Hamilton considered that the cavalry should be replaced entirely by mounted infantry. This was supported to a considerable extent by Lord Roberts. In any case the lance was abolished in March 1903, although the sword survived, described as a mediaeval toy by Ian Hamilton. The order abolishing lances was rescinded in 1908 and the lance survived as a weapon of war until 1927.

Haig was one of a number of cavalry officers who gave evidence. He had noted the effectiveness of cavalry armed with modern rifles in South Africa and even when they were armed with carbines in Sudan. His evidence read:

The ideal cavalry is that which can fight on foot and attack on horseback, and I am thoroughly satisfied from what I have seen in South Africa that the necessity of training cavalry to charge is as great as it was in the days of Napoleon.

Cavalry (though in a few situations it may be strengthened by the support of mounted infantry) will be able to act successfully without it, but mounted infantry cannot act strategically alone and independently of cavalry. For horsemen armed with firearms only (though highly-trained as cavalry) cannot cope successfully with cavalry either in attack or defence . . .

To take away from cavalry its power of assuming the active offensive by mounted action, by depriving it of the *arme blanche*, is to withhold from it a considerable advantage without any compensating gain.

He also gave evidence about the need for cavalry regiments to have their own transport. His evidence was reported by *The Regiment* of March 1903:

Amongst the all-conflicting evidence that has been given before the War Commission it is refreshing to read the very practical suggestion put forward by Colonel D Haig CB, 17th Lancers, concerning the equipment of cavalrymen. He advocates the provision of light regimental transport to carry the daily requirements of men and horses. Colonel Haig's suggestion strikes at the root of our immobility during the recent Boer campaign. Equipped as he was with an unnecessarily heavy saddle and wallets, a nosebag of horse food, rifle, sword, lance, great coat, blankets and other paraphernalia, the cavalryman looked more like a travelling showman than a death dealing soldier. No one knows better than a cavalryman himself how all these goods and chattels retarded his progress in pursuit of the wily Boer, and to what extent they were responsible for knocked-up horses.

Haig's views were sent in a private letter to Lord Jessel,[3] a Conservative Member of Parliament and former officer in the 17 Lancers, from Piershill Barracks, Edinburgh, on 2 April 1903, in response to a letter from Jessel, seeking his opinion:

Many thanks for your letter. Personally I think our regiments of Cavalry should be armed in equal proportions viz. half the Cavalry should have swords; the other half lances – but I believe that a good hog spear would be better than the existing long lance. There is no doubt that the latter is

224

an impediment when scouting and when dismounted, but I don't think it is wise to abolish the lance.

Strategical reconnaissance must culminate in a tactical collision if the enemy possesses Cavalry; we want the lance for this.

I have expressed my opinion to the War Compt. very strongly that I consider Cavalry (properly trained) should fulfil all the requirements of mounted troops, and that the Mounted Infantry should be abolished.

No country can afford to maintain mounted troops of different values.

It is rather a long story, but if you have a desire to discuss the question further, I'll come and call on you next time I am in London – I shall be there next week as I am a Member of a Committee which meets at Aldershot on Mon., Tues. and Wedy. next week on questions concerned with Cavalry equipment, sword, etc.

Thanking you for the interest you have taken in our arm.

This letter was sent to Lady Haig in February 1930, under cover of the following letter from Lord Jessel , from his house in South Street, Mayfair:

Some time ago Sir Frederick Maurice[4] wrote to the *Times* requesting anyone who had any letters from the Field Marshal to forward them to him. In turning over some documents, I found an interesting letter to myself on the subject of Lances. After the Boer War on the initiative of Sir Ian Hamilton, a movement was on foot to abolish cavalry and substitute mounted infantry. The idea was strongly resisted by several members of the House of Commons, who had served in Lancer regiments, viz. Captain Sinclair (afterwards Lord Rathcreedan[5]), Sir William Younger[6] and myself. We pointed out that the experience of one War was not sufficient criterion and that the British Army had to operate all over the world. In the Great War no mounted infantry was used and the cavalry campaign in Palestine was one of the greatest achievements of the War. I forward the letter in the hope it may be of some use and should be glad to have it returned when copied.

With kind regards.

PS I have just remembered that when I was Deputy Director of Remounts at the War Office we wrote a letter to the Field Marshal asking for his views about the cavalry at the end of 1918 or commencement of 1919. There was a strong movement as there is now, to abolish the cavalry and no longer use horses. The Field Marshal wrote a despatch to the Army Council in which amongst other matters, he stated that, if the Germans had had any cavalry left in 1918, they could have driven a wedge between the British and French Armies. I hope that it will be possible for you to obtain from the War Office the despatch containing these views.

The War Office did not have a separate despatch on this subject; Lord Jessel may have been thinking of the Field Marshal's final First World War despatch, which includes the following paragraph:

The absence of hostile cavalry at this period (the German offensive, March 1918) was a marked feature of the battle. Had the Germans had at their disposal even two or three well-trained Cavalry Divisions, a wedge might have been driven between the French and British Armies. Their presence could not have failed to have added greatly to the difficulties of our task.

Apart from his evidence on the armaments appropriate to modern cavalry, Haig was evidently questioned by the Elgin Commission on the subject of regimental spirit. His splendidly tongue-in-cheek response was:

I am not in a Highland regiment, but I fancy there are a good many non-Highlanders in them; anyhow, they get the traditions, and Englishmen joining get to believe they are Scotchmen. There is a little leaven of Highlanders that leavens the lot.

Douglas Haig's appointment to become Inspector-General of Cavalry in India was announced in early August 1903. It appeared in the press as follows:

Colonel Douglas Haig, CB, ADC, who has recently been selected to succeed General Sir E Locke Elliot[7] as Inspector-General of Cavalry in India, is only forty-one years of age, and since his return from South Africa where, during the greater part of the recent war, he was Chief Staff Officer to General Sir John French, he has commanded with conspicuous success the 17th (Duke of Cambridge's Own) Lancers – the old 'Death or Glory Boys'. By the time he arrives in India, Colonel Haig will have

226

entered upon his forty-third year. No case is recorded in the annals of the British Army in India of an Officer being appointed to a post of such distinction and importance at anything like so early a period in his career. In Colonel Haig's case the exception is thoroughly well merited. His service comprises a brilliant series of accomplishments and achievements. It was in the 7th (Queen's Own) Hussars that Colonel Haig's military record commenced. This was in 1885. After leaving the Staff College where he was the most brilliant student of his year, he went to Egypt, where he took part in the battles of Atbara and Omdurman, was mentioned in despatches and obtained a brevet majority. After the fall of Khartoum he joined General French, who was in command of the Cavalry Brigade at Aldershot, and has been closely associated with him ever since. In South Africa, Colonel Haig acted as Chief of Staff to General French's Cavalry Division until the army was split up, and then became commander of a field column.

Before leaving for India, Haig was invited to Balmoral.

### Diary for 3 October 1903

Reached Aberdeen about 11 am. Breakfast alone with Lord Selborne[8] (1st Lord of Admiralty) at refreshment rooms and leave at 12.20 for Ballater. Get to Balmoral before 3 pm and was driven at great pace by coachman.

### 4 October 1903

His Majesty presents me with the CVO in recognition of services which I rendered in the past and would render in the future as IG of Cavalry in India, and as 'mark of personal esteem' also a stick as a remembrance of my visit. After lunch drove with His Majesty and Prince Alexander of Teck[9] to Gelder Shiel. We had tea and walked home. Sat next the King at dinner.

### Letter to Henrietta dated 4 October from Balmoral

After lunch today I drove with His Majesty to Gelder Shiel (I think) where we walked about ½ mile to see a waterfall and then took tea in a place which the late Queen used to like very much. His Majesty was in the best of spirits and is sending you a haunch of venison. He asked me your station tho' he remembered the postal station. I told him Thurston. Then fully an hour after, when we were at tea, he got out an envelope and, without saying anything, wrote your address on the back of it, and then said to me 'I have put it down so as not to forget it'. I mention all this so that you may know whence the haunch came when it arrives, and that the King has taken all the trouble himself about sending it. His Majesty has desired me to write to him when I go to India!

Douglas Haig arrived in Bombay on 30 October 1903. He travelled from there to Simla.

### Letter to Henrietta dated 5 November 1903

I left Bombay on Saturday afternoon last week. We got to Kalka about 7 am on Monday. As a rule one has to drive in tongas taking a few light things with one while the heavy baggage follows by bullock cart. The Engineer of the new Simla Kalka railway ran a train for my convenience. We left at 8.30 am. The line is a very narrow gauge (about 2ft.). The curves were very sharp and gradients extremely steep, so we had to go slowly and got here without running off the rails. This is certainly a more comfortable means of getting along than the tonga. I found a pony etc. sent by Hamilton to meet me, and I went at once to Snowdon where he stays with Lord Kitchener. We had tea and a pleasant chat with Lord K. till it was dinner time. The latter was dining out, but I dined at Snowdon with Hubert Hamilton and the personal staff.

On Tuesday I saw Lord K. in his office and discussed Cavalry matters, upon which questions he and I are quite agreed. I also took over my own office which is in the same building as Lord K's.

Tuesday night I dined with the C. in C. There was a big dinner party of 30. Lady Curzon[10] was there, but not HE the Viceroy,[11] as the latter slipped over the tail of his pony when riding up a slope and got kicked. A clot of blood seems to have formed, and so he is staying still in bed until it becomes absorbed. Lord K. makes a excellent host and gave us a capital dinner. The Viceroy's band played afterwards. K. brought a French cook out with him when he took command.

People seem to keep late hours at Simla. It was almost midnight before the guests left Snowdon and Lord K. asked me to sit down and have a chat and a whisky and soda, so that it was after 12.30 before I left his house.

The Chief is looking very fit and well, and is in the best of spirits. I think that already K. has done a vast amount of good. Lord K. wired home; 'Haig has taken over. Has he been made a Major General yet? I hope this will be done'. In any case I wear the uniform and am called MG.

The response from the War Office was noted in Haig's diary:

**7 October 1903.**
    . . . the reply stated that I wd. be gazetted a substantive Colonel
    and Brigadier General. In 6 months time on recommendation of
    Lord Kitchener my name wd. be considered for promotion.

## Letter to Henrietta from Allahabad 12 November 1903

I got here from Simla yesterday morning, and have been busy inspecting
the 4th Bengal Lancers. I take the regiment here out for 24 hours work
in the field. I enclose a programme of the sort of things I see.

    I don't think I told you that I went over my house at Simla. A very
nice one and just the right size. It stands on hill above Annandale where
there is a Polo ground, and quite close to my office. It is more or less
furnished, and you know I bought a few extra things from General
Smith- Dorrien,[12] the last occupant, but I wd. be much obliged if you
would send me out a good writing table. The one I have in my bedroom at
the flat wd. do, and a couple of nice arm chairs and a good chair for the
writing table.[13]

    I wd. like to make my own room comfortable. It is 19 ft 9 in. by 14
ft. 6 in. I'll get a good carpet here but wd. like curtains to cover four doors
4 feet wide and 7 ft 6 in. from where the curtain rods are. The room has
pink on the walls and white paint.

    The climate is quite pleasant here at nights tho' they say they have
had terribly hot weather this year. Allahabad is an old cantonment with
fine houses and trees etc. I leave on Saturday for Lucknow where I spend
a week, then to Fyzabad for 3 days and on to Jhansi for a camp of
exercise and get to Rawal Pindi on 2nd December with Lord K.

## Letter from Lucknow 19 November

I came here on Sunday morning and leave again next Sunday evening for
Fyzabad. My Brigade Major and I have had a Bungalow lent us here and
every arrangement made for us by the 5th DGs. I spent Monday and
Tuesday inspecting them, and yesterday and today the 6th Cavalry.
Tomorrow I have them both out bivouacking about 20 miles apart for
reconnaissance and field service duties and return Saturday.

    You will have seen that poor Lord K. has broken his leg. This will
upset all his plans for the winter and is a great disappointment to us all
for he always makes things go, wherever he is. I was to have been with him
at the big manoeuvres at Pindi.

## Letter from Jhansi 26 November 1903

You ask after my health. Many thanks, I feel very well indeed. I get lots of exercise, mental and physical. If you glance at the programme of my inspections which I sent to you, you will see that I spend 3 days as a rule with each regiment and bivouac with them on the nights they are out . . . .

You would be surprised at the amount of baggage and stuff I have to go about with – horses and clerks and office boxes and orderlies. I am half ashamed at the number of bullock waggons required to convey all this stuff to and from the station. Then they fire a salute of guns when I come and go at each station, so 'l'arrivée' is most impressive at times – especially for the regiments, for they are not quite certain what to expect.

## Letter from Darapoor, 20 miles West of Jhelum, 29 December 1903

I spent Xmas in camp at Lala Musa: it is a junction on the N.W. Railway between Wazirabad and Jhelum. Colonel Biddulph[14] of the 19th Lancers is with me and has his hawks.

We left Lala Musa on the 26th and moved to Dingah – about 15 miles westwards. It took 16 camels to carry our camp and kit – some were very wild as most of the good ones had been requisitioned for the recent manoeuvres – so there was a good deal of delay in getting along. Then when the camp did start a passing train frightened one of the brutes and he threw his load and disturbed some of the others – so it was after sunset (5.30 pm) before the camp reached Dingah. The latter is a very old town with narrow streets paved with bricks. We stayed in the Dak Bungalow, quite a well-built house. It was from Dingah that Lord Gough[15] set out to fight the battle of Chilianwallah. During the night the camelmen from Lala Musa ran away (but without their pay!). So we got another lot at Dingah – a much better lot.

On Sunday we moved to Rusool. On the way I rode over the battlefield of Chilianwallah, where Gough made rather an ass of himself. We sent on the hawks in the morning and we killed some Obarah (a kind of bustard) quite close to the obelisk where most of the dead are buried. Rusool is on the Jhelum. It is famous as the spot where the water for the Jhelum canal is drawn off the river of that name. Alexander the Great[16] also crossed the river at this point and defeated Porus.[17]

We stayed in the rest Bungalow at Rusool and yesterday crossed over the river to this place. We left the tents and heavy things at Rusool to move lower down the river to a place opposite Jalalpoor. We brought 4 ponies over. They jumped into the boat from the sand after a little coaxing. Another boat conveyed our servants and cooking things etc. Col. Biddulph and I crossed in a small skiff.

As I think I told you I am looking round the country with a view to conducting a Cavalry Staff Ride in this district in February; and at the same time we get some sport with the hawks and an occasional shot. But this is not a good country for snipe. Yesterday we killed 2 geese with the Peregrine hawks. It seems wonderful how these small birds can tackle such a much bigger and stronger one.

Tomorrow we work back via Jalalpoor to Ramnagar on the Chenab, and then to Wazirabad. I leave the latter place on 3rd January for Delhi to direct some manoeuvres in that vicinity.

The two baskets with the mess kit, knives, forks, plates etc. do very well, and I was able to start off on this trip without any bother. I shall have my own mess at the manoeuvres and also at the Staff Tour in February. Secrett takes general charge and does very well.

The climate here is perfect at present. Every night we have a fine big fire as it freezes. By day the sun is bright and warm.

## Letter from Nowshera 29 March 1904

At present I am staying with the 8th Cavalry in rooms in their Mess House. This is most comfortable and leaves me free to have my meals where I like, but there is another Cavalry regiment here and a Colonel commands the station, who all want to entertain me and I hear say that the Officer Commanding the 8th (who is the most junior) had no right to invite me before them. So you see how difficult it is to please them all. But, as you know, I have my work to do, and what with bivouacs and parades, I don't give them much time for entertainment.

Smith Dorrien was awfully kind at Quetta and insisted on providing me with all kinds of supplies for the journey, and also for the 24 hours I spent in bivouac near Quetta. I left Quetta last Friday and arrived here about 4 am on Monday. I spent about 6 or 7 hours in Lahore on Sunday morning on my way here, so it was not a bad journey. I had a cooking carriage though I don't think the natives care very much whether they have a cooking carriage or not, as they carry their own metal charcoal 'sizzries' as they call them, and cook just as well in the adjoining compartment as in the cooking place I find.

You can imagine what an amount of baggage I have. It is not any trouble to me as it is moved to and from the train by Govt. transport (carts and people) but I think it is an unnecessary expense to Govt. as I give a warrant in payment for carrying it – about 6 or 7 bullock cart loads! I have so many different kinds of uniform and also plain clothes for hot and cool places, the 'office' and a heap of useless papers. The Babu's bed or 'lounge' as he calls it with office table and chair, besides my cooking and mess arrangements.

Then there is the Dhobi's bundle (stock in trade) including a particular piece of wood (which to me looks like any other piece of wood) but which he assured me makes all the difference to the way the shirts are done up (I think he irons on it). But all the bundle is usually on the gentleman's back, like the world on the shoulders of the man of ancient mythology. Of course I could not do without the Dhobi, but next year by having headquarters at Meerut I can reduce the office and kit very considerably besides having a more agreeable winter for myself as I could arrange to have a few days off between the different towns.

I finish here on Friday and leave at midday for Umballa and Simla. I therefore hope to get to Simla next Sunday afternoon (3rd April) and will be able to get things in order before Lord K. arrives. He is sure to put me on to do or work out all kinds of Cavalry questions, including 'the cost' to Govt. of my proposals.

## Letter from Simla 1 September 1904

I think General French thought that he might have got the Bombay Command which General Hunter got this time last year. There are four 'Commands' as they are called; – Punjab, Bengal, Bombay and Madras. There was never any doubt about Kitchener coming as Commander in Chief, though I know the latter would much prefer a billet such as Cromer has in Egypt.

The C in C in India really has very little power. All the Supply, Transport and Finance are under an individual called the 'Military Member of Council'. That is to say that Lord K may order men to Thibet but he does not know whether they will starve or not because he has nothing to do with the supply arrangements. Such a system is obviously ridiculous. It is like a pair of horses in double harness without a coachman.

The latter ought to be the Viceroy but he has too many things to attend to already, even if he was capable of discharging such duties, which the majority of Viceroys are not. At home the 'Military Council' represent the coachman now. Of course there must be some confusion in the War Office at home after such a thorough shaking up, but I doubt if it is right to call it 'chaos'. Throw into a tank a number of bodies of varying sizes and weights and you have the present state of affairs. There is bound to be a 'settling down' and a re-arrangement of bodies which have got into unsuitable places. But I feel sure that the system of Army Control which has been started is a sound one. I don't mean Arnold-Forster's[18] scheme, about which I don't know enough to pronounce an opinion.

You doubt whether Alan (Fletcher[19]) is 'clever enough' for the job! The so-called sharp people very often disappoint us or cheat or have some other drawback such as being disagreeable, bad-tempered, etc. All I

232

require is people of average intelligence who are keen to do their jobs properly. Alan is well up to this standard and is most unselfish and tactful, so I find it a pleasure to go about with him.

I am also fortunate in my Brigade Major (MacAndrew[20] of the 5th Bengal Cavalry). You remember I chose him on account of what I saw as an Intelligence Officer in S. Africa. I think his father was Provost of Inverness and lost all his money in the Glasgow Bank crash. The appointment of Brigade Major is an annual one but I have taken M on for another year. He is most thorough and arranges everything so well and without fuss.

I have also taken on a stout little party called Colonel Middleton[21] of the Bengal Cavalry as Assistant Director of Cavalry Manoeuvres for the winter. He is a pleasant little man – something like French, and curiously enough he married a niece of French's. I sent him to Meerut and Peshawar last week to see the various generals in those parts, and explain the arrangements which I wished made for the Camps in the Punjab. There has been very little rain yet in that part of India, so he had an unpleasant journey and came back with a bad cold, but did all I wanted. Middleton commanded his regiment for 2 years in Tirah as a Major, then for 5 years as a Lieut. Colonel and has still 2 more years to run as CO. So you can understand COs. of Native Cavalry Regiments are fairly antiquated.

I have given you a long story today in case I may be short of time for next week's mail.

## Letter from Jhansi 17 November 1904

Yours of 24th October reached me last Saturday night (12th Nov.) at Meerut before I left for here. Quite a quick mail. Many thanks for it, and for all the trouble which you took to send me a camera. It has not turned up yet, but will no doubt arrive in time: meantime Alan has a splendid camera of his own and has taken a good many pictures of various men and places: you will of course have copies.

He went off to Agra to see the Taj yesterday but I expect him back tomorrow forenoon. I thought it was the only chance of him seeing it as I won't be so near Agra again this winter. I have 4 regiments in camp here and have been busy every day since I arrived (last Sunday). I finish on Saturday and leave next morning for Lucknow.

We are staying in the Bungalow of the 1st Lancers' Colonel. He is out in camp with his regiment so we have the whole place to ourselves and 3 trappers to take us about. I was going into camp originally but there was a case of anthrax among the mules, and so the camp in which the animal was, was put in quarantine for a fortnight, and the other regiments were also separated for fear of contagion. So it was decided that I wd. be better placed for reaching the various camps from Jhansi than if I was actually in one of the camps away from the main road.

At Lucknow we are to stay with Maj. Gen. Sir Elliot who used to visit Navan occasionally in days gone by for hunting. I shall only be there 'till Thursday as I have to be at a camp near Delhi on the Friday morning. It is lovely weather here now; bright cold mornings and cold evenings the moment the sun goes down. It seems to me much colder than when I was here last year in December. There has been a good deal of snow already in the hills which doubtless makes a difference here also.

Please thank Percy for his kindly wishes 'to make a pile for me'! But I believe I have as much money as is good for me! I have some good ponies and horses and enjoy myself pretty well without feeling the want of money. Too much luxury is ruining the country (I mean England) and also the Yankees!!

## Letter from Lucknow 23 November 1904

I am staying with Sir E. Locke Elliot. He commands the Lucknow Division and spends much time on the race course which he has in splendid order and in a sound financial condition.

I have been inspecting the Royals who are stationed here. They have had a difficult time finding out how to keep horses fit in India and generally settling down as none of the officers had ever been out in India with a Cavalry regiment before.

## Letter from Gurgaon, near Delhi 1 December 1904

I left Lucknow on Thursday evening last and got to Delhi next morning – rode out southwards to the Koitah (about 11 miles) where I stayed in Adam Khan's Court – a fine big dome of a place now used as a Police Officers' rest house. I supervised some Cavalry manoeuvres on Friday night and Saturday and got in to Camp here on Sunday morning.

I see that you are still excusing yourself for assisting the enemy and travelling in the German subsidized Mail boats, alias Commerce Destroyers! I am going to travel home by the Messageries Maritimes Steamer leaving Bombay on 20th April, because the P&O decline to give me a cabin to myself unless I pay an extra fare. The Messageries give me a 3 berth cabin for a single fare & £20 extra – and a bathroom to myself! As the steamers leaving in April are so crowded I shall be much better off on the French boat, besides encouraging 'l'entente cordiale'.

## Letter from Aurangabad 14 December 1904

I left Mhow on Sunday morning early. We slept in our carriage and so had a good rest on the Sabbath and got here very comfortably on Tuesday morning. We got out at Daulatabad, about 8 miles from this, and went over the old fort.

It is really a wonderful old place – a single hill with the sides of rock cut shear down for a hundred feet or more, and a great ditch hewn out of solid rock all round. Then the entrance into the fort is only big enough to admit one man at a time, and it is cut into the side of the hill through solid rock, so that it comes out (after winding about for 100 yards or more with torches) in the centre of the hill. After then ascending some winding steps one gets about 3 parts of the way up, and then there is the remains of an iron cage in which a fire was lighted after it had been drawn over the stairway. A hole is cut through the rock to the outside to admit air and cause a draught through the fire. Then still higher there is a spring of water said to come from the mountain ridge about 2 or 3 miles away.

All this was made about 800 years ago or more by the Mahrattas. Aurangzeb[22] besieged the place for three years in 1600 odd. I mention all this to let you see what wonderful old castles there are in India, about which there are no books written and few people know about. It would be a revelation to those of the New World I fancy. Also it would open the eyes of the self satisfied scientists of the present day to see Aurangzeb's water system which still supplies the city here. He brought water from the hills 6 or 7 miles distant in stone pipes; that is stones with long holes drilled in them, and the ends of each laid alongside and cemented. The pipes and fountains are still in use! How much of London will be standing in 2200? I got some tobacco made in Aurangzeb's time and fired some powder made by his people!

I am really pretty busy – some 35 officers or more here for a Staff Ride. Sir Archibald Hunter joins me tomorrow as a spectator. We work across the hills from here to Adjunta and then I take a train on Wednesday 21st at Jalgaon (near Bhusawal Junction) for Meerut where I spend Xmas.

## Letter from Meerut 23 March 1905

I have started on that physic, but I scarcely want such things as I am very fit, thank you. Hubert Hamilton (K's Mil. Sec.) and Sclater[23] (the QMG) have much more need of these sorts of things. They seemed to be worn out and in need of a rest. They have had a terrible winter helping K to fight Curzon over the system of Army Administration in India. K seemed very fit and well and in the best of spirits.

I did not go to see Curzon when I was in Calcutta, as I was so busy, but I see from the papers that he has taken to his bed and was unable to attend the council meeting yesterday. He is doing his utmost to defeat K over this proposal of his to abolish the Military Department. It is sad to see so much energy wasted on fighting amongst themselves, especially by a man like Curzon who poses as a great statesman. K is very far seeing and I cannot see how the Government at home can support Curzon in this, which is mainly a military question.

Curzon has kept putting off sending the despatch home (this includes a dissenting minute from K) for no good reason at all, but really in the hopes of the Government at home going out or something happening to prevent a decision being arrived at. However K, who is most patient, has insisted on action being settled one way or another by May so that if he does not get his way he can resign and leave for home in that month.

I was astonished at K's concentration. He could think and talk to me about little else, and one afternoon spent over 2 hours explaining the whole case and reading me the choice passages from his despatches on the subject.

I am going out on Sunday to the Kadir for the annual pigsticking meet.

## Letter from Meerut 30 March 1905

I had a capital time at the Kadir though my horses had never seen a pig before. I went by train from here to a station beyond the Ganges on the line to Moradabad, called Gujraula, and rode from there about 13 miles to camp. The latter was about 35 miles from here by road at a place called Sherpur. We sat down 60 for dinner. The tents were arranged in a square amongst trees, and our horses were put in another wood about half a mile away to keep the flies which they attract at a distance.

There were between 200 and 300 horses at the camp and each officer could enter two horses for the Kadir Cup. Altogether 120 horses competed in the first round; this was the biggest number attending any meeting. Three horses compete in a heat, and the one who gets first spear remains in the second and so on. I was lucky and won both my first heats.

We had 30 or 40 elephants, after which followed the line of beaters at 30 or 40 yards distance. When one was not riding, one got a good view of what was going on, from the back of an elephant. Everything was very well run. From a printing press to print the daily programmes and the menus, to cut flowers from Meerut and ice from Agra daily!

The weather was perfect. We started the first day at 7.30, stopped about ¾ hour for lunch and went on till after 6 pm. Frank Wormald in

236

the 12 Lancers broke his collar bone and one or two others got a shaking, but otherwise there was no serious accident. So everything went off well.

As already noted Douglas Haig went home on leave on a Messageries Maritimes boat in April, arriving in England on 5 May. A totally unexpected event – marriage changed his life. A brief description of how he met his future wife, the engagement and marriage are given in the following chapter. His diary for this period has no entries covering these events and there are no surviving letters to his sister. The next letter to Henrietta was written on the boat, in which the General and his wife travelled to India, for the General to resume his appointment as Inspector General of Cavalry.

Notes
1. Lieutenant General Sir Drury Drury-Lowe (1830–1908) commanded the 17 Lancers from 1866–1879. His moment of glory came at the Battle of Ulundi (1879) when he led the 17th in a charge. Sir Drury had been knocked off his horse by a spent bullet, but remounted and was able to obey the order of Lord Chelmsford to 'Go at them Lowe'. (Anglesey says that he couldn't remount and the charge was actually led by the second in command.)
2. Victor Alexander Bruce 9th Earl of Elgin KG, GCSI, GCIE (1849–1917) was Viceroy of India 1894–9 and Secretary of State for the Colonies 1905–8. He was Treasurer of the King's Household.
3. Herbert Merton Jessel CB, CMG, (1866–1950) had been a captain in the 17 Lancers. He was a Conservative Member of Parliament 1896–1906 and 1910–18. He became a peer in 1924.
4. Major General Sir Frederick Barton Maurice KCB, known as 'Freddie' (1871–1951) was commissioned into the Derby Regiment in 1892. He served in South Africa, England and the War Office. He went to the Staff College in 1913. He 'retired' after publishing a letter in the press accusing Lloyd George of lying about the strength of the British Army in March 1918.
5. Cecil William Norton 1st Baron Rathcreedan (1850–1930) was an MP from 1892 to 1916, when he was promoted into the House of Lords. He had served in the 5 Lancers and been Brigade Major at Aldershot in 1881–2. He held several junior Government posts.
6. Sir William Younger Bt.(1862–1937) was a Member of Parliament, who briefly was member for a constituency in the Borders and eventually Haig's neighbour after Haig moved into Bemersyde. Younger's home was Ravenswood, just across the River Tweed from Bemersyde.
7. Lieutenant General Sir Edward Locke Elliot KCB, DSO (1850–1938) was an Indian Army officer. He was responsible for several mobile columns in South Africa and was Haig's predecessor as Inspector

General of Cavalry in India. He became a lieutenant general in 1906 and retired in 1911.

8. William Waldegrave 2nd Earl of Selborne KG, GCMG, (1859–1942) was First Lord of the Admiralty from 1900 to 1905. He subsequently became High Commissioner in South Africa. He commanded the 3rd Battalion The Hampshire Regiment.

9. His Serene Highness Prince Alexander of Teck became Major General the 1st Earl of Athlone KG, GCB, GCMG, GCVO, DSO (1874–1957). He was commissioned into the 7 Hussars in 1894 and served in Sudan (Haig mentions him briefly in his account of that campaign). He served in South Africa, where he won his DSO. In the First World War he was with the 2 Life Guards, became a brigadier in 1917 and honorary major general in 1918. He was created Earl of Athlone at the time in the war when the Royal Family changed their name to Windsor. He was Governor General of South Africa from 1923 to 1928 and Governor General of Canada from 1940 to 1946. He was much liked in these appointments.

10. The first Lady Curzon was Mary Victoria Leiter, daughter of Levi Zeigler Leiter of Washington. She died in 1906, after which Curzon married Grace Hinds, daughter of J. Monroe Hinds, at one time US Ambassador to Brazil.

11. George Nathaniel Curzon KG, GCSI, GCIE, (1859–1929) was an MP from 1886 to 1898, when he became Viceroy until 1904. He had been created Baron Curzon of Keddleston before becoming Viceroy. He became an Earl in 1911 and Marquess in 1921. Of his many senior Governmental appointments Secretary of State for Foreign Affairs (1919–24) was the most notable.

12. General Sir Horace Lockwood Smith-Dorrien GCB, DSO (1858–1930) was commissioned into the Derby Regiment in 1876. He was one of five survivors of the Battle of Isandlwana. He was in India and took part in the Tirah campaign, then the Sudan campaign, where he commanded a Sudanese battalion. He was a successful commander in the Second Boer War and was promoted to major general. After further service in India he became the GOC.-in-C. Aldershot before Haig. In 1914 he commanded 2nd Corps after the death of Lieutenant General Sir James Grierson. His action in turning on the Germans at Le Cateau gave the British Expeditionary Force some respite, but he was forced by French to resign. He became Governor of Gibraltar in 1918. He died in a car accident in 1930. His soldiers are said to have considered that he must be a good general, because his flow of bad language was equal to theirs! Perhaps this was one of the benefits of his education at Harrow!

13. The writing table, nice arm chairs and good chair for the writing table can be seen in the photograph of General Haig's sitting room at his house in Simla.

14. Most probably Lieutenant Colonel Stephen Francis Biddulph, Indian

Army, who retired in 1910. Presumably his original regiment in the British Army was the 19 Lancers.

15. Lord (Hugh) Gough was attempting to conquer the Sikhs and occupy the Punjab, following the First Sikh War of 1845–6. In January 1849 he fought a 12,000 strong Sikh army at Chillianwala, on the River Jhelum and was soundly defeated, losing 132 officers killed and total casualties of nearly 2,500. Gough claimed a victory. The military authorities in London decided to retire Gough as superannuated and incompetent.

16. Alexander the Great (356–323 BC) crossed the Hindu Kush into Northern India in 328 BC, moving into the Punjab in the spring of 326 BC. He crossed the Indus and reached the River Hydaspes, before his Macedonian army refused to go any further and Alexander returned home.

17. One of the Princes against whom Alexander fought was Porus, who fought gallantly and was badly wounded, then captured. Alexander was so impressed with him that, instead of killing him – the usual practice – he befriended him. Porus became Alexander's ally and was left in charge of much of the conquered territory when Alexander retreated. He was assassinated some time between 321 and 315 BC.

18. The Right Honourable Hugh Oakley Arnold-Forster (1855–1909) was MP for West Belfast from 1899–1906, then for Croydon from 1906 until he died. He was Secretary of State for War from 1903-06.

19. Lieutenant Colonel Alan Francis Fletcher was born in 1876 and commissioned into the 17 Lancers in 1897. He remained Haig's ADC throughout the 1914–18 war. Anyone who has been an ADC knows that no outstanding intellect is required!

20. Major General Henry John Milnes MacAndrew (1866–1919) was commissioned into the Lincolnshire Regiment in 1866, but transferred into the Indian Army in 1888. After his time as Haig's brigade major he stayed in India in staff appointments. In 1915 he became Brigadier General Staff of the Indian Cavalry Corps, before being given command of the 5th Indian Cavalry Division in the Middle East in 1916. He died accidentally in a fire.

21. Colonel Herbert John James Middleton born 1856, commissioned 1876, became a colonel in 1905, retired in 1913. He was in the Indian Army throughout his career.

22. Aurangzeb was the last of the great Moghul Emperors (1618–1707). He was a devout Muslim and persecuted the Hindus in his empire. He didn't succeed in taking Daulatabad, but it fell after his death to Shah Jehan and the Nizam of Hyberabad.

23. General Sir Henry Crichton Sclater KCB (1855–1923) was commissioned into the Royal Artillery in 1876 and served in Egypt, Ireland, Aldershot and South Africa before becoming Quarter Master General in India in 1904. He commanded a division in India. He became Adjutant General to the Army in 1914.

# Chapter 9

# Marriage, India and the
# War Office

## 1905 – 1908

Douglas Haig went home on leave in spring 1905, arriving in early May. He was invited by the King to stay at Windsor for Ascot races. The invitation seems to have been rather a last minute affair and Haig was described by one of the household as the 'extra' guest. One of the Maids of Honour on duty that week was the Hon. Dorothy Vivian,[1] known as Doris. She and her twin sister Violet were both Maids of Honour. Their brother, George (Lord Vivian), was in the 17 Lancers and had been badly wounded at Tarkastad (see letter to Henrietta dated 22 September 1901). Surprisingly, George had never introduced his sisters to his Commanding Officer, although they were all at the finals of the Inter-Regimental Polo in 1903. Also Haig had written to Lady Vivian, George's mother, to re-assure her that his wounds would not be mortal.

The meeting between Haig and Doris at Windsor in June 1905 was therefore their first. By the end of the week they were engaged to be married, having only officially been introduced to each other on Thursday evening. This arme blanche approach to courtship seems mainly to have taken place on the golf course on Friday! Haig and Doris were playing against the Duke of Devonshire and a lady, whose name has not been recorded. The Duke was a remarkably bad golfer and was a visitor to most of the bunkers on the course. This left plenty of opportunity for Haig to talk to the lady with whom he had obviously fallen so dramatically in love.

The next morning, Saturday, they arranged to play golf again, this time before breakfast. No golf was played, however, and Haig proposed. He had intended that they should find a quiet seat, where he would propose, but there was none to be found. At this he blurted out 'I must propose to you standing!' Doris's comment was; 'This was very abrupt and I must say unexpected, but I accepted him.' A first introduction on Thursday evening followed by proposal and acceptance of marriage on Saturday before breakfast could reasonably be described as 'abrupt' or indeed 'very abrupt'.

On Saturday afternoon Haig was playing golf at Sunningdale in a foursome with his brother John. Between the thirteenth and fourteenth holes they were accosted by a mounted orderly, who brought a letter ordering Haig back to Windsor Castle for the remainder of the weekend. The King and Queen seem to have been thoroughly amused by the whole episode. The King said to Haig; 'What do you mean coming to my house and trying to take away one of the Queen's best Maids of Honour?' To Doris he said that she must do her utmost not to interfere with the military work of my 'best and most capable General'. Queen Alexandra wrote to Lady Vivian, a letter which Haig took with him when he called on her to ask permission to marry her daughter. The original letter is now in the Museum of Edinburgh Lady Vivian had at first refused to see him, but Haig in his turn refused to go away. Eventually his persistence and the Queen's letter won the day and permission was given.

Among the letters of congratulations received by the couple was one from St. John Brodrick, Secretary of State for War in 1901–2.

34 Portland Place
London, W.
June 30th '05

Dear Miss Vivian,

Will you think me intrusive if I write a line of very warm congratulation on your engagement? When we were labouring in 1901–2 I used to hear from returning officers one chorus of panegyric of the ideal staff officer, who from the first had made the reputation of his chiefs, and I always knew whose name would follow the preamble. I do not suppose there is a more popular, appreciated or successful officer in the Army, and I wish you joy with all my heart.

Yours v. truly,

St. John Brodrick

The marriage took place in the Private Chapel in Buckingham Palace. It was an extremely happy one, which ended only on the death of the

241

Field Marshal in January 1928. There were three daughters and a son.

Major General Douglas Haig and his bride travelled to India in the Messageries Maritimes ship, *Ville de la Ciotat*, which left Marseilles on 30 August.

## Letter to Henrietta written from SS *Ville de la Ciotat*, 3 September 1905

We expect to reach Port Said about 8 or 9 tonight so I must write you a line to tell you of our journey since we left you in Paris. Doris and I had a very comfortable journey to Marseilles, where we arrived at 9.30 a.m. on Wednesday morning. The servants had already arrived and gone off with the baggage to the docks which are only some 10 minutes in a cab from the station.

The *Ville de la Ciotat* was alongside the jetty and we walked on board without any hustle. Secrett took us to our cabin and reported 'all correct'. She is a fine big ship for this part of the world, and as there are very few passengers, Doris and I have been given each a cabin adjoining with a door communicating between the two. We have also been given a third cabin for our baggage, so, as far as accommodation goes, we could not be much better off. I don't think the feeding is as good as on board the ship on which I came home, but possibly the good fare which you provided for us at home may make one look at things in a different light.

The steamer which arrived at Marseilles two days before we left had had a terrible tossing in the Mediterranean, but we have not felt it. The wind however has been with us and yesterday and today it has been quite hot. Friday our port holes had to be shut but our cabins were still cool as we have an electric fan in each one.

The days have passed quite pleasantly. Doris is an excellent traveller and is always cheery and ready to make the best of things. We sit at table with a Frenchman and his wife, the Judge of the High Court of Noumea. Quite pleasant people, and we talk French all the time. We have 'café au lait' between 8 and 9 and breakfast at 12 o'clock, dinner at 6.30 p.m. A simple life and early hours, but you can have many more meals if you like, i.e. one between each of those I mention, namely early tea, afternoon tea (4 p.m.) and again tea at 9 p.m. and 'sandveges' for the hungry.

On Wednesday we saw the eclipse very well about noon. Shadows thrown by ropes etc. on deck were quite curious as one side was quite as firm as usual, while the other was fleecy and irregular. The latter was 'thrown by the moon' we were told by a scientific cove on board!

The Haigs reached Bombay on 13 September. They stayed at the Taj Mahal Hotel as guests of Sir Pratap Singh. Doris described meeting Sir Pratap:

> Sir Pratap Singh called on Douglas in the afternoon. He was a dear old man and insisted on our being his guests at the hotel. He and Douglas had played many a game of polo together. In riding clothes he did not look imposing, but in the evening when we dined together he was very gorgeous in rich embroideries and bejewelled turban, which Douglas explained to me he had put on to do honour to us.

## Letter from Snowdon, Simla, 21 September 1905.

Doris and I got here on Sunday afternoon. We had a most comfortable journey from Bombay. A good deal of rain had fallen a few days previously so that there was no dust, and as the sky was cloudy it was quite cool – indeed the part of the journey from the top of the Ghants along by Manmar and Khandhwa was cooler than I have often felt in December.

The Managers of the G.I.P. and East Indian railways gave me my usual cooking carriage as a compliment and I only paid the ordinary 1st class for Doris and self. From Kalka here we drove in a landau instead of the usual tonga. So altogether our journey was a most comfortable one, and Doris stood it very well indeed and never seemed at all fatigued or was once put out with the knocking about.

Lord Kitchener was still in town when we arrived here but he had made every preparation for our reception, and sent us a most friendly telegram of welcome which reached us during the railway journey. His carriage met us just before we got into Simla, and we drove straight to his house. It is a most comfortable one. We have very nice rooms and everything is arranged with great taste by Lord K. himself. His cook (a Frenchman) is excellent. So Doris and I were alone here on Sunday and Monday and on Tuesday Lord K. arrived.

I think it was a good plan to let us settle down quietly before his arrival, for although he is most kind and hospitable, he is rather shy and somewhat ponderous. This style of man unintentionally causes a feeling of awkwardness about him, and might have prevented us settling down as quietly as we have done. He is really awfully kind, and Doris and he seem to get on first rate. On Tuesday night he took us to the Theatre. He has a box there.

Relations between him and Curzon are still a good deal strained. This is not to be wondered at seeing what a liar Curzon has shown himself to be. C. is now going round trying to ingratiate himself as much as possible and cause people to forget his unpopularity of the past 6 yrs. Lady C. is playing up in that direction also. Poor K. on the other hand quietly went off to Kangra and Kulu to see that the sufferers from the earthquake of March last had been attended to.

Doris and I think of moving to the Hotel on Saturday. We have very nice rooms there but K. seems quite delighted to have us here and so possibly we may have to stay on a bit longer.

### Letter from Multan 25 October 1905

Doris is back at the Cecil Hotel, and seems delighted to be in her own rooms after the ceremony of Viceregal Lodge. She writes to me sometimes 2 or 3 letters a day telling me of the goings on there. I hope to go to Meerut about 4th Nov. better address Doris without 'c/o I.G. of Cavalry' as several of her letters have come on to me first.

After Douglas Haig had left Simla on 2 October to carry out his tour of inspection in the north-west, Doris went to stay at Viceregal Lodge. Lord and Lady Curzon were packing up and leaving Simla, Curzon having resigned his post as Viceroy.

Doris described the formality of Viceregal Lodge in her book, *The Man I Knew*.

My host and hostess could not have been kinder although they were so busy packing up to leave India. His Excellency was rather alarming, having a habit of asking rather sarcastic questions round the dinner-table, and as each of our turns came, we trembled. There was an outstanding difference between him and my previous host, Lord Kitchener. The latter was a silent man, with his mind full of military plans, shy in society and forbidding by his indifference to conversation around him, whilst Lord Curzon, a much cleverer man, never ceased talking and loved display and admirers round him. I could not help being amused at the pomp carried on, even when there were no outside guests. I had, though alone, to go so many steps forward as the Viceroy came down and make my curtsy in the same formal way as at large parties.

The Curzons left Simla on 25 October. There was considerable speculation as to whether or not Lord Kitchener, who had been away on military duties, would return in time for the Curzons' departure and if he did return would he and Lord Curzon shake hands. To quote David Gilmour:[2] 'Kitchener returned reluctantly for the occasion, grumbling that it was not very pleasant to shake hands with a man who had called him a liar.' It seems that each considered the other to be a liar!

Curzon was succeeded in November by the Earl of Minto,[3] who had been an outstanding Governor General of Canada. The handover was complicated by the arrival of the Prince and Princess of Wales[4] for a tour of India. The 'Review' referred to in the letters of 8 November and 13 December, below, was in honour of the Prince and Princess.

### Letter from Simla 8 November 1905

Tomorrow is mail day, but Doris and I are leaving in the morning for Meerut, so I must write you a line this evening to catch it. We have fires all day long here now, and Simla is already quite deserted looking. Most of the shopkeepers have gone to the plains for the winter, and the bulk of the Officers are en route for Calcutta. Many more Officers seem to have gone there this winter than usual. I expect that in view of the reshuffling of duties which is expected at Army Headquarters when Minto arrives, they are afraid that their interests might be neglected if they were absent at Simla.

So many Cavalry regiments are now on the move to the manoeuvres at Pindi (there are to be 16 there) that I can't do much inspection work at present. I shall therefore be at Meerut 'till about the 20th then go to Allahabad for 4 days and then work my way North to Pindi, getting there on 2nd December with Doris. Sir Bindon Blood[5] has asked us to stay with him for the camp. I, however, go into Camp on Monday 4th December as the manoeuvres begin on the 2nd.

We shall have pretty hard work while the Camp lasts as the troops will be fighting all Tuesday, Wednesday and Wednesday night until Thursday midday. The Review is on the Friday. I leave as soon as possible for a small Cavalry Camp near Lucknow where 4 regiments will be concentrated. This will finish my inspection up to Xmas.

Doris has settled everything here capitally – paid all the bills, docketed receipts, etc. etc. so that I have not had anything to fuss about at all. She might have been taught 'account keeping' by yourself!

### Letter from Jarwal Road 13 December 1905

You ask me about 'the General Staff' and 'what part I am to play in it and when'. I personally have heard nothing officially about taking any part in it yet. With the new Govt. there is no knowing what new departure may not be made. Haldane[6] must have some pluck to take over the post of Secy. of War. I heard from French two weeks ago that he hoped matters

245

would soon be resolved for me to come home. I hope however that I shall be able to finish my winter's work, i.e. remain in India 'till 15th April. In any case my time (3 years) is up on October 30th and Doris and I could spend the summer very pleasantly in Kashmir, if I am not require at the W.O. So I don't care much whether I go to the W.O. or not at present.

You will read all about the manoeuvres and the Review in the papers, so I need not enter into details. I went to Camp on Monday 4th December. On Tuesday we had a lot of Cavalry fighting with a big charge before the Prince and Princess just before lunch, in which I was said to have been successful. Wednesday and Wednesday night there was a general action, and the Southern Army, to which I belonged, fell back on Pindi. The troops marched most of the night, and we got into Camp at Pindi Thursday afternoon – some of the Northern troops not 'till late that night. So it was a hard time for troops.

On Friday we had the big Review – 50,537 of all ranks on Parade. Personally I had 64 Squadrons and 4 R.F.A. Batteries (about 8,000 horses) under my orders. It was a grand show and everything went off without a hitch. This was very creditable considering that there had been no rehearsal, and the space in which this large body of troops had to manoeuvre was somewhat restricted.

Doris and I dined with Lord Kitchener on the Friday night, and went to sleep in our railway carriage after dinner, leaving at 6 a.m. on Saturday for Meerut. I was at Meerut on Sunday and started again that night for Lucknow and this place where we have a small Cavalry Camp 'till Saturday.

We picked Guy up at Meerut and brought him along with us. He seems very fit and is enjoying himself. I am glad to have him with me as he has no swagger at all and is ready to do anything.

At the dinner at Pindi Doris went to dinner with the Prince. The latter gave her their 2 photos for me as a memento of their visit and gave Lord K. a silver vase. I shall be here 'till Sunday, then I go on to Allahabad and back to Meerut by the 21st Dec. for Xmas.

## Letter to Oliver Haig, Douglas Haig's nephew from County Camp, near Lucknow 13 December 1905

Herewith a few lines to wish you . . . very many happy New Years and much happiness. I have not heard from you for a long time so I don't know where you are to be for Xmas. I was so glad to hear of the safe arrival of your little daughter and I trust that she and Esme[7] are now very fit and well. I spent a long time last week at the manoeuvres at Rawalpindi for the Prince of Wales. Doris went with me and stayed with Sir Bindon Blood in Pindi when I was in camp. The Review was a grand sight – over

246

fifty thousand troops were present. I had all the Cavalry and Horse Arty. under me at the Review – 64 squadrons – in line they covered nearly 4,500 yds.

Doris is now at Meerut where we have a bungalow. I go back there on the 21st to spend Xmas. The 17th are now settled there. I had some goodish games of polo with them before I went to Pindi. Old Nicholls (playing very bold!) nearly knocked Portal over; entirely old N.T's fault and tho' on my side I damned him freely – all he said was that he ought not to be put on a side to play against his Colonel! I suppose the temptation to knock the latter over was too much for him.

## Letter to Henrietta from The Residency, Hyderabad (Deccan) 11 January 1906

I left Bangalore on Sunday afternoon and got here Monday in time for dinner. Wolseley Haig (the 1st Asst. Resident) met me at the station. Guy Brooke and I are staying with him and his wife Beatrice – a very kind nice woman. My Brigade Major with the office Babu etc. got out at the station before this and went direct to Bolaruan to be ready for my inspection of the 13th Hussars which I begin on Saturday. Wolseley Haig[8] has another house at Bolaruan which is close to the Cavalry lines, so we move up there tomorrow.

I received a letter from Esher[9] this morning cracking up Haldane the new S.of S. for War like anything. Then towards the end of the letter he writes 'There is only one change not yet made, which Haldane must make. It is to put you in Hutchinson's place. I have never let him alone for a day since he took office on this subject. I have wanted to get you back here in that place for two years – the whole tone of Army Officers and their education will have undergone a change which will recast the Army.'

## Letter from Aurangabad 26 January 1906

. . . I have heard no word indicating any desire on Mr Haldane's part that I should be brought home soon to help in starting a General Staff, so I have got the refusal until the middle of February of a house at Mashobra (about 2 or 3 miles out of Simla) for the summer. It is quite a nice situation and nicer than Simla which is very crowded now. If you have no plans for the summer, the change out here would do you good, and you could picnic in the woods all day long – and in the autumn visit Kashmir etc. and return to England when my appointment is up in Nov. next.

## Letter from Meerut 8 February 1906

I had a long letter from French by last mail, dated 14th January, in which he writes 'I think there is every chance of the billet about which we talked being vacant within the next six or eight months, and then there is no doubt about you being called upon to fill it,' and further he says 'You may hope to be installed in Pall Mall by next autumn.' I'll send you the letter when I have answered it. This, I think, will be a very good arrangement for Doris and me, especially as I see by your letter that you propose to go to America this summer.

Everyone I hear from speaks well of Haldane, so the advent of the Radicals is certainly of great advantage to the Army in substituting him for Arnold-Forster. French seems to like him very much and the 'Army Councillors', Hubert Hamilton writes me 'have now the spirits of schoolboys home for their holidays'. So far at any rate things seem to be going well for the Army . . . .

## Letter from Meerut 15 February 1906

There have been several accidents out pig sticking during the last fortnight. Four officers (2 each week) were mauled by panthers. Last Thursday Obbey Beauclerk was out. He was on some of Alan Fletcher's horses as the latter broke his collar bone pig sticking the previous week and could not go. Obbey saw a panther in some grass, galloped at it but his horse shied off and he missed with his spear. The panther sprang on the next man who however speared him in the neck. Panther and man rolled on the ground, the former worrying him like a big cat does a mouse. Talbot of the 17th Lancers then came up and tried to stick the animal but it caught his spear in its mouth and mauled his hand badly. Some others finally arrived on the scene and despatched the panther.

The bites of panthers are much more poisonous than those of tigers. Luckily they had some antiseptics on the spot, and by means of a motor the wounded men were in hospital before 6 hours had elapsed. I am glad to say that all are doing well, but the Drs. have had to cut them about a great deal to get rid of poisoned flesh. The previous week one fellow was bitten by a panther on the thigh. He stupidly went on riding thinking little about it, so that by dinner time he became nearly stupid from the effects of the poison. He is now believed to be out of danger but has had a terrible bad time of it poor fellow. . . . I think the want of water in the district brought so many panthers near the river, and made them so fierce, because it is most unusual for them to attack until wounded.

## Letter from Peshawar 28 March 1906

I told you a fortnight ago that I had received a hint that I might be required at the War Office very soon. About a week ago I got 2 letters from Esher and one from General Lyttelton offering me the Directorate of Training. The former said Mr Haldane was very anxious for me to come home and assist in schemes of reorganization, and both he and the King were desirous that I should accept the billet. Although called 'Training' the department also deals with 'War Organization' and 'Home Defence' so that it is the most important Directorate in the General Staff at the present time.

General Stopford holds the appointment at the present time, but he expects to be given the Home District when Bully Oliphant's[10] time is up in July. Though the appointment is not vacant 'till then, Mr Haldane wishes me to come home as soon as I have finished my winter's work here. I hope to leave Bombay either on the 28th April or 12th May but will telegraph as soon as the date is fixed.

## Letter from Rawalpindi 3 April 1906

I am still quite uncertain when I shall leave for England. On the one hand Lord Esher writes that Haldane is anxious for me to go home as soon as I have finished my winter's work; on the other hand General Lyttleton, who is Chief of the General Staff, telegraphs (in reply to one from me asking for passage by mail of 28th April) that vacancy is 'not 'till 9th August and returning earlier would involve resignation of present post and payment of passage'. I am not prepared to do this as it would mean a loss of about £600 pay and the best part of £200 for our passages.

On the other hand Reuter announced a few days ago that Gen. F. Stopford had been appointed to the command of the Home District. This at once makes the required vacancy so I expect before long I shall be ordered home. I'll send you a telegram as soon as my plans are fixed up. Doris and I go to our railway carriage tonight and start at 5 a.m. tomorrow en route for Mashobra.

We are quite ready to start at the end of this month or not 'till July. Personally the life at Mashobra would be more agreeable for the summer than an office in Pall Mall! Still it is a very great honour to be sent for at this critical time to help to decide the future organization of the Empire's forces. So I ought to be thought very lucky.

Haig was very clear about the importance, to the future shape of the British Empire's forces, of the work being carried out by Haldane at the War Office. He must also have been well aware that his appointment to the War Office at this time was important from the viewpoint of his own career. As things turned out the appointment was of critical importance to Britain at the start of the First World War. In the first place Haldane and Haig negotiated the agreements under which the British Empire provided military and naval support when war broke out. The structure included for the first time the appointment of a Chief of the Imperial General Staff. Secondly the work created a British Territorial Army whose timely arrival in France, after the heavy casualties of Mons and First Ypres, may well have made the difference between the Expeditionary Force's survival and its defeat. Haig's diary follows the meetings and discussions, which led to the momentous and creative changes under Haldane's leadership as Secretary of State for War. Thirdly, the composition of Field Service Regulations, published in 1909, provided the structure used by the Army throughout the First World War.

Before this, however, the War Office finally got its act together and recalled Haig to England as soon as possible at the Government's expense! He was to be considered to be on leave until the appointment of Director of Military Training became vacant, but may well have been expected to take part in the discussions in an unofficial capacity – such are the devious ideas of the Whitehall warriors! This in fact is exactly what Douglas Haig did. Shortly before leaving Simla Haig had a final discussion with Kitchener and was asked to help to persuade the Secretary of State to accept some changes to the organization and structure of the Indian Army, with a rather unrealistic side-swipe at the cost of allowances in the British Army. Kitchener's points were noted in Haig's diary.

**6 May 1906.**

Doris and I lunched with Lord Kitchener at 'Wildflower Hall'. Lord K. in good form and had a long talk with him. He wishes me to do what I can about the following points:-

1. Home Governments to refrain from interfering in matter of railways and reorganization scheme. Railway of Kotal River especially necessary, because it can be continued to Gandawah.
2. S.of S. for War to write supporting him in matter of sanitation of cantonments, which was originally made for soldiers but now overcrowded with natives etc. Water insufficient in May.
3. He (Lord K.) approves of reduction (temporarily) of Indian Garrison by 10,000 men, but thinks Home Government

should not insist on this, because India pays for all of them in India. He would be glad to take recruits at 17 and 18 and train them in hills.

4. He wishes to abolish the 3 Commands and have 3 Inspector Generals – Gaselee and Hunter have accepted extension on these conditions. Change to be brought in early in October. Each I.G. to have a good military secretary and a D.A.G. and 2 A.D.C.s. Smith Dorrien will act for 4 months during Hunter's leave as L.G.C. and G.O.C. Divn. – clearly showing no need for L.G.C. Gov. Gen. in Bombay and Hunter approve of this.

5. Indian Division is a much larger unit than a British Divn. So K. thinks an officer on getting command of one should become a Lt. General.

6. Army at home expensive chiefly owing to allowances. He would make these annual grants. Cost of Army should be £22,000,000 instead of £24,000,000.

The Haigs left Bombay on the P&O s.s. *Arabia* on 12 May. The journey from Simla to Bombay was very hot. As Douglas Haig said:

We have a reserved compartment and get 2 maunds of ice in at Umballa which keeps carriage cool . . . . Get 2 maunds of ice at Jhansi about 3 p.m. This keeps temperature down to 103° in carriage – others up to 112° . . . .

They arrived in London on 1 June, were met at Paddington by Henrietta and stayed with her at 21 Princes Gate. They made their home there until they leased a cottage near Farnborough and bought Trunk House at Cove in 1907. The Press report on Douglas Haig's appointment was as follows:

The appointment of Major-General Douglas Haig as Director of Military Training at Headquarters has given the greatest satisfaction to the mounted branches of the Army. The Cavalry Committee established at Aldershot does much excellent work, but its functions are more restricted than is commonly supposed. It does not influence policy; its duties being mainly confined to details of equipment and like matters. If it were not that Sir John French is a fearless champion of the cavalry, and that in Ireland and elsewhere there are cavalry officers of uncommon energy and enthusiasm, the cavalry of the British Army would not now be in the excellent state in which we see it. The force has not hitherto been adequately represented at headquarters, but the authorities have now a great opportunity before them. There is an abundance of keen and earnest young cavalry officers with all the experience of South Africa behind them. When Mr Haldane gives practical effect to the General Staff, which he soon must do, he should hasten to include not a few of our talented cavalry officers in its composition. It was an encouraging sign that an eminent cavalry officer like General Haig has been given an important appointment at headquarters, but strong cavalry representation in the counsels of the War Office would have prevented some errors being made in the recent past. Recruiting for the cavalry was suspended too long, in order to benefit the infantry, and the result has been that our cavalry regiments have in many instances been short of men, while horses have been more than adequate in number. What is required is that the cavalry arm of the Service shall have a proper recognition at headquarters and its interest shall receive the consideration it well deserves. The transfer of an officer on promotion from the infantry to the Royal Dragoons recently was an event which placed in a strong light the disadvantage to which the cavalry are yet subject. It has caused some strong feeling, and we hope it gives a warning to Mr Haldane. The matter requires to be further explained for the reply in the House of Commons explains nothing.

Soon after his arrival in England Haig reported to the War Office and was immediately included in the discussions and planning over which Haldane and Lord Esher presided. Having stayed the weekend of 6 to 8 June at Windsor Castle, Haig met Haldane for the first time on the 9th. His diary reads as follows:

**6 June (Windsor Castle)**
Doris and I go by train to Windsor. The servants had been sent on before. We were given a large suite of rooms in the Victoria Tower – sitting room, bed & dressing room and bath room, tho' the decorations were not very artistic. Their Majesties were very late, having been to see the procession of boats at Eton (this held today instead of the 4th of June which was a Bank holiday). Dinner at 9 o'clock. Both the King and Queen welcome us most

kindly; – thought Doris 'looking so much better' and 'prettier' – 'hair better done' etc. After dinner I had a long talk with the King, who did not play bridge. Lord Milner also a guest.

## 8 June

Doris and I play golf before breakfast. Leave Windsor about 12 o'clock by motor. Doris sits inside with the Queen. I am on the box next the chauffeur. The latter a skilled 'mechanic' but a moderate coachman and shakes the car about by stopping and checking abruptly.

At Buckingham Palace the Queen gets out and receives her letters on the doorstep like the rest of mankind. Says she is sorry she has no lunch to offer us (She had only come to town for a few hours to see Princess Victoria) and insists on our getting into motor again to be driven to Princes Gate.

## 9 June

I motor to Aldershot where I stay with General French at Govt. House to meet Mr Haldane. The latter is a big fat man but with a kind genial face. One seems to like the man at once.

Govt. House so full that I have to stay with the A.D.C.

## 10 June

I have two walks with Mr Haldane before and after lunch. He seems a most clear headed and practical man – very ready to listen and weigh carefully all that is said to him.

## 11 June

Leave Farnborough Station with Mr Haldane and his private secretary Colonel Ellison[11] for London. Attend Conference on Territorial Army at War Office. Lord Esher is President, and there are some 40 odd members. It is known as the 'Duma'. Committee sit 'till 2 o'clock. Return to War Office after lunch and see General Lyttleton (Chief of General Staff) and General Sir Frederick Stopford (now Dir. of Mil. Training).

## 12 June

My late Staff in South Africa dine with us at Princes Gate. Major Greenly (12 Lancers) now on the General Staff. Major Legard (17 Lancers) now at Staff College. Major Farquahar, a gentleman at large from Johannesburg!

## 13 June

Attend 'Duma' as usual. The Militia Officers seem afraid their force will disappear if placed under the 'County Associations' and are anxious to remain under the War Office.

Receive a letter from War Office that Army Council had decided my pay is to be £1,200 instead of £1,500. Write to Ellison and ask if this has been done with Mr Haldane's knowledge, because if so, I would like to reconsider my acceptance of the appointment.

## 15 June

The 'Duma' meets today at 11.45 and at 12 o'clock Mr Haldane comes and addresses the meeting. He is very complimentary on the work which has been done. A sub committee is to assemble on the question of the Militia on Tuesday 26th. I am to attend the meeting.

Receive letter from secretary to the S. of S. for India, asking me call at India Office Thursday next to see S. of S., Mr Morley.[12]

Attend 7th Hussars Regimental dinner. About 47 Officers present. General Hale in chair and Lt. Colonel Walter commanding regiment. I sit next Colonels Lawley and Holdsworth. Dalgety and Wormald opposite. Regiment is at Norwich.

Have an interview with Mr Haldane by latter's request. He tells me that letter received by me on Wednesday night had been sent without his knowledge and that he will see that my pay of £1,500 is not touched.

## 21 June

Interviewed by Mr Morley the Secretary of State for India. He seems to take a broad-minded and sensible view of Indian affairs. It was 1.30 before we parted. Mr Morley expresses the hope that I will apply to him if he can inform me on any subject or assist me in any way.

## 6 June

Attend sub-committee of the 'Duma' to consider Militia questions. Some 20 or more Colonels of Militia regiments present. On question of reinforcing Regular Army over sea, all most anxious that militia should only be sent in 'Battalion units' and not as drafts. It was 6.30 before I left the War Office.

Dinner of Staff College graduates. Sir Evelyn Wood in chair. Sit at the end of the table opposite him with Hubert Hamilton on my right and Colonel Wilson (Education Dept.) on my left.

## 27 June

Committee meeting at 2.30. Impossible to get Militia Officers to agree to wishes of War Office Council, namely to provide drafts for Army in the Field, instead of expanding the Regular Army. Some are willing to supply 'companies' when required. So these sign paper to that effect, remainder sign to go abroad as Battalions.

## 28 June

Doris and I lunch with the Duchess of Buccleuch at Montagu House[13] at 2 o'clock. A large table and one for the children with few occupants! The Duchess explains that she always expects many to turn up for lunch and she expresses the hope that when I am at the War Office I will come in regularly. The Duke says much the same and also remarks that I must feel that I can go whenever it suits me. Very kind of them!

## 9 July

Mr. Haldane addresses the 'Duma'.

Doris consults Dr. J. Phillips. He stops her bicycling, motoring or playing golf etc. We leave for Aldershot and stay with General French at Govt. House.

## 11 July

Motor to Jolly Farmer (Bagshot) where French and I mount our horses and ride towards Wishnevor Cross. Pilcher's Bde. engaged in attack operations through the woods. Get back to Govt. House in time for lunch.

Esher arrives and he, French and I discuss the possibility of Turks supported by Germans attacking Canal and Egypt.

About 2.30 or 3, during this discussion, I get attack of ague. The General is very kind, lights fire and gets me hot water etc. Anxious for me to stay on, but I insist on going and Doris & I leave by 4.15 train for London.

Sir Lauder Brunton[14] comes to see me at 9.30 p.m. and prescribes. He advises me to go to Tarasp, Switzerland.

## 12 July

Rather weak after yesterday's attack of fever. After lunch go to House of Commons and hear Mr. Haldane make his statement on the Army. He speaks for 2 hours and 40 minutes without a check!

## 16 July

Attend at Mr. Haldane's room in House of Commons. Discuss measures for putting resolutions into effect. Esher and General Mackinnon[15] come in later. Haldane's secretary, Ellison, Lucas and Acland also present.

Dine at Reform Club with Sir Lauder Brunton to meet certain men interested in improving the manhood of the Nation, firstly by reducing infant mortality and secondly by drilling boys and youths etc.!

## 17 July

Meeting at War Office of 14 Colonels of I.Y. regiments. Lord Scarbrough, Harris etc. They recommend that I.Y. be enlisted for service overseas like the Militia.

## 19 July

Attend meeting in Mr. Haldane's room at House of Commons to arrange details of 'Territorial Army'. Mr. F.E. Smith has moved the adjournment of House to call attention to Mr. Haldane's scheme.

## 20 July

Meeting in Hamilton Gordon's[16] room at War Office. Colonel Ellison, H. Gordon, Heath (of A.G. Dept) and self. We decide to commence by starting 17 Divns. for Territorial Army (say 450,000 men) on the basis of population.

Dine at Marlborough House. A dinner of Anglo Indians. Sit next Sir Godley (permanent Sec. at India Office) and Sir Acland (who accompanied H.R.H. on Indian tour).

On 21 July Haig left for Tarasp. His doctor, Sir Lauder Brunton, was anxious that he should subject himself to the full cure at the spa before recuperating at Pontresina for a number of days. He duly received permission to stay in Switzerland until 23 August, returning to duty on the 25th. As he had been working at the War Office from early June, when he was meant to be on leave, his request seems entirely

256

reasonable. Ironically his appointment as Director of Military Training came into effect on 11 August, when he was still in Tarasp. At Tarasp he was in the care of a Dr Vogelsang, who prescribed the amount of the waters he should drink, what exercise he should take and what his diet should be. At the end of Haig's stay at Tarasp Dr. Vogelsang was pleased to announce that his liver had been reduced by two centimetres. The diary does not describe by what method the measurement was carried out.

While at Hotel Waldhaus at Vulpera-Tarasp he wrote on 5 August to Gerald Ellison as follows:

I don't know how much to thank you for your kindness in arranging for me to stay on until I have finished my course of waters! It was really good of you to have thought of this in the midst of all your work, and I am most grateful to you.

I have written to the C.G.S. and told him I propose (in accordance with the advice of the Dr. here) to remain here 'till the 16th and then go to Pontresina (Hotel Kronenhof) for a week as 'Nach Kur'. This will enable me to reach London on Friday 24th and I shall attend office next morning. Any day after that will suit me to attend on the S. of S.

Yes – many thanks – these waters have done me a heap of good. My medico yesterday declared that my liver was back to its normal size and he added 'it is not to say that the improvement can be felt, but I can measure it with an ordinary measure'!

With best wishes for a pleasant time during your short leave, and again thanking you for your kind thought very much.

**Diary for 12 August 1906, written while at Tarasp**

Write to F.2. Section, War Office (Finance) asking that pay be issued to me from 11th inst. when Stopford vacated appointment of D.M. Training. If any difficulty to refer the matter to S. of S.

**25 August (Princes Gate)**

Doris walks with me to War Office. Mr. Haldane (S. of S.) sees me about 4 p.m. He has discussion with Colonel Ellison and myself on question of Territorial Army and finally tells me to form Committee and call in from time to time anyone whose presence I think necessary.

Mr. Haldane, Colonel Ellison and Colonel Shiba of the Japanese Army dine with us at Princes Gate. Mr. Haldane leaves about 11 p.m. because he is to start early tomorrow for Marienbad.

**28 August**

Meeting of officers in my department at 3 p.m. when we commence work on Territorial Army scheme. We continue 'till nearly 6 p.m.

**29 August**

Go War Office early, Doris walks there with me. Have discussion with General Miles[17] re conversion of Militia Garrison Artillery into Militia Field Artillery. Some 10,000 men required for duty as Field Artillery men for ammunition columns on mobilization – only some 5,000 available. After lunch see the C.G.S. (Lyttleton). At 3 p.m. meeting of officers of my Department on Territorial Army scheme. Captain Montgomery keeps notes and is to work out 'actuarial' calculations.

**4 September**

Leave by 9.45 train. Meeting with Volunteer Officers from all parts of England. All against County Associations. Adjourn at 1.30 'till 2.30 and then discuss scheme for training National Army. Catch 4.55 train for Farnborough.

The above programme reflects the fact that the Haigs had taken a small house, Coombe Farm, near Farnborough. Douglas Haig did not like living in London because he found it too airless and he missed riding in the early mornings before going to the War Office.

**5 September**

Meeting at War Office to consider estimates. Sir Fleetwood Wilson President. Generals Miles and Heath[18] also on Committee with myself. Commandants of Shoebury, Hythe and Chatham consulted.

**6 September**

Meeting at War Office with certain Yeomanry Officers who had been invited to come and discuss questions with me. Lord Scarbrough makes proposals for I.Y to do advanced Guard Cavalry work but stipulates 'no extra training'. I told them straight, that would be impossible, but that I.Y. could do work of Divisional squadron and remainder of I.Y. be ready to take field after 3 months methodical training after mobilization.

Lunched at Willis's with Lovat[19]. Mr Haldane also present,

258

Scarbrough, Shaftesbury, Lawson, Meyrick and the Colonel of the Middlesexes – 19 in all. Afterwards, have a long talk with Haldane who quite agrees to my proposals for the Territorial Army.

### 7 September
Black pony put in trap about 10 a.m. for me to see if trap (a new one) suitable. Pony kicked & ran off breaking new cart. I had to run to catch 10.20 train.

Sent for by Mr. Haldane at War Office about 3.30. Showed him scheme for Yeomanry; also gave him copy of proposals for training Territorial Army. Then got Col. Gordon to S. of S.'s room; he showed in detail how far our scheme had progressed. S. of S. said he thoroughly agreed with all we had done.

Caught 6 p. m. train.

### Letter to Colonel Gerald Ellison, Private Secretary to Haldane. Written from Sherborne 11 September
I have been thinking over the discussion which we had with the Finance specialists yesterday.

Our object, in my opinion, should be to start a system of finance suited to the 'supposed situation', i.e. a great war requiring the whole resources of the nation to bring to a successful end.

Even if the proposed system cost more in peace, it should be inaugurated provided that it is more practical in war. The Swiss system seemed to me to be exactly what is wanted to 'root the Army in the people'. Although the County Association as originally organized may not be workable, there must be some local authority or Council representing the area from which men, supplies, transport, etc. are required.

I return to London Thursday evening. When do you come up again? I was sorry not to have been able to read your paper on the Staff yesterday, but as you saw I had a heap of stuff to get off before leaving for this place. Some 70 or 80 Officers here including Esher. A most interesting scheme, but some of the solutions not very practical to my thinking.

### Letter to Ellison dated 15 September from the War Office.
Herewith continuation of the 'Magnum Opus' to date for your remarks please.

I trust that there will be no splitting up of the scheme into parts and handing over the A.S.C. part (say) to the Q.M.G. to work out in detail, until our Committee is satisfied with the plan as a whole!

I quite agree with your memo. on the General Staff.

Forgive so short a line.

## Letter to Ellison from War Office 17 September

Re the application of principles contained in Chap. 1 and 11 of the papers re Territorial Army which I sent you, I think it will be almost impossible to apply a limit of age to Battalions, say 17 to 25, at the commencement of the scheme on account of difficulty of peace training. I have therefore started to work out the possibility of forming Battalions in peace of say 12 Companies, which on mobilization, would form a Service Battalion of 8 Companies, and the remaining 4 Companies expand to a second Battalion.

Please think over this, and give me your views at your leisure. But whatever principle we decide on, the details and application must of course be worked out by local men in the Grouped Regimental District.

There is one point which I hope you will impress on the S. of S., and that is that we must be clear regarding the functions of the Militia and must not hesitate to put his conclusions into practice.

On 20 September Henrietta Jameson persuaded Douglas Haig to go with her to a séance with a medium. Haig clearly took the whole event in a light-hearted spirit. He recorded in his diary that he asked the medium to ask the spirits how the Territorial Army should be organized. She apparently thought a 'company basis' would be better than a 'battalion basis'! Haig then said that she told him that he:

... was influenced by several spirits – notably a small man named Napoleon, who aided me. That it was in my power to be helped by him for good affairs but I might repel him if his influence was for bad though he had become changed for better in the spirit world. I was destined to do much good and to benefit my country. Asked by me how to ensure the Territorial Army Scheme being a success, she said '. . . thought governed the world. Think out the scheme thoroughly, one's thoughts would then be put in so convincing a manner that the people would respond (without any compulsion) and the national Army would be a reality.' She could not bring Napoleon to me, but I must think of him and try to get his aid as he was always near me.

It may or may not have occurred to the medium that her leg was being pulled, but on the whole she seems to have been a good match for the General!

## 12 November

At 3.30 go to House of Commons and see S. of S. in his private room there. Military Members have raised difficulties on question of reorganizing Militia. Seems to me only an excuse to show that they are angry because S. of S. does not consult them enough! Get back to War Office and see C.G.S. He is very shirty and tells me not to be absent on Saturdays without his approval! He wants all papers from S. of S. to be given to him at once – not my affair as these papers go to him before coming to me! Result of Lucas not stirring him up sufficiently – no doubt he has been tackled by Miles!

## 14 November

S. of S. sends for me re procedure in coming Session. See C.G.S. (still rather snuffy). At 3 p.m. attend committee meeting of General Parsons'[20] Committee re conversion of R.G.A. (Royal Garrison Artillery) to Field Artillery. Parsons excellent on his Committee and puts the destructionists Miles and Crutchley[21] in their places.

## 11 December

Furniture from my office in Pall Mall being moved to new War Office in Whitehall. Do not go to London.

## 2 January 1907

Meeting with Ellison & General Ewart[22] also Mr. Liddel (a law officer of the Crown) re Bill for Territorial Force. Meeting at noon. At 3 p.m. Sir Guy Fleetwood Wilson (Dir. of Finance) come and see me to make out data on which estimate of cost is to be framed. Receive kind letter from Mr. Haldane. He writes that he means to go straight ahead and stand or fall by his scheme.

## 3 January

Amend leaflet with General Miles (leaflet is to go to Press to explain the new organization). Fleetwood Wilson [the Treasury's Sir Humphry!] comes to my room during the

261

operation and criticizes severely the way in which he has been ignored in the matter of the new scheme.

During the afternoon I go to Miles's room with Ellison and work out data on which non-regular Reserve is to be calculated. We are to meet at noon tomorrow with F. Wilson. A terrible day of criticism, but some progress made notwithstanding!

## 15 January

First meeting of Committee on Territorial Army presided over by General Miles. Present: Fleetwood Wilson – self – General Robb[23] (from Colchester), Gorringe – Ellison and Heath as secretaries. We consider 'references' by General Douglas (A.G.) but impossible to work on such detailed instructions since latter in many essential points differs from Haldane's scheme.

## 16 January

Attend lecture in R.U.S.I. on Swiss Military system. Mr. Haldane in chair. A very crowded meeting. Many no doubt hoping to have a go at Haldane after the lecture. But H. finds it necessary to attend to business at House and so leaves before discussion. A wise proceeding!

## 18 January

Meet in C.G.S.'s room with General Sir B. Duff (C. of S. India), Sir N. Lyttelton, Generals Ewart and Hutchison present. Differences in Home and Indian organization are discussed.

S. of S. asks me today to arrange for Cavalry manoeuvres in Scotland.

## 4 February

Parsons' committee reassemble at 11.30 a.m. I write minute of dissent to the recommendation that only Divisional Ammunition Columns are to be made up of non-regulars. Am summoned to S. of S. twice this afternoon.

## 8 February

Dine with Mr. Haldane to meet Prime Minister (Asquith), but latter falls ill at last moment. Sit between Sir Geo. Murray of the Treasury and Ponsonby (P.M.'s Sec.).

## 15 February

Leave for Knowsley with the S. of S. and his two secretaries (Col. Ellison & Lord Lucas[24]). Some dozen militia Colonels there to meet Haldane. Only a couple of ladies at dinner. After they had left the dining room the S. of S. explains his scheme confidentially. Lord Derby[25] and his son Eddie Stanley promise that they will do all they can to help. After half past eleven before we leave dining room and the conversation is kept up in the smoking room 'till after 2 o'clock! Though scheme meant end of Militia Colonels – all pledge to support it.

## 25 February

Go to House of Commons at 3 p.m. Mr. Haldane brings in his Scheme of Army Reorganization. He begins speaking about 3.50 p.m. and speaks without a stop or even an effort until 7.10 p.m.! I had a good seat behind the Speaker's chair, but the C.G.S., who comes in late, takes my seat and I sit on the arm! C.G.S. remarks during speech that Mr. Secretary Haldane is going much further than he (Sir N.L.(C.G.S.)) had approved! – and that he does not remember many things announced as part of the scheme.

## 8 March

Dr. Phillips sent for and he comes about 9.30 p.m.

## 9 March

Doris going on well as possible. So by her request motor with Blair to Sunningdale to play golf. Receive telephone message from Henrietta there (about 5.30) 'Daughter born about 4 o'clock. Everything going on well.'

## 17 April

Christening of baby at Chapel Royal.

The baby was christened Alexandra Henrietta Louisa. The godparents were the Queen (represented at the Chapel by Lady Emily Kingscote), Henrietta Jameson, the Duchess of Buccleuch (Louisa) and Doris's great-uncle Walter Vivian.

## Letter to Henrietta dated 21 April from Trunk House

I had a most interesting forenoon yesterday. I met Mr. Haldane at the Colonial Office a little before 11 o'clock and attended the Colonial

Conference with him. The Chief of the General Staff and the Q.M.G. and Director of Operations were also there. At 11 o'clock Mr. Haldane took his seat on Lord Elgin's right. The latter presides.

The Premiers were sitting at a horse-shoe table on each side of him in order of seniority of the Colonies. Deakin who made the good speech on Friday night was on Elgin's left with his defence minister – the latter v. ugly with a goat like beard & spectacles, on the whole like old Kruger. Next was Dr. Jim, then Moor from Natal, then Botha & his interpreter & Dr. Smart (of Cape Colony).

On Haldane's right came Sir W. Laurier & Bordon (of Canada), then representatives of New Zealand and Newfoundland and assistants further down the table – 2 short hand writers in the centre of the horse shoe but at a small table apart; secretaries at tables round the walls of the room. We had 4 hard chairs placed for us behind Haldane.

The latter made a short speech of 20 minutes explaining our organization and ended with a motion for the Conference to adopt. All the Premiers then spoke in turn – all very patriotic. His speech was v. well received and all asked that it should be published. His motion was also agreed to. The latter practically creates an Imperial General Staff and so puts 50% on to the value of the General Staff.

It was nearly 2 before I got away, so I only caught the 3 p.m. train.

## Diary for 1 May 1907

S. of S. interviews me re quota to be asked for from Counties for Territorial Force. 3 p.m. Meeting of Territorial Army Committee. Arrange to ask Army Council for definite statement as to what proportion of regulars to non-regulars is permissible for the several arms. Having got this, it devolves on Adjutant General to find the required numbers of men.

## 3 May

Ellison comes to my room and discusses memo on future powers of the I.G. of Forces. Seems to create two Kings – the I.G.F. in opposition to the C.G.S. We agree best to delay action on memo until it can be further discussed.

## 6 May

S. of S. sends for me and tells me that Esher had wired him Friday night that he (E) cannot continue to serve him etc. (all because Haldane has told Esher not to treat memo on duties of I.G.Forces as an official document!). The S. of S. went to York and on return to London last Sunday found out Esher's movements from his secretary, meets him at Paddington on way to see the King. S of S. discusses memo with him.

The S. of S. wishes me to see Esher with him. Latter arrives about noon – quite amenable and remarks 'atmosphere at Court unsuitable to touch on subject'. Memo gone through and given to amend. Again go through memo with Esher and together we alter certain points and add some paras re inspections. Send copy to S of S. and one to Esher.

## 7 May

Meeting in S of S's room at 11 a.m. Present Stopford, Miles, Mackinnon, the 'Law Officers of the Crown', Ellison, Colonel Gordon, Lucas and self. Decide that area for Territorial Army shall be the 'London County'- two Divisions to be raised in it and a Brigade in City of London. Stopford is opposed to idea of Divisional organization but S of S firm on that point.

## 10 May

Meeting re organization Territorial Force medical Services. To meet Surgeon General Keogh. Agree that there are no insurmountable difficulties.

## 14 May

Arrange principles on which Transport for Territorial Army is to be organized. Present at meeting Q.M.G. (Sir Wm. Nicholson[26]), Sir E. Ward (the Sec.), Generals Benson[27] and Clayton [28](Transport Department), Ellison and self.

## 24 May

C.G.S. sends for me because he wishes to know whether the S of S proposes to put the Notes 'Training Territorial Forces' on table House of Commons at once. We have meeting in S of S's room and General Miles sent for. We go through main paras of memo. C.G.S. quite friendly. It is agreed that I should revise memo with General Miles.

## 28 May

Attend House of Commons. Territorial and Reserve Forces Bill in committee. Attack of Militia partisans (of which much had been heard) comes to nothing.

On my way from station to Trunk House, horse falls and

throws me from cart on my head. Slightly stunned for a minute and unable to feel my legs, but soon all right and drive home.

## 29 May

Do not go to London as head rather sore. Get up for lunch and ride afterwards with Doris.

## 30 May

S of S sends for me and I attend meeting in his room. Present Lord Esher, Colonel Repington[29] (Military correspondent *Times*), Ellison and self. Discuss possibility of meeting Lord Salisbury's wishes re Militia becoming 3rd Battalions – also possible concessions which may be necessary in House of Lords to get Bill through.

At 4 p.m. meeting of 4 Military Members in S of S's room, also Generals Miles, Mackinnon and self to discuss paper on Training Territorial Army. The A.G. (Douglas) put up by General Miles is rather obstructive. S of S quite firm and I am instructed to carry out revision of a few details.

## 31 May

Again bothered with correction of 'Notes on Training' – a memo which S of S wishes to lay on table of House of Commons and which General Miles (for some reason) wishes to block. See C.G.S. and Miles and come to agreement. C.G.S. to give memo as now corrected to S of S. I see latter before lunch and explain situation to him.

Lord Scarbrough calls at 3.30 re Yeomanry. Thinks concessions as to enlistment good, but wants further concession for time-expired men re-engaging.

See C.G.S. afterwards and send the famous memorandum to printers for another Proof!

## 24 June

Catch 8 p.m. express at Euston for Perth. Colonel May joins me at station.

## 4 July

Wet morning. Operations in neighbourhood of Cloan. Ride to where Battery of Volunteer Artillery are position with Scots Greys. Find General Leach 'commanding' guns and squadrons and generally meddling with all and sundry. Operations rather a farce. S of S telegraphed for, to meet opposition leaders in House of Lords, as latter wish to make amendments to Army Bill. London express stopped at Auchterarder about 10 p.m.

Large dinner party including Prince Arthur of Connaught[30] and officers of the Greys.

## 5 July

Arrive Euston about 8 a.m. Find Doris very well; she had been staying at Princes Gate and went last night to Stafford House Ball, but had not met many old friends.

Busy day of meetings at War Office. Lord Salisbury attends committee in S of S's room. Esher and A.G. present. About 4 p.m. Lord Scarbrough and Lord Middleton (late Brodrick) came to talk to me about Yeomanry.

## 6 July

Meeting Army Polo Club. I am President. Final of Inter-Regimental Tournament – 20th versus 11th Hussars. The former win. Best team.

## 8 July

Doris and I dine with her mother at 27 Chesham Place and go on to a ball given by Lady Nunburnham, Grosvenor Square. Doris dances a good deal and we both enjoy ourselves. Home at 1 a.m. by Doris's request!

## 9 July

Leave for Bulford. Stay with Colonel Birkbeck, the Commandant of Cavalry School at Figheldean. Walk over to Netheravon before dinner.

## 10 July

Leave Figheldean about 8 a.m. See 2 Batteries of Horse Artillery practise. Lunch at Gunner's Camp and attend critique afterwards. Ride to Camp of Lancashire Artillery Militia. 4/1 paid for each horse daily but all risk taken by the owners. Training on Plain for 8 weeks. About 30% of Brigade are regulars. Dine at Cavalry School, Netheravon.

## 11 July

Ride out about 8.15 a.m. to see R.H.A. practise. After seeing 1 Battery I rode across and see the Lancashire Artillery drilling. A well horsed battery and they drill well. Then, to Cavalry School where I see the class of sergeants and remounts. A very good show.

Lunch at Abington House with Col. Birkbeck and catch 3 p.m. train for London.

Douglas Haig returned to Tarasp once again in late July to take the waters under the care of Dr Vogelsang, who said that he was in better physical shape than the previous year. He arrived back in England on 29 August to find the baby '. . . has grown greatly and is very strong and well – some 15lbs. in weight'.

His book, *Cavalry Studies – Strategical and Tactical* was published whilst he was away. The publisher was Hugh Rees Ltd. of Pall Mall and was part of the Pall Mall Military Series. It covered five Staff Rides, carried out during Haig's time as Inspector General of Cavalry in India in 1903 to 1905. He was helped with the book by a retired Royal Engineer Colonel called Sir Lonsdale Hale, who was a learned military academic, regularly called 'an old fool' by Douglas Haig, but entirely as a term of endearment! The book received some very favourable reviews as he described in a letter to Henrietta, written from Trunk House, Cove on 31 August 1907:

> Doris and I got back here about 7 o'clock on Thursday after quite a good journey. Our train from Dover reached London about 5.25 – about 20 minutes late only, which is not bad for the Paris train. We gave our keys to one of Cook's agents and came on direct from Waterloo. The heavy baggage followed by next train and we got it here by 9 o'clock. London seemed close and stuffy, and I think it was best to come direct here. Your goddaughter has grown a lot , and seems very well and happy. I went to office yesterday. Most of the Army Councillors are on leave but there are a number of committees being held, which is keeping the 'Directorates' busy. I leave here on Monday at 10 a.m. for Salisbury for the Dorsetshire manoeuvres and I'll arrange to be in London on Thursday in time for dinner. My address will be c/o Mr Wiles, Kingsbury Square, Wilton, Wilts. I called at Rees' yesterday. He said the book had been much favourably reviewed in many papers. This morning I have copies of a number of the reviews. The *Westminster Gazette* is especially friendly and ends up;

>> 'If the writer of this notice knew how to give higher praise than he has done he would unhesitatingly give it; and if space admitted he would delight in doing his best to describe the operations and put forward

the lessons of each and all the lessons with such infinite pleasure and – subject to the tenacity of his understanding – with so much profit."

One could not well be praised more highly.

The book also attracted the attention of the enemy, as Haig quite clearly recognized the Germans to be. A certain Major Max von Poseck wrote to Haig and said how interested General von Kleist had been and 'highly pleased with most of your principles'. It appears that only 353 copies of the book were printed, at least in the first edition and there is no evidence of any reprints. It is not known at what price it was sold, but it is not likely to have been a great money-spinner for either the author or the publisher!

**Diary for 15 September**
Doris and I leave Euston for Leighton Buzzard to stay with Mr. Leopold Rothschild for the Aldershot Command manoeuvres. Party consists of Lt. General Oliphant, Major Ostertag (German Attache), Major von Reuter (German War Office), Major Hyderbuch (German General Staff), Doris and self, Colonel May (my assistant Director of Military Training), Captain and Lady Sybil Grant (Coldstream Guards), Colonel Du Cane (R.F.A.), Miss Du Cane (sister), Lady Lurgan with our host and hostess. Motor from station to Ascott, have tea and go round gardens, stables etc. Dinner 8.30.

Haig had met Leopold de Rothschild[31] at Tarasp and Pontresina where they were both taking the waters and they had become friends. Evidently the War Office had asked the Rothschilds to invite the three German officers and to treat them 'with rather special civility', as Doris Haig later wrote. Her account continued:

Mrs Rothschild asked me to make myself very agreeable at dinner, because one of these officers was to take me in. I thought him extremely common, but tried to carry out what I had been asked to do – apparently so successfully that, during dinner he became very drunk and proceeded to make love openly – daring to call me 'Suesse Doris.' The whole party laughed.

Douglas Haig seems to have taken it all very calmly and continued to be civil to the man, who eventually apologized. He was apparently so impressed with Haig that he sent him his photograph!

Towards the end of 1907 Haig's job title changed to Director of Staff Duties, but he continued to carry out the same work as he had as Director of Military Training. He presumably thought the change was so unimportant that he does not mention it in his diary. The press, on the other hand, made the following comments on War Office Changes:

> Several important military changes take place in consequence of the vacation of the post of Director of Staff Duties by Lieut-General Hutchinson. His place will be filled by Major-General D. Haig, the Director of Military Training, who will be succeeded by Brigadier-General A.J. Murray, the principal Staff Officer under General Sir John French at Aldershot. The latter will be promoted to Major-General. The vacancy at Aldershot is expected to be filled by the appointment of Colonel W.R. Robertson. This however is not finally certain, as Lieut-General Smith Dorrien, the new Aldershot Commander, has to be consulted first.

A press report of a very different type describes:

**Shooting party at Sandringham (January 13th 1908)**
The party for the last week of the Sandringham winter season was larger than usual, and it included one or two newcomers. The Duke and Duchess of Roxburghe[32] were there, and the Queen walked and talked much with the dainty American peeress, and will probably attend the big ball she proposes to give in June. Sir Henry and Lady Evelyn Ewart, General Douglas Haig and his pretty but very delicate-looking wife, Mr. and Mrs. Willie James, Lord Claud Hamilton and Miss Jane Thornewill, Lord Burton's sister-in-law, together with some shooting men, made up the party. The most depressing weather did not prevent the Queen and the other ladies from joining the guns at lunch, and this meal, which is usually served in a cosy marquee, is the cheeriest event of the day at Sandringham. The fare, although not so elaborate as at some of the shoots given by ambitious millionaires, is by no means Spartan, and it is always piping hot, while the Royal servants lay the table and wait with as much ceremony as at a meal indoors.

**Diary 18 January**

Ride in the morning with Princess Victoria, Doris and Colonel Arthur Davidson.[33] We go through Ammer Village and have a gallop along grass lanes and home through fields. I ride a brown horse bought for the Queen.

General Sir George Higginson[34] arrived today. He was a guest here with me 10 years ago. My weight then 11.8 the same as his – now I am 12st.11lbs. and he is still the same. He remembers as an Eton boy seeing the King christened. He is now 82 yrs. of age and just as fit as he was ten years ago.

**19 January**

Today is being held to commemorate General Gordon's death. The ladies with the Queen drive to Church at 11.30. The gentlemen with one or two exceptions walk and are joined by the King and the remainder (who had driven at 12 o'clock). A bell gives a few tolls and we all walk in. The Commandments followed by a sermon are then read. The preacher (Hon. Tyrwhitt) takes as his text 'What manner of child shall this be?' and asks for subscriptions for the Gordon Boys Home near Woking. £92 is collected.

After lunch the King shows us round the gardens, stables, etc. I alone of all the party am taken by the King to see 'Persimmon' who broke his pelvis 2 weeks ago. The Queen is feeding him with carrots.

**27 January**

Dine with Mr. Sidney Webb[35] (41 Grosvenor Road). Mr. Haldane sits on Mrs. Webb's right – Arthur Balfour on her left. I am next Balfour with Mr. Mackinder on my left. About a dozen altogether. A plain simple dinner – whiskey & soda and lemonade offered to drink – and brandy after dinner.

In the evening a reception of the officers attending the School of Economics (about 30) and their professors.

**2 February**

Motor with Blair and Kiggell[36] to Staff College where Mr. Haldane and Ellison join us about noon. Consider steps necessary to enlarge Staff College to extent of 22 students. Lunch with Commandant (General Henry Wilson).

After lunch I explain my scheme for creating a number of War Schools. Mr. Haldane much pleased and says that he will arrange to find money for both. It is 5 p.m. before we leave the College.

## 3 February

Travel to London with Blair. Meet Walter Bagot who was at Sandhurst with me. Recently in charge of Chinese coolies – says Transvaal now given back to Boers! and life impossible there.

King and Crown Prince of Portugal were murdered on Saturday.

Doris and I dine quietly together at Princes Gate.

## 7 February

Put forward names of 14 general Staff Officers for appointment as 2nd grade G.S. Officers to Territorial Force.

Receive letter from Major Poseck asking leave to publish Essay on my Cavalry Studies in the Militaer Wochen Blatt. He is staff officer to General von Kleist, Inspector-General of Cavalry.

## Letter to Mr Haldane dated 18 March from the War Office

You will no doubt remember that two Batteries of the Lanarkshire Artillery Volunteers were turned out for special training last summer, and were brigaded with Regulars for about 10 days at the Scottish manoeuvres. The chief object of this was to enable us to form an opinion as to the standard of efficiency, which Volunteer Artillery could reach under the condition then existing. I attach a letter from Colonel May who, as Asst. Director of Training, accompanied me specially to watch the work of this Artillery.

I fully agree with what he writes, and am of opinion that what was done by these sections of Volunteer Artillery shows that they can become mobile enough, even under the old system of training, to take part in field operations. I did not however see this Artillery at practice but Colonel Wing's report on Allen's (Sheffield) Corps, 4th West Riding of Yorkshire, dated 9th August last, seems sufficient testimony on this head. His words are 'the practice was very satisfactory'. Wing is now Staff Officer for R.H. and Field Artillery to the C in C at Aldershot, and his opinion is that of an expert of today. Copy of Wing's report is attached.

In discussing the question of the standard of efficiency to which Volunteer Artillery can be brought, it seems highly important to notice that very great changes are being made with the view of providing better means for training. Briefly put they amount to the following:

1. The Volunteer Artillery is now to be organized as Field instead of Garrison, and will be formed in Artillery Brigades with Q.F. guns (quick firing).

2. A Divisional Artillery Commander and Staff is provided to direct the training throughout the whole year.
3. The training of officers and N.C.O.s of the Territorial Artillery by means of the Regular Training Brigades.
4. The methodical association of Volunteer Artillery with Regulars at training centres and camps.

Lastly the General Staff Officer in each Division of the Territorial Army brings the General Staff at Army Headquarters into close touch with the Territorial Force, so that the results of what is being done will be closely watched and proposals for improvement in organization and training will be carefully thought out, and put forward as necessity demands.

For these reasons I deprecate any change in the policy of creating a 2nd line Army complete in all arms and services.

## Diary 19 March

In House of Commons Mr Haldane reads out a letter which I had given him, stating value of territorial Field Artillery. Lord Roberts had remarked in House of Lords that 'they were a danger to the Country'. Give Mr H. papers re the Field Service Regulations.

## 22 April

Feel unwell so do not go out riding. Doris sends for Dr. about noon. Have much pain.

Haig was seriously ill with influenza, complicated by yet another bout of malaria. His high temperature lasted for some days. Doris considered that he was also run down by the long hours and hard work he had been doing at the War Office. After he was better she took him to Folkestone for a week to recuperate.

## Diary 28 July 28

C.G.S. tells me that the King wishes Graham to be given some Staff appointment. As H.M. asks for anything C.G.S. wishes his desires complied with. Graham is not fit for General Staff, in my opinion so I go and see A.G.'s department and ask them to provide for him.

Lunch with Mr Haldane to meet Sir E. Grey[37] (S of S for Foreign Affairs). Winston Churchill (Board of Trade) and General Ellison there too.

Mr. H goes off early and we discuss Army reorganization.

**Press Cutting about the Autumn Manoeuvres – entitled 'The Manoeuvres Scheme'**

I understand that this year the army manoeuvres will be on a much larger scale than for many years past. An enormous tract of country, having roughly, Salisbury Plain for its centre, and extending from Middlesex to Gloucestershire, is being acquired for the purpose. Of the Expeditionary force of six divisions, four are permanently quartered in the South of England, the other two being in Ireland, and it is expected that the former will all take part in the proposed operations. There will in addition be a cavalry division of twelve regiments and four batteries of horse artillery so that the number of troops that will take part in the manoeuvres will be between 40,000 and 50,000 men. In addition each of above five divisions will carry out their preliminary training on some spot of the ground that has been acquired, that of the cavalry being probably on Salisbury Plain. The latter will this year be commanded by Major-General Douglas Haig, who holds at the War office the post of Director of Staff Duties, and who, next to Sir John French, is our finest cavalry leader. He may be expected to employ this arm in a very different way than was the case last year. Spectacular charges will give place to a more modern concept of the horse soldier's role, and a large scheme of tactical reconnaissance will be undertaken.

**16 October**

Go to War Office early. Great Conference and War Game held under C.G.S. About 50 or 60 officers present representing all branches of the Army. Object of scheme is to arrive at decision as to our war system for Field Service Regulations.

Lunch with Mr. Haldane. Ellison and General Murray also there.

**4 November**

Meeting in C.G.S.'s room about the formation of an Imperial General Staff.

**5 November**

Finish discussion on my paper on Imperial General Staff and C.G.S. agrees to have it printed and sent to Colonial Premiers.

**7 November**

Doris asks me at 3.45 a.m. to call Secrett to send him for the Dr. By 5.25 they come to tell me that a little girl has been born and mother and daughter doing very well.

**24 November**

At 5 o'clock Henrietta calls at War Office for me. We drive to Peckham Rye and attend a spiritualistic séance. Mr. Husk, medium. The whole is a great fraud.

Dine with Sir J. French. We have a happy evening together and settle many things.

**27 November**

Mr. Haldane sends for me to tell me that Wilson, Commandant of the Staff College, has been crabbing Territorial Force.

**15 December**

Meeting in Mr. Haldane's room with C.G.S., Sir Fred. Bordon and General Hoad to consider my paper on the Imperial General Staff. Sit 'till nearly 7 p.m.

**16 December**

At office at 10 o'clock and correct proof of Imperial General Staff paper with C.G.S. 'till 12 o'clock. Arrange for copies to go to the Colonial office.

**18 December**

Motor with Kiggell to Staff College. Sir Wm. Nicholson (C.G.S.) makes annual inspection. Our Memorandum on the formation of an Imperial General Staff posted to Australia and New Zealand.

**23 December**

Meeting in S of S's room re motors for use in War. Du Cros, the head of Panhard Works, there.

Meeting of Military Members regarding Field Service Regulations. Present Sir Wm. Nicholson (C.G.S.), Sir C. Douglas (A.G.), Sir H.Miles (Q.M.G.) and the M.G.O., also Colonel Adye and myself. Proof generally agreed to. It has been over 5 years in the writing!

## 25 December

Doris and I spend a quiet & happy Xmas at Trunk House.

## Notes

1. Vivian family. Hussey Crespigny Vivian 3rd Baron Vivian GCMG, CB (1834–1893) was a diplomat, who became Britain's first ambassador in Rome 1891–3. He had a son and three daughters. George (1878–1940) was in the 17 Lancers in both the Boer and First World Wars. Dorothy (Doris) (1880–1939) and Violet (1880–1962), twins, were both Maids of Honour to Queen Alexandra. Violet never married (she told her great nephew and niece that she never married because no man ever measured up to King Haakon of Norway!) Alexandra (1882–1963) was a Lady of the Bedchamber to Queen Elizabeth the Queen Mother. She married, in 1911, Lord Worsley, eldest son of the 4th Earl of Yarborough, who was in the Royal Horse Guards and killed at 1st Ypres in October 1914. Lady Vivian, who died in 1926, was Louisa Duff, sister of Sir Charles Assheton-Smith of Vaynol, North Wales.

2. *Curzon* by David Gilmour, published by John Murray, p.342.

3. Gilbert Elliot-Murray-Kynynmound 4th Earl of Minto KG, GCSI, GCMG, GCIE (1845–1914) had previously been Governor General of Canada from 1898–1904. He was Viceroy from 1905–10. As a young man he had been a noted amateur steeplechase rider, winning the Cheltenham Gold Cup and completing the Grand National.

4. The future King George V and Queen Mary.

5. Sir Bindon Blood GCB (1842–1947) was commissioned in 1860 and retired in 1907. He served most of his career in India. He commanded the army in the Punjab at the time (1902) of the murder of an Indian cook by soldiers of the 9 Lancers and was surprised that the affair caused 'such silly excitement' in Simla. He was seemingly proud of his descent from Colonel Blood, who stole the Crown Jewels in Charles II's reign. He was Churchill's commanding officer in the Malakand Field Force. As will be seen from the above dates he lived until the age of ninety-nine.

6. Richard Burdon Haldane 1st Baron Haldane (1856–1928) was arguably Britain's best ever Secretary of State for War, the post he held from 1905–1912. During this time he and Haig reorganized the Army, so that it was fit for war in 1914, with the Regular Army being supported by an efficient Territorial Army of all arms. One of the lost opportunities of the First World War was the formation of Kitchener's New Army, which failed to build on to the existing Territorials. Haldane was hounded out of office in 1915 as the result of a press campaign claiming that he was pro-German. Haig personally delivered the first copy of his *War Despatches* to Haldane with an inscription expressing his admiration for Haldane's work as Secretary of State.

7. Esme Armstrong Crabbe, Oliver Haig's wife.

8. Lieutenant Colonel Sir Thomas Wolseley Haig KCIE, CSI, CMG, CBE

(1865–1935), a cousin, was commissioned into the Seaforth Highlanders. He joined the Indian Political Department in 1891 and was based in Hyderabad. After retiring from service in India he joined the office of the Lord Lyon King of Arms, where he became Albany Herald.

9. Reginald Baliol Brett, 2nd Viscount Esher GCB, GCVO, (1852–1930)was Permanent Member of the Committee of Imperial Defence 1905–18, as well as serving on the Committee of Enquiry into the South African War and being Chairman of the War Office Reconstruction Committee. His wife was Eleanor Van de Weyer, daughter of a Belgian ambassador to London. They had four children.

10. General Sir Laurence James Oliphant KCB, KCVO, born 1846, became a general in 1911, retired 1913.

11 Colonel Sir Gerald Francis Ellison CB, (1861–1947) was commissioned into the North Lancashire Regiment in 1882, transferring first to the Royal West Surrey Regiment in 1891 and then to the Royal Warwickshire Regiment in 1898. He had served at Aldershot and in South Africa in staff jobs before becoming private secretary to the Secretary of State for War (Haldane) in 1905-08. He was a key member of the group reforming the Army.

12. John Morley, 1st Viscount Morley of Blackburn OM (1838–1923) was a Liberal Member of Parliament, elected in 1892. He was a noted orator and writer. He became Secretary of State for India in 1905, a post he held until 1910. His influence on Indian administration was one of firmness in dealing with alarming symptoms of sedition. He became Lord President of the Council in 1910 until 1914. He never married and the title died with him.

13. The Duke and Duchess of Buccleuch's London house was Montagu House, Whitehall. He was the 6th Duke of Buccleuch and 8th Duke of Queensberry. She was the daughter of the 1st Duke of Abercorn and sister of Lady Lansdowne. Luncheon was laid for twenty-eight every day the Buccleuchs were in residence, on the basis of open house, with the butler deciding who was to be admitted. The present Department of Defence was built in the garden of Montagu House, which was purchased by the Government in 1913. A grandson of the Buccleuchs married Haig's second daughter.

14. Sir Lauder Brunton was a leading physician of that era.

15. General Sir William Henry Mackinnon KCB, KCVO, was born in 1852 and commissioned into the Grenadiers in 1870. After service in Malta and Madras, his career was thenceforward concerned with the Volunteer Army, firstly as a colonel, then as major general of the Imperial Yeomanry during the South African War. He was Director General of Auxiliary Forces in 1904–7, then of Territorial Forces.

16. Lieutenant General Sir Alexander Hamilton Gordon (1859–1939), was commissioned into the Royal Artillery in 1880. He served in Malta, South Africa and was an instructor at the School of Gunnery. He was in

Army Headquarters from 1904-08. In 1910 he went to India as Director of Military Operations. In the First World War he commanded IX Corps 1916–18, but was replaced in September 1918.

17. Lieutenant General Sir Herbert Scott Gould Miles GCB, CVO was born in 1850 and commissioned into the Royal Munster Fusiliers in 1869. He served in Aldershot before becoming Commandant of the Staff College in 1898–99. In 1904-08 he was Director of Organization at Army Headquarters. He became QMG in 1908. He was put out to grass in 1913 as Governor of Gibraltar. Haig found him maddeningly obstructive, but they were good personal friends. Lady Haig records how, when Miles was staying with the Haigs at Farnborough, the two generals bought from Hamley's a dummy broken egg, which they put on the drawing-room carpet. Lady Haig hit the roof, but eventually saw the joke! This must be one of the best possible ways of 'bonding' with another general!

18. Major General Charles Ernest Heath CVO, CB was born in 1854 and was commissioned into the Duke of Cornwall's Light Infantry in 1873. He transferred into the Army Service Corps in 1890. He was i/c administration at Aldershot in 1905-07. He became Director of Transport and Remounts at Army Headquarters/the War Office in 1907–11.

19. Lord Lovat, the Earl of Scarbrough, the Earl of Shaftesbury, the Hon. W.A.W. Lawson and Sir T.C. Meyrick were all prominent leaders in the Voluntary Army in their part of the country.

20. Lieutenant General Sir Lawrence Worthington Parsons born 1850, commissioned 1870, became a lieutenant general in 1909 and retired in 1912.

21. Major General Sir Charles Crutchley was born in 1856 and commissioned into the Scots Fusilier Guards in 1874. He was based at Headquarters British Army from 1889 to 1909 with a role in army organization, ending up as director.

22. Lieutenant General Sir John Spencer Ewart KCB was born in 1861 and commissioned into the Cameron Highlanders in 1881. He served in Egypt, Malta and South Africa before going to Army Headquarters. He was Military Secretary to the Secretary of State from 1904-06 and Secretary of the Selection Board. In 1906 he became Director of Military Operations at Army Headquarters/the War Office, the Adjutant General from 1910–14..485

23. Major General Sir Frederick Spencer Robb KCB, MVO (1858–1948) was commissioned into the Durham Light Infantry in 1880, served in Aldershot, Sudan and Army Headquarters, before commanding a brigade in Eastern Command. He became Major General i/c Administration at Aldershot in 1910 to 1914. He was Inspector Gen85eral of Communications in France in 1914 and Military Secretary to the Secretary of State for War in 1914–16.

24. Auberon Thomas Herbert, 8th Baron Lucas and 11th Baron Dingwall

(1876–1916) was private secretary to the Secretary of State for War 1907–8, then Under Secretary of State for War and a Member of the Army Council 1908. He joined the RFC in the First World War and did not return from a flight over enemy lines in 1916.

25. Edward George Villiers Stanley 17th Earl of Derby KG, GCB, GCVO, CB (1864–1948) was commissioned into the Grenadiers and served as private secretary to Lord Roberts in South Africa. He had a long and distinguished career in politics including Secretary of State for War in 1916–18. With his many connections in the Voluntary Army he was an important ally for Haig. His son died before him and he was succeeded by his grandson.

26. Field Marshal Lord Nicholson GCB (1845–1918). After Woolwich he was commissioned into the Royal Engineers. He served in India from 1871 to 1900. He was Military Secretary to Lord Roberts in South Africa and Director of Transport. After the Boer War he went as Military Attaché to Japan, before becoming QMG in 1905. He became a general in 1907 and in 1908 became the first CIGS. He was promoted to field marshal in 1911 and raised to the peerage in 1912 on retirement from the Army.

27. Major General Sir F.W. Benson became honorary colonel of a Canadian Regiment in 1905.

28. Major General Frederick Thomas Clayton CB, born 1855, commissioned into the Warwickshire Regiment in 1876, served in China, South Africa and became a transport specialist as Assistant Director of Transport for the Army in 1902–6. He was Director of Supplies at the War Office, then major general i/c administration in South Africa from 1911.

29. Colonel Charles Repington (1858–1925) was a highly influential correspondent with the *Times* and subsequently the *Morning Post*. He drew attention to the shell shortage in France in 1915. His influence on military policy was such that he was referred to as 'the twenty-third member of the Cabinet'.

30. Prince Arthur of Connaught (1883–1938) was commissioned into the 7 Hussars, before transferring into the Royal Scots Greys in 1907. He served in the First World War as one of Haig's ADCs. He was Governor General of South Africa from 1920–23.

31. Leopold de Rothschild, (1845–1907), banker and third son of Baron Lionel de Rothschild lived at Ascott House, Wing, Bucks. The house had been bought by Baron Mayer Rothschild and handed over to Leopold and his wife. They created an outstanding garden. The house now belongs to the National Trust.

32. Henry John Innes-Ker, 8th Duke of Roxburghe, KT, MVO (1876–1932) was commissioned into the Blues and served in the South African and First World Wars. She was Mary Goelet from New York.

33. Colonel Sir Arthur Davidson KCB, KCVO, born 1855, was equerry to the King from 1902.
34. General Sir George Higginson GCB, was born in 1826 and commissioned in 1845 into the Worcester Regiment. He retired in 1893.
35. Sidney (1859–1947) and Beatrice (1858–1943) Webb were leading members of the Fabian Society and promoters of industrial democracy. They were instrumental in founding the London School of Economics and Political Science in 1895 with funds left to the Fabian Society.
36. Lieutenant General Sir Launcelot Edward Kiggell KCB (1862–1954) was commissioned into the Royal Warwickshire Regiment in 1872. After two years as an instructor at Sandhurst he served in South Africa. He became Director of Staff Duties at the War Office in 1909. He was Haig's Chief Of Staff from 1915 to January 1918.
37. Edward Grey 1st Viscount Grey of Falloden and 3rd Baronet KG, (1862–1933) was Secretary of State for Foreign Affairs from 1905 to 1915. He was a friend of Haig's at Oxford.

# Chapter 10

# War Office and Chief of the General Staff in India

## 1909 – 1911

1909 started with Haig still in the War Office as Director of Staff Duties, but by April he had been offered the appointment of Chief of Staff in India. After some days of thought and discussion with others he accepted the appointment, but deferred taking it up until the autumn. He was totally committed to completing his work with Haldane and gave himself from April until early October to do so. Meantime the pattern established during the previous three years continued.

**Diary for 1 January 1909**
Quiet and happy day with Doris. Ground white with snow. Dinner off a fine turkey from Radway.

**2 January**
Send motor to meet Doris's mother, her sisters Violet and Alexandra who come from London. Christening of baby at Cove Church. Violet, Alexandra and self proxies. Child called Victoria – Doris – Rachel.[1]

**3 January**
Doris and household very busy packing up in view of our move to London for 3 months. The child's nurse gave notice at 7 a.m. this morning. An awkward hour for such an announcement but the woman is slovenly and will be no great loss.

**5 January**

Call on General French at Horse Guards. We agree entirely on scheme of training for Cavalry Division.

Call at 1 Hill Street which was handed over to me at 12 o'clock. Secrett and other servants have made good progress in getting things unpacked. A van had left Trunk House last night and boxes delivered at 9 o'clock this morning. Wire Doris to bring our Indian rugs as the dining room rather bare.

**15 January**

Preside over Committee on the organization of depots and reserve Batteries for Field Artillery on mobilization. General Hoad brings scheme for General Staff in Australia.

**19 January**

Discussion on Territorial Force. 11 General Staff Officers of Divisions present and give their experiences. Much good work has been done.

**22 January**

General Hoad brings the Eddison 'phonograph' for me to see. A wonderful invention and saves shorthand writer.

Meeting at Horse Guards with General French and 2 Cavalry brigadiers. Generals Byng, Allenby, Fanshawe[2] and Lindley[3] regarding;

(a) training of officers for riding at Olympia.
(b) training of Cavalry Division.

Fix date for Staff Ride 1st March to 6th.

Mr. Haldane sends for me re Education Scheme and his speech on Estimates.

**26 January**

Lunch with Mr. Haldane. Sir Edward Grey (Sec. for Foreign Affairs) and Br. General Aston[4] form the party.

Doris and I dine with Lord Sanderson to meet Lord Northcote[5] recently returned from governorship of Australia. Sit next to Lady Margaret Charteris.[6] A wonderful old lady of 75.

## 3 February

Dine with Doris's mother and go to see the 'Englishman's Home'. The play shows what is likely to happen if this country is invaded. It is extraordinary how the play draws crowded houses every night and how impressed the audience seem to be with the gravity of the scenes. I trust that good may result and 'universal training' may become the law of the land, but for myself the performance was not an interesting sight. I felt that the incapacity of the people in defending their homes was disgusting.

## 12 February

Doris and I dine with Scarbroughs at 21 Park Lane. Take Mrs. Churchill in to dinner. Have long discussion with Winston Churchill[7] on Sword and Lance as weapons of today for Cavalry. Also on the general policy for Home Defence.

## 15 February

Meet Colonel Ponsonby[8] who had been in Berlin with the King last week. German Court most friendly, but officers of Army and Navy still hostile. Kaiser gives State Ball not to amuse his subjects but 'to teach deportment' and so they dance 'Polonaise' and 'Parnes' etc.

Kimberley dinner at Ritz Hotel. Doris calls for me and we go on to Londonderry House but crowd so great we do not get in!

## 16 February

Meeting to fix Staffs for manoeuvres. Murray and Adye present. General Ewart brings paper dealing with W.F. scheme and states his branch has arrived at conclusion that we only need transport to enable us to operate 3 marches from a railway. On this our line of communications can be modified!

Doris attends opening of Parliament. The Queen had given ticket.

## 18 February

Lunch with Mr. Haldane and walk with him to House of Commons. We discuss objects for which Army and Expeditionary Force exist. He is in doubt whether to organize to support France and Russia against Germany and perhaps Austria. I point out that, by organizing, war may be prevented.

## 15 April

Sir O'Moore Creagh[9] comes to see me. He is going to Paris to recover from influenza. Asks me to go to India as his Chief of Staff. I decline saying that I am fully engaged on the Imperial General Staff scheme and other important matters, but after a short reconsideration ask that I may be given a week to think it over.

## 3 May

Scatters Wilson[10] comes to see me re work on General Staff with a view of preparing himself for post of Military Secretary India.

Lunch with Sir O'Moore Creagh. I have accepted the appointment.

## 14 June

Lunch with Mr. Haldane. Winston Churchill, Generals Murray and Ellison of the party. Churchill has returned to the fold and there is much more rejoicing over the return of the prodigal than over the viands and wines etc.!

## 23 June

Receive letter from Sir Dighton Probyn[11] telling me that the King will promote me to be a K.C.V.O. in Birthday Gazette.

## 25 June

Birthday Gazette appears this morning. Many congratulations received from officers attending Staff Ride. They drink my health.

## 12 July

Take Doris and the 2 children to Garden Party at Buckingham Palace. Owing to the threatening weather first part of entertainment given in Throne Room where stage erected. Xandra very good and holds on to my hand. Doris carries baby in her arms for a bit, then sends nurse home with her.

## 14 July

Dine with Mr. Haldane to meet Mr. Balfour.[12] Generals Ellison and Murray the other guests. We talk about Home Defence and the organization of the forces of the Empire. Mr. Balfour goes off about 11 p.m. to House of Commons saying that he will see that there is no break in continuity when his party gets in.

## 15 July

Meet Mr. Balfour in the street. He remarks that he enjoyed last night and begins to renew his conversation of then.

Sir Wm. and Lady Nicholson, Doris's mother, her sister Alexandra and Miss Hughes, General Pulteney,[13] Captain Anderson, Lord Vivian and Scatters Wilson dine at Princes Gate and all seem to enjoy themselves.

## 11 August

Telegram this evening from Miss Charlotte Knollys[14] saying that the Queen wishes Doris and children to go to Balmoral.

## 16 August

Doris starts for London and Scotland with 2 children and 2 nurses.

Doris wrote:

On hearing of our departure to India, for Douglas to take up his new appointment, the Queen is sorry for me leaving the children, and insists on having us to stay. We have a delightful time, and the Queen thoroughly enjoys playing with the children; my only fear is that they may get spoilt. It was touching to find rooms arranged as nurseries and every smallest detail thought out by the Queen herself.

## Diary 25 September

Reach Balmoral about 3 o'clock. Colonel Frederick (Deputy Master of the Household) has lunch ready for me. Colonel Fairholme (Mil. Attache, Paris) arrives with me. After lunch walk out on to the golf links and see McKenna and Sidney Greville playing golf. Large party staying at the Castle. Count Benckendorf (Russian Ambassador), Mr McKenna[15] (1st Lord of the Admiralty), Lord Rosebery,[16] Shackleton[17] of South Pole fame, Sir Alan Young etc. etc. Sit opposite the King at dinner between Lord Rosebery and Greville. Lecture after dinner by Shackleton.

## 26 September

Go to Church at Craithy. After Church motor to Mar Lodge with the King for lunch. Get back in time for tea. Sit next the

King at dinner. Have talk with Mr. McKenna about Navy and need for General Staff. But ignorant of war or its needs!

## 27 September
Lunch with King on the moor. Sit on his left at lunch. The Prince of Wales opposite. Take leave of His Majesty after lunch and go back to Balmoral. Catch 1.50 train at Ballater.

## 6 October
Go to office about 10.30. Hand over report Cavalry Training to Captain Howell. Go to India Office and say goodbye to Lord Morley and the Permanent Under Secretary and also the Master of Elibank. I leave a card on Sir B.D.Duff as he is so busy and several officers waiting to see him. Return to War Office and say goodbye to Mr. Haldane and many others. About 2 o'clock hand over to my successor General Kiggell and go to lunch with Henrietta.

## 7 October
A great number of friends to see me off. Bee, Mary, Hugo and Wolseley Haig. Sir Wm. Nicholson (C.G.S.), General Murray (D.M.T.), General Kiggell, my successor, W. Adye, Braithwaite,[18] Colonel Hole, Colonel Haldane,[19] Alan Fletcher, Edmund Talbot, Beresford and many others.

## 8 October
Sail on *Mantua* at 10 a.m. Passengers keep on arriving with great piles of luggage. One lady and her nurse and child left on the pier.

A press cutting of the time said:

Major-General Douglas Haig it is understood has been selected to serve in India as Chief of Staff to General Sir O'Moore Creagh the new Commander-in-Chief. General Haig is at present Director of Staff Duties at the War Office, and has filled many important appointments. He was for some years Inspector General of Cavalry in India and is believed to hold the record among Cavalry Officers for rapidity of promotion. Twelve years ago he was a Captain in the 7th Hussars, but he has been a Major-General for nearly five years; and thus in seven years he passed through the rank of Captain, Major, Lieutenant-Colonel and Major-General. He owes this rapid promotion of course to the two campaigns in which he took a very conspicuous part – the Sudan War and the South African War. In the latter campaign he was for some time Chief of Staff to General Sir John French, and especially distinguished himself in the fighting around Colesberg. General Haig is a native of the Midlands, and when at home lives near Warwick.

Apart from the ludicrous description of Haig as 'a native of the Midlands' this is an accurate summary of his career. Another press cutting quotes a brother officer as saying 'I would rather have Haig's luck than a licence to steal horses'. But of course luck was only part of the reason for his fast promotion after a slow start!

The journey to Bombay on SS *Mantua* was pleasant and uneventful. Sir Douglas and Lady Haig were accompanied by John Vaughan, by now Lieutenant Colonel, commanding the 10 Hussars, who were stationed in India. Doris Haig records a curious incident when a fortune teller in Port Said foretold Haig's future. She said:

We found a wonderful man at Port Said who foretold Douglas's future like reading a map. The Great War was described and the anxieties and responsibilities it entailed. Douglas would be successful in everything that he undertook, and would save the country. Honours would be showered on him, but he would be much concerned about the sufferings around him.

**Diary for 22 October**
Arrive Bombay about 5 a.m. Land at 9.30. Met by Mr. Cheers (confidential clerk) and Furreed my dressing boy (who first joined me in December 1886 at Secunderabad). Mr. Cheers had arranged to get him. Also a Goanese butler and an ayah for Doris. We go to Taj Mahal Hotel and find Sir Pratap Singh (Maharajah of Idar) waiting for us. We are guests at the Hotel. Motor with him in afternoon to some Arab Stables and on to Gwalior's house beyond Malabar Hill. Dine with Craigie at Yacht Club.

**23 October (journey to Simla)**
Leave at 3 p.m. by Punjab express. Doris and I have C of S's saloon. Quite comfortable.

## 25 October

Get to Kalka about 4 p.m. Send baggage on by train and Doris and I leave in C's [Commander in Chief's] motor at 9 a.m. very shaky going round corners. Get to Simla about 1.15. Met by Chief's brougham and go to lunch at Snowdon [C.-in-C.'s house]. After we drive to 'Kenilworth' which Wapshare had taken for us for 2 months.

## 26 October

Go to office and go round and make acquaintance with all and sundry.

## 13 November

Mr Azizuddin (an Afghan by birth) in Criminal Intelligence Dept. lunches with me. He attributes the unrest and secret societies in India to Curzon – thinks Lord Kitchener 'afraid'. States that in a month's time assassinations will begin in both England and India.

The Haigs went on a sight-seeing tour in Rajasthan from 2 to 6 December, returning to Calcutta on 8 December.

## 15 December

Meeting of Advisory Committee. The Viceroy (Lord Minto) arrives from Madras. We all go to Government House to meet him. He expresses a wish to have a long talk with me, but as he is going off again tomorrow to Darjeeling, it seems difficult to arrange!

## 25 December

Our dinner party for Xmas – Sir Pratap Singh, General and Mrs Kitson[20] (Q.M.G.), Colonel Beaton, Colonel Headlam, Neil, Doris and self – 8 in all.

## 26 December

Mail arrives when out riding. No letter from Henrietta or Nurse about the children, so Doris fussing.

## 29 December

Doris and I play golf at Tollygunge after lunch. Most people have gone to the races!

Dine with Lt. Governor of Bengal at Belvedere. After dinner

there is a dance. Doris goes to supper with 'His Honour' and has to eat a good one for once! Get back about midnight.

## 1 January 1910

The usual 1st of Jan. parade takes place this morning. Ride the chestnut arab, 'Knight of Deccan', who is looking very well. Go to Treasury Gate at 7.45 and join H.E. the C in C. We ride together to Government House. Start then in procession with the Viceroy. An enormous crowd of natives looking on. There is no 'salaaming' to the Viceroy and natives an impassive, sullen, sleepy looking lot.

Doris and I motor to Tollygunge Steeplechases and lunch there with the Lt. Governor, Sir E. Baker.

## 8 February

Attend meeting Legislative Council at 11 a.m. Press Bill passed. Sit till 6.45 p.m. with short break for lunch. Some excellent speeches especially Mr Sinha's (Law Member of Council). He speaks out pluckily against sedition. Burdwan calls Keir Hardie[21] a 'white coolie'! At end of debate the Viceroy announces liberation of 'deportees'. The argument ceases to be political and becomes 'anarchical'!

## 10 February

Meeting in my Office at 11 a.m. to decide how to employ 9 extra lakhs which have fallen available to be used before 31st March. There is a shortage to date of 179,000 rifles. I consider the position serious and ask for 16,000 at once. S of S has asked for an explanation. Duff being there and having approved of deficiency, as C of S., I am in a difficult position!

## 12 February

Ride with Doris as usual before breakfast.

At office at 10 o'clock. About 11 a.m. an A.D.C. from the C in C arrives and says Sir O'Moore wants to see me at once. I go to Treasury gate. The Chief shows me a telegram from 'Wodehouse' saying that party which had gone to Khyber had not returned – feared the worst etc. etc. We go to see the Viceroy and Secretary of Foreign Office called in. In an hour's time wire is received signed 'Johnstone and Hewitt' the names of 2 ladies who had visited Khyber and sent wire to Chief as a joke!! Truly forward and badly brought up females.

## 10 March

Admiral Slade[22] comes to see me re blockade of Incleran Coast to stop arms traffic.

## 12 March

Wire comes of raid near Bannu – 2 squadrons of 14th Lancers and 200 rifles of 57th Rifles sent to intercept them. Captain Stirling (57th Rifles) killed. 6 raiders killed and 5 wounded. Our losses 5 killed and 12 wounded.

## 2 April

Arrive Simla 4.30 p.m. We have taken a new house 'Holly Oak' and find it nicely arranged. Doris had given directions to Mrs Cheers to have curtains, chair covers, etc. made.

## Letter to General Sir Gerald Ellison written at Simla 14 April 1910

Sir Arthur Barrett (Adjutant- General here) goes home on Saturday on 6 months leave. He will call at the W.O. to see the C.I.G.S. first of all to ask if he may discuss questions with you and others in the office. I have told him that I would write to you about him. He is a good straight fellow, but more of an outdoor soldier than organizer. Indeed the A.G. Division here is only beginning to realize what its legitimate duties are. Still you will be able to give him your ideas and make suggestions for the better organization of the Army of the Empire of which the Army in India forms an important part. I am telling them here that the first point to decide is 'What you propose to put into the Field', and then work back to all that is necessary for the maintenance of that Field Force, and Internal Security.

We are gradually getting the General Staff going here. Hamilton Gordon arrived two weeks ago, and is gradually getting into the way of things. He will be a great help.

I am sorry to see that Mr. Haldane was so poorly during the winter, but conclude from his speeches in the Commons that he is quite fit again. What a pity it is that he has to associate with such a pack of rascals as Lloyd George & Co! They seem to be ruining the country in trade; and in reputation also by working at Redmond's bidding!

I spent some weary hours in the Legislative Council in Calcutta listening to speeches by our Indian brothers. But on the whole the latter are a satisfactory lot and mean to do their duty to the Government and the Country.

We are to have a couple of Divisions out for training next December if all goes well, and will manoeuvre against each other. You should come out here for a change and have a look round!

Forgive a hurried line and let me hear when you have a spare moment how things to go with you.

## Letter to General Ellison dated 8 June 1910

CHIEF OF THE GENERAL STAFF SIMLA 8. VI. 10

MY DEAR ELLISON,

I was delighted to get your most interesting letter of 13th May. It was nice of you to find time to write in the midst of all your hard work. The papers which you enclosed re. the 3 kinds of Reserves of the T.F. are interesting reading, and show how much you have done to develop the original scheme. It is good to hear that you are getting to grips with our R.E. friends! I am inclined to think that they hold almost as peculiar place in the Indian Army as at home. I was astounded the other day to be told that the C.R.E. of a Division can hold his appointment for as long as he chooses to remain up to the age limit 56! I am glad the Depots are really taking shape at last! What has old Miles been about to allow such progress to be made? It must be a satisfaction to Mr. Haldane to be in office while some of the fruits of his great labour are beginning to appear! Give him my best respects!

Here we are jogging along fairly steadily and people are beginning to grasp what the work of a General Staff really means. But as you know the organization of A.H.Q. is a peculiar one! We all have a 'dual capacity' viz. Staff Officers and Departmental Officers! but I can only talk to the 'Commander – in – Chief' but on no account to the 'Honble. Army Member' though he is one and the same person. Of course we make the system go, and all credit is due to Lord K. for having done away with the 'old Military Department' with its separate head. But under our existing system the C. in C. is kept in Calcutta in the winter settling numbers of administrative questions instead of being able to go on tour and visiting the troops. Sir O'Moore means to tour much more in the coming winter, and has been discussing how to arrange to carry on business. The Chinese are apparently pressing us all round our N.E frontier and on the Burmese frontier also. I question whether the Foreign Office in London and our people in Pekin are quite alive to what is going on. There is a stretch of independent tribal territory East of Bhutan about which very little is known and into which the Chinese have already penetrated while we are discussing what to do!

The internal situation is not good whatever the Politicians may say, especially in the Punjab where people act more and talk less than in Bengal and Bombay. The Arya Samaj is undoubtedly doing much harm

291

in the Army and should be tackled at once. The Punjab Government
under Dane seem very weak in the circumstances.

Confidential For Genl. Ellison's personal information.

(Sgd.) D.H.

9.vi.10

## Diary entry for 6 May 1910

The King is ill. This morning's Bulletin stated that His Majesty's
condition gives cause for grave anxiety. This evening's states that
the King is worse, and that his condition is critical.

## 7 May

News arrives about 9.30 a.m. that the King is dead. His Majesty
died last night at 11.45 p.m. Doris goes to telegraph office and
wires Miss Knollys 'Please express to Queen and Princess
Victoria our deepest sympathy stop and with the Household we
mourn. Doris and Douglas Haig.'

## 8 May

All engagements are of course cancelled. Doris and I go to
church. Short funeral address on the King's death. The Viceroy
present.

## 12 May

King George Vth proclaimed in front of Town Hall. With C in
C Staff from HQ assembled at Viceregal Lodge 4.45 p.m. and
accompany Viceroy to the Ridge. Guards of Honour etc.
and trumpeters from 10th Hussars.

## 20 May

Day of mourning throughout Empire. Funeral Service for King
Edward at noon. Viceroy and C in C with their staffs attend.

## Letter to Henrietta dated 11 August from Simla

We have been busy arranging to send troops to Tibet – and now the
Minister at Pekin wires that the Chinese will be responsible for the lives
of our agents and others in Tibet. I hope we need not have to send the
troops there now, as the expedition will run away with a vast amount of
money which we can ill spare from military funds at present. Altho' only
a very small force is going the difficulties of the road make transport
work very costly. The railhead is only 320 ft. above the sea and in 20

miles the road rises to cross a pass 12,000 ft. above sea level. The rains too are terrible in those parts at present.

We had great discussions in the Legislative Council last Saturday over the renewal of the Seditious Meetings Act. The Viceroy had been ill with the 'flu but was able to preside. We sat from 11 a.m. to 4 p.m. without rising. There were some good speeches. The Hindoos opposed the bill, but of course it was carried without difficulty. I had a Bengalee (Bupendranath Basu) to dine on the Sunday. He has a difficult position, as his own people think him too mild in his opposition, and if he says anything too strong he is reprimanded by those in authority in the Council!

On Monday Doris and I dined at Viceregal Lodge to see 'The Thief'. Lady Eileen[23] acts extremely well. And tho' the play was an expurgated edition of the original French play, there was quite enough left in to give free scope to Lady E's talent. That young lady would make a fortune on the stage, but such sensational acting must be very bad for a young girl. She gets quite exhausted after the 2nd Act which is a long one.

We had to have supper and did not get to bed till all hours.

A wire has just come offering John Vaughan the Cavalry School at Netheravon. The post is not vacant till next January. He will do well there and I am glad he has got it.

## 18 August

Write to C in C to remind him that 15th September is last date on which relief force can leave Quatong for Gyantor and return before the passes close. A month is also required to collect supplies for the relief force. So decision should be given soon whether expedition is to be abandoned for this year.

[The above refers to a possible expedition into Tibet, first mentioned in mid-June. The expedition did not take place because the Chinese guaranteed the safety of the British agents, based in Tibet.]

Leave with Colonel Hudson[24] by 12.42 train for Saugor Cavalry School.

## 20 August

Arrive Saugor at 1.40 a.m. General Wapshare[25] and 2 of his Staff meet me and drive me to Cavalry School. We walk round School before breakfast. I am much annoyed at way in which work is held up and keenness of Staff damped by delay in issuing Army Order authorizing opening of School. Delay is due to opposition

on part of Sir R. Scallon (Sec. Army Department) and Financial
Department (Fleetwood Wilson).

## 10 October (Simla)

Lecture at Theatre by Colonel Drake (Marines) of Quetta Staff
College on 'World Politics'. As President of the Council, I
propose thanks to the Viceroy.

In the evening Farewell Ball to Lord and Lady Minto. (I receive
the guests. No ladies on committee to avoid any quarrelling!)

## 11 October

We get home from Ball at 3 a.m. All went off well and the Mintos
seemed to enjoy themselves.

Leave by 12.40 train for Rawal Pindi. Doris goes to stay at
Viceregal Lodge.

## 2 November (Quetta)

Go round Staff College with General Capper. Call on Sir H.
MacMahon.[26] We discuss situation on frontier etc. Dine at Staff
College.

## 3 November

Inspect Staff College. See senior term individually. About 11.30
give short address. Leave Quetta for Simla at 3.40 p.m. with
Captain Charteris.

## 12 November (In train for Calcutta)

Doris and I leave by 12.40 train for Calcutta About 10 miles
from Kalka a waggon belonging to goods train in front of us,
had run off the line. Mr. Wood (of Railway Board) is on our
train. He gets a European railway driver from the 11 o'clock
train and we go on to see the scene of the derailment. We unload
waggon and get it on to the rails and send it on to the next
station, about ½ mile away. Finally we get to Kalka about 7.30
p.m. The mail train kept for us. (My dressing boy Furreed left
behind. He missed the train!).

## 14 November

Arrive at Howrah Station, Calcutta, about 7 a.m. (railway time).
About an hour late! Secrett meets us with motor. Find Water
Gate Quarters very fresh and clean. The rooms have been newly
painted and done up generally.

Dinner at Belvedere to meet the Viceroy and Lady Minto. The Lt. Governor of Bengal, Sir E. Baker, makes a pleasant little speech, avoiding political questions and dealing only with the social side of life. Lord Minto replies much on the same lines. Singing after dinner and get away about 11.45 p.m.

## 16 November
Dine with Calcutta Turf Club. Banquet in Race Stand to Lord Minto. Mr. Dudley Myers presides and makes good speech. So also does the Viceroy. Stands and grounds illuminated. Ladies allowed in after dinner.

## 21 November
Go with Doris to Government House to meet the new Viceroy – Lord Hardinge of Penshurst.[27] Wear white uniform; warm morning for those in thick cloth kit. Viceroy's Council on right of entrance and on left the Government officials of Bengal, then HQrs Staff consisting of 4 (C of S, QMG, AG and MS) with C in C, then the Judges, Consuls etc. Lord Hardinge introduced to each in turn. We get away by 11 o'clock.

State dinner at Government House. Two tables (about 78 at No. 1 table and 60 at No. 2). Lord Minto proposes Lord Hardinge's health. Latter responds and proposes Lord Minto's health. Lord Minto replies with a most touching speech, and evidently much broken at his approaching departure. Lady Hardinge speaks to me after dinner. She is delighted that Doris is here.

## 23 November
Go with Doris to Government House to see the Mintos off. They leave at 12.45 a.m. As soon as guns have finished salute, Lord Hardinge enters Throne room and the acting Home Member (Mr. Earle) reads Proclamation given at Balmoral last August, signed by Mr. Morley.

## 2 January 1911
Parade as usual for Queen Empress Proclamation. The Viceroy and C in C ride at a foot's pace! State Dinner at Government House. I sit next the Roman Catholic Archbishop who is on my left and the American Consul on my right.

## 4 January

Advisory Council at 11 a.m. At 3 p.m. the committee under General Barrow[28] meets to consider blocks in promotion occurring in Native Army. Colonel Bingly[29] and myself present as members. Doris and I dine quietly at Government House.

## Letter to General Ellison written from Aurangabad 13 January 1911

I was very pleased to hear from you, and I thank you greatly for sending me 'Ian Hamilton's book!' It was kind of you to remember me. Since hearing from you I got another copy from Mr. Haldane, so I have passed on the one you sent me to Hamilton Gordon.

I am very sorry indeed to see that you have been in bed and in the Dr.'s hands.

I trust that you are already all right again, and very fit to carry on the great work which you have had in hand for the past five years. It is a good thing for the Army that Mr. H. is still to remain at the W.O. You must now concentrate on the Sapper position.

I think Mr Haldane's preface to your Book is excellently put together, especially his remarks on the 'basic principle' – the Navy. We have been asked our views on the Persian railway question, and I have strongly insisted on adhering to the 'basic principle' and to construct the line from Karachi along the sea coast to Bander Abbas, thence the line to run to Yezd and Teheran etc. Bander Abbas commands the Straits and also the Persian Gulf. We ought to fortify B.A. (or at any rate be ready to occupy it in case of emergencies) and to make the change of gauge there under the guns of our fleet.

The development of Seistan should also be by direct line from Karachi – on no account to extend the Nuchki line – that will merely give us over to the Russians (or Germans) where they have consolidated themselves in Persia! Let us stick to the sea coast as long as we can. What do you say?

You will have to hurry up with your Reserves 'after six months' war! The Germans seem to be going ahead in every direction with the utmost assurance and energy, so that the crisis is sure of coming before many years are over. Their action in the Baghdad railway, Persian Gulf questions, Dutch sea defences, etc. etc. all point in the same direction.

Besides getting the General Staff and Regular Army here organized as well as we can, I am pressing to have the Volunteers encouraged in every possible way. The European population (British) is now considerable and in the event of a great National crisis we must be able to spare some Divisions from India. Indeed by withdrawing a certain

296

number of them, internal security would be an easier problem under certain circumstances.

I only arrived here this morning from Calcutta to attend some manoeuvres which Sir E. Barrow is directing, but I have to be back in Calcutta by the 22nd to attend the Council as the C in C is on tour in Burma. It is rather a waste of time, as my 'Indian Colleagues' talk such a lot, even worse than Mr H's pals in the House of Commons on the TF Bill!!

We had a useful Staff Tour, and a Conference last month at Rasul (near Jhelum). I had several of the Administrative Staff from AHQ out. Enclosed from the DAG shows that our efforts have not been wasted. Please destroy it.

### Diary 3 February (Crown Prince of Germany's visit)

Crown Prince of Germany (Prinz Wilhelm) arrives at 4.30 p.m. Public reception. Full dress reception at Government House. Viceroy meets the Prince at Station. State dinner in full dress. Count zu Dohna, commanding Guard Cavalry Division the head of Prince's Staff. He stayed at Salisbury Plain during Cavalry training in autumn of 1908.

### 4 February

11 a.m. meeting of committee on Trans-Persian railway project. Doris goes to Hospital at 7 a.m. and returns at 11. [She was doing a three months' nursing course at the Residency Hospital, Calcutta. She had organized a Home-Nursing Corps of European women.] She leaves at 2.15 to play golf at Barrackpore with the Crown Prince.

Leave at 3 p.m. in launch to stay at Barrackpore. Party Lord and Lady Hardinge, the C in C and Lady Creagh, Colonel Wilson (Military Secretary) and Mrs., Doris and myself, besides H.I.H. the Prince and some of his Staff including General von Dohna, Lieutenant Zioleltitz and Sir Harold Stewart.

### 6 February

The Wilsons and I leave Barrackpore by launch at 9.30 a.m. Doris stays on. The Prince stays in bed to avoid going to Darjeeling!

## 13 February

Doris and I dine at Government House. Crown Prince at dinner. A small party. My eye rather painful from a tennis ball hit whilst playing yesterday at Treasury Gate.

## 14 February

Call in Dr. Williams to see my eye which is still painful. Cover it up and douch it with boric lotion. Doris in good form looking after medical operations!

## 15 February

Go through appreciation of situation on Burma frontier with C in C. Order 300 mules from Madras and mobilization equipment for 1 Indian Battn. and Batty. Mountain Artillery to go in some ship. After lunch sent for by C in C because the Viceroy has ordered that in the event of Hertz's expedition being ordered to drive Chinese from Pienma, command should devolve on Military Officer. The Viceroy has sent file to be put before C in C! Chief wires to G.O.C. Burma top send Colonel of 89th P. [Punjabis?] to front if not already there.

## 17 February

Leave in motor at 6.45 a.m. for golf at Tollygunge.

See Tanner[30] at 10 a.m. and arrange about measure to be taken in Burma before rains break end of April.

Play 2 chukkas of polo.

Dine with Jenkins (Home Department) and Carlyle (Revenue and Agriculture) at Bengal Club. About 50 or 60 at dinner. 2 tables. I sit on Carlyle's right.

## 18 February

Foggy morning but motor to Tollgunge and play golf with Doris.

Go with Tanner to see C in C. Give proposals re Burma to Chief, who agrees to them and passes them to General Grover[31] (Sec. Army Department).

## 1 March

Attend Legislative Council. A great waste of time. Go there again after lunch till 4.30 p.m. Leave for Ghaziabad at 6.50 p.m.

## 24 March (Calcutta)

Take case to C in C re Burma-Chinese frontier.

Play polo for Legislative Council against Viceroy's team. Our team:

Fuzzie Graham
Mr Fremantle of the U.P.
Self and Malik Umar Hayat Khan. (Tiwana.)

The latter like a Bashi-bizook but unable to gallop as he has not played for years and has done himself too well recently. We were therefore handicapped by him. We play only four chukkas and win 5 goals against none! Our opponents are:

Colonel Maxwell
Major Keely
Captain Forester
Captain Muir

Doris and I dine at Government House. Sir E. Baker also there.

From 25 March until 29 March the Haigs went on a sightseeing tour of Benares, followed by inspection of some units by Douglas Haig at Saugor.

## 12 May Simla
At 7.30 a.m. receive private wire from Lord Haldane asking if I would like to be considered for Aldershot Command. Reply 'Yes I would'. At 10 a.m. go to Snowdon to see the C in C re action against Turkey on account of interference on Shatt el Arab and Persian Gulf.

## 13 May
Ride out to Naldera with Doris. We were at lunch and ready for golf when an urgent telephone message reached me through Mashobra Office that the Viceroy wishes to see me on important business at the Retreat. I change at once and ride to the Retreat where he is staying the weekend. The Viceroy shows me wire which he has received from S of S India asking if my services can be spared to succeed General Smith-Dorrien in December at Aldershot. 'If so is the appointment desired by him?' Viceroy replies that my services can be spared but the C in C and he hope that I can remain in India till after the Durbar.

I get back to Naldera about 8 p.m. and find Doris anxious as to what had become of me owing chiefly to Sir T. Wynne's alarmist reports of a revolution.

**Telegram from Viceroy to Secretary of State for India 14 May 1911 12 p.m.**

Please see your telegram of 12th. General Haig. He will be very pleased to accept the succession to General Smith-Dorien if selected; we can spare him. In case he is selected, the Commander-in-Chief and I would be glad if we may retain his services until after the Durbar, but he could of course go if he is wanted earlier.

**20 May**

Ride with Doris to lunch with the Viceroy and Lady Hardinge at the Retreat. After lunch H.E. discusses the organization of the Army Department and sees no use for 2 secretaries – i.e. secretary for Finance as well as the secretary of the A.D.

Following telegram arrives from S of S just before we leave: 'General Haig. Your telegram of 14th inst. There is no objection to his retention in India until after the Durbar if selected to succeed General Smith-Dorrien.'

**27 May**

Horse Show at Annandale. Ride with Doris and MacAndrew and arrive about 11.30 a.m. My grey 'Fiddlesticks' gets second prize for ponies. Doris's 'Lucky Girl' gets first prize for hacks. Viceroy very sorry his big English horse does not get a prize. He and Lady Hardinge come early. Mrs Donie, wife of the Lt.-Governor of Punjab, gives away the prizes. Get back about 7 o'clock.

**17 June**

Coronation Fete at Annandale. 6000 gate tickets sold by noon. Rain comes down heavily at 1.45 p.m. but clears away and afternoon and evening fine. Dinner at 7.45 p.m. I take in Lady Hardinge. Fireworks (Ludevic Porter responsible). Not very good, partly due to wet.

**18 June**

Kind letter received from Lord Haldane dated 2nd June; 'a great satisfaction to me that you are coming home to take over

300

Aldershot. This has been my own strong wish for some time past. You will find a good deal to do.'

## 22 June

Coronation Day. Attend service 11 o'clock in full dress. Write to Lord Haldane.

## 6 July

Meeting Annandale Fete Committee. We made R7000 odd after paying all expenses. We decide to give R3000 to charities and R4000 to pay off Club debt.

Lunch at Viceregal Lodge.

## 14 July

Play polo in afternoon. Ground very slippery. My pony slips up and I fall on my head.

Preside at Staff College Club dinner held in the 'Chalet'. About 65 present. A record attendance. C in C as guest. We have no speeches. A great improvement.

## 16 July

Receive letter from Sir H. Smith-Dorrien wanting to know if we will take over all his furniture at Aldershot. I reply we might take certain things at a price!

## 22 July

Receive telegram from London; 'Xandra quite well again'. As we have not heard before that she was ill we are rather anxious.

## 23 July

Letter from Louie (Doris's mother) saying that Xandra and Nurse have come to London. Surgeon (Burghard) called in and advised immediate operation to remove glands. To be done on the Monday after mail left. So we know meaning of yesterday's wire.

## 30 July

Telegram from Henrietta; 'Xandra quite well'. I reply thanking her telegram and add 'Please send children seaside East coast Broadstairs recommended'.

Doris receives depressing letters from her mother telling her details of Xandra's operation and she is much upset.

301

## 5 August

Telegram from Henrietta; 'Children arrived all well Broadstairs'. Also from Neil; 'Both children looking splendid'.

## 10 August

Reuter, date London 10th August; 'It is officially stated that General French has been appointed Chief of the Imperial General Staff . . . . Sir D. Haig Commander at Aldershot'. (Three months have elapsed since I received Lord Haldane's telegram (12th May) offering me appointment.)

## 12 August

In reply to telegram from Viceroy, Secretary of State wires that 'he has informally ascertained from War Office that General Haig is to succeed to the Aldershot Command and that the appointment of General Lake to succeed General Haig is concurred in.

By November preparations were being made for the Durbar in honour of the new King George V and Queen Mary in Delhi. They arrived on 7 December.

## 1 December

Ride out to inspect Cavalry Camps with C in C. Breakfast with Neil at Cavalry Division Camp and ride home with Miss Creagh, Doris and Neil. Latter rather pleased with Miss C![32]

Doris and I lunch with Captain Allanson at Government of India Camp. A wonderful place. Several drawing rooms and sitting rooms, some 'Reserved for Executive Council'! Billiard room, card rooms etc. etc. The whole cost £30,000. Allanson also doing Bengal Camp. He brings the Governor and all his servants from Calcutta, feeds them and sends them back free of all expense!

## 2 December

Rehearsal of Review. I leave Camp with Doris and Miss Creagh and take them to Flag Staff. Meet C in C at level crossing near Review ground. Review begins at 10 a.m. Keighley (Bodyguard) represents the King. It takes an hour to ride round troops. Review finishes at 1.40.

Receive English mail. Kiggell writes situation still strained with Germany.

302

**3 December**

Meeting C in C's Camp of all G.O.Cs. (Divisions and Brigades) upon yesterday's march past. Reception tents (6 in all) of Lt.-Governor of Punjab burnt in two minutes about 4.50 p.m. Result of electric wires fusing. All silver, glass, etc. burnt.

**5 December**

At 10 a.m. the Viceroy arrives and we go through rehearsal of State entry. Mr. Du Boulay represents the King. The large tent in which Ruling Chiefs presented to King's representative burnt down soon after the ceremony.

Rehearsal Durbar. I do not go but take Doris to visit some of the Rajahs' Camps – Kashmir, Sikkim, Cooch Behar, etc. Kashmir has some fine carvings (dark walnut) along whole front of camp and also old embroideries of the Kashmir shawl type lining state tents.

Sir H. Smith-Dorrien comes to see me. He tells me it cost him £4,500 to get into Government House, Aldershot! Big dinner C in C's Camp.

**7 December**

Leave Camp 8.30 a.m. and ride with the Q.M.G. (Kitson) to Fort. C in C rides by long route and is nearly late; breaks his sword belt and finds difficulty in getting another! The King and Queen arrive at 10 a.m. Governors of Provinces, Viceroy's Council, Commanders of Armies and self as C.G.S. introduced by Viceroy. Their Majesties shake hands with us all. The King rides in procession at a walk through Delhi to Ridge where address is presented. We get to Camp about 12.30.

**11 December**

Presentation of colours to 7 British regiments. A perfect parade. Men stand like rocks.

**12 December**

Leave by motor about 9.30 for the Durbar Arena. Doris and I have excellent seats in front row opposite the King and Queen. We walk about till noon. Then Viceroy arrives with procession and full escort, their Majesties wearing crowns and robes. Chiefs and high officials make obeisance to the King. Their majesties walk to thrones in the centre and a proclamation is read. The King reads an announcement that Delhi will now be the Capital of India. Some from Bengal indignant at 'partition of Bengal' being renounced at bidding of the disaffected. All over by 2 o'clock. State Dinner. About 110 present. After guests seated the King and Queen come in. Viceroy makes a speech proposing His Majesty's health. After dinner huge crowds come to reception.

## 13 December

Garden Party at Fort. The King and Queen show themselves on balcony overlooking the Bala like the Mogul Emperors of old. Great native fete held on Bala. The Hall, Mosque, Diwani-Kas, etc. lit up by electricity at night.

## 14 December

Ride to Review ground. Cold frosty morning and we ride about to keep horses warm. Their Majesties come at 10 o'clock. Everything goes off well. I have never seen troops march past better, or Cavalry gallop in better order. Divisions march past by Brigades in mass. Great blocks of Infantry look splendid. Investiture. The Queen given G.C.S.I. by the King. I receive the K.C.I.E. During investiture there is a cry of fire, but shouts of 'sit down' stops a panic. A tent (4 from the Queen's) was burnt in 3 minutes – occupied by Lord Crewe's secretary.

## 15 December

Lt.-General Sir P. Lake[33] comes to see me and I hand over various papers concerning the General Staff.
At 2 o'clock motor to Review stand for Assault-at-Arms and Races. Excellent Musical Ride by 17th Lancers. Dinner in Camp.

## 16 December

Photo of all in C in C's Camp. Their majesties leave at 12 noon – the King for Nepal and the Queen immediately after for Agra.

## 17 December

Many friends come in the morning to bid us goodbye. Leave by Coronation express for Bombay.

The Haigs returned home on board the P&O ship SS *Oceana*, which left Bombay on 23 December. Doris was seriously ill on the journey; she had dysentery, thought to be as the result of sleeping in a damp tent at the Durbar. The ship's doctor at one stage thought she would not survive.

They had originally intended to join Willie and Henrietta in Egypt, but this plan was cancelled because of Doris's illness. Instead they broke their journey in Marseilles and Paris, arriving back in London on 11 January 1912. They were met at Charing Cross Station by 'many friends' but, for once, not by Henrietta.


Notes
1. It might seem that the Haigs' second daughter was given second class treatment as regards her baptism and godparents. Whereas her elder sister was baptized in the Chapel Royal, with the Queen and Duchess of Buccleuch as godmothers, the second daughter had to make do with the local church and members of her immediate family as sponsors. Eventually Princess Victoria became a godmother and the baby was named Victoria after her, Doris after her mother and Rachel after her grandmother (Rachel Veitch).
2. Lieutenant General Sir Edward Arthur Fanshawe KCB (1859–1952) was commissioned into the Royal Artillery in 1878. He served in Ireland and Wessex and was a colonel at the start of the First World War. During the war he commanded a division and finally V Corps.
3. Major General John Edward Lindley, born 1860, commissioned into the 1 Dragoons in 1881. He served in Britain and Ireland, commanding the Cavalry School in 1905–7. He commanded the Welsh Division in 1913. He died in 1925.
4. Probably Colonel Sir George Grey Aston KCB, born 1861, commissioned into the Royal Marines 1879, he served in South Africa and was an ADC to the King. He had taught both at the Royal Naval College and the Staff College.
5. Stafford Henry 1st Baron Northcote (1846–1911) was, with Downer and Fitzroy Newdigate, one of the founders of the Australian federal constitution. He was created a peer in 1900 and was Governor General of Australia in 1903–11.
6. She was born Lady Margaret Butler, daughter of the Earl of Glengall. She was the widow of Lieutenant Colonel the Hon. Richard Charteris, Scots Guards, who died in 1874. She died in 1915.
7. Sir Winston (1874–1965) needs no explanation. Although having many disagreements with Churchill, Haig remained on friendly terms with him and greatly admired what he achieved as Minister of Munitions. Readers will have noted that 'young Churchill' appeared briefly in the Sudan Chapter 4 of this book. Haig thought little of Churchill's books on the Sudan and South African campaigns.
8. Lieutenant Colonel Sir Frederick Edward Grey Ponsonby KCVO, CB, was born in 1867 and commissioned into the Grenadier Guards. He became assistant private secretary to the King in 1910. He died in 1935.
9. General Sir Garret O'Moore Creagh VC, GCB, GCSI (1848–1923) was

commissioned into the 95 Foot in 1866. Within four years he had trans-ferred into the Indian Army and the remainder of his career was in India, including command of a brigade in the China Expedition of 1900-01. After commanding a division and two years as Military Secretary in the India office he succeeded Kitchener as Commander-in-Chief of the Army in India. His VC was won in the Khyber Pass in 1897.

10. Lieutenant Colonel Sir Matthew Richard Henry Wilson Bt. CSI, DSO (1875–1958) was commissioned into the 10 Hussars in 1897. He served in the South African War and retired in 1912. He was an MP from 1914–1922, but served in the First World War in command of the Middlesex Hussars. As well as winning a DSO he was mentioned in despatches.

11. General Sir Dighton Macnaghten Probyn VC, GCB, GCSI, GCVO, ISO (1833–1924) was extra equerry to the King. He had a distinguished career with the Indian Army, including the founding of Probyn's Horse, an irregular Sikh unit. He won his VC during the Indian Mutiny. He was a great favourite with the Royal Family and died in Sandringham in what had been Queen Victoria's bedroom.

12. Arthur James Balfour, 1st Earl of Balfour KG, OM, (1848–1930) was Leader of the Opposition at the time of the meeting with Haig, having been Prime Minister in 1902–5. He was awarded an Earldom in 1922, the customary reward for having been Prime Minister (even for three years). He held many senior offices of state during his career, but is chiefly remembered for his declaration about a National Home for the Jews. He died unmarried in 1930.

13. Lieutenant General Sir William Pulteney KCB, DSO, (1861–1941) was commissioned into the Scots Guards in 1881. He served in the Congo, Uganda and Ireland before being given command of 6th Division in Ireland in 1910. He commanded III Corps throughout the First World War.

14. The Hon. Elizabeth Charlotte Knollys was the sister of the 1st Viscount Knollys. She was a Lady of the Bedchamber to Queen Alexandra from 1870 to 1925. She died in 1930.

15. Reginald McKenna (1863–1943) was elected to Parliament in 1895. In 1908 he became First Lord of the Admiralty, where he persuaded his colleagues that Britain should invest heavily in Dreadnoughts at the time that Germany was building up its fleet. He became Home Secretary in 1911 and Chancellor of the Exchequer in 1915. He resigned with Asquith in 1916 and became Chairman of the Midland Bank until his death.

16. Archibald Philip Primrose, 5th Earl of Rosebery KG, KT, (1847–1929) was honorary colonel of two Territorial Army units. He married the daughter of Baron Mayer de Rothschild of Mentmore, which was passed to him and his wife.

17. Sir Ernest Henry Shackleton CVO (1874–1922) was born in Ireland. He

took part in four Antarctic expeditions, under Scott in 1901–4, in 1908–9, in 1914–17 and in 1921–22. He died of angina and influenza on his last expedition and is buried in South Georgia.

18. General Sir Walter Pipon Braithwaite (1865–1945) was commissioned into the Somerset Light Infantry in 1886. He served in South Africa and England before going out to Quetta to command the Staff College in 1911. He was General Sir Ian Hamilton's Chief of Staff at Gallipoli, before commanding a division in France. In 1918 he commanded IX Corps in the 100 days' campaign with conspicuous success.

19. General Sir James Aylmer Lowthrop Haldane KCB, DSO (1862–1950) was commissioned into the Gordon Highlanders in 1882. He served in India, returning to England in 1899. He was attached to the Japanese Army in Manchuria in 1904–5. This was followed by a number of staff appointments in England. He commanded a brigade in 1912–14, then 3rd Division 1914–16. He commanded VI Corps from 1916–19.

20. Major General Sir Gerald Charles Kitson KCVO, CB, CMG was born 1856, commissioned into the KRRC in 1876 and became a general in 1907. His career included command of the Royal Military Colleges in Canada and England. He commanded a brigade in India and became QMG India in 1909. He went on to command a Division in India in 1912.

21. James Keir Hardie (1856–1915), Socialist leader. He entered Parliament as an Independent Labour candidate in 1892, but lost his seat in 1895. He returned to Parliament in 1900 as Member for Merthyr. His early death was said to be due to depression as the result of the onset of the First World War.

22. Admiral Sir Edmond John Warre Slade KCIE, KCVO (1859–1928), joined Royal Navy in 1872, became a captain in 1899, C.-in-C, East Indies 1909–12. Retired 1917. In retirement he became vice chairman of the Anglo Persian Oil Company.

23. Lady Eileen Elliot (1884–1938) was the eldest of the three beautiful daughters of the Viceroy, Lord Minto. She married Lord Francis Montagu-Douglas-Scott, son of the 6th Duke of Buccleuch. Lord Francis was ADC to Lord Minto. He was very badly wounded at First Ypres, but settled after the war in Kenya, where he and his wife established a remarkable estate, called Deloraine.

24. General Sir Havelock Hudson KCIE (1862–1944) was an Indian Army officer throughout his career. This included the China Expedition of 1900-01. He was commandant of the Cavalry School at Saugor in 1912. In 1914 he was BGGS Indian Corps, followed by GOC 8th Division in 1915–16. He returned to India to become Adjutant General in 1916.

25. Brigadier General Richard Wapshare was born in 1860 and served in the Indian Army throughout his career, except for the first two years after commissioning, when he was a Royal Marine. He was commandant of the Cavalry School at Saugor from 1910–12, ie Hudson's predecessor. He was given command of a brigade in 1912.

26. Major Sir Horace Westropp McMahon Bt DSO was born in 1863, commissioned into the Royal Welsh Fusiliers in 1885 and retired in 1907.
27. Charles Hardinge, 1st Baron Hardinge of Penshurst KG, GCB, GCSI, GCMG, GCIE, GCVO (1858–1944) had had a long career in the Diplomatic Service before becoming Viceroy in 1910 to 1916. His wife was a Lady of the Bedchamber to Queen Alexandra.
28. General Sir Edmund George Barrow GCB, was born in 1852 and commissioned into the 102 Foot in 1871. He transferred into the Indian Army in 1877 and served in India for the whole of his career (except for two months in Egypt in 1882). He commanded the Northern Army briefly in 1908 and the Southern Army from 1908–12.
29. Colonel Alfred Horsford Bingley CIE was born in 1865 and commissioned into the Leinster Regiment in 1885. He transferred into the Indian Army two years later. He was on the Staff at Army Headquarters from 1901–11.
30. Colonel John Arthur Tanner CB, DSO was born in 1858 and commissioned into the Royal Engineers in 1877. He served in India from 1906 and was appointed GSO 1 at Army Headquarters in 1910.
31. Lieutenant General Sir Malcolm Henry Stanley Grover KCIE, CB, was born in 1858 and commissioned into the 89 Foot in 1877. He transferred into the Indian Army the following year. Apart from four months on the Suakin Expedition in Sudan in 1885, the remainder of his career was in India. He commanded a brigade in 1907–8, was Inspector General of Cavalry in 1908–11 (a curious appointment for an infantry officer), Secretary of the Army Department in 1911–12 and a Divisional Commander in 1912.
32. Miss Gerard Beatrice Creagh was born in 1887. She was a niece of General Sir O'Moore Creagh. She married Neil Haig in 1913.
33. Lieutenant General Sir Percy Henry Noel Lake KCMG, CB,(1855–1940) was Haig's successor as Chief of the General Staff in India. He was six years older and was commissioned into the East Lancashire Regiment in 1873, twelve years before Haig was commissioned. He served in Egypt/Sudan, Ireland, England and, for several years, in Canada. He commanded a division in India in 1911–12, before becoming CGS. He was C.-in-C. Mesopotamia in 1915, but was a failure and returned home.

# Chapter 11

# Commander in Chief, Aldershot

## 1912 – 1914

The Haigs arrived in London on the evening of 11 January and stayed in Willie and Henrietta's house at Princes Gate. Douglas Haig comments on the comfort of the house and the excellent dinner that evening, despite the Jamesons still being away in Egypt and there being a new butler and other staff.

**Diary 12 January**

Walk with Doris to War Office. Lord Haldane very pleased to see me, also Kiggell and others. Bring K back to lunch at Princes Gate. Return to Office and see Military Secretary. He is to let me know the date on which I am to take over at Aldershot. Smith-Dorrien had evidently asked that he be kept on full pay till Salisbury is vacant for him, viz. March 1st. Meet General French in Cavalry Club. General Headlam dines quietly with us at Princes Gate

**13 January**

Leave by 12.15 train for Kineton to go Radway. The 2 children waiting for us on platform at Kineton. A very happy surprise. Two pretty little girls in red coats and green hats! Doris and the 2 children and I motor to Radway and we have tea with the bairns. Doris telegraphs to Henrietta , to Cairo. 'Arrived here. Children very well. So grateful for your motherly care of them. Doris.'

**14 January**

Children come in to see us at 8 a.m. Cannot make their Mother and Daddy out. Doris and I go to Church. A Rev. Robinson has replaced old Miller who died more than a year ago. The Church has more people than formerly.

Dr Oldmeadow comes to see Doris. He pronounces her lungs and heart quite sound. Xandra's gland which showed after operation has disappeared now. We walk after lunch with the children.

## 22 January
Doris and I go to Aldershot. Allot rooms at Government House etc. and decide on what improvements are wanted.

## 29 January
Meet Lady Smith-Dorrien at Government House Aldershot and go through her furniture.[1]

Douglas Haig went at the end of January to fish in Ireland with his sister and brother-in-law, Henrietta and Willie Jameson. Seemingly the fishing was good, but there was hard frost and the country was covered with ice. After Ireland he went to stay with his nephew Oliver Haig at Ramornie, Fife, near to the Haig whisky distillery. Douglas Haig had become a non-executive director of John Haig and Co. in 1894, when the company was founded. He had retired from the board in 1898, but rejoined in 1912 and remained a director until his death in 1928. Oliver Haig had joined the board in 1896 and played an active part in the management of the company.

## 20 February
Ride with Oliver to Markinch. See Wilkinson[2] the new Manager of J.H. & Co. Seems a sensible fellow with sound ideas regarding organization of England into areas for sales. He is to see Ferguson (Manager of H. and H.). H. and H. have paid 7% during last 3 years but they seem to have little capital.

## 22 February
Ride with Oliver to Leven and see Mr. William Shepherd. My loan account is now £9,300. He thinks I have done very well to reduce it so much. Fife Coal is a very sound investment. Price of shares down at present owing to possibility of coal strike. Caledonian Hotel property of J.H. & Co. now. Manager not doing so well must be changed. Leven has developed in a surprising way.

310

**26 February**

Doris and I call on Mr Burghard 86 Harley Street – the surgeon who operated on Xandra. He tells us that there is no reason for anxiety. She should lead a healthy open air life. Every 3 or 4 months neck should be examined to see if glands are disappearing on other side to scar. He advises no lessons and to aim at making her into a regular country girl.[3]

During the afternoon Doris and I go to Mawers and finish purchase of furniture.

Dine with Sir John French at the Carlton. Doris goes home about 10 p.m. and I talk on with him till 11.30.

**27 February**

Nicholas, 12th Lancers, comes up from hunting in Wilts and dines with us. We go to see the Durbar in the Kinomacolor after. Good but scarcely gives full idea of the brilliance of colour and glittering jewels of actual ceremony.

**28 February**

Go with Doris in morning and choose a gold wrist watch – a present from the ladies of Simla for instructing them in First Aid and Home Nursing duties.

**29 February**

The Prime Minister's (Asquith) negotiations with miners seem to have failed and general strike threatened. Our new motor (a Hudson) comes for us and we motor to Aldershot. On the way we call at Mawer's and buy furniture for the drawing room. Captain J Charteris R.E. is to be my Asst. Mil. Sec. and Captain D. Baird, 12th Cavalry, Aide de Camp.[4] They meet us on arrival. We stay at the Queen's Hotel as Government House is not ready yet.

**1 March**

Take over Aldershot Command today as C in C. Go to office at 11 a.m. and go round the General Staff with Br. General Davies. General i/c of Administration takes me round his Officers afterwards. He had come specially from leave to meet me.

Lord Worsley,* R.H.G. comes to report as extra A.D.C. in accordance with orders received from War Office.

---

* 'Woolly' Worsley married Alexandra, Doris Haig's youngest sister, in 1912. He was killed at 1st Ypres in 1914. She was a widow until she died in 1963.

Charteris, in his life of Haig, says that Aldershot viewed Haig and his staff with some suspicion. Much of the General's service had been abroad and particularly in India, and Charteris and Baird, who he brought with him, were Indian Army officers. The local wags referred to them as 'the Hindoo invasion'.

### Diary 4 March

Leave Radway at 12 o'clock in shut hired car from Kineton. We have to get out at foot of hill[5] to walk up! Car sticks after going a short way up; driver reverses and goes up backwards. Rain falls heavily. Three or more stops. And Secrett puts stones to hold wheels etc. Finally motor breaks down altogether. And the driver gets a bike lent to him to go into Kineton to fetch another motor. Returns with an open one and it is raining and blowing hard. Doris and I sit in broken down car till 2.30 or more and only get to Banbury at 3. Catch 3.45 train and reach Aldershot at 6.30 p.m.

### 7 March

Leave Farnborough at 9.18 a.m. for London. Attend meeting of Selection Board at War Office. Sir Wm. Nicholson presiding. Sit next to Sir Neville Lyttleton. Generals Miles and Henry Wilson lunch with me at Marlborough Club. Return to Aldershot by 5 p.m. train.

### 13 March

Doris and I go to Jr. A. & N. Stores and buy glass and dinner service etc. for Government House. We allow for parties of 36 which means getting a large quantity. Motor to Aldershot arriving at 2 o'clock.

### 14 March (Aldershot)

Ride out at 9 a.m. See a Company of Bedfords entrenching. Several with coats on! Many could not use pick and shovel.

Play golf with Doris until she goes to meet children arriving from Radway.

Find careful test of our Artillery ammunition shows that half our fuzes are bad!

### 22 April (Inspections)

Leave Government House in motor at 10 a.m. for Oxford. General Davies[6] and Charteris accompany me. Secrett with baggage goes in motor lorry starting at 8 a.m.

312

## 23 April

Motor to Brill and consider position of general advance guard. Return to Oxford and walk round the colleges after lunch. Meeting with Directing Staff at 5 p.m.

## 24 April

Start about 9.30 a.m. for Wantage and Newbury. Some 15 motor lorries brought from Aldershot to demonstrate practically the work done at a 'rendezvous' and the 'refitting points' of a Division. Get back to Oxford at 3 o'clock. Call on Principal of B.N.C. Conference at 8.30 p.m.

## 25 April

Work indoors at supply of ammunition etc. before a battle which is to take place beyond Brill. Also work out organization and location of Staff and others of A.H.Q., General H.Q. and I.G. of Communications.

Lunch with Dr. Bussel, the Vice Principal of B.N.C. The Principal (Heberden) comes to see me when at lunch.

## 28 April

Do not go to church as motor fetches Sir Lonsdale Hale and brings him and his daughter to lunch. He comes about 1.30 and enjoys himself greatly. We send him back in motor.

## 30 April

Ride at 9 a.m. and have meeting at 11.30 with General Morland re 3 Coys. of Scots Guards, Dorsets and Loyal N. Lancs. who are to receive colours from the King.

Play golf with Doris in the afternoon. I win by 1 hole.

## 1 May

Leave for London at 9.47 a.m. Attend the Selection Board at 11.30 a.m. Finish by 12.30 when Sir J. French holds first meeting of C in C's in his room. Smith Dorrien and Grierson[7] present – also two Directors, Kiggell and Murray.

Catch 2.5 train at St. Pancras and arrive Bedford a little after 3. Start in motor at once and drive about 60 miles, getting back to hotel about 7 p.m. Stay at Swan Hotel. Quite comfortable. Davies and Charteris accompany me. Our Object is to work out Scheme for the Command Staff Tour.

## 3 May

Fix up scheme for Staff Tour and leave with General Davies for London. Dine at Buckingham Palace. This is the second state dinner. The 'Opposition' attend including Mr. Balfour, Bonar Law[8] etc. and Lord Rosebery. I sit next Austen Chamberlain[9] and we discuss Russian, Persian, German and Italian politics. The King speaks to me about his visit to Aldershot. He is anxious to give as little trouble as possible. Get home about 12.

## 15 May The King and Queen's visit to Aldershot

Rehearsal of presentation colours at 9 a.m. Receive wire that the King's departure is delayed as King of Denmark died in Hamburg yesterday. The King and Queen arrive at Pavilion at 4 o'clock. I meet them at gate near Guard of Honour. Generals Robb and Davies, Colonel DuCane D.A.A.Q.M.G. and my 3 A.D.Cs. accompany me. Have tea with Their Majesties and at 5.30 ride through the Lines to Flying Corps on Cove Common. Very windy for flying. Doris and I dine with Their Majesties. The King tells us he had seen Queen Alexandra just before coming here.

## 16 May

Cold blustery morning. Start at 10 a.m. 3 Cavalry Regiments (Bays, 11th Hussars and 19th Hussars) carry out evolutions under Kavanagh.[10] Then R.H.A. under Haney take up series of positions and fire upon flagged enemy. K.R.R. attack Miles Hill from North, crossing canal by extemporized bridges – tarpaulin covers used chiefly. At 3.30 the King gives the Colours to Scots Guards, Dorsets and Loyal N. Lancs. The King and Queen come to tea at Government House. We ask wives of 5 Brigadiers. After tea Their Majesties go round the Connaught Hospital.

## 17 May

Start at 10 a.m. Their Majesties visit Electric Power Station, then go to country N. of Tunnel Hill. 7th Fusiliers and section of Fd. Artillery operate southwards. General Haking explains general situation. Then Howitzer Brigade (Furse) shows how guns directed, means of observation from balloon. See wireless and at 4 p.m. go to Flying Corps and Aircraft Factory. On to Staff College where officers pass the King one by one. We have tea there and get back at 7 p.m.

**18 May**

Motor to Bordon with the King and Queen and Doris, starting at 10 a.m. Get on horses at Artillery Mess (the ladies remain in motors). Ride through lines. See Somerset L.I. attack position etc. Brig. General Landon[11] in charge of arrangements which are good. M.I. then shows system of training. His Majesty rides to motors on road but the Queen had gone off to see some jumping and missing the road back is 15 minutes late. Get back at 1.15. At 4 p.m. go to Cambridge Hospital with Their Majesties. The Queen leaves at 3 o'clock and takes Doris to the Louise Margaret Hospital.

General and Lady Archie Murray and Colonel and Mrs Hancox dine with us at Government House.

**19 May**

Go to Pavilion (Royal residence at Aldershot) at 10.45 and walk with Their Majesties to All Saints Church where Parade Service is held. Representatives from each Corps. attend. The King sees troop file home after Church. We are photoed with Their Majesties.

Violet (Doris's sister) comes to stay with us. Doris, Violet, Charteris and I dine with Their Majesties.

**20 May**

Go to Pavilion at 9.45 a.m. The King is very nice to me and thanks me for all that I have done. And presents us with photos in his drawing room. His Majesty tells me to put in orders a note of his appreciation.

I see attack on Caesar's Camp by Suffolks and Co. of R.E.

The King's message of appreciation, dated 22 May, was as follows:

The King has commanded the General Officer Commanding-in-Chief to convey to all ranks of the Aldershot Command His Majesty's appreciation of the state of the troops and of the operations which he saw carried out. His Majesty was particularly struck by the fine military bearing and discipline of the troops, the intelligent keenness displayed by all officers and men, and the sound system of training obtained in the units of the Command. His Majesty also expressed the pleasure, which both he and the Queen felt at being again with his troop at Aldershot. His Majesty further commanded the General Officer

Commanding-in-Chief to convey to all serving in the Aldershot Command his satisfaction with all that he had seen, both in barracks and in the field.

In July Haig was appointed Colonel of the Regiment of the 17 Lancers. The following telegram was received from Sialkot on 13 July:

All ranks desire express warmest satisfaction on your appointment as Colonel of Regiment and beg accept heartiest good wishes from all. Commanding 17th Lancers.

And from Lieutenant Colonel W.A. Tilney the Commanding Officer, sent from Suez; he was presumably on his way home on leave:

Rejoicings congratulations all ranks regiment your appointment. Tilney.

### Diary 7 September

Doris and I leave by 9.19 train. We get out at Vauxhall and leave her luggage at Victoria. Then call on Sir James Gildea[12] at Queen Anne's Gate – the office of the S.S.F.A. at 10.30 a.m. We settle the whole business satisfactorily and Doris very pleased. We then walk to Motcomb Street where Doris interviews maids and engages one. We lunch at Princes Gate and I take her to catch the 2.2 p.m. train for Margate, where she is joining the children. I leave St. Pancras at 2.40 p.m. for Thetford. Camp in the Abbey Park.

### 9 September

Motor to Chippenham (Cambs.) where 1st Division is camped. See Lomax and call on Mrs. Tharpe to thank her for her hospitality.

Division v. Division Manoeuvres begin today at 1.15 but mounted reconnaissances start 3 hours earlier. Motor to Attleborough and see General Davies 6th Bde. pass. Then on to Mundford where we take to horses. Meet General Lawson commanding 2nd Division. He omits to issue orders for night halt in time so troops have to settle down in bivouacs after dark. Order for halt should be given by 5 p.m. for a Divn. Lawson has outposts on line of river Brandon – Thetford. At 9 p.m. I motor to Elveden and go round outposts of 1st Divn. Then to Brandon and see 4th Gds. Bde. in outposts covering that place. 6th Bde.

has 2 Coys. on outpost duty in Thetford. Nasty cold night and the troops have no tents.

## 10 September

Away at 4 a.m. Ride across heath on S. of Brandon. Neither Lawson nor Lomax are keen to attack, though the scheme requires each to act offensively. After a certain amount of skirmishing I stop operations at 11.30. Wet day. Lomax[13] goes to bivouac at Culford. Lawson to Elveden. I hold conference outside School room at Elveden. Very wet heavy showers. Get back to camp at 3.30 p.m. Wet night.

## 11 September

Command Training begins today. Whole command advances in column on one road. Trains of 2nd Division in rear of fighting troops. Wet day. Change direction of Divisions to their standing camp so that troops may have tents. Excellent exercise for staff. Have much trouble at Thetford in getting the train so change to road to Brandon. Lomax had given his Division an hour's halt for dinner and so blocked train in Thetford. Take motor about 4 p.m. and go to see Colonel McMahon commanding marked enemy at Warren Farm near Hillborough. Give troops tot of rum tonight.

## 12 September

Move camp to grass fields outside N. gate of Buckenham Tofts. I ride over for conference at 11 a.m. at Hall. General French had come over by motor from near St. Ives. He attends conference and says he is much pleased. We go round a few of the camps with him. Recommence operations at 5 p.m. Reconnaissance of enemy's outposts and position from South Pickering via Rowley Corner to Warren Farm. Today much finer. Ride in afternoon to Warren Farm across country and return along outpost line about 7 p.m.

## 13 September

Issue orders at midnight. Ride out at 4 a.m. Just light enough at 4.45 to recognize anyone at a couple of yards distance. Lomax advances to attack position without an advanced guard! Sound cease fire about 8.30 and get back across country to camp shortly after 9 o'clock. Have conference at 3 p.m. on night's operations.

Issue special idea and my appreciation of situation for Army Manoeuvres.

## 14 September

Have conference in servants' hall at 11 a.m. on scheme for Army Manoeuvres. General Allenby commanding Cavalry Div. and Colonel Vaughan C.G.S.O., Captain Howell 2nd G.S.O.[14] and Hutcheson 3rd. G.S.O. come over from Newmarket after night operations and return after lunch. Issue instructions to Cavalry and orders to Red force.

## 15 September

Ride over to Methwold and go round camps of 1st Divn. I find some at Church Parade and others playing football after Church. A tournament of 6 a side, 10 minutes each way. After lunch go over to Euston Park where Cavalry Division arrived today. I think they should have had a rest day between Cavalry training and Army Manoeuvres.

## 16 September

Army Manoeuvres begin at 6 a.m. today. Advance in 3 columns. We make long halt on this line. Blue force evidently entrained on line Hitchen- Gamlingay and is digging position near the Gogmagog hills. Lord Cadogan[15] very kind. I go over and have bath in the afternoon. We stay in the village school at Culford.

## 17 September

Send on Morland with line Bde., a Bde. of Field Artillery and a Batt. of howitzers via Newmarket to report to General Allenby commanding Cavalry Division near Dullingham. With remainder march via Dulham to line Cowlinge-Huldon. Blue occupies his position River Hill Worsted Lodge. His mounted troops attack Haking in command of Advanced Guard of 2nd Division near Little Thurlow in afternoon. My H.Q. in Wickhambrook School. Just after we get there about 4.30 p.m. the King arrives to see me. I give His Majesty tea.

## 18 September

Send on Cavalry at 5 a.m. from Little Thurlow to seize and hold the high ground between Burtlow and Haverhill till relieved by Infantry. 2nd Division to march on Camp's Green and drive back whatever met. 1st Division to high ground near West

318

Wickham as reserve under my orders. Cavalry get high ground at Wigmore Pond without opposition. Relieved by Bde. of 2nd Division. Heard enemy advancing to attack from Bartlow and Saffron Walden. Order Lomax 1st Div. to occupy position West Wickham to 'Park' Slundy Camps with Bde. in reserve in rear of his left. Intend to take offensive with 2nd Divn. and Cav. Divn. Enemy's 4th Division come on so fast that have to hold the position with 2nd Division. Enemy attack me in position instead of me attacking him and Cavalry Division comes upon the rear of his 4th Divn. when all engaged with my 2nd Divn. The Blue 3rd Divn. and Territorial Bde, have 'formed front to flank' on communications in Bedford to Birmingham. Cease fire about 6 p.m. My H.Q. in Haverhill. I stay in Farmhouse Mill (Mrs. Low).

**19 September**
Motor to Cambridge. Lunch at University Arms and attend Conference at 2.45 in Trinity Hall. The King present. Sir J. French sits on His Majesty's right and Colonel Seely the S of S of War on his left. I am called upon first to explain my operations as C in C of Red Force. I think my remarks were well received. Grierson followed; then French. His criticisms especially on the strategic value of Cambridge were not much thought of.

Catch 4.45 train for King's X and reach Farnborough 7.40 p.m.

Charteris gives a very different version of the Cambridge conference. He says:

The manoeuvres ended near Cambridge, and the conference took place in the great hall of Trinity College. All the most distinguished officers of the Army and many of the dignitaries of the University were present, and H.M. the King himself presided. Haig had been opposed in the manoeuvres by Sir James Grierson, and the two Commanders were called on to describe and explain their operations.

Although Haig had written out a clear and convincing statement of his views, and held the paper in his hand throughout the Conference, he did not refer to it when he spoke, but to the dismay of his staff attempted to extemporize. In the effort he became totally unintelligible and unbearably dull. The University dignitaries soon fell asleep. Haig's friends became more and more uncomfortable; only he himself seemed totally unconscious of his failure.

It will be noted that Charteris puts the conference in a different college to that shown in the diary, but it seems likely that Trinity, rather than Trinith Hall, was the correct college. Also, Charteris was in Bulgaria before 2 October, a lengthy journey from England by train, for which he may well have had to start before 19 September. Perhaps his version of events was received second hand.

## Diary 21 September

At 9 a.m. give the Smith-Dorrien Cup for Companies attack exercise to 3rd Battalion Coldstream Guards. 7 squadrons and 120 companies had entered for the Competition. Then go for a ride and attend office at 11 a.m.

Golf with Doris in afternoon.

## 23 September

Ride out and meet Colonel Greenly 19th Hussars and have a talk about the manoeuvres. He tells me that information had not been passed on from Cavalry Division to O.C. Regiments! Go to office 11 o'clock.

Play golf with Doris and go to London by 6.10 train. Bee and Jessie staying at Princes Gate.

Once again Haig had been ordered to do another cure to try to prevent further attacks of malaria and the liver troubles which resulted from the attacks. Rather than go once again to Tarasp, he and Doris went to Llandrindod Wells.

## 25 September

We leave by 11 a.m. train from Euston. Through carriage to Llandrindod and luncheon car as far as Stafford. Arrive at Llandrindod at 4.15 p.m. and go to Montpellier Hotel. We have nice bright rooms and things seem comfortable. Dr Ackerley comes to see us at 8.45 p.m. He stays till nearly 10.30 p.m. and goes carefully into all our ailments and medical history.

## 30 September

Dr. Ackerley thinks me, for my age (51), the fittest man he has seen for a long time. This after testing my blood pressure.

## 2 October

Bulgaria, Serbia, Montenegro and Greece reported to be mobilizing today against Turkey. Wire from Charteris from Legation,

Sofia – 'Is official attachment here possible?' I reply 'I agree better apply officially.'

## 8 October
Write to Charteris today to Sofia to tell him not to hurry home.

## 9 October
Montenegro declared war on Turkey today.

The following news cutting had been kept by Haig:

> The proclamation of the King of Montenegro to his people, published in Friday's *Daily Mail*, is so striking a document that we cannot resist quoting it verbatim:
>
> > My hopes of finding a method by which Old Servians might be able without bloodshed to liberate themselves from their sufferings have not met with success. That is why, although it weighs heavily on my heart to break the peace of Europe, there remains to me no other course than to handle the sword – that sword which, assuredly not without honour, Montenegrins have followed to Nikshitch, Antivari and Dulcigno. Montenegrins, ours is the cause of justice. *Alea jacta est* – the die is cast – and God and Servia in good fortune will help us to extend that fortune to our brothers in misery. By the blessing of God, of St. Peter of Montenegro, and of all the saints, may the dreams of my first youth, when in poems I foretold this memorable day, be realized and kindle the breasts of my people with faith to march beyond the limits of this Montenegro! Long live Montenegro! Long live the Balkan Alliance!

How Sir Walter Scott would have loved such a proclamation! It breathes the very spirit of his Highland Chieftains."

## Diary 11 October
I wire this morning to Charteris at Sofia 'to withdraw at once from Balkan States in accordance with Army Council's Orders'.

## 22 October
At the dentist (McKechnie) 29 Queen Anne Street at 9 a.m. Tooth which was badly stopped at Simla last year and split, then

crowned at Bombay last December, was cause of my visit. Have gas and it is removed by 11 a.m.

Catch 11.45 train for Aldershot. Play golf with Baird after lunch.

## 23 October
Inspect 5th D.Gs. and the Liverpool Regiment on their arrival to this Command.

Major P. Howell, Staff College, gives a most interesting lecture on the Balkan situation in the Prince Consort's Library.

## 24 October
Inspect the 1st and 3rd Battalions of the Grenadier Guards on their arrival to this Command.

## 14 November (staying with Oliver Haig in Fife)
At lunch receive following telegram – O.H.M.S. War Office London. To General Douglas Haig, Ramornie, Ladybank, Fife. 'Secretary of State would like to see you here on official business at eleven thirty tomorrow. Please come if possible reply General Sir John French'. Arrange to leave by night mail to London. We shoot duck and pheasants after lunch.

## 15 November
Get to London 7.45 a.m. Go to Grand Hotel and bath and change. Meet General French and Sir A. Paget[16] at War Office at 11 a.m. French explains the gravity of the situation. We all see Colonel Seely the S of S for War together. I am told Command for which I have been selected, and my Staff etc.

Get back to Farnborough in time for lunch 2 p.m.

## 17 November
I motored to London and attended meeting at 11 a.m. at General Grierson's house at 9 Cadogan Gardens.

General French, Grierson, Sir A. Paget, Brig. Gen. Henry Wilson present.

## 20 November
Go to London by 9.47 train and attend meeting of 17th Lancers Association at 11 o'clock, then see Military Secretary and General French at War Office. Situation seems more warlike today.

Lunch with Henrietta at Princes Gate. Return to Aldershot by 5 p.m. train. Henrietta comes to station.

**22 November**

Lunch at Farnborough Hill with the Empress Eugenie.[17] Grand Duchess Vladimir of Russia[18] had motored down from London. I sit on right of Empress at lunch. She speaks French all the time and is most friendly and bright. After lunch we go round the museum in which are relics of Napoleon I and III and Prince Imperial.

John Vaughan arrives in afternoon to stay and lectures on French Cavalry in 1912.

**2 December**

Ride with Baird. Leave by 12.14 train for London. Lunch at Princes Gate with Henrietta and Willie. Dinner at Princes Gate including Percy Chubb.[19]

**4 December**

Doris and I go to London 9.19 train.

Selection Board 10.30 a.m. See General French privately after. No change in situation though things seem 'damped down' for the moment. Try on khaki uniform and give Doris lunch at the Cavalry Club. Buy Xmas presents at Asprey. Return Aldershot by 5 p.m. train.

**22 December**

Attend Service at Scotch Church 11 a.m. when Dr. Fleming from St. Columba's London consecrates window presented by the Cameron Highlanders. All come to lunch including Dr. Sims.

**23 December**

Generals Grierson and Rawlinson arrive to stay – also Walter Vivian[20] and Violet. The latter motor down from London.

The King visited Aldershot again in both 1913 and 1914. His notes of appreciation were as follows. They were addressed from the Royal Pavilion, Aldershot Camp:

14 May 1913

On the conclusion of my visit I wish to express my satisfaction with the energy and progress which characterizes the whole life of the Aldershot Command. I was glad to find marked development in the work and administration of the Royal Flying Corps, and what courage and esprit de corps animates all ranks of this newly formed arm. The display by the 5th Dragoon Guards was an interesting example of the improved training of recruits and horses throughout the Cavalry, which I understand is largely due to the system in force at the Cavalry School. It was gratifying to see the keen manner in which the Territorials were carrying out their training under somewhat unfavourable weather conditions, and to realize that Officers and men were giving up their short holiday to make themselves efficient members of our Citizen Army. In the officers Gymkhana Club and the recent great increase of recreation grounds for the men, I recognize that physical exercises and sport are not overlooked as essential factors in the training of the soldier. The Queen and I always enjoy passing a few days in the Camp, and it is especially satisfactory to me that I have these opportunities of seeing the different Arms of the Service at their daily training.

21 May 1914

It has been a great pleasure to the Queen and myself again to visit Aldershot for the fifth time since my Accession and to be accompanied on this occasion by the Secretary of State for War, and the Chief of the Imperial General Staff, and the Adjutant General. I wish to express my satisfaction with the consistent progress in the practical training and tests of the Troops under your Command, and with the keen co-operation with which all ranks work for efficiency. It was evident to me what order and method govern the working of Departments concerned with Barracks, Supply, Transport, Mobilization Stores, Physical Training and the care of sick men and horses. I am glad to note the steady development of the Royal Aircraft Factory and of the equipment of the Royal Flying Corps, and I am confident that by inspection and research everything possible is being done to minimize the perils of flying and to decrease the number of lamentable accidents to gallant Officers and Men. The equitation of the men and training of the horses of the 1st Cavalry Brigade impressed me with the successful results of modern stable management throughout the mounted branches. In the

Cavalry Club and new Soldier's Club at Bordon, I appreciate the efforts being made to brighten and widen the barrack life of the Soldier. The Queen and I always look forward to our visit to Aldershot; and I welcome these opportunities of becoming more closely acquainted with the life and training of my Army.

## Diary 21 February
Called on Sir C Douglas I.G.F. re Depots and the training of recruits. Motored back to Aldershot with Nicholas, 12th Lancers.[21] Dinner of 14.

## 20 April
Butler[22] and Charteris motor from Aldershot and go over ground for Staff tour, joining me at Littlehampton.

## 25 April
Doris and I and children motor back to Aldershot after lunch.
I preside at annual meeting of Golf Club.

## 27 April
Go to London by 12 o'clock train and attend meeting at Cavalry Club of John Haig & Co. Mr Gourly present. Declare dividend of 2%. Very hot weather.

## 30 June
Left Farnborough 8.30 a.m., caught 10 o'clock train at Charing Cross. Met Generals Grierson and Allenby, forming English mission. Captain Banbury[23](Grierson's ADC) & Baird – also Secrett was of the party. At Boulogne reserved carriage etc. for us. Met at Hotel Crillon, Place de la Concorde, by Colonel de la Panoves (French Military Attaché). Dined at Café de la Rue, Rue Royale.

## 1 July
Called on General Joffre, Conseil Superieur de la Guerre,[24] and General Belin (Etat Major de l'Armee) at Ministere de la Guerre, also on M. Messienary in Rue St. Dominique.
Leave by 12.20 train Gare de l'Est, arrive Chalons about 2.30 ... Reach Camp de Mailly at 4.40 – call on heads in the Camp.

## 2 July

Ride out at 4 o'clock – v. hot weather. Present: General Castelnau of Conseil Superieur de la Guerre,[25] General Foch, Commanding 20th Corps,[26] General Balfourier,[27] Commanding 11th Division. Get back about 1 o'clock.

Dine with Foch. Wet evening. Captain Loos accompanies us.

## 3 July

Start at 4. Wet Morning. Division assembles, deploys and attacks. Morning keeps up [wet weather presumably].

Lunch at home but dine with Foch. Sit on Castelnau's left. We listen to band afterwards playing marches.

## 4 July

Start 4.30. Division attacks, shorter morning. Division formed in mass and we inspect it. Troops very steady. They march past and we take the salute. We ride home at head of 69th Regiment.

Dine with General Balfourier. Foch left for Nancy.

## 5 July

Left in motors about 9.30. Go via Sommesous and Fere Champenoise to Sezanne, North to Ste. Prix and Champaubert the West to Vauchamp and Mont Mirail. Lunched and went over battlefield. Got back about 6 p.m.

## 6 July

Out by 4.45 a.m. – advanced guard scheme. After critique, demonstration by Artillery. Rode home with Colonel Moger, commanding the Artillery. Lunch with General Balfourier at 11.30 and catch 2.30 train for Paris.

Dine with Sir F Bertie at British Embassy. General Joffre present.

It was clear to Haig that the 'Preparatory Prologue' was very nearly at an end. Arrangements for a series of training exercises had been made, for instance Brigade Training in June, an Administrative Staff tour in July and Cavalry Division Training in August. The last one certainly could not have taken place, but training continued at the highest possible intensity until the end, whilst everyone watched what was happening on the Continent with great anxiety. During this time Haig's diary was a much more spasmodic affair than previously or as it was to become after the war had started. There are brief entries in

July and early August and not every day. He records one sad event; he attended the funeral of his old friend Bully Oliphant in the Guards Chapel on 10 July.

Haig crossed over to France on 15 August, the start of the 'epic drama of four years and one hundred days'.

## Notes

1. Some of the furniture the Haigs bought from Smith-Dorrien is still at Bemersyde.
2. Thomas Wilkinson became chairman in 1936 and was responsible for the Haig company's expansion, particularly overseas.
3. Apart from the fact that she hunted, it is hard to visualize Lady Alexandra as a 'country girl'. She married in 1941 Rear Admiral Howard-Johnston, by whom she had two sons and a daughter. The marriage was dissolved in 1954. She subsequently married Lord Dacre of Glanton. She died in 1999.
4. General Sir Harry Beauchamp Douglas Baird KCB (1877–1963) was commissioned into the Indian Army in 1897. He stayed in the Indian Army until he became Haig's ADC in 1912. He was known as Dolly.
5. The hill was Edgehill, notably steep and with severe bends.
6. Lieutenant General Sir Francis John Davies KCB (1864–1948) was commissioned into the Grenadier Guards in 1884. He served in West Africa, South Africa and Army Headquarters before joining Aldershot Command firstly as GSO 1, then Brigade Commander and BGGS in 1910. He went to the War Office as Director of Staff Duties in 1913. In the First World War he commanded firstly a division then two different corps before becoming Military Secretary to the Secretary of State for War in 1916–19.
7. General Sir James Moncrieff Grierson KCB, KCVO, CMG (1859–1914) was commissioned into the Royal Artillery in 1877. He served in Egypt, Sudan, Berlin as Military Attaché, China, Army Headquarters as DMO, Aldershot as a divisional commander and from 1912 as GOC.-in-C. Eastern Command. He was on his way to France as GOC II Corps in 1914, when he died of a heart attack. He was well known to be greatly overweight and unfit.
8. Andrew Bonar Law (1858–1923) was a Conservative party politician, who succeeded Balfour as leader of his party. He was Prime Minister from 1922 to 1923, when his health gave out. Two of his sons were killed in the First World War.
9. Sir (Joseph) Austen Chamberlain KG (1863–1937) was the son of Joe. He entered Parliament in 1892 as a Unionist. He was Chancellor of the Exchequer from 1903-06, Secretary of State for India 1915–17 and Foreign Secretary 1924–28.
10. Lieutenant General Sir Charles Toler McMurrough Kavanagh KCVO,

KCB, DSO (1864–1950) was a dashing cavalry commander, who was more noted for his failures than his successes. He was commissioned into the 10 Hussars in 1884. He was in command of the 1 Cavalry Brigade at Aldershot from 1909–13, followed by a Cavalry Brigade in India in 1914. He was GOC Cavalry Corps from 1916–19.

11. Major General Herman James Shelley Landon CB (1863–1946) was commissioned into the Warwickshire Regiment in 1879. He served in India 1906–10 and commanded the 3 Brigade at Aldershot from 1910–14 and three different divisions during the First World War.

12. Colonel Sir James Gildea had been an officer in the Royal Warwickshire Regiment. He had seen the need for funds to help the widows and orphans of soldiers and sailors, many of whom were experiencing great hardship. He founded the Soldiers' and Sailors' Families Association in 1885. This evolved into today's SSAFA, a charity which continues to help widows and orphans of servicemen.

13. Lieutenant General Samuel Holt Lomax (1855–1915) was commissioned into the 90 Foot (Scottish Rifles) in 1874. Having been AAG in II Corps in 1902-04, he commanded a Brigade and from 1910 1st Division at Aldershot. He was in command of this Division at First Ypres when he was hit by shellfire in5 Hooge Chateau (Haig's Headquarters) on 31 October 1914 and badly wounded. He died of his wounds the following April.

14. Brigadier General Philip Howell (1877–1916) was commissioned into the Indian Army in 1897 and transferred into the 4 Hussars in 1913. In 1912 he was a major at the Staff College. During the First World War he served in Salonika and was killed in 1916. He was one of Haig's protégés.

15. George Henry Cadogan, 5th Earl Cadogan KG (1840–1915) was a Conservative Minister and Lord Lieutenant of Ireland. He was the first Mayor of Chelsea in 1900. The Cadogan family has continued to be kind to the Army by providing a house in Chelsea for the use of the Major General Commanding London District.

16. General Sir Arthur Henry Fitzroy Paget GCVO, KCB (1851–1928) was commissioned into the Scots Fusilier Guards in 1869. He served in Ashanti, Sudan, Burma and South Africa. He was C.-in-C. Irish Command in 1912–14.

17. Empress Marie Eugenie Ignace Augustine de Montijo (1826–1920) was the widow of the Emperor Napoleon III. After the death of her husband she moved to Farnborough. Her son the Prince Imperial was killed in the Zulu War.

18. Grand Duchess Marie Alexandrine Elisabeth Eleonore of Mecklenburg-Schwerin (1854–1920) married the Grand Duke Vladimir in 1874. He was the brother of the Emperor Alexander III and uncle of Tsar Nicholas II

19. Percy Chubb was an American business man, who was regularly offering to make Haig's fortune! Haig never bit.

20. The Hon. Walter Warrick Vivian (1856–1943) was Doris Haig's uncle. He and his niece Violet lived together in North Wales and Anglesey. Walter ran the Vaynol Estate until the owner, his nephew Sir Michael Duff, came of age. He was a particular favourite of Haig. They used to have long and animated discussions of a wide range of topics, notably over breakfast!
21. Basil Gordon Nicholas, born 1885, was commissioned into the 12 Lancers in 1905. He had been General O'Moore Creagh's ADC.
22. Lieutenant General Sir Richard Harte Keatinge Butler KCB (1870–1935) was commissioned into the Dorset Regiment in 1890. He was a GSO 2 at Aldershot from 1911 to 1914. He then commanded the 2nd Battalion Lancashire Fusiliers in 1914. He was BGGS then MGGS 1st Army before becoming Deputy CGS to Haig from 1915–18, when he took over command of III Corps until 1919.
23. Charles William Banbury, born 1877, was commissioned into the Coldstream Guards in 1899. He had been Grierson's ADC since 1909.
24. Maréchal Joseph Jacques Cesaire Joffre (1852–1931) was the French Army's Commander-in-Chief at the start of the First World War until 1916, when he was replaced disastrously by Nivelle. His victory at the Marne in 1914 saved France. Haig was fond of him, but did not always admire his military decisions.
25. General Noel Joseph Edouard de Curieres de Castelnau (1851–1914) commanded the French 2nd Army in 1914. Like Joffre he was rather old for the job.
26. Maréchal Ferdinand Foch (1851–1929) was a highly energetic aggressive leader, always happier in the offensive rather than the defensive. As 'Generalissimo' in 1918 he and Haig worked effectively together, although they did not always agree on how to deal with the immediate situation. Foch wrote a most generous commendation of Haig after his early death in 1928. It is interesting that the three British Generals who visited France in July 1914 were all between seven and nine years younger than their French counterparts.
27. General Maurice Balfourier commanded XX Corps in the Somme campaign, then XXXVI Corps. He was awarded the GCMG for his part in the Somme campaign. He was the real hero of Verdun. He was sent into retirement by Pétain in 1917.

# Index

330

arrival South Africa, 118
at Clifton College, 12, 13
at Omdurman, 92–101
at Orwell House
  Preparatory School,
  12
attends John Ruskin
  School of Art, 17
avoids capture by Boers
  near Carolina, 176
awarded CB and
  appointed ADC to
  King, 219
awarded KCVO, 284
birth of children, 263,
  275
born Edinburgh 1861, 10
commands mobile
  columns, 182
commissioned into 7
  Hussars, 20
elected to the Bullingdon,
  16
enters Brasenose College,
  14
enters Royal Military
  College, Sandhurst,
  18
gives evidence to Elgin
  Commission, 223,
  224
in Battle of Eland's
  Laagte, 123–9
in Battle of the Atbara,
  82–7
involved in writing
  Cavalry Drill Book,
  59
meets and proposes to
  Doris Vivian, 241
nominated for Staff
  College by Duke of
  Cambridge, 37
plays polo for Oxford at
  Hurlingham, 15
publishes Cavalry Studies,
  268
receives KCIE, 304
replaced by Erroll, 162–3
rescues Egyptian sergeant,
  84
returns to 7 Hussars at
  Norwich, 110
returns to 7 Hussars in
  India, 38
returns to India with
  bride, 242
said to be colour blind, 36

selected to command 17
  Lancers, 182
stationed at
  Secunderabad, 25
visits Australia with
  Beresford, 30–1
visits French Cavalry, 37
visits German Cavalry,
  42, 45–58
visits USA with British
  Polo team, 23
wins Anson Memorial
  Sword, 19
Haig, Esme, 246,
Haig, George, 23, 24
Haig, Hugo, 13, 47, 77, 85,
  175, 178, 189, 190,
  200, 286
Haig, John (Bee), 12, 23,
  240, 286
Haig, John, 11
Haig, Lieutenant Colonel
  Neil, 169, 288, 302
Haig, Oliver, 1, 5, 192, 199,
  246, 310
Haig, Sir T. W., 247, 286
Haig, Lady Victoria,
  subsequently Montagu-
  Douglas-Scott, 284,
  309
Haig, William, (brother), 14
Haig, William,
  (grandfather), 11
Haking, Lieutenant General
  Sir R. C. B., 60, 143
Haldane, General Sir J. A.
  L., 286
Haldane, Lord, 1, 2, 3, 245,
  247, 248, 249, 250,
  252, 254, 255, 256,
  257, 262, 263, 264,
  265, 266, 270, 273,
  274, 275, 281, 282,
  283, 284, 286, 290,
  291, 296, 297, 299,
  301, 302, 309
Hale, Colonel Sir Lonsdale,
  1, 161, 164, 268, 313
Hale, General, 254
Hamilton Gordon,
  Lieutenant General Sir
  A., 256, 259, 265, 290,
  296
Hamilton, General Sir B.,
  186
Hamilton, Lieutenant
  Colonel G. H. C.
  (Ghazi), 205, 220

Hamilton, Major General
  H. I. W. (Hammy), 200,
  228, 235, 248
Hamilton, General Sir Ian
  (Johnny), 128, 134,
  174, 213, 223, 296
Hamilton, Lord, 67, 270
Hampshire Regiment, 26
Hancox, Colonel H. P., 315
Hardie, Keir, 289
Hardinge of Penshurst,
  Lady, 295, 297, 300
Hardinge of Penshurst,
  Lord, 295, 297, 298,
  299, 300, 302, 303,
  304
Harrison, General Sir R., 67
Hathaway, Major Dr, 143,
  146
Headlam, Major General Sir
  J. E. W., 288, 309
Heath, Major General C. E.,
  258, 262
Heberden, Dr, 16, 313
Hely-Hutchinson, Sir W. F.,
  132, 199
Henderson, Colonel G. F.
  R., 60, 61
Henniker, Major General Sir
  W. C. G., 188, 189
Hickman, Colonel, 186
Hicks Pasha, 66
Higginson, General Sir G.,
  271
Hildyard, General Sir
  Henry, 60, 141
Hitchcock, Tommy, 23
Hoad, General, 275, 282
Holdsworth, Colonel 'Ugly',
  254
Hole, Colonel, 286
Household Cavalry, 166
Houston, Bobby, 23
Howell, Brigadier General
  P., 286, 318, 322
Hudson, Principal
  Frodsham, 15
Hudson, General Sir H., 293
Hughes, Miss, 285
Humphries, Regimental
  Sergeant Major, 33
Hunt, Colonel, 31
Hunter, General Sir A., 82,
  83, 84, 92, 184, 232,
  235, 251
Hutcheson, Captain, 318
Hutchison, Lieutenant
  General, 262, 270

333

Hutton, Lieutenant General
Sir E. T. H., 171
Hyderbuch, Major, 269

Imperial Light Horse, 124,
128, 129, 130, 131,
138, 141

Jameson, Henrietta neé
Haig, 1, 3, 5, 23, 32,
33, 34, 35, 40, 46, 48,
50, 51, 68, 69, 70, 72,
74, 75, 76, 81, 84, 86,
87–92, 101,102, 103,
111, 112, 116, 132,
133, 141, 147, 150,
151, 161, 167, 168–78,
227, 228–36, 242, 243,
244, 245, 247, 248,
251, 260, 275, 286,
301, 302, 305, 309,
310, 323
Jameson, William, 5, 23, 24,
41, 172, 177, 192, 195,
199, 305, 309, 310,
323
Jessel, Lord, 1, 224, 225,
226
Joffre, General J. J., 325
Jones, Major General I.,
184, 187, 188
Joubert, General Piet, 151

Kadir Cup, 236, 237, 248
Kavanagh, Lieutenant
General Sir C., 202,
203, 314
Keighly, Major V. A. S., 302
Kelly-Kenny, General Sir T.,
165, 166
Kemp's Regiment, 212
Keogh, Surgeon General,
265
Khalifa, 66, 83, 89, 92, 100,
101
Kiggell, Lieutenant General
Sir L. E., 271, 286, 302,
309, 313
Kimberley, 160–6
King's Royal Rifle Corps,
314
Kintore, Earl of, 31
Kissingen, 51, 52, 53
Kitchener, Field Marshal
Earl, 3, 62, 66, 67, 69,
72, 83, 86, 92, 95, 96,
97, 98, 101, 102, 103,
105, 152, 161, 163,

164, 165, 169, 175,
178, 181, 182, 183,
185, 187, 189, 190,
192, 195, 203, 219,
228, 229, 232, 236,
243, 244, 246, 250,
288, 291
Kitchener's Horse, 164
Kitson, General, 288, 303
Kitson, Mrs, 288, 303
Knollys, Miss C., 285, 292
Knollys, Sir Francis, 103
Krause, Commandant F.,
178
Kritzinger, General P. H.,
186, 187, 188, 190,
193, 194, 195, 196
Kruger, P., 115, 117, 123,
170, 175

Ladysmith, 125–166
Lake, Lieutenant General Sir
P. H. N., 302, 304
Landon, Major General H.
J. S., 315
Laurier, Sir W., 264
Lawley, Colonel R., 205,
207, 219, 254
Lawrence, General The
Hon. H., 222, 223
Lawson, Major General,
316, 317
Laycock, Brigadier General
J. P., 117, 162, 163,
164, 171, 172
Le Gallais, Lieutenant
Colonel P. W. J., 79,
83, 89, 94
Leach, Major General Sir E.,
266
Legard, Major, 191, 193,
199, 253
Lewis, Lieutenant Colonel
D. F., 98
Lindley, Major General J.
E., 282
Lindsay Gordon, Adam, 4
Lipton, Sir T., 172, 199
Locke Elliot, Lieutenant
General Sir E., 226, 234
Lomax, Lieutenant General
S. H., 316, 317, 319
Long, Colonel C. J., 159
Longford, Earl of, 213
Loos, Captain, 326
Lovat, Lord, 258
Loyal North Lancashire
Regiment, 313, 314

Lucas, Lord, 263, 265
Luck, General Sir George, 5,
30, 58, 182
Lukin, Major General Sir H.
T., 189
Lund, Major, 201
Lyttleton, General The Hon.
Sir N. G., 105, 185,
186, 189, 248, 253,
261, 262, 263, 264,
265, 266, 274, 275,
312

MacAndrew, Major General
H. J. M., 189, 233, 300
Macdonagh, Lieutenant
General Sir G. M. W.,
60
Macdonald, Major General
Sir Hector, 96, 97, 98,
102
Mackinder, Mr, 271
Mackinnon, General Sir W.
H., 256, 265, 266
Mahdi, 66, 93, 99, 101
Mahmoud, Emir, 82, 85,
86, 87, 104
Mahon, Lieutenant General
Sir B. T., 79, 83, 84
Malan, Commandant A. H.,
188
Malet, Sir Edward, 50
Malet, Lady Ermyntrude, 50
Manchester Regiment, 125
Martin, Lieutenant Colonel,
101,
Mary, Queen, 245, 246,
302, 303, 304, 314,
315, 324, 325
Maurice, Major General Sir
F. B., 225
Maxim gun, 67, 82, 83, 84,
85, 96
May, Colonel, 269
McCalmont, General, 68
McCracken, Brigadier
General F. W. N., 157,
158
McKechnie, Mr, 321
McKenna, The Rt. Hon. R.,
285, 286
McMahon, Major Sir H.
W., 294
McMahon, Lieutenant
Colonel N. R., 317
*Melik*, 96
Messienary, M., 325
Methuen, Field Marshal

335

Slade, Admiral Sir E. J. W., 290
Slatin, Sir R. C., 100, 102, 104
Smith-Dorrien, General Sir H. L., 229, 231, 270, 299, 300, 301, 303, 309, 313, 320
Smith-Dorrien, Lady, 310
Smuts, Dr J.C., 114, 183, 196, 197, 205, 207, 208, 209
Solly-Flood, General Sir Frederick, 25
Somerset Light Infantry, 315
South Africa, 2, 113–55, 156–80, 181–217
South African Light Horse, 183
Spion Kop, 159, 160
Sprigg, Sir G., 211
Stanley, Lord, 263
Stein, Margaret, 10
Stephenson, Major General T. E., 199
Stewart, Sir H., 297
Steyn, M., 185, 194, 207
Stirling, Captain, 290
Stopford, Lieutenant General The Hon. Sir F. W., 141, 249, 253, 257, 265
Sudanese troops, 88, 90, 92, 104
Suffolk Regiment, 148, 149, 158, 159, 315
Swaine Colonel L. V., 45, 46
Sykes, Christopher, 67
Symons Major General Sir P., 132

Talbot, Colonel Lord Edmund, 170, 172, 286
Tanner, Colonel J. A., 298
Teale, RQMS Reginald, 39
Teck, Prince Alexander of, 81, 227
Terraine, John, 41
Territorial Army, 2
Tharp, Mrs, 316
Thomas Cook & Co., 74
Thomson, Lieutenant, 199

Thornewill, Miss J., 270
Thornton, Captain, 198
Tilney, Colonel W. A., 316
Tucker, Lieutenant General Sir C., 165
Tullibardine, Marquess of, 89

Van de Venter, General Sir J. L., 209
Van Reenen, Commandant, 191
Vaughan, Major General J., 90, 110, 116, 117, 118, 145, 175, 176, 287, 293, 323
Veitch, Rachel, 5, 11,
Victoria, Princess, 67, 253, 271
Vivian, The Hon. A., 281, 285
Vivian, Lady, 240, 241, 281, 285, 301
Vivian, Lord, 5, 240, 285
Vivian, The Hon. V., 240, 281, 315, 323
Vivian, the Hon. W., 263, 323
Vladimir, Grand Duchess, 3, 323
Vogelsang, Dr, 257, 268
Von Kleist, General, 268, 272
Von Poseck, Major M., 269, 272
Von Reuter, Major, 269

Walter, Lieutenant Colonel, 254
Wapshare, Brigadier General R., 293
Ward, Sir E., 265
Warwick, Daisy, Countess, 5,
Warwick, Guy, Earl of, 171, 172, 246, 247
Warwickshire Hunt, 5, 41
Watson, Colonel, 159
Wauchope, Major General A.G., 91, 143
Webb, Beatrice, 3, 271
Webb, Sidney, 3, 271
Wernher, Sir J., 114

Western Province Mounted Rifles, 206
White, Colonel, 204, 206
White, Field Marshal Sir G., 116, 123, 129, 134, 135
Wilhelm, Crown Prince, 297, 298
Wilhelm II, Kaiser, 46, 50, 283
Wilkinson, T., 310
Williams, Colonel, 183, 184
Williams, Dr, 298
Wilson, Colonel, 255
Wilson, Colonel H. F. M., 297
Wilson, Field Marshal Sir H., 275, 312, 322
Wilson, Lieutenant Colonel Sir M. R. H., 284, 285
Wing, Colonel, 272
Wolseley, Field Marshal Viscount, 66, 147, 181
Wood, Field Marshal Sir Evelyn, 1, 4, 37, 40, 45, 51, 52, 53, 54, 67, 71, 77, 79, 89, 102, 104, 105, 106, 118, 142, 147, 150, 172, 177, 255
Wood, Mr, 294
Wormald, Major K., 201, 236, 254
Worsley, Lord, 311
Wyndham, Colonel G. P., 118, 202, 203
Wynne, General Sir A. S., 199
Wynne, Sir T., 300

York, Duchess of, subsequently Queen Mary, 67
York, Duke of, subsequently King George V, 67
Young, Sir A., 285
Younger, Sir William, 225
Yule, Brigadier General J. H., 131, 132

Zioleltitz, Lieutenant, 297
Zu Dohna, Count, 297